Home Engagement in Diplomacy

Diplomatic Studies

Series Editor

Jan Melissen
(*Leiden University and University of Antwerp*)

VOLUME 23

The titles published in this series are listed at *brill.com/dist*

Home Engagement in Diplomacy

Global Affairs and Domestic Publics

Edited by

Jan Melissen, HwaJung Kim, and Githma Chandrasekara

BRILL

LEIDEN | BOSTON

Cover illustration: Formas abstractas (1929) by Joaquín Torres García (Uruguayan, 1874–1949). Sourced from Artvee and free of copyright restrictions.

The Library of Congress Cataloging-in-Publication Data is available online at https://catalog.loc.gov

Typeface for the Latin, Greek, and Cyrillic scripts: "Brill". See and download: brill.com/brill-typeface.

ISSN 1872-8863
ISBN 978-90-04-73836-2 (paperback)
ISBN 978-90-04-73832-4 (e-book)
DOI 10.1163/9789004738324

This book is printed on acid-free paper and produced in a sustainable manner.

Contents

Notes on Contributors

Githma Chandrasekara

is an independent researcher and communications consultant based in Sri Lanka. She a junior fellow and editorial assistant with *The Hague Journal of Diplomacy*, and a graduate of the advanced M.Sc. in International Relations and Diplomacy at Leiden University, The Hague Campus, in the Netherlands.

Andrew F. Cooper

is University Research Chair, Department of Political Science, and Professor, the Balsillie School of International Affairs, University of Waterloo, and an Associate Research Fellow at the United Nations University Institute on Comparative Regional Integration Studies (UNU-CRIS), Bruges, Belgium. His latest book is *The Concertation Impulse in World Politics Contestation over Fundamental Institutions and the Constrictions of Institutionalist International Relations* (Oxford: Oxford University Press, 2024).

Scott Harrison

(Ph.D., History) is a research fellow at Simon Fraser University's David Lam Centre for Asian Studies. He was the Senior Program Manager of Northeast Asia and Engaging Asia pillars at the Asia Pacific Foundation of Canada, where he worked for over a decade. His research and activities are driven by "connecting histories, shaping futures." Harrison examines Canada-Asia/Indo-Pacific relations through non-central government/para-diplomacy; global Indigeneity and Indigenism; reconciliation; business, policy, and strategy; and developing Asia-related competencies for Canadians, as well as Japan's history, diplomacy, and politics, along with Asian Cold War history.

Anna Geis

is professor of International Security and Conflict Studies at Helmut Schmidt University / University of the Federal Armed Forces Hamburg (Germany). Her research areas cover issues of legitimacy of military interventions, security governance, recognition of non-state armed actors, German security policy, and transitional justice.

Quinton Huang

is an M.A. student in History at the University of British Columbia, and was a junior research scholar at the Asia Pacific Foundation of Canada from 2020 to

2022. He holds an A.B. in History and East Asia Studies from Brown University, and is a board member of the global nonprofit Strait Talk. His current research focuses on the global connections and networks underlying squatter settlements in postwar Hong Kong, as well as histories of migration, intercultural exchange and information in early modern to 20th century East and Southeast Asia.

HwaJung Kim

Ph.D., serves as a research professor, selected by the National Research Foundation of the Ministry of Education, Republic of Korea, in mid-2021, at the Institute for International and Area Studies, Graduate School of International Studies, Ewha Womans University, and she works for the Korean Association for Public Diplomacy since 2020.

César Jiménez-Martínez

is an assistant professor in the Department of Media and Communications at the London School of Economics and Political Science. His research examines the mediation of nationhood, paying attention to phenomena such as nation branding, digital nationalism, and more recently protests at the nation-state level. He is author of Nation Branding in the Americas: Contested Politics and Identities (with Efe Sevin and Pablo Miño, Routledge 2025), Media and the Image of the Nation. He has received several awards, including the 2021 Anthony D. Smith Award in nations and nationalism, and the 2023 ICA Award in public diplomacy.

Christian Lequesne

is professor of Political Science at Sciences Po. He was Director of the Center for International Studies (CERI) at Sciences Po and Director of CEFRES in Prague. He was also LSE-Sciences Po Alliance Professor at the LSE. He is co-director of the European Review of International Studies. His current research focuses on the sociology of diplomatic practices. Recent publications include *Ministries of Foreign Affairs in the World, Ethnographie du Quai d'Orsay. Les pratiques des diplomates français; Le diplomate et le Français de l'Etranger. Les pratiques de l'Etat envers sa diaspora* (to be published in English in 2026).

Jan Melissen

is Editor-in-Chief of *The Hague Journal of Diplomacy*. As a think-tanker-turned-academic, he is a senior fellow at the Institute of Security and Global Affairs at Leiden University, The Hague, and a professor in the Department of Political

Science, University of Antwerp. He is a faculty fellow with the Centre for Public Diplomacy at the University of Southern California, Los Angeles. He received the International Studies Association (ISA) Distinguished Scholar Award in Diplomatic Studies in 2022.

Christian Opitz

is a post-doc researcher at Helmut Schmidt University / University of the Federal Armed Forces Hamburg (Germany), where he works on the project "*Recasting the role of citizens in foreign and security policy?*", funded by the German Research Foundation (DFG). His research focuses on the domestic politics and dynamics of foreign and security policy, the transformation of the diplomatic profession, and the broader evolution of modern democratic political systems.

Hanna Pfeifer

is Head of Research Area "Societal Peace and Internal Security" at the Institute for Peace Research and Security Policy at the University of Hamburg (IFSH). Her research is interested in domestic and international dynamics of order and violence. She works at the intersection of political science research on violence/conflict, foreign policy analysis and international relations, and the area studies on West Asia and North Africa (WANA).

Anna Popkova

is an associate professor at Western Michigan University School of Communication and an allied faculty member at the Global and International Studies program. Her research on public diplomacy and international strategic communication examines the public diplomacy efforts of such non-state actors as transnational advocacy networks, citizen diplomacy communities, and dissenting diasporas. She is the editor of *Disruption and Dissent in Public Diplomacy* (2025, Palgrave Macmillan), and published in journal including the *International Journal of Communication, International Communication Gazette, The Hague Journal of Diplomacy, International Journal of Strategic Communication, Place Branding and Public Diplomacy*.

Allison Scott

holds a Bachelor of Arts in Applied Diplomacy with a concentration in International Law from DePaul University. She is the author of "Liminality: The Realm of Diplomacy" in *Creating Knowledge* (2023). Her research and policy interests are Diplomacy and Human Rights Law.

Toshiya Takahashi

is professor of International Relations at Shoin University, Japan. He started a Ph.D. study at the London School of Economics and Political Science and received his Ph.D. from the Australian National University. His research interest is conceptual aspects of security, Japan's security and foreign policy, and security in multilateralism. He is a Member of the APEC Study Center of Japan and the APEC round table with the Ministry of Foreign Affairs of Japan and the Ministry of Economy, Trade and Industry of Japan. He is the Author of *China in Japan's National Security: Domestic Credibility* (Routledge, 2020).

Geoffrey Wiseman

is professor and Endowed Chair in Applied Diplomacy in the Grace School of Applied Diplomacy, DePaul University, Chicago. A former Australian diplomat, serving in Stockholm, Hanoi, and Brussels and advisor to the Australian Foreign Minister, Gareth Evans, he has also worked in the Strategic Planning Unit of the Office of the United Nations Secretary-General and as peace and security program officer at the Ford Foundation. He has taught at the University of Southern California and the Australian National University. With Pauline Kerr, he co-edited *Diplomacy in a Globalizing World: Theories and Practices* (Oxford University Press).

Yun Zhang

is professor of International Relations at Nanjing University, China. He obtained Ph.D. in law from Peking University and Ph.D. in international relations from Waseda University. He was an associate professor at Niigata University, Japan. His research expertise includes China-Japan-U.S. relations and Asian international relations. He held positions at Free University of Berlin, the Massachusetts Institute of Technology, the University of Hong Kong, National University of Singapore, and Peking University. He has authored seven monographs, including *Unpacking the Dynamics of Japan-China Mutual Mistrust* (The University of Tokyo Press, 2020). *Sino-Japanese Relations in a Trilateral Context: Origins of Misperception* (Palgrave Macmillan, 2017).

Štěpánka Zemanová

Ph.D., is an associate professor and Head of the Department of International Studies and Diplomacy at the Faculty of International Relations, Prague University of Economics and Business. In her capacity, she oversees the design and implementation of undergraduate and graduate programmes specialising in international studies and diplomacy. In the past, she served as a working group member to establish the Global International Relations Section in International Studies Association. Currently, she is the secretary of this section. Her research interests cover economic diplomacy, economic statecraft, international sanctions, and international human rights protection's political and economic aspects.

Introduction

Jan Melissen, HwaJung Kim and Githma Chandrasekara

In recent years, governments across the world have been putting more effort into talking to their home citizens – the smallest units of society – about global affairs. International events have a significant impact on people's daily lives, and a number of Western countries, on both sides of the Atlantic, have recently witnessed how the electoral vote can have far-reaching consequences for a country's foreign policy agenda. In the West and beyond, we see that governmental relations with individuals conducted through organisations standing for sectors of civil society are increasingly seen to be falling short of public expectations. Emotions often run high around foreign policy issues ranging from war and terrorism to migration and environmental threats. The question of how to engage with individual citizens on global affairs is not an easy one, and the past offers little guidance. Governmental engagement with citizens is on the agenda of democracies and their leaders, as well as that of authoritarian powers and the studies in this book show that the practice of such domestic engagement on international issues is still at an experimental stage. They also demonstrate the importance of bearing in mind that experiences with such dialogues vary across cultures and political systems.

This project grew out of a long-standing interest in innovation and experimentation in diplomacy, which is a fundamental feature of its practice.[1] Paradoxically, throughout history these characteristics of diplomatic practice have gone hand in hand with a certain organisational inertia within foreign ministries as government institutions and a professional diplomatic culture that is generally comfortable with the status quo. Trying out new modes of engagement and incorporating new kinds of activities have been part of diplomacy since ancient Near Eastern envoys carting cuneiform tablets on camels' backs travelled to distant kingdoms. Nonetheless, *experimentation* in new modes of engagement has received less attention in academic research than more institutionalised forms of innovation that left a discernible paper trail in diplomatic archives, the media and individual diplomats' reminiscences.

As the title *Home Engagement in Diplomacy* suggests, this volume is about the interdependence and dialogue between governmental diplomacy and the

---

1 Melissen 1999.

societies it serves. Diplomatic work is meant to help society and the national economy, but, as this volume argues, the state–society relationship is a two-way street, based on the principle of mutuality. Sub-state actors, social movements and individuals in society have the potential to affect the practice of diplomacy and therefore, to an extent, their agency impacts on diplomacy itself. We call this dynamic 'home engagement', and we refer to the direct interaction between diplomacy and people in domestic society rather than non-state actors representing them.

All of this deserves more scholarly attention from students of diplomacy, who, we suggest, would do well to reflect on the trend that foreign policy-related concerns are increasingly touching base with society. This proposition implies that definition should be seen as an activity on the cusp of the society of states and global society, as one involving not only professional diplomats, but also a wider circle of practitioners and 'ordinary' people who are outsiders and stakeholders or, indeed, participants in the diplomatic process. This volume, therefore, reflects an appetite for more research on the marginal practices of diplomacy, thus acting on the scholarly hunch that a better understanding of what appears peripheral in diplomacy matters. We even speculate, audaciously, that a better grasp of practice on the boundaries of the diplomatic world may help us to see part of the outline of future mainstream practices. As two co-editors of this work have argued elsewhere, 'an understanding of things peripheral in diplomatic practice may inform us about shifts in professional culture and what is commonly assumed to be the hard core of diplomacy'.[2]

This book is equally a deliberate effort in research collaboration with scholarly input and insights from Europe, Asia and the Americas. It is grounded in the confidence and optimism that a broad geographic scope of analysis is necessary for our understanding of simultaneous occurrences worldwide and home engagement as an emerging practice in dissimilar social settings. Among the more specific drivers of this book is our casual observation of the contradiction that public opinion, at least in the Western world, appears to be less interested in the world's high politics, but appreciably more concerned about the effects of regional and global crises on their perceived national security, their personal sense of safety and their material well-being. Debates on the external relations agenda increasingly reflect the needs and wants of society at large and in democracies where populism is on the rise, the public articulation of governmental priorities on foreign policy is often plainly anti-elitist.

---

2   Kim and Melissen 2022.

The social mechanisms behind the politicisation of diplomacy are of academic and practical interest. It is hardly surprising, then, that foreign ministries and their staff, the most obviously identifiable flag bearers of diplomacy, seem to be paying greater attention to domestic conversations on international affairs. They do so as it is part of the bread and butter of their profession, but also for reasons that include a clear sense of professional self-preservation. What does this boil down to in terms of research? There is a whole set of questions on the domestic dimension of diplomatic practice that is begging for better answers than the study of diplomacy and international relations (IR) theory can presently offer, and this book can only begin to answer them. Therefore, the first chapter sets the scene by first interrogating the conceptual and theoretical origins of the 'domestic deficit' in diplomatic studies and IR. Broadly speaking, this book upholds eclecticism as an approach that is more fitting for exploratory research, and we shy away from the kind of imposed coherence across chapters that would run the risk of missing out on insights that 'do not fit'. The authors of this book examine home engagement in diplomacy through multiple conceptual lenses and are inspired by different social science theories, perspectives and levels of analysis.

We do not contest that diplomatic adaptation and experimentation with societal dialogues is becoming more urgent in the face of long-held sentiments that diplomats are out of touch with society and that the mediation of those dialogues in addressing international challenges is optional. However, the thematically connected studies in this book do not guess at the risks of the *absence* of domestic diplomatic engagement, nor do they discuss in depth the politics of efforts to reverse any trends towards expanded state–society dialogue in liberal-democratic or authoritarian settings. We equally resist making specific policy recommendations or prescriptive 'to-do' lists aimed at solving governmental conundrums associated with home engagement in diplomacy. Alternatively, we advance the straightforward proposition that long-lasting practice advice and policy recommendations will only make sense when they are rooted in academic attempts to fathom social phenomena and based on sustained empirical rather than sporadic observation and mere opinion-making.

The studies in this volume are a first systematic effort to compensate for what is arguably an impermissible omission in the received wisdom on diplomacy's parameters and potentialities. The eleven chapters all have abstracts of their main argument as well as keywords that point to the foci of their analysis. Rather than summarising chapters in this Introduction, Chapter 1 introduces some of the authors' main findings in the context of a conceptual discussion, theoretical contextualisation and a more applied middle-range analysis of home engagement in diplomacy.

Bibliography

Kim, HwaJung and Jan Melissen. 'Engaging Home in Diplomacy: Introduction'. *The Hague Journal of Diplomacy* 17 (4) (2022), 611.

Melissen, Jan, ed. *Innovation in Diplomatic Practice* (Basingstoke: Palgrave Macmillan, 1999).

CHAPTER 1

Theorising and Debating the Domestic Deficit in IR and Diplomatic Studies

Jan Melissen and Githma Chandrasekara

Summary

This chapter explores the often overlooked domestic dimension of diplomacy, emphasising the integration of societal engagement into diplomatic studies. We propose the notion of 'home engagement' to highlight the mutual relationship between diplomacy and the domestic publics, focusing on the agency of citizens as stakeholders in foreign policy. By critiquing the historical neglect of state–society interactions in international relations (IR) theory, foreign policy analysis and diplomatic studies, we argue that this oversight has sustained an elite-dominated view of diplomacy, marginalising citizens' roles in domestic and international contexts. The concept of the accelerated societisation of diplomacy illustrates our take on a more integrative view of contemporary diplomatic practice. With a grounding in democracy theories, particularly deliberative and participatory frameworks, we demonstrate how these models can inform and transform diplomatic practices. Globalisation, crises and the rise of populism have heightened public interest in foreign policy *outcomes*, requiring new methods that recognise citizen agency and adapt to the changing sociopolitical complexities of global affairs. The chapter positions home engagement as a critical area of scholarly focus, advocating for a research agenda that bridges the gaps between diplomacy, governance and societal dynamics. Drawing from interdisciplinary perspectives, we underscore the potential of home engagement to describe diplomacy as a process co-constituted by societal actors, more specifically citizens. This reframing calls for a more inclusive framework for understanding and practising diplomacy, reflecting the centrality of state–society interactions in addressing contemporary global challenges.

Keywords

state–society relations – citizen participation – deliberative governing – democracy theory – IR theory – foreign policy analysis – diplomatic studies

1   Introduction

This book analyses home engagement in diplomacy as a separate and distinct practice, and it does so for two main reasons. Firstly, diplomacy increasingly takes diplomats themselves outside the sphere of networking, communicating and negotiating with their peers. The book and this chapter hope to make a modest contribution to knowledge about diplomacy as an activity that puts greater demands on career diplomats, as well as political appointees, as 'boundary spanners' who engage with home society, including its citizens. Secondly, and following from this point, our focus hopes to help erode classical understandings of diplomacy in favour of a new conceptualisation that gives pride of place to its multifaceted societal dimension. The depth of state–society dynamics has received little attention from scholars who embrace statism implicitly or with theoretical conviction. Here, it may serve as a reminder that, around the turn of the century and later, other key aspects of diplomatic engagement with citizens were still not deemed worthy of attention. Consular affairs were smugly situated outside the realm of 'real' diplomacy by the majority of diplomatic professionals and their academic followers. In another kind of exclusion ritual among traditionalist students of diplomatic practice, public diplomacy was initially described as a 'term for propaganda conducted by diplomats' rather than diplomacy's public dimension.[1] Today, in both of these fields of diplomatic practice, the governmental dialogue with increasingly assertive home citizens, and by implication their agency, is evident and recognised. We argue that the time is right for diplomatic studies to fully embrace the domestic state–society dimension of diplomacy and take into account the nation's citizens and, as this chapter and book argue, people's agency – not as a sideshow but as a more critical element in the evolving essence of diplomacy.[2]

The first part of the chapter sets the scene by seeking to understand how international relations (IR) theory, foreign policy analysis and diplomatic studies have largely turned a blind eye to people as the smallest units within international or global society. We offer reasons why that omission encourages a myopic view of contemporary diplomacy and consider the meaning of diplomacy's accelerated societisation. In Sections 3–6, the second half of the chapter, we turn to different types of theorising on approaches and mechanisms of governmental engagement with society. We examine relevant works

1   Berridge and James 2001, 197.
2   Jönsson and Hall 2005.

of literature from various disciplines on perspectives of public policy, governance, democratisation and deliberation that seem transferable to the study of diplomacy.

2   IR, Foreign Policy Analysis and Diplomatic Studies: Theories, Concepts and Blind Spots

2.1   IR *Theory: Realism and the Absence of the Domestic Scene*
This section addresses the gap between practice and theory. As such it leans towards a sociology of theories, and with a central claim: most academic reflection on international relations and diplomacy has failed to capture the past and present reality of diplomacy's domestic dimensions. A review of mainstream IR theory for the purposes of this chapter is challenging. It needs to balance its analytical neglect of the domestic dimension with the fact that such theory has proven remarkably resistant to seeing the practice of diplomacy as theoretically relevant. The grand traditions of international thought see diplomacy variously as a tool of foreign policy, as a practice, as an institution of the society of states, and as a bundle of practices that may or may not contribute to the making of world politics.[3] The realist tradition and its understanding of international politics as the struggle for power between sovereign states mostly remains the first reference because of its association with the assumed realist worldview of old-school diplomats. Like the other main traditions in IR, realist theory lags significantly behind real-world developments which highlight the increasing interconnectedness between global affairs and the concerns of domestic publics.

The classical realism of founding scholars such as Carr and Morgenthau left scope for reflection on the societal and transnational dimensions of politics as well as discussion on diplomacy's often neglected contribution to international politics. Such aspects, increasingly visible in global affairs, have been effectively sacrificed in the neorealist and neoclassical realist theoretical paradigms.[4] Neorealists do not explain international politics outside the dynamics of the relative power capabilities of the great powers in the international system. Therefore, they do not explain diplomacy as being related to foreign policy or as an expression of state behaviour. Domestic societies are naturally outside their epistemic gaze. Neorealist analysis of state behaviour, aimed at the finding of scientific laws, is based on the methodological assumption that

---

3   Sharp 2018.
4   Ripsman, Taliagerro and Lobell 2016, 74.

systemic dynamics are determinant in explaining foreign policy and, hence, the diplomatic behaviour of states.[5] As far as domestic society is concerned, the intellectual curiosity driving this book runs against the view of those who merely assert systemic impact on domestic politics. As to the reverse picture, in the eyes of neorealists, neither domestic structures nor political leaders determine foreign policy, themes that have been addressed in neoclassical realism and foreign policy analysis.

Neoclassical realists' contribution to their in-school argument with their neorealist cousins comes down to the fact that, for them, 'the nature of state–society relations can have a significant impact on the strategic behavior of states', even though many scholars have questioned whether this is a key theoretical concern.[6] However, the limitations of their theoretical assumptions are of interest. Neoclassical realists neglect diplomacy but argue that they have much more to say about foreign policy choices and grand strategy than neorealism, constructivism, *Innenpolitik* approaches or liberal IR theories, a subset of such theorising.[7] Here it is important to underline that their conception of the domestic scene is narrowed to the political institutions of national society rather than taking the wider view that societal groups as well as individuals make up society, and that domestic politics remains altogether resistant to neoclassical theorising.[8] Moreover, in the more recent literature Ripsman, Taliaferro and Lobell make a point of distinguishing between foreign relations in a situation of domestic state–society harmony and one of state–society discord.[9] This kind of dichotomous classification does not consider present-day concerns with the effects of the politicisation of both society and government, the impact of polarisation in society on the formal political process, and populist foreign policy as a presumed reflection of people's preferences that are unrepresented by political institutions and unmediated by societal organisations. Neoclassical realism, then, is an IR research programme that is not equipped to address some of the most pressing concerns in Western state–society relations as it only embraces a limited range of present-day state–society dynamics. Theoretically, it ultimately adheres closely to the neorealist primacy of systemic preferences. As Narizny concludes convincingly, '[t]he more it [neoclassical realism] reveals that domestic factors mat-

---

5   Narizny 2017, 160.
6   Ripsman, Taliaferro and Lobell 2016, 74; Legro and Moravcsik 1999, 45.
7   Ripsman, Taliaferro and Lobell 2016, 2–5.
8   Legro and Moravcsik 1999, 45. See also Rose 1998.
9   Ripsman, Taliaferro and Lobell 2016, 70–72.

ter, the less it will be able to sustain its justifying assumption that systemic pressures deserve analytical priority'.[10]

If we want to find out more about the home dimensions of international behaviour, it may help to first climb down from abstractions such as the system of states and shared beliefs about state behaviour in the international system. Rather than viewing states as actors, liberal theory proposes to place individuals and collectives and their agency in society as constitutive of politics, the claim being that the state is an institution that aims to be representative of the identities and preferences of people and organised groups in society.[11] Like the other grand IR traditions such as realism and constructivism, though, mainstream liberalist thought has relatively little to contribute to our understanding of diplomacy because of its actor-centric rather than 'relationalist' focus. In short, missing in mainstream IR theory is the key point that international relations and, hence, the constitution of global affairs cannot be imagined without diplomacy.[12] This equally applies to constructivist, identity-focused theory, with its systemic bias and habit of focusing on identities that are fluid but relations that are relatively fixed, conceived as mutual signalling or interaction rituals, rather than seeing them as part of the social that is fluid in world politics.[13] So far, the project of a 'new constructivism' that would privilege relations and processes over more or less fixed properties is, at best, a work in progress.[14]

2.2 *Foreign Policy Analysis: The Domestic Scene as a Decision-Making Environment*

The lack of IR interest in state–society relations overlooks the agency of citizens in favour of groups and civil society organisations that are taken for granted as their accepted representatives. Still, moving the discussion in the right direction, in the aftermath of the Cold War, Moravcsik rightly pointed out that 'state–societal relations – the relationship of states to the domestic and transnational social context in which they are embedded – have a fundamental impact on state behavior in world politics'.[15] From here, one would imagine, it is a small step to recognise and interrogate foreign pol-

---

10   Narizny 2017, 178.
11   See also Moravcsik 1997, 516–519.
12   Rebecca Adler-Nissen, 'Relationalism or why diplomats find international relations strange', in Sending, Pouliot and Neumann 2015, 284–308.
13   Wong 2021.
14   McCourt 2022, 39–44.
15   Andrew Moravcsik, in Slaughter 2017, 33.

icy and diplomacy as projects and processes in which citizens as unrepresented individuals matter.

The research field of foreign policy analysis (FPA) is largely separated from IR theory and almost completely divorced from diplomatic studies, the object of study of which is a larger concept than FPA.[16] Foreign policy analysis, especially its psychological and leader-focused orientation, basically sees the domestic sphere as an environment that constrains governments in foreign policy and, by implication, the nature and scope of their diplomatic action.[17] As a subfield of political science, FPA does not communicate easily with IR theory; it generally ignores the existence of diplomatic studies, and any integrating attempts to remedy some of these disconnects show that much work needs to be done.[18] FPA research does not see how individuals in society matter much beyond the institutions that represent them, or as respondents in opinion polls and voters in electoral democracies. FPA's fixed gaze is limited to the participation of institutions and groups, including non-state actors, in the formal political process and their influence on policy outcomes. In FPA's largely positivist research tradition there seems to be little scope for critical theorising. In the work of Alden and Aran, however, we see an appreciation of a more pluralist domestic environment and a more critical understanding of what is actually meant by the 'domestic environment'.[19] Beyond the narrow conception of the domestic sphere as a territorially bounded space, both the historical record of globalisation and the current reality of transnational flows of ideas and opinions point in the direction of roles for people independent of the actors representing them.

Conceptual historical research can help guide critical FPA that is more inclusive, characterised by transnational processes that affect people, with domestic institutions aiming to represent them and with globalised civil society. Leira argues that 'foreign policy emerged when the external affairs of states were questioned domestically – in a process closely related to the emergence of a public sphere and a relatively free press [in Europe] during the eighteenth century'.[20] In his view, FPA should not overlook 'the generative effects of foreign policy: the processes that produce, and continually constitute it, as a space of action'.[21] Understanding the nation-state as pluralist, as a society

---

16   Sharp 2016, 271.
17   Brummer 2020.
18   Kaarbo 2015.
19   Alden and Aran 2017, 65.
20   Leira 2019, 188.
21   Leira 2019, 196.

that includes individuals and does not stop at territorial borders, would be significant in FPA. Increasing domestic interchange between government and citizens on a range of topics points to the perceived relevance of people's agency outside the sphere of formal politics and, hence, foreign ministries' recognition of the importance of dialogue with the whole of society. As expressed in a forum discussion at the root of this book project:

> The importance of enhanced state–society dialogue on foreign affairs is now firmly on the radar of national governments in, for instance, the United States, Germany and South Korea, where the phantom of unreachable or fickle publics has swung policy-makers into action. Efforts at informed dialogue and the support of 'ordinary people' at home, on a variety of international questions affecting domestic welfare, safety and security, can be seen as symptoms of the changing nature of foreign policy and the politicisation of diplomacy. The stakes can be high.[22]

2.3　IR and Diplomatic Studies: More Oversight

The study of diplomacy and the 'grand theories' in IR and 'mid-level' theories in foreign policy analysis largely pass one another like ships in the night. For example, IR neorealists and students of diplomacy seem to live in different worlds. Students of diplomacy depict the world as a *society* of states rather than a structurally determinative system characterised by rivalry between its main units. Bull's 20th-century description of international society as 'a group of states, conscious of certain common interests and values, [that] form a society in the sense that they conceive themselves to be bound by a common set of rules in their relations with one another and share in the working of common institutions' is under considerable pressure in today's geopolitical world, but it is still a valid working definition.[23] Both research traditions nonetheless have one basic feature in common: their wholehearted identification with a 'Westphalian' conception that privileges the sovereign state as the paramount actor in global affairs.[24]

At this point, it is pertinent to point out where, broadly speaking, mainstream IR theory and diplomatic studies part company. Adler-Nissen explained very well that the substantialist, or essentialist, that is, actor-centric, approach of IR generally fails to recognise that diplomacy is much more than a foreign policy tool, and this applies *mutatis mutandis* to the actor-centric view

---

22　Kim and Melissen 2022, 611–612.
23　Bull 1977, 13.
24　Windler 2017, 260–262.

of decision-making at the centre of attention within FPA.[25] Both IR and FPA overlook diplomacy as a process in continuous flux that helps construct the national interest, contributes to the constitution of global affairs and co-determines outcomes in international politics. For us, world politics is un-imaginable without diplomacy and would be pretty much a jungle without the institutions and processes of diplomacy. Diplomacy as a constitutive and regulating mechanism makes the business of international politics what it is. Students of diplomacy conspicuously emphasise their dedication to the anal-ysis of *relations* as the unit of analysis, in contrast to IR's system-focused and actor-centric research.

Relations, not just between states but also within complex multi-actor net-works, may be seen to constitute the operational principle of diplomacy. Maintaining such relations has always been and remains part and parcel of large swathes of contemporary practice. The logic of relational networking across national boundaries makes much diplomacy an activity that can and often does precede the pursuit of interests and can hence be better under-stood cross-culturally and, in academic terms, by borrowing from sociology rather than rationalist political science and its IR offshoots. Instead of a world of states – and without denying the importance of states and govern-ments as an important fact of international life – a larger picture then be-comes visible. This requires an ontological shift. Transnational problem-solving networks connect the domestic and international spheres in which trends in international relations do not stop at the national borders of nation-states. In this line of thinking, Slaughter, in a book meant to persuade academ-ics and policymakers that the individual practitioner is in the first place *homo sociologicus* rather than homo economicus, suggests 'a person driven as much by the desire to belong and connect as by her individual goals'.[26] According to this argument, it becomes problematic to designate diplomatic studies as a subfield of IR. Diplomatic studies is an interdisciplinary field that continues to develop with valuable input from various disciplines and fields, including history, sociology, psychology, geography, communication, law and political theory. Within the diverse and evolving realm of global affairs, and following the intellectual curiosity driving this book, the IR frame furthermore runs the risk of downplaying the analysis of key domestic dimensions of diplomacy. In fact, the domestic societal playing field and political realities that we perceive

---

25   Rebecca Adler-Nissen in Sending, Pouliot and Neumann 2015. See also Jönsson and Hall 2005.

26   Slaughter 2017, 69.

as a given in the everyday experience of diplomats have equally escaped the attention of many academic students of diplomacy.

This book prefers the terms 'home engagement' and 'domestic engagement' (or even 'participatory diplomacy') over 'domestic diplomacy', a term that may give the impression of being an oxymoron as diplomacy is conventionally seen to be about relations between rather than within collectives. In his reflections on three pairs of words constructed with the adjective 'domestic' – *domestic diplomacy, domestic public diplomacy and domestic foreign policy* – Sharp observes that the emergence of the term 'domestic' in a diplomatic context might be an indication of the questioning of identities which belong to political spheres either inside or outside the nation-state. As he spells out:

> to characterize some of the relations between governments and some of their own people as diplomacy might well reflect acceptance of a more nuanced and, indeed, more accurate understanding of the ways in which peoples relate to one another, both within international boundaries as well as across them, than that provided by the single inside–outside frame of the sovereign state system.[27]

Critical theorists take this argument one step further. They do not specifically theorise the domestic dimension of diplomacy but roundly dismiss the state-centric definition of diplomacy as 'a discourse of recognition and authority (re)performed by sovereign states to exclude non-sovereign others'.[28] Constantinou and Sharp have taken this argument in favour of an inclusive definition to its logical conclusion, with the relativist point that any objective definition of diplomacy is exclusive and intolerant vis-à-vis other uses of the term or the recognition of non- or sub-state practices as diplomacy.[29] In this view, diplomacy can be practised in different subnational, transnational and international spheres, at different levels of governance and social experience, and by sovereign and non-recognised international actors.[30] Alternatively, the plea for more global collaboration and what has been called a humanity-centred diplomacy, away from *raison d'état* thinking, can take a more normative slant. Zaharna proposes three broadly defined principal purposes for practitioners of public diplomacy, as communicators and

---

27   Sharp 2016, 279.
28   McConnell, Moreau and Dittmer 2012, 804. See also Constantinou 2015; Cornago 2013, 48–54.
29   Constantinou and Sharp 2016, 20.
30   Constantinou 2013.

'boundary spanners of humanity': collective problem-solving, mediating human diversity and responding to human needs.[31] From yet another angle, concerned about the nation-state and people's agency in international affairs rather than the motives for global collaboration, Chapter 2 in this book, by Jiménez-Martínez, critiques that mainstream diplomatic studies fall into 'methodological statism'. In his view, an uncritical and largely un-questioned emphasis on the role of the state rests on the simplistic assump-tion of the stable and uncontested nature of the nation-state within clear geographic and identity boundaries. Critical theory then looks at diplomacy without conceptually neglecting the domestic sphere as one that needs to be opened and where, in fact, diplomacy is equally at work. Yet critical theo-rists have by and large not deemed the study of *public* diplomacy, including its domestic dimension, worthy of their attention. Meanwhile, over the past twenty years public diplomacy – the largest subfield in the study of diplo-macy – has attracted limited productive theorising. The 'public' strand of research receives close attention in our discussion as it includes attention for the general public, audiences and common people in the analysis of diplomacy.

2.4   *Accelerated Societisation of Diplomacy and Domestic Engagement*

Public diplomacy studies have boomed quantitatively, in terms of their schol-arly and grey literature output, and as such, this research orientation within diplomatic studies has strengthened its interdisciplinary nature. The sizeable amount of normative work on public diplomacy has contributed to the atten-tion paid to diplomatic studies outside academia, and it speaks for itself that governments have shown pragmatic interest in the sophistication of their public diplomacy toolbox. Gregory has authoritatively described public diplo-macy as 'an instrument used by states, associations of states, and some sub-state and non-state actors to understand cultures, attitudes and behavior; build and manage relationships; and influence thoughts and mobilize actions to advance their interests and values'.[32] This description of the concept re-quires some contextualisation. Firstly, public diplomacy research, with inputs from different academic disciplines and fields, has made the concept more rather than less 'fuzzy' and indisputably less theorised than would be helpful to advance this young academic field. Describing the field's academic evolu-tion, Pamment and his colleagues put it this way: 'few would maintain that [public diplomacy] has traditionally been a concept supported by strong the-

---

31   Zaharna 2022, 161–162.
32   Gregory 2024, 2.

oretical insights and sophisticated theoretical development'.[33] Another leading voice concluded that we 'do not yet have a theory or even competing
theories of PD'.[34]

Secondly, although Gregory's integrating definition does not, strictly speaking, exclude the domestic domain, it effectively reflects the scholarly consensus that public diplomacy is about *international* communication and relationship building with publics outside national borders. Studies in the first two
decades of this century have mostly barred or discouraged attention for communication and relationship building in the domestic sphere. The pioneering
work of Huijgh is a notable exception. She advances the plausible argument
that 'in a global environment where domestic (security) concerns are increasingly linked to international events domestic politics has become part of the
diplomatic process'.[35] Equipped with field observations of the diplomatic
world on four continents, and realising that both academics and diplomats
needed to be persuaded, Huijgh argued tirelessly in favour of 'diplomatic activity with a domestic consciousness'.[36] With that assessment, Huijgh was well
ahead of much theory and practice. Today it seems a run-of-the-mill statement that *all* diplomacy has a domestic dimension. According to Cooper, in
an argument rightly underscoring the connection between politics and diplomacy, this insight gained ground after the rise of populism in Western democracies.[37] As the day-to-day work of public diplomacy is increasingly woven
into the fabric of mainstream diplomacy, it does indeed make sense to refer
to it as diplomacy's public dimension – and, as we argue in this book, to include the public dimension at home.[38]

Making sense of sprawling public diplomacy research over the past decades
is not for the faint-hearted. It seems a productive way forward to identify
different types of logics that reveal the field's 'nascent theories', supplemented
by a line of thought that takes us conceptually in a different direction.[39] In
recognition of diplomacy's wide-ranging public dimension, *public* diplomacy
may be usefully seen as part of the process of diplomacy's accelerated *societisation*. As Kelley observed and elaborated in his book *Agency Change*, diplomacy has become enmeshed with society.[40] In conventional narratives about

---

33   Pamment, Fjällhed and Smedberg 2024, 54.
34   Gilboa 2023, 18.
35   Huijgh 2019, 37 (originally published in 2011).
36   Huijgh 2019, 35. See also Huijgh 2012; Pisarska 2016.
37   Cooper 2019, 36–50.
38   Gregory 2024.
39   Pamment, Fjällhed and Smedberg 2024.
40   Kelley 2014.

diplomacy, society has, however, been pretty much missing, no doubt due to the traditionally statist bias of the field. The rather circumscribed historical understanding of the societal dimension within diplomatic studies is now being revised. Important recent scholarship on the emerging system of states in early modern Europe shows, for instance, how relationships within a mosaic of actors that cannot be captured with contemporary binaries (e.g. state–non-state, formal–informal, professional–non-professional) co-constituted diplomacy as a transnational social practice on the winding path of its professionalisation and institutionalisation.[41] As a multidirectional activity across and within nation-states, diplomacy was and is practised on the cusp of the evolving international system, and ditto transnational relations.

At this point there is advantage in highlighting the deeper societal roots of diplomacy today. Diplomats and the often sizeable proportion of other public officials in overseas missions represent their state and 'whole of government', as well as the interests of regions and cities; they facilitate private commercial interests; they promote the culture, identity and core values of the nation-state; and consular staff have a duty of care vis-à-vis nationals abroad. Diplomats work *for* and *with* home, and wherever they are, they heed the needs and wants of their home economy and society and must take the political persuasion of their government, official directives and changing policies into account. What is central and what is peripheral in diplomacy, as a bundle of networked activity that is state-led or not, may then sometimes seem a matter of perspective.

Our argument that the state-centred diplomatic process is co-determined by state–society relations brings the whole of society into focus, including the certainty that the foreign policy establishment is an object of different types of people engagement. Individuals and groups in society that matter are not always organised, they may or may not feel represented by widely recognised non-state diplomatic actors, and they may or may not be easily reachable, but that does not deprive them of agency. Not just civil society organisations that are legitimate in the eyes of government, but additionally disintermediated individuals who are further removed from the ways and jargon of government, experience the domestic consequences of events and crises abroad. In contrast to the accepted and somewhat stale terminology of a 'whole-of-government' process, 'joined-up government' or 'multi-stakeholder governance' on foreign policy issues, there is less talk in official circles about the need for a 'whole-of-society' approach. Even so, there seems to be an increasing need for more inclusive domestic engagement when shaping foreign policy agendas.

---

41   Windler 2017; Tremml-Werner and Goetze 2019.

From here it is a small step to recognise that the less formalised sphere of diplomacy-at-home brings the perception and experience of its practice closer to the arena of domestic politics. As a further matter, there can be little doubt about the multidirectional drivers of home engagement. They may, for instance, originate in issue-driven popular discontent, existential concerns within the executive branch of government regarding the damaging effects of politico-emotional trends and political polarisation, or the growing interest in the effectiveness of diplomacy by legislators within parliaments who see diplomacy as an activity serving society, and as such accountable to elected politicians. As we discuss in the following part of this chapter, engaging home in diplomacy is characterised by diverse process aspects, discrete mechanisms and functions. Domestic engagement, as far as it is a government-initiated practice, often includes the overarching aims of diplomatic constituency creation and the promotion of trust in government. This is the hard core of domestic engagement as the two-way renegotiation of state–society relations. Ultimately, yet importantly, domestic engagement at the initiative of the foreign ministry is often connected with diplomatic practices ranging from consular assistance, commerce and security concerns to the making of policies on, for instance, sustainability issues or human rights. It also addresses concerns ranging from specific citizen anxieties about the homeland impact of foreign developments and crises to harvesting knowledge and promoting diversity of thought or, alternatively, managing the corrosive effects on the foreign policy establishment of popular discontent or even *sotto voce* worries about rising emotions and polarisation on international issues.

3 Approaches and Mechanisms of Domestic Engagement

3.1 *Understanding 'Domestic Publics' in Diplomacy*

As domestic actors and people become more vocal across various channels, from social media to public forums and grassroots movements, their potential influence on foreign policy decisions increases, prompting states to develop strategies that not only align with their foreign policy objectives but also resonate with the preferences and aspirations of their domestic constituencies. The growing public interest in foreign affairs, particularly in the aftermath of transformative global events such as the 9/11 attacks in 2001, reflects broader democratisation, globalisation and advances in information technology.[42]

---

42   Headley and van Wyk 2012.

Such trends have been reinforced by impactful events and developments, such as the wars in Ukraine and Gaza and the sharp political responses in the Western world to migration and refugee flows. These and other factors have contributed to a more informed citizenry and stronger and more assertive civil societies, potentially enhancing public participation in policy processes.[43]

These shifts have coincided with the emergence of new concepts such as 'people diplomacy', 'domestic public diplomacy', 'citizen diplomacy' and 'participatory diplomacy', reflecting an evolving practice that challenges conventional notions of diplomacy.[44] However, it would be a mistake to overlook, based on Western experience, that domestic engagement practices are not uniform across different national, cultural or political contexts, nor are they a democratic privilege. Takahashi's contribution to this volume (see Chapter 5), for instance, sheds light on the limitations of Japan's non-state actors and people diplomacy. While the role of non-state actors in diplomacy has expanded in many Western countries, their influence remains marginal in countries such as Japan, where a hierarchical state–society relationship persists. The challenge for non-state diplomatic actors in such contexts lies in gaining social legitimacy and engaging more deeply in global networks, often requiring support from the national government.

One of the critical issues in understanding domestic engagement in diplomacy is defining who constitutes the 'domestic publics'. In Chapter 3 of this volume, Opitz, Pfeifer and Geis explore the evolving meaning of '*the public*' in German domestic public diplomacy, particularly in the context of foreign and security policy. They highlight that the term 'public' is rarely conceptualised in academic debates and point out the diversity within the domestic publics. These authors note that domestic publics are not a homogeneous mass; instead, they consist of diverse communities with varying levels of influence and representation. While the relevance of foreign publics for achieving foreign policy goals has long been recognised, there is growing acknowledgement that domestic publics are just as crucial in enabling or restricting foreign policy implementation and success. In line with the discussion in our introductory chapter, Opitz, Pfeifer and Geis conceptualise the public engaged in diplomacy, both at home and abroad, as two sides of a single practice of public diplomacy.[45] Their empirical research and this dual focus highlight once more the need for a nuanced understanding of how state–society relations shape both international and national diplomatic endeavours.

---

43   Kim 2020; Headley and van Wyk 2012.
44   Choi 2019; Huijgh 2012; Sharp 2016.
45   Opitz, Pfeifer and Geis 2022.

In Chapter 9 of this volume, Popkova further enriches this discussion by analysing the efforts to make citizen diplomacy in the United States more inclusive and representative of its *diverse domestic publics*. Citizen diplomats in local communities play a crucial role in implementing state-supported citizen diplomacy programmes by engaging with international visitors. However, little attention has been paid to who these citizen diplomats are and the extent to which they reflect the diversity of their local communities. Popkova draws on Fraser's concept of 'subaltern *counterpublics*',[46] which refers to parallel discursive arenas where members of subordinated social groups create and circulate counter discourses. These counterpublics can in principle function both separately from and in opposition to the dominant public sphere, although they often oscillate across different spaces. This complexity highlights the importance of addressing diversity and representation in citizen diplomacy, particularly at a time when evolving political dynamics may deprioritise the value of citizen involvement in foreign policy. The strength of these initiatives lies in their ability to authentically 'tell the American story', a goal that remains vital amid such challenges.

In Chapter 4 of this volume, Lequesne adds another dimension to the discussion by examining *'home diplomacy' beyond a nation-state's borders*. He argues that home diplomacy should not be limited to building relationships with citizens within national boundaries but should also include engagement with the national diaspora living abroad. Lequesne points to the French consular services' engagement with French citizens living overseas as an example of how home diplomacy can extend beyond territorial boundaries. This extraterritorial dimension of diplomacy highlights the importance of considering both territorial and non-territorial relationships in any comprehensive analysis of home engagement in diplomacy.

3.2   *Diplomacy and Democracy: An Evolving Relationship*

The relationship between diplomacy and democracy is undergoing significant transformation. Traditional diplomacy, long conducted behind closed doors and resistant to public scrutiny, is now intersecting with the democratic imperative for inclusivity and public engagement. This shift has been driven by the rise of non-electoral participation mechanisms – such as public consultations, citizen assemblies and participatory budgeting – that engage domestic publics more directly in decision-making processes.

---

46   Fraser 1990.

Van Deth observes that such mechanisms enhance the legitimacy of foreign policy decisions by bridging the gap between state actors and citizens.[47] However, they can also disrupt established diplomatic norms by introducing new dynamics and actors. The central premise for advancing democratic representation in foreign policy is not to undermine the professional foreign service. Instead, it ensures that diverse actors can participate in policymaking. The concept of *'foreign-policy-as-public-policy'*[48] epitomises this change, advocating for diverse voices to contribute to and participate in foreign policymaking, fostering democratic legitimacy and reflecting the complexities of contemporary societies.[49] This trend signifies a move towards more inclusive governance models, with state actors increasingly tasked with fostering deliberative environments aligned with foreign policy goals.[50]

The authors of this volume make noteworthy efforts to refine the conceptual framework for engaging home in diplomacy by integrating democratic theories. For example, Harrison and Huang, in Chapter 10, introduce the concept of a *'democratic diplomatic middle ground'* where state, non-central government and domestic society actors interact in a shared space to collaboratively design and implement policy. Drawing on assemblage theory and co-production, this framework emphasises public participation in policymaking and advocates for involving local communities, either through 'top-down' inclusion by the state or 'bottom-up' initiatives by civil society. Using the example of Canada–Asia municipal twinning, Harrison and Huang illustrate how this democratic diplomatic middle ground allows various actors to influence the evolution of identities, capacities and diplomatic relationships.

This marks a welcome step forward in advancing the intersection of diplomatic studies and democratic theories. However, it also raises an important question: is it only diplomatic studies that stands to benefit from engaging with democratic theories, or are democratic theories themselves ready to embrace and be enriched by this cross-fertilisation? Exploring this reciprocity could open new pathways for understanding how participatory principles evolve when applied to complex international and transnational settings. Such cross-pollination could deepen insights into both fields, revealing how democratic frameworks adapt and gain relevance in addressing global challenges while reshaping the practices and norms of diplomacy. By doing so, the democratic diplomatic middle ground framework not only enriches the study

---

47   van Deth 2021.
48   Mesquita and Belém Lopes 2018.
49   Mesquita and Belém Lopes 2018.
50   Pfeifer, Opitz and Geis 2021.

of interstate diplomacy and international organisations but also underscores the transformative potential of integrating democratic theories into traditionally hierarchical domains such as diplomacy.

Zhang's contribution to this volume (see Chapter 6) furthers this discussion with the concept of *'internal societization of diplomacy'*, which involves a political community-building process between the state and society within a domestic context. While existing literature primarily focuses on the external accelerated societisation of diplomacy as in public diplomacy, Zhang shifts the focus to how domestic political processes affect a state's diplomatic relations with other countries, for instance, by withdrawing support from or punishing powerful politicians. This perspective highlights the importance of including diverse voices in diplomatic processes to enhance the democratic quality of foreign policy. At the same time, it raises critical questions about the adaptability of traditional diplomatic actors, political leaders and political parties fighting off a crisis of legitimacy to new forms of engagement.

3.3   *Participatory Governance in Diplomacy*

Diplomacy is not just about representation; next to that is the 'making of world politics' and governing as a system of rule and control. Sending, Pouliot and Neumann argue that governing is about influencing other actors' behaviour in order to realise specific goals, and they make a point that can be applied to the central claim in this book:

> If governing becomes progressively more important in the realm *between and beyond borders*, then not only will diplomats have to bring skills in representation to bear on the task of governing, but their effectiveness as diplomats will also depend to a large degree on their ability to work with and through other actors.[51]

In recent years, the rise of *participatory, consultative governance* – a form of innovation arguably not limited to democracies – has gained momentum within diplomatic practices, reflecting a broader trend of involving citizens more directly in decision-making processes.[52] This approach is increasingly recognised as vital in a world shaped by political shifts, such as the rise of populism, the growth of socio-political movements and adjustments such as the expansion of digital communication platforms.[53] These changes have em-

---

51   Sharp 2009; Sending, Pouliot and Neumann 2015, 17–19, our emphasis.
52   Forde 2020.
53   Bächtiger et al. 2018.

phasised the need for governments to engage with their domestic audiences, many of whom may feel marginalised or inadequately represented by existing political institutions. They highlight the increasing role of participatory governance as a response to contemporary challenges.[54]

The study of diplomacy can usefully borrow and apply concepts and insights from public administration, a well-established academic field, with a focus on central government and executive branch collaboration with non-state actors. Within public administration, mainly branched off from political science, participatory governance is characterised by state-sanctioned processes that enable citizens to voice opinions and vote on policy matters, thereby directly influencing policies that impact their lives.[55] By doing so, it integrates citizens into the policymaking process, allowing them to deliberate on crucial issues such as resource allocation and state authority. In contrast to traditional governance systems that operate primarily through representative democracy, participatory governance is designed to complement and improve these systems. The point is not to reject the constitutional principle of representative democracy but to enhance democratic quality and state performance through institutional reform, bringing citizen engagement to the forefront.[56] Fung argues that participatory governance strengthens the core values of democratic systems, such as legitimacy, effectiveness and social justice.[57]

Is participatory governance a potentially powerful tool for enhancing domestic or even democratic engagement in the field of foreign policy and diplomacy? The literature suggests that participatory governance is a viable and valuable tool for addressing complex policy issues, especially in areas involving multiple stakeholders and groups in society with diverse points of view, as is the case of foreign policy. Hence, participatory governance can be particularly effective in handling contested policy areas. Complex issues involve multiple stakeholders – including government officials, private sector actors, civil society groups and affected communities – and organisations with different perspectives, abilities and mandates.[58] By facilitating dialogue and negotiation, participatory processes can generate more inclusive decision-making and policy solutions that incorporate local knowledge.[59] This capacity to bring together diverse voices makes them a tool for enhancing democratic

---

54   Pfeifer, Opitz and Geis 2021.

55   Wampler and McNulty 2011, 6.

56   Wampler and McNulty 2011.

57   Fung 2015.

58   Komendantova, Riegler and Neumueller 2018.

59   Rodriguez and Komendantova 2022.

engagement.[60] In this manner, the practices of participatory governing can be seen as a *mechanism of societised diplomacy*, an actionable approach to 'domestic diplomacy' as governing rather than representation.

Nevertheless, viewing participatory governance solely through the lens of conflict management and governance efficiency reflects a managerial perspective. A significant strand of deliberative scholarship advocates a deeper, more transformative role for such processes, seeing them not just as a way to smooth over differences but as an opportunity for systemic change. Building on this viewpoint, this chapter introduces the concept of '*deliberative governing*', which provides a more encompassing framework for understanding and advancing these practices. This term will be explored in detail in Section 3.5, offering a robust foundation for examining governance in the context of diplomacy.

Psychological theories provide further insights into the challenges of participatory diplomacy. Group dynamics and decision-making studies highlight how the tendency towards consensus can sometimes undermine deliberative principles. Cognitive biases, such as confirmation bias and groupthink, can lead participants to reinforce pre-existing beliefs rather than engage in open discussion. Kim's contribution to this volume (see Chapter 7) explores these dynamics to understand how empowerment theory can explain cognitive and emotional factors in participatory diplomacy. She argues that empowering marginalised voices is an essential component of participatory diplomacy, regardless of the specific mode of governance. Her framework thus offers insights into how different political systems – whether liberal or illiberal – shape the behaviour of states towards their citizens.

3.4   *Raising the Quality of Public Participation*

Democratisation theory can inform the study of diplomacy when the gaze of the latter is no longer limited to the international realm, and this area of political science theorising adds a healthy dose of pragmatism to our earlier IR-centred conceptual and theoretical discussion. The main descriptor in this discussion is participatory governance, which encompasses both *participatory democracy and deliberative democracy*. Participatory democracy involves large groups of citizens directly engaging in decision-making processes, while deliberative democracy typically features smaller, more focused groups involved in in-depth discussions.[61] Both forms aim to strengthen democratic

---

60   Rodriguez and Komendantova 2022.
61   Carson and Elstub 2019.

values by promoting active participation and enhancing the quality of citizen engagement.

Deliberative democracy emphasises fair, reasoned discussions among citizens, fostering inclusive decision-making. Its primary focus is on creating informed and thoughtful dialogues to improve the decision-making process.[62] It challenges traditional representative democracy by advocating for more open, transparent and accountable systems.[63] Unlike participatory democracy, deliberative democracy places special emphasis on meaningful public engagement, the idea being that this strengthens the democratic quality of governance, aligning it more closely with inclusivity and responsiveness.

3.5   *Deliberative Governing in Diplomacy*

One way to describe the central theme of this book is that it lifts the application of deliberative democracy principles – a well-established framework in political theory – into the realm of diplomacy, applying them to issues of national decision-making and foreign policy. We prefer to use the more encompassing term '*deliberative governing*'. It harmonises with our previous definitional emphasis on diplomacy as governing, and it offers a more nuanced approach than merely transposing the principles of deliberative democracy from the domestic to issues in the international arena. This framework is not just about replicating existing democratic engagement models; it adapts and refines them to suit the distinct challenges of diplomacy, where the stakes are often higher, the information more sensitive and the interplay of domestic and international pressures more complex.

Deliberative governing, in this context, then provides a framework for engaging domestic publics in discussions about foreign policy, encouraging dialogue that considers a range of perspectives, preferences and values before arriving at policy decisions. By grounding itself in reasoned debate, mutual respect, reciprocity and a balanced distribution of communicative power,[64] deliberative governing aims to create a political environment where citizens contribute to policymaking in an informed and equitable manner. This approach addresses modern democratic or consultative deficits by ensuring broader and inclusive representation in policymaking.[65] It ensures greater representation, consultation and participation by integrating the domestic publics into the development of foreign policy. Non-electoral participation,

---

62   Hendriks and Lees-Marshment 2019.
63   Forde 2020; OECD 2020.
64   Bächtiger et al. 2018.
65   Bächtiger et al. 2018.

as van Deth highlights, is becoming increasingly important, particularly as citizens seek to engage with policy areas that directly impact their lives even outside the voting booth.[66] When it comes to the foreign policy sphere, these insights suggest that diplomats and policymakers must develop new tools and mechanisms to facilitate a dialogue that acknowledges both expert input and public values. The societal dimension of diplomacy, then, is not merely about consulting citizens – it is about empowering them to influence outcomes in meaningful ways. That requires a tailored approach distinct from typical domestic policy processes, and as governments experimenting with deliberative governance have experienced, it is a tough assignment.

The extent to which elements of the public can influence foreign policy varies by issue, and global issues arguably bring the general public closer to the government-wide sphere of external relations, for example, in areas such as environmental and climate policy. As global challenges become more complex, there is growing recognition that public participation can enhance the legitimacy of foreign policy decisions. Deliberative governing helps bridge the gap by ensuring that foreign policy decisions incorporate a broader range of perspectives and values from the public.[67] In contrast, 'hard' foreign policy and in particular national security issues traditionally rely more on specialised knowledge, limiting public involvement due to the executive's reliance on intelligence services. Public support is nonetheless an asset, and many diplomats will have personal memories of how significant public opposition to government policy can be perceived as uncomfortable or as a threat to the certainties of bureaucratic life.[68]

Thus, deliberative governing in diplomacy represents an evolved approach that harnesses democratic principles in a way that aligns with the demands of contemporary diplomacy. Rather than imposing domestic consultation frameworks directly onto international relations, it strategically adapts them, fostering a diplomatic environment where public input is both feasible and meaningful without compromising the operational integrity of specialised diplomatic tasks. This nuanced approach helps reconcile the often polarised relationship between government action and public expectation, leading to a foreign policy that is more resilient, transparent and in touch with the values and concerns of the society it serves.

---

66   van Deth 2021.
67   Pfeifer, Opitz and Geis 2021.
68   OECD 2020; Pfeifer, Opitz and Geis 2021.

3.6   Models of Deliberative Processes

Institutionalising deliberative practices is neither straightforward nor at the top of any official priority list in the foreign policy and diplomacy of states. It is interesting to observe, though, that international organisations also have a stake in democratic governing. The Organisation for Economic Co-operation and Development (OECD) highlights several models of deliberative public engagement, including citizen recommendations on policy questions, evaluations of ballot measures and permanent deliberative structures.[69] These models underscore the diverse applications of deliberative governing and its potential to improve policy outcomes, build public trust and enhance democratic engagement. The OECD outlines three main routes: establishing permanent deliberative structures, mandating deliberative processes under certain conditions and allowing citizens to initiate such processes – but all require strong institutional support and commitment to inclusivity.[70]

One of the most prominent examples of deliberative governing in practice is the rise of citizens' assemblies and deliberative mini-publics.[71] These assemblies, which consist of randomly selected citizens, are tasked with deliberating on specific policy issues and providing recommendations to policymakers. Citizens' assemblies have been used in various countries to address topics such as electoral reform, climate change and urban planning.[72] The strength of these assemblies lies in their representativeness and their ability to engage citizens in discussions about complex policy issues. For instance, participatory mechanisms for Climate Action Plan 2050 organised by the German Federal Ministry for the Environment represented a sophisticated form of a mini-public, with citizens' recommendations making their way into political programmes.[73]

3.7   Evidence on Deliberative Governing in Practice

Empirical evidence from various participatory and deliberative practices demonstrates how these models can transform governance by enhancing citizen involvement in decision-making. Bua and Escobar discuss how democratic innovations have reimagined and deepened citizen involvement in gover-

---

69   OECD 2020.

70   OECD 2020.

71   Pfeifer, Opitz and Geis 2021; Lacelle-Webster and Warren, 2021; Green, Kingzette and Neblo 2019.

72   Lacelle-Webster and Warren 2021.

73   Pfeifer, Opitz and Geis 2021.

nance.[74] For instance, India's Right to Information campaigns have empowered citizens to hold public officials accountable, while Uganda's participatory constitution-making process in 1995 provided a platform for citizens to contribute to drafting a new constitution, enhancing legitimacy and public support for the constitutional framework.[75] These and other examples in the sphere of domestic politics may offer lessons for integrating deliberative democratic principles into diplomatic practices.

Deliberative governing can impact diplomatic practices by incorporating domestic voices into international policymaking. The European Union's Citizens' Dialogues serve as a notable example of how deliberative democracy can bridge the gap between foreign policy elites and the broader public.[76] These dialogues provide a platform for citizens to engage directly with EU policymakers on issues such as climate change, migration and economic policy, thus demonstrating their potential to engage in the foreign policy decision-making processes.[77]

In Chapter 3, Opitz, Pfeifer and Geis contribute to this discussion by examining how 'domestic public diplomacy' has evolved to include more dialogical formats, allowing citizens to participate in discussions about foreign and security policy by German state actors. They use critical junctures in German foreign policy in the last three decades as opportunities for diplomats and politicians to redefine interaction with the public, showcasing how inclusive engagement can politicise foreign policy and empower citizens to influence decisions that affect their lives.[78] While these instances show the potential for a participatory approach to diplomacy, they also reveal significant challenges in balancing inclusivity with effective governance.

As briefly mentioned in the introduction to this book, deliberative governing's application varies significantly across different political and cultural contexts. In Japan, for example, public deliberation is seen to deepen democratic practices within a liberal democratic system, often focusing on local assemblies and consultative forums.[79] In contrast, such practices in China represent an effort to reflect the influence of ancient Confucian traditions that prioritise social harmony and collective decision-making and introduce deliberative el-

---

74   Bua and Escobar 2018.
75   Wampler and McNulty 2011.
76   OECD 2020.
77   Susen 2017.
78   Falk 2004; Tallberg and Uhlin 2012
79   Tang, Tamura and He 2018.

ements within its authoritarian system of government.[80] These contrasting approaches demonstrate the adaptability of deliberative governing to different political systems and cultural contexts, highlighting its potential to influence governance in both democratic and illiberal, even dictatorial settings.

In Chapter 7, Kim's comparative analysis of domestic public engagement in diplomacy, namely the Arirang Mass Games of authoritarian North Korea and the Participatory Diplomacy Center of democratic South Korea, underscores how different political contexts shape domestic engagement in diplomacy. North Korea's state-driven Arirang Mass Games, while effective in projecting state narratives and their function as a form of mass mobilisation and propaganda, do not result in dialogue about international issues. An engaged citizenry in an authoritarian state can become a means of coercion, compelling the public to make sacrifices for the country's survival. By contrast, South Korea's Participatory Diplomacy Center emphasises informed citizen participation as a democratic and inclusive approach. These diverse examples reveal that while the specific forms and outcomes of domestic engagement practices can vary greatly across political systems, they have somewhat comparable implications for diplomatic practices: governments increasingly seem to realise that they need to reconcile domestic expectations with the international obligations of the state.

4   People's Agency and Identity in the Digital Age

The increasing adaptation of digital technologies has reshaped the participatory landscape in governance.[81] Digital tools, such as the internet and blockchain technology, were initially expected to radically transform participatory mechanisms and democratise governance. While these technologies have not revolutionised participation as anticipated, they have enhanced existing practices.[82] Digitalisation has facilitated broader citizen engagement by making participation more accessible and efficient. Moreover, it has shifted the focus of citizen participation from merely providing input to actively overseeing decision-making and implementation processes.

Within diplomatic studies, Manor has enriched work on digital diplomacy with research on how digital diplomacy targeting domestic publics can make an impact on society's and citizens' interpretation of news and events in

---

80   Tang, Tamura and He 2018.
81   Dean 2023.
82   Dean 2023.

global affairs. Diplomatic practitioners in increasingly mediatised foreign ministries are then visual narrators. Manor concludes that 'domestic digital diplomacy constitutes a significant shift, or disruption, in diplomatic practice as diplomats no longer face the world with their backs to the nation. Domestic digital diplomacy represents the creation of a new and profound relationship between diplomats and their citizens.'[83]

The online environment gives more opportunities for engagement with government to sub-state actors and social networking platforms. In a wider sense, the digital sphere offers opportunities for enhanced people's agency, which starts with citizens' active, critical and well-informed reflection on foreign policy issues and diplomatic encounters covered in the media. Spectatorship theory complements conventional democratisation theory. Felicetti emphasises that not all participants in domestic dialogues on foreign policy issues should be considered potential co-creators of government policies. Positive spectatorship can hence be pragmatically theorised as a form of political agency, a characteristic of people who develop an independent understanding of political issues while relating to others. This nuanced, critical perspective should not be overlooked in discussions about deliberative democracy and its participatory practices.[84]

In Chapter 2, Jiménez-Martínez highlights the overall potential for digital participation to challenge state authority. Digital media platforms have enabled more individuals to engage in national debates and challenge state-controlled narratives. This phenomenon, part of a broader process of 'digital nationalism', raises questions about the role of citizens in shaping national identity and policy.[85] Conflict and contestation are nonetheless rarely acknowledged, as this author cautions, with existing studies only marginally addressing dissent and disruption.[86]

Digital media have contributed to several trends in national identity representation: nations are increasingly portrayed as communities of consumers, the participatory affordances of digital media allow diverse actors to represent the nation, and this diversity leads to more significant fragmentation and polarisation. Acknowledging the role of citizens in representing the nation does not imply treating all voices equally. States, with their greater access to material and symbolic resources, continue to play a dominant role in shaping national identity. Nonetheless, digital media have disrupted traditional state

---

83   Manor 2024, 177.
84   Felicetti 2022.
85   Mihelj and Jiménez-Martínez 2021.
86   Pamment 2021.

narratives, forcing governments to contend with a more complex and contested public sphere. Future debates should, therefore, address tensions between 'top-down' and 'bottom-up' perspectives, exploring when these approaches may align or conflict.[87]

5   The Elite View and Inequality in Domestic Engagement

Incorporating deliberative governing principles into diplomacy presents both
challenges and promising opportunities. Deliberative processes require time,
resources and commitment from state and non-state actors, which may not
always be feasible when international negotiations accelerate. Furthermore,
deliberative forums can be vulnerable to co-optation by powerful interest
groups, undermining their democratic potential. Integrating domestic engagement practices into diplomatic strategies requires careful balancing. Traditional diplomatic actors must foster deliberative environments aligning
with their foreign policy goals while ensuring that the domestic publics are
meaningfully involved in decision-making. Achieving this balance requires
reassessing the role of domestic engagement in diplomacy and recognising
the importance of engaging citizens in foreign policy discussions.

One of the critical challenges in this regard is the tension between expertise
and public participation. While there is growing recognition of the value of
public input, research by Hendriks and Lees-Marshment reveals that political
leaders often value public engagement for pragmatic, epistemic and instrumental reasons rather than for democratic ones.[88] They highlight a 'participatory dissonance' between leaders' appreciation for public insights and their
preference for informal, organic engagement with citizens over formal consultation processes.

This dissonance between participatory ideals and practical implementation reflects the complexities of incorporating public input into diplomacy.
Political elites recognise the instrumental value of public engagement in
shaping foreign policy and their preference for informality is massively reinforced in the context of populist leaders' imagined relationship with the public versus national elites. This theme is explored in Chapter 8 by Wiseman
and Scott, who examine how this tension has played out in the United States
across two politically distinct presidential administrations: those of Republican Donald J. Trump (2017–2021) and Democrat Joseph R. Biden, Jr

---

87   Pamment 2021.
88   Hendriks and Lees-Marshment 2019.

(2021–2025). Their study suggests that the nature of diplomacy's domestic engagement depends significantly on an administration's commitment to democratic or pluralist norms. This underscores the challenges of creating meaningful and democratic engagement mechanisms in complex, politicised and polarised environments.[89]

Another challenge is the potential for domestic engagement practices to exacerbate existing inequalities. Participatory governance initiatives often aim to include marginalised and underrepresented groups in decision-making processes, but there is a risk that more powerful actors may co-opt these initiatives or that they may reinforce existing power dynamics.[90] Ensuring domestic engagement practices are genuinely inclusive and representative seems to be crucial for their legitimacy.

In this volume, Zemanová (see Chapter 11) addresses this challenge by examining the role of a largely overlooked group – youth – as non-state actors in diplomatic engagement. Often underrepresented in both national and international decision-making, youth have significant potential to shape diplomatic agendas through grassroots initiatives. Zemanová analysis of the Junior Diplomat Initiative, active in cities such as Prague, Geneva, Paris and Tbilisi, illustrates how a student-led project has evolved into an international platform for grassroots diplomacy. These initiatives bring fresh perspectives to the diplomatic sphere, underscoring the importance and complexity of integrating youth voices in foreign policy, while also highlighting the broader benefits and challenges of making diplomacy more inclusive.

6   Diplomacy through Public Engagement: Systemisation and Transnationalisation

Despite these challenges, domestic engagement practices offer significant opportunities for enhancing the practice of diplomacy. By incorporating public deliberation and participation into diplomatic strategies, states can enhance the legitimacy and effectiveness of their foreign policies, align them more closely with the interests and values of their domestic publics, and strengthen their international standing. The growing emphasis on participatory and deliberative governing reflects a broader shift towards more inclusive forms of governance, which have the potential to inform the practice of 'diplomacy-as-governing'.

---

89   Boswell, Dean and Smith 2023.
90   Popkova and Michaels 2022.

While deliberative processes offer numerous benefits, they are not a pana-
cea for democratic and governance challenges. They are less effective for urgent decisions, binary questions or issues heavily influenced by national security concerns. Deliberative processes seem best suited for values-driven
dilemmas, complex problems requiring trade-offs and long-term issues beyond short-term electoral incentives.[91] Furthermore, the practical implementation of deliberative democracy faces logistical challenges, the need for inclusive participation and difficulties in integrating deliberative outcomes into
existing political structures. These limitations underscore the need for a
nuanced approach that combines different democratic mechanisms to address governance challenges effectively.

The 'systemic turn' in the literature on deliberative democracy is worthy of
attention as it emphasises understanding deliberation as part of a broader
democratic system.[92] This approach examines how different deliberative processes interact with established institutions and contribute to the overall
democratic framework.[93] Rather than focusing on a single institution or process, the systemic approach advocates for a balanced interplay between various deliberative sites, recognising that each has strengths and weaknesses.
This perspective offers a comprehensive understanding of how deliberative
practices can be integrated at different governance levels, including transnational and global contexts. For instance, the European Union's consensus-
seeking approach exemplifies a deliberative strategy applied at the supranational level, fostering cooperation and dialogue among Member States.[94]

The application of deliberative democracy principles to the society of states
is particularly compelling, as diplomacy often lacks the strong institutional
frameworks found in domestic governance. Deliberation and persuasion are
essential in international settings where traditional coercive power is limited.[95] In these contexts, transnational public spheres and global civil society
play a critical role, offering platforms for marginalised groups and ideas that
might otherwise be excluded from established political structures. The development of these spaces may be important for our understanding of how deliberation can contribute to democratic governance at multiple levels, both
within and beyond national borders.

Global deliberative democracy, though less explored, offers an avenue for
enhancing democratic engagement. International deliberative processes,

---

91   OECD 2020.
92   Mansbridge et al. 2012.
93   Smith 2018.
94   Eriksen and Fossum 2018.
95   Bächtiger et al. 2018.

where panels from different countries discuss shared policy issues, provide valuable insights for supranational governance. An example is the 2019 Citizens' Dialogue in The Hague, where citizens from different countries engaged in cross-national deliberations on global issues. These dialogues demonstrate the feasibility of global deliberative processes, despite challenges related to representation and even something as straightforward as translation.[96] Global and transnational deliberative processes offer a way to achieve meaningful citizen input at a level where traditional democratic mechanisms fall short. These processes are complicated and in their infancy, but they can potentially bridge the gap between domestic publics and international decision-makers, ensuring that global policies reflect a broader range of perspectives and values.

7   Concluding Remarks

This introductory chapter seeks to reinvigorate the diplomatic studies research agenda by exploring how states engage with their domestic publics on diplomatic matters. The many engagements that we have identified strongly intimate that this is a largely underexplored and yet potentially rich area for the study of diplomacy. We see an urgent need for academic research to look beyond traditional actors and practices, to include citizens and recognise people agency in international affairs. By engaging with debates across various social science disciplines, we highlight the inclusion and omission of state–society interactions in IR theory, foreign policy analysis and diplomatic studies. We argue that a more comprehensive empirical and theoretical understanding is needed about how domestic publics are or can be integrated into diplomatic processes. Such engagement will come slowly but surely more into focus in the practice and study of diplomacy, as the case studies in this book show. It matters for diplomatic studies to research the boundaries of state practice and embrace the notion of domestic societal engagement in diplomacy, as a multidirectional and multilevel process. The ways in which state–society relations relate to diplomacy, going way beyond public diplomacy's external focus, deserve to be researched in more depth and included in the future canon on diplomacy.

---

96   OECD 2020.

Acknowledgements

The co-authors are deeply grateful to Jorg Kustermans, Christian Opitz, Paul Sharp and Geoffrey Wiseman for their valuable and insightful comments.

Bibliography

Adler-Nissen, Rebecca. 'Relationalism or why diplomats find international relations theory strange'. In *Diplomacy and the Making of World Politics*. Eds. Ole Jacob Sending, Vincent Pouliot and Iver B. Neumann (Cambridge: Cambridge University Press, 2015).

Alden, Chris and Amnon Aran. *Foreign Policy Analysis: New Approaches* (London and New York: Taylor & Francis, 2017).

Bächtiger, Andre, John S. Dryzek, Jane Mansbridge and Mark Warren. 'Deliberative Democracy: An Introduction'. In *The Oxford Handbook of Deliberative Democracy*, eds. Andre Bächtiger, John S. Dryzek, Jane Mansbridge and Mark Warren (New York: Oxford University Press, 2018), 1–31. styled-content>/styled-content> 10.1093/oxfordhb/9780198747369.013.50.

Berridge, G. R. and Alan James. *A Dictionary of Diplomacy* (Basingstoke: Palgrave, 2001).

Bezerra, Carla de Paiva and Murilo de Oliveira Junqueira. 'Why Has Participatory Budgeting Declined in Brazil?'. *Brazilian Political Science Review* 16 (2) (2022). DOI 10.1590/1981-3821202200020001.

Boswell, John, Rikki Dean and Graham Smith. 'Integrating Citizen Deliberation into Climate Governance: Lessons on Robust Design from Six Climate Assemblies'. *Public Administration* 101 (2023), 182–200.

Brummer, Klaus. 'Comparative Analyses of Foreign Policy'. In *The SAGE Handbook of Research Methods in Political Science and International Relations*, eds. Luigi Curini and Robert Franzese (London and Thousand Oaks, CA: SAGE, 2020).

Bua, Adrian and Oliver Escobar. 'Participatory-Deliberative Processes and Public Policy Agendas: Lessons for Policy and Practice'. *Policy Design and Practice* 1 (2) (2018), 126–140. DOI 10.1080/25741292.2018.1469242.

Bull, Hedley. *The Anarchical Society: A Study of Order in World Politics* (Basingstoke: Macmillan, 1977).

Carson, Lyn and Stephen Elstub. 'Comparing Participatory and Deliberative Democracy'. *Research and Development Note, newDemocracy*, 2019. https://www.newdemocracy.com.au/wp-content/uploads/2019/04/RD-Note-Comparing-Participatory-and-Deliberative-Democracy.pdf.

Choi, Kwang-jin. 'Peoplomacy vs Diplomacy: The Diplomatic Evolution'. USC Center on Public Diplomacy, 19 March 2019. https://www.uscpublicdiplomacy.org/blog/ peoplomacy-vs-diplomacy-diplomatic-evolution.

Constantinou, Costas M. 'Between Statecraft and Humanism: Diplomacy and Its Forms of Knowledge'. *International Studies Review* 15 (2013), 141–162.

Constantinou, Costas M. 'Everyday Diplomacy: Mission, Spectacle and the Remaking of Diplomatic Culture'. In *Diplomatic Cultures and International Politics: Translations, Spaces and Alternatives*, eds. Jason Dittmer and Fiona McConnell (London and New York: Taylor and Francis, 2015).

Constantinou Costas M., Pauline Kerr and Paul Sharp. *The SAGE Handbook of Diplomacy* (London: SAGE, 2016).

Cooper, Andrew F. 'Adapting Public Diplomacy to the Populist Challenge'. *The Hague Journal of Diplomacy* 14 (1–2) (2019), 36–50.

Cornago, Noé. *Plural Diplomacies: Normative Predicaments and Functional Imperatives* (Leiden and Boston: Martinus Nijhoff, 2013).

Dean, Rikki. 'Civic Participation in the Datafied Society | Participatory Governance in the Digital Age: From Input to Oversight'. *International Journal of Communication* 17 (2023), 3562–3581. DOI 1932–8036/20230005.

Eriksen, Erik and Jan-Erik Fossum. 'Deliberation Constrained: An Increasingly Segmented European Union'. In *The Oxford Handbook of Deliberative Democracy*, eds. Andre Bächtiger, John S. Dryzek, Jane Mansbridge and Mark Warren (New York: Oxford University Press, 2018), 842–855.

Falk, Richard. 'The Changing Role of Global Civil Society'. In *Global Civil Society: Contested Futures*, eds. Gideon Baker and David Chandler (London: Routledge, 2004), 69–84.

Felicetti, Andrea. 'Casting a New Light on the Democratic Spectator'. *Democratization* 29 (7) (2022), 1291–1309.

Forde, Catherine. 'Participatory Governance in Ireland: Institutional Innovation and the Quest for Joined-up Thinking'. *Administration* 68 (3) (2020), 1–20. DOI 10.2478/ admin-2020-0013.

Fraser, Nancy. 'Rethinking the Public Sphere: A Contribution to the Critique of Actually Existing Democracy'. *Social Text* 25–26 (1990), 56–80.

Fung, Archon. 'Putting the Public Back into Governance: The Challenges of Citizen Participation and Its Future'. *Public Administration Review* 75 (4) (2015), 513–522. DOI 10.1111/puar.12361.

Gilboa, Eytan, ed. *A Research Agenda for Public Diplomacy* (Cheltenham: Edward Elgar, 2023).

Green, Jon, Jonathon Kingzette and Michael Neblo. 'Deliberative Democracy and Political Decision Making'. In *Oxford Research Encyclopedia of Politics*, 2019.

https://oxfordre.com/politics/view/10.1093/acrefore/9780190228637.001.0001/acre fore-9780190228637-e-917.

Gregory, Bruce. *American Diplomacy's Public Dimension: Practitioners as Change Agents in Foreign Relations* (Cham: Palgrave Macmillan, 2024).

Headley, James and Jo-Ansie van Wyk. 'Debating the Public's Role in Foreign Policy'. In *Public Participation in Foreign Policy*, eds. James Headley, Andreas Reitzig and Joe Burt (Basingstoke: Palgrave Macmillan, 2012), 3–20.

Hendriks, Carolyn M. and Jennifer Lees-Marshment. 'Political Leaders and Public Engagement: The Hidden World of Informal Elite–Citizen Interaction'. *Political Studies* 67 (3) (2019), 597–617. DOI 10.1177/0032321718791370.

Huijgh, Ellen. 'Introduction: Public Diplomacy in Flux: Introducing the Domestic Dimension'. *The Hague Journal of Diplomacy* 7 (4) (2012), 359–367.

Huijgh, Ellen. *Public Diplomacy at Home: Domestic Dimensions* (Leiden and Boston: Brill Nijhoff, 2019).

Jönsson, Christer and Martin Hall. *Essence of Diplomacy* (Basingstoke: Palgrave Macmillan, 2005).

Kaarbo, Juliet. 'A Foreign Policy Analysis Perspective on the Domestic Politics Turn in IR Theory'. *International Studies Review* 17 (2) (2015), 189–216.

Kelley, John Robert. *Agency Change: Diplomatic Action Beyond the State* (Lanham, MD: Rowman & Littlefield, 2014).

Kerr, Pauline and Geffrey Wiseman. *Diplomacy in a Globalizing World: Theories and Practices* (New York: Oxford University Press, 2018).

Kim, Hwajung and Jan Melissen. 'Engaging Home in Diplomacy: Introduction'. *The Hague Journal of Diplomacy* 17 (4) (2022), 611.

Kim, Younhee. 'Citizen Participation in Korea'. In *Routledge Handbook of Korean Politics and Public Administration*, eds. Chung-in Moon and M. Jae Moon (London: Routledge, 2020). DOI 10.4324/9781315660516.

Komendantova, Nadeja, Monika Riegler and Sonata Neumueller. 'Of Transitions and Models: Community Engagement, Democracy, and Empowerment in the Austrian Energy Transition'. *Research & Social Science* 39 (2018), 141–151.

Lacelle-Webster, Antonin and Mark E. Warren. 'Citizens' Assemblies and Democracy'. In *Oxford Research Encyclopedia of Politics*, 2021. DOI 10.1093/acrefore/978019022 8637.013.1975.

Legro, Jeffrey W. and Andrew Moravcsik. 'Is Anybody Still a Realist?'. *International Security* 24 (2) (1999), 5–55.

Leira, Halvard. 'The Emergence of Foreign Policy'. *International Studies Quarterly* 63 (1) (2019), 187–198.

Manor, Ilen. 'Domestic Digital Diplomacy: Digital Disruption at the Macro and Micro Levels'. *The Hague Journal of Diplomacy* 19 (1) (2024), 145–183.

Mansbridge, Jane, James Bohman, Sariya Chambers, Thomas Christiano, Archon Fung, John Parkinson, Dennis Thompson and Mark Warren. 'A Systemic Approach to Deliberative Democracy'. In *Deliberative Systems: Deliberative Democracy at the Large Scale*, eds. John Parkinson and Jane Mansbridge (Cambridge: Cambridge University Press, 2012), 1–26. DOI 10.1017/CBO9781139178914.002.

McConnell, Fiona, Terri Moreau and Jason Dittmer. 'Mimicking State Diplomacy: The Legitimizing Strategies of Unofficial Diplomacies'. *Geoforum* 43 (2012), 804–814.

McCourt, David. *The New Constructivism in International Relations* (Bristol: Bristol University Press, 2022).

Mesquita, Lucas and Dawisson Belém Lopes. 'Does Participation Generate Democratization? Analysis of Social Participation by Institutional Means in Argentine, Brazilian and Uruguayan Foreign Policies'. *Journal of Civil Society* 14 (3) (2018), 222–240. DOI 10.1080/17448689.2018.1496307.

Mihelj, Sabina and César Jiménez-Martínez. 'Digital Nationalism: Understanding the Role of Digital Media in the Rise of "New" Nationalism'. *Nations and Nationalism* 27 (2) (2021), 331–346. DOI 10.1111/nana.12685.

Moravcsik, Andrew. 'Taking Preferences Seriously'. *International Organization* 51 (4) (1997), 513–553.

Narizny, Kevin. 'On Systemic Paradigms and Domestic Politics'. *International Security* 42 (2) (2017), 155–190.

OECD (Organisation for Economic Co-operation and Development). *Innovative Citizen Participation and New Democratic Institutions: Catching the Deliberative Wave* (Paris: OECD Publishing, 2020). DOI 10.1787/339306da-en.

Opitz, Christian, Hanna Pfeifer and Anna Geis. 'Engaging with Public Opinion at the Micro-Level: Citizen Dialogue and Participation in German Foreign Policy'. *Foreign Policy Analysis* 18 (1) (2022). DOI 10.1093/fpa/orab033.

Pamment, James. 'Does Public Diplomacy Need a Theory of Disruption? The Role of Nonstate Actors in Counter-branding the Swedish COVID-19 Response'. *Journal of Public Diplomacy* 1 (1) (2021), 80–110. DOI 10.23045/jpd.2021.1.1.080.

Pamment, James, Alicia Fjällhed and Martina Smedberg. 'The "Logics" of Public Diplomacy: In Search of What Unites a Multidisciplinary Research Field'. *The Hague Journal of Diplomacy* 19 (1) (2024), 49–83.

Pfeifer, Hanna, Christian Opitz and Anna Geis. 'Deliberating Foreign Policy: Perceptions and Effects of Citizen Participation in Germany'. *German Politics* 30 (4) (2021), 485–502.

Pisarska, Katarzyna. *The Domestic Dimension of Public Diplomacy: Evaluating Success Through Civil Engagement* (London: Palgrave Macmillan, 2016).

Popkova, Anna and Jodi H. Michaels. 'Who Represents the Domestic Voice? Diversity, Equity and Inclusion in Citizen Diplomacy'. *The Hague Journal of Diplomacy* 17 (4) (2022), 669–678.

Ripsman, Norrin M., Jeffrey W. Taliaferro and Steven E. Lobell. *Neoclassical Realist Theory of International Politics* (Oxford: Oxford University Press, 2016).

Rodriguez, Fernando S. and Nadejda Komendantova. *Approaches to Participatory Policymaking Processes: Technical Report* (New York: United Nations Industrial Development Organization, 2022). https://www.unido.org/sites/default/files/unido-publications/2022-12/PPM-WEB-final.pdf.

Rose, Gideon. 'Neoclassical Realism and Theories of Foreign Policy'. *World Politics* 51 (1) (2019), 144–172.

Sending, Ole J., Vincent Pouliot and Iver B. Neumann. *Diplomacy and the Making of World Affairs* (Cambridge: Cambridge University Press, 2015).

Sharp, Paul, 'Diplomacy in International Relations Theory'. In Pauline Kerr and Geoffrey Wiseman. *Diplomacy in a Globalizing World: Theories and Practices.* (New York: Oxford University Press, 2018).

Sharp, Paul. *Diplomatic Theory of International Relations* (Cambridge: Cambridge University Press, 2009).

Sharp, Paul. 'Domestic Public Diplomacy, Domestic Diplomacy, and Domestic Foreign Policy'. In *The Transformation of Foreign Policy: Drawing and Managing Boundaries from Antiquity to the Present*, eds. Gunther Hellmann, Andreas Fahrmeir and Milo Vec (Oxford, online edition, Oxford Academic, 2016). DOI 10.1093/acprof:oso/9780198783862.003.0012.

Slaughter, Anne-Marie. *The Chessboard and the Web: Strategies of Connection in a Networked World* (New Haven, CT: Yale University Press, 2017).

Smith, William. 'Transnational and Global Deliberation'. In *The Oxford Handbook of Deliberative Democracy*, eds. Andre Bächtiger, John S. Dryzek, Jane Mansbridge and Mark Warren (New York: Oxford University Press, 2018), 856–868. DOI 10.1093/oxfordhb/9780198747369.013.22.

Susen, Simon 'Jürgen Habermas: Between Democratic Deliberation and Deliberative Democracy'. In *The Routledge Handbook of Language and Politics*, eds. Ruth Wodak and Bernhard Forchtner (Abingdon: Routledge, 2017), 43–66. DOI 10.4324/9781315183718.ch3.

Tallberg, Jonas and Anders Uhlin. 'Civil Society and Global Democracy: An Assessment'. In *Global Democracy: Normative and Empirical Perspectives*, eds. Daniele Archibugi, *Mathias Koenig-Archibugi and Raffaele Marchetti* (Cambridge: Cambridge University Press, 2012), 210–232.

Tang, Beibei, Tetsuki Tamura and Baogang He. 'Deliberative Democracy in East Asia: Japan and China'. In *The Oxford Handbook of Deliberative Democracy*, eds. Andre Bächtiger, John S. Dryzek, Jane Mansbridge and Mark Warren (New York: Oxford University Press, 2018), 791–804. DOI 10.1093/oxfordhb/9780198747369.013.42.

Tremml-Werner, Birgit and Dorothée Goetze. 'A Multitude of Actors in Early Modern Diplomacy'. *Journal of Early Modern History* 23 (2019), 407–422.

van Deth, Jan W. 'What Is Political Participation?'. In *Oxford Research Encyclopedia of Politics*, 2021. https://oxfordre.com/politics/view/10.1093/acrefore/9780190228637.001.0001/acrefore-9780190228637-e-68.

Wampler, Brian and Stephanie L. McNulty. *Does Participatory Governance Matter? Comparative Urban Studies Project Exploring the Nature and Impact of Participatory Reforms* (Washington, DC: Woodrow Wilson International Center for Scholars, Comparative Urban Studies Project, 2011).

Windler, Christian. 'From Social Status to Sovereignty: Practices of Foreign Relations from the Renaissance to the Sattelzeit'. In *Practices of Diplomacy in the Early Modern World c. 1410–1800*, eds. Tracey A. Sowerby and Jan Hennings (Abingdon: Routledge, 2017), 254–266.

Wong, S. 'One-upmanship and Putdowns: The Aggressive Use of Interaction Rituals in Face-to-Face Diplomacy'. *International Theory* 13 (2021), 341–371.

Zaharna, R. S. *Boundary Spanners of Humanity: Three Logics of Communications and Public Diplomacy for Global Collaboration* (Oxford: Oxford University Press, 2022).

CHAPTER 2

Citizens as Problems or Resources: Power, Diplomacy, and the Contested Voice of the Nation

César Jiménez-Martínez

Summary

Works in public diplomacy, nation branding, and soft power generally disregard conflict and disorder, depicting the relationship between states and citizens as harmonious and productive. This is a relevant blind spot that overlooks several social, political and technological transformations – such as the emergence of digital media – which have destabilised the monopoly of states over the representation and communication of the nation. Actors outside the state nowadays have greater capacity for cultivating and disseminating alternative versions of national identity which may disrupt those produced by authorities. This chapter outlines these transformations, focussing on two areas where tensions between states and citizens are notorious. The first one refers to episodes of protest, when, due to their coverage by different forms of media, the perception of political elites as the main conduit of the national voice becomes unsettled. The second one denotes attempts by authorities to incorporate citizens within processes of national representation and communication, through apparently 'bottom-up' initiatives that may cast people as resources or as individuals to be disciplined about their 'correct' identities. An acknowledgement of these tensions has relevant implications for the study and practice of public diplomacy and nation branding, opening empirical and normative questions about the role of ordinary citizens in the task of representing and communicating the nation. Moreover, it interrogates the extent to which democratic ideals of participation and representativeness align with a set of initiatives that to date have prioritised the concentration of symbolic power in the hands of the state.

Keywords

Nation Branding – Public Diplomacy – Nationalism – Media – Digital Nationalism – Protests – Bottom-up Participation – Latin America

1 Introduction

In April 2021, when the lives of people around the world were still shaken by the Covid-19 pandemic, a new nation brand manifesto was unveiled by the authorities of Colombia. Drawing on more than 1,500 surveys and focus groups with Colombians and foreigners, the manifesto promised to distil the country's national essence into a single sentence: 'The most welcoming place on earth'. Seeking to leave behind past associations with terrorism and state violence, the slogan intended to entice foreign investors, businesspeople, and tourists under optimistic and auspicious promises about this Latin American nation-state. Yet only a few days later tens of thousands of people took to the streets of cities such as Cali, Bogotá, Pereira and Medellín, demonstrating against corruption as well as taxes and healthcare reforms proposed by the government of then-president Iván Duque. The protests were met with censorship, misinformation and police brutality, including dozens of deaths, human rights violations and accusations of sexual abuse.[1] On social media, celebrities such as Shakira, J Balvin and Malumna expressed support for demonstrators and condemned the reaction of authorities, while the country's right to host the 2021 edition of the Copa América football tournament was removed. Unsurprisingly, the branding campaign portraying Colombia as the most welcoming place on earth was quickly withdrawn, with promotional consultants stating that carrying on would have been a hypocrisy.[2]

This was not the first time in Latin America that state attempts at constructing and circulating specific versions of national identity were questioned or undermined by citizens. Similar episodes had occurred in Brazil in 2013 and six years later in Chile, when massive protests unsettled official narratives about these nation-states being harmonious, successful societies, attractive for visitors and global capital, as well as worthy of higher political influence.[3] They are consequently examples of governments not only failing to engage, but entirely colliding with 'home'. Yet these tensions have been rarely studied by scholars focussed on the overseas representation and communication of nation-states. Works in public diplomacy, nation branding and other soft power initiatives generally depict the relationship between states and citizens as harmonious and productive, overlooking struggles, conflict and disorder.[4]

---

1 Pineda Castro 2022, 9.
2 Miño 2022b, 176.
3 Jiménez-Martínez & Dolea 2024, 40.
4 See however the special issue by Kim & Melissen 2022; as well as Pamment 2021; Zaharna & Uysal 2016.

The possibility of citizens disrupting and fracturing accounts produced by authorities is therefore an important blind spot that deserves to be scrutinised. The authority of modern states is underpinned both by force and by attempts to legitimise such authority through the use of symbolic forms.[5] Simply put, states claim to have not only a monopoly on violence, but also a monopoly on the domestic and overseas representation and communication of the nation. However, several political, economic and social trends, including the development of digital communication technologies, have markedly destabilised the second monopoly, with a greater number of individuals claiming to speak on behalf of the nation.[6] Fresher outlooks are consequently needed to examine the role of ordinary individuals in an increasingly fickle environment.

This chapter aims to contribute to these discussions, overviewing some of these shifts and shedding light on tensions that need to be acknowledged and examined. I will look at these transformations by first sketching the contingent and constructed nature of nation-states. Since the dawn of the latter, the production and circulation of versions of national identity have been the primary concern of governments and diplomats, who rely on coercive and symbolic power to communicate a human group about their supposedly common features, as well as their adherence to a set of individuals as leaders. However, as I outline next, these practices have been radically altered as a consequence of broader social trends, with other actors, especially ordinary people, having the capacity to cultivate and disseminate alternative versions of national identity.

I will then focus on two areas where tensions between states and individuals are particularly notorious. The first one refers to episodes of protest, where the inevitable, sometimes violent frictions that emerge from the plurality of views of social life become visible. Due to their coverage by national, international and alternative forms of media, outbreaks of social unrest interrogate whether states should necessarily be perceived as the sole or main conduit of the national voice, or whether other actors can be seen, at least temporarily, as equally valid agents. The second one centres on how, partly due to these tensions, states have increasingly sought to incorporate citizens within processes of national representation and overseas communication. While often celebrated by practitioners and academics, these attempts at integration raise important questions about the role that the inhabitants of nation-states

---

5   Thompson 1995, 15.
6   Mihelj & Jiménez-Martínez 2021.

should have in these activities, and whether citizens are simply perceived as mere resources to extract national 'essences', or individuals to be disciplined about 'correct' forms of collective identity.

Two relevant caveats need to be stressed. First, my account emerges from the perspective of media and communications, with particular emphasis on activities such as public diplomacy and nation branding. I have done my best to address debates from relevant fields such as diplomacy, international relations, nationalism as well as social movements, but there will inevitably be omissions. Second, the arguments charted here primarily focus on Latin America. With few exceptions,[7] the continent has been largely neglected in discussions about public diplomacy and nation branding, notwithstanding the enthusiastic embracing of these practices by local governments during the last two decades. Further literature is therefore needed about a region that has not only eagerly adopted nation promotion, but where the relationship between states and citizens has historically been characterised by discord and contestation.[8] I am nonetheless confident that the perspectives outlined in this chapter will be of relevance for other settings, beyond the specificity of the cases outlined below.

2   The State Monopoly on Representation and Communication

Although the term 'nation-state' is used on an everyday basis, historians, political scientists, sociologists and anthropologists, among others, have engaged in heated debates about its meaning as well as how it relates to the notions of 'nation', 'state' or 'country'. In broad terms, perennial or primordial theories argue that the nation is a historically and ethnically rooted human formation that precedes the creation of the centralised political and legal organisation known as the state. Conversely, modernist approaches stress the foregoing nature of the state, underscoring its role as originator of contemporary nations, especially during the 19th and the first half of the 20th century.[9] States are not however fixed, coherent entities, but, as scholars in sociology, international relations and diplomacy emphasise,[10] they are constituted by a multiplicity of actors who fall back on different roles and responses when dealing with the environment they operate in.

---

7   e.g. Fehimović & Ogden 2018.
8   Chasteen 2003, xix; see also Hobsbawm 2016.
9   For a summary of debates, see Mylonas & Tudor 2021.
10   e.g. Haugevik & Neumann 2021; Leddy-Owen 2020.

These discussions become more nuanced when examined through a Latin American lens. The word 'nation' has had different connotations across the continent, with 'patria' (fatherland) being the preferred expression used throughout the period in which Latin American creoles were fighting for their independence from European empires.[11] Likewise, despite their crucial role in the development of nationalism, Latin American states have generally been fragile, facing recurring episodes of social, economic and political upheaval and typically depending on the support of local landowning and military oligarchies.[12] Most significantly, Latin American nation-states are undoubtedly a modern phenomenon. Since the 16th century, struggles to forge and impose – sometimes violently – collective identities have taken place across the continent to create, foster and communicate the sense of being one people among the Europeans who moved to the New World, original indigenous communities, African slaves, as well as the descendants of these and other groups that subsequently migrated to these territories.[13] The states formed after local elites achieved independence from the Spanish and Portuguese empires consequently faced the task of constructing new nations, most of which remain in place until today.[14]

Discussions on power are fruitful to examine both the origin and maintenance of these nation-states. According to Thompson, power is 'the ability to act in pursuit of one's aims and interests, the ability to intervene in the course of events and to affect their outcome.'[15] He distinguishes four types of power: economic, political, coercive and symbolic. While modern states depend on all of them, Thompson echoes Weber when holding that two of these types of power are crucial to sustain state authority: *coercive*, which refers to the use, or threat of using, physical force to confront hazards or insubordination; and *symbolic*, that is, the reliance on representational devices to encourage and uphold the rightfulness of specific people and institutions as bearers of political power.[16] Flags, mythical creatures, portraits of indomitable rulers, as well as narratives of heroes and valiant pasts, among many others, were introduced by political elites to *perform* nation-states as tangible and visible, as well as to convince – not always successfully – a

---

11   Chasteen 2003; Lomnitz 2000.

12   Eakin 2017; Hobsbawm 2016; Miller 2006.

13   Eakin 2017; Larraín 2011; Radcliffe & Westwood 1996.

14   Chasteen 2003, xix.

15   Thompson 1995, 13.

16   Thompson 1995, 15.

human community of their shared ties and their allegiance to a particular set of individuals as leaders.[17]

The above powers can be applied both internally and externally. Although war is perhaps the most obvious example of coercive power, states have also targeted segments of their own populations, such as during the military campaigns against indigenous groups in Chile, Argentina and Guatemala,[18] or the many episodes of human rights violations committed by the dictatorships that governed the continent in the second half of the 20th century.[19] Likewise, symbolic power can be used to communicate versions of national identity to individuals and organisations based overseas. Some typical examples are the world fairs of the 19th century, the employment of propaganda at times of armed conflict, the reliance of governments on international public relations agencies, and more recently, nation branding and public diplomacy.[20] Consequently, as mentioned earlier, states not only claim a monopoly on violence but also a monopoly on the representation and communication of the nation.

Diplomacy is underpinned by such monopolies. One of the many definitions of diplomacy outlines it as 'the conduct of relations between sovereign states ... in world politics by official agents and by peaceful means.'[21] This definition is symptomatic of traditional approaches, which stress that only a specific group of individuals, carefully chosen by the state – such as intellectuals or civil servants – have the right to represent and speak on behalf of the nation. However, as Billig notes, '[the] voice of a nation is a fiction; it tends to overlook the factional struggles and the deaths of unsuccessful nations, which make such a fiction possible.'[22] That is because nation-states are far from being harmonious and stable formations. On the contrary, they are spaces of continuous conflict and transformation. Specialists in Latin America have for instance criticised Benedict Anderson's account of the origin of modern nations, which holds that nominally equal 'imagined communities' emerged during the wars of independence fought by creoles against Spain.[23] They conversely note that these imagined communities were more an aspiration than a reality, with important segments of the population – those who were indigenous, black, female and/or poor – left out of the versions of collective identity

---

17   Chasteen 2003; Eakin 2017; Ku 2022; Zaharna 2022.
18   Miller 2006, 204.
19   Larraín 2011.
20   Cerda 2018; Miño 2022a; Pryluka 2023.
21   Bull 1977, 156.
22   Billig 1995, 71.
23   Anderson 1991.

crafted by local elites.[24] In turn, these 'unimagined' individuals embraced, rejected or transformed the representational devices manufactured by the state, sometimes producing their own interpretations and symbolic outputs to communicate what the nation is or should be.[25]

Definitions of diplomacy like the one above therefore fall into what I have elsewhere called *methodological statism*.[26] With that, I mean an emphasis on the role of the state as the sole or main driver behind nationhood processes, disregarding the significance of other agents as well as the unstable, fluctuating and contested nature of nation-states. The latter point is key. Nation-states are continuously re-created, both in everyday life and on extraordinary occasions; they are sources of identity, units of political and cultural organisation, ways of structuring the world, projects to mobilise people, as well as principles of legitimation to justify the quest for different types of power and their exercise.[27] A more productive approach is therefore proposed by Paul Sharp, who conceptualises diplomacy as 'a discrete human practice constituted by the explicit construction, representation, negotiation, and manipulation of necessarily *ambiguous* identities.'[28] That approach opens the door for acknowledging that a greater number of actors, outside the state as well as outside the geographic and symbolic boundaries of the nation, take part in cultivating, communicating and contesting versions of national identity.

3   Challenging the Monopoly: From National Mass-Media to Digital Nationalism

In the late 20th and early 21st centuries, debates about globalisation and cosmopolitanism predicted that nations would be replaced by different units of political organisation and identity attachment.[29] These views were however founded on a spurious opposition between the national and the global. Globalisation is structured through the prism of nations,[30] and nation-states are international projects, whose existence presupposes other comparable and equivalent units.[31] However, while globalisation did not threaten the existence of the nation, developments associated with it contributed to weaken

---

24   Chasteen 2003; Miller 2006; Radcliffe & Westwood 1996.
25   García Canclini 1995; Itzigsohn & vom Hau 2006.
26   Jiménez-Martínez 2023, 98; see also Leddy-Owen 2020, 1088.
27   Calhoun 1997; Hobsbawm 2016; Leddy-Owen 2020; Mihelj 2011; Shahin 2021.
28   Sharp 1999, 33, my emphasis.
29   e.g. Beck 2000.
30   Mihelj 2011.
31   Calhoun 1997.

the relative monopoly enjoyed by political elites to represent and communicate it as a homogeneous whole.[32]

That does not mean that struggles were non-existent in previous eras. In Latin America there is a rich history of social movements challenging accounts produced by both authoritarian regimes and democratic governments, questioning narratives about who belongs and does not belong to the national community, as well as the conditions of such belonging.[33] Advances in global communication media however contributed to making these contestations more visible, facilitating the construction and circulation of alternative versions of national identity at an unprecedented speed and geographical scope. Corporations, NGOs, terrorist groups, social movements and many other individuals and organisations are nowadays more capable of expressing their objectives and agendas in national terms, sometimes undermining the monopoly of the state as the sole representative of the nation.[34]

These developments are part of the longer and entwined history of nation-states and the media. Media organisations and technologies – both printed and electronic – are 'paradigmatic institutions' that concentrate symbolic power and have a dual nature as both active agents as well as terrains where different actors pursue their objectives.[35] Although the interests of the media and political elites do not always align, the media have been crucial tools for nation-building, with Karl Deutsch stating that social communication was essential for 'the relatively coherent and stable structure of memories, habits and values' that sustain national communities.[36] Subsequent studies have emphasised that, thanks to their spatial reach, naturalisation of routines, standardisation of language, as well as the prominence given to specific symbols and narratives over others, the media, especially the mass-media, have contributed at varying degrees to the instilling, shaping and maintenance of a sense of national identity, solidarity and belonging among geographically separated individuals.[37] Although by no means the only cause behind these processes, the media have played a substantial role in making nations tangible and naturalising them as frameworks to organise social life and structure the world.[38]

---

32   Jiménez-Martínez 2020.
33   Chase-Dunn, Morosin, & Álvarez 2017; Itzigsohn & vom Hau 2006; Radcliffe & Westwood 1996.
34   Eakin 2017; Gerbaudo 2017; Skey & Antonsich 2017.
35   Thompson 1995, 17.
36   Deutsch 1966, 75.
37   Anderson 1991; Billig 1995; Eakin 2017; Mihelj 2011; Thompson 1995.
38   Skey 2022.

The media have also been acknowledged as key tools for shaping overseas perceptions of a nation-state. The histories of propaganda, psychological operations and international public relations emphasise how governments have relied on communicative practices to construct, circulate and manage specific portrayals of a nation-state.[39] These discussions received a further impetus in the early 2000s, with the global spread of concepts and practices such as nation branding, public diplomacy and soft power. Although their definitions may vary, they often refer to a set of media-centric initiatives which draw on strategic communication to construct, disseminate and safeguard 'new' or 'improved' versions of national identity to advance political or economic goals.[40] The centrality of the media has also been felt within diplomatic circles. Scholars have noted that diplomacy is progressively mediatised, with communication technologies becoming inseparable from the key tasks of national representation, communication and negotiation.[41]

Classic works on the media and the nation-state[42] stress the former as centripetal forces that create a forum where dominant imaginaries, narratives or myths about the nation are developed, sustained, renewed and contested. Significantly, these arguments emerge from the study of the mass media. Implicitly or explicitly, many of these works acknowledge that, due to technological, economic and legal barriers, only a reduced set of individuals – such as political elites or those working in the media industries – have historically had the resources and capacity to construct and circulate symbolic forms pertaining to the nation. The participatory design, ease of use and relatively low cost of digital technologies have however produced an important transformation, with a greater number of actors potentially able to communicate their views about themselves and the collective identities they associate themselves with. More specifically, digital media have contributed to three significant trends, which are part of a wider process of 'digital nationalism'.[43] First, due to the prevailing political economy of digital platforms, nations are increasingly imagined and communicated as communities of consumers, as in the cases of nation branding and the broader phenomenon of economic nationalism. Second, the participatory affordances of digital media have enabled a greater number of actors to act on behalf of the nation, making national identities potentially more diverse but also unpredictable. Third, this diversity has

---

39   Taylor 1997.

40   Aronczyk 2013, 34.

41   Aguirre Azócar & Erlandsen 2018; Melissen 1999; Pamment 2014.

42   e.g. Anderson 1991; Deutsch 1966.

43   Mihelj & Jiménez-Martínez 2021, 332; see also Schneider 2018; Shahin 2021.

been accompanied by a greater fragmentation and polarisation, with people gripping to niche and sometimes extreme forms of nationalism.[44]

State attempts at sustaining a dominant version of national identity have consequently been weakened, with other actors capable of cultivating and disseminating alternative narratives. Looking at the case of Pakistan, Kalim and Janjua hold that 'the common man' (sic) is currently a more significant actor in nationalism, given that digital media facilitate 'the construction and dissemination of democratized bottom-up discourse.'[45] Similar accounts have been charted in studies about China, Russia and Central Asia, Iran and India.[46] That does not, however, mean that the era of common narratives is over or that the contemporary media environment is an even playing field. States continue to have at their disposal a greater amount of material and symbolic resources in comparison to ordinary citizens.[47] In addition, digital technologies are not neutral, with algorithms, interfaces, and commercial and political interests restricting the types of collective identities that can be communicated.[48] Notwithstanding these imbalances, the above observations point out that, despite attempts at monopolising the representation and communication of the nation, states are only one among several actors involved in these processes. Official narratives compete with accounts emerging from outside the state as well as from outside national boundaries.

Scholars in diplomacy have effectively acknowledged these trends,[49] yet a significant number has interpreted them from an administrative viewpoint, calling for governments to adopt an even more centralising role to bring order to a chaotic communication environment.[50] Although well-intended, these approaches perpetuate methodological statism. They are underpinned by positions that ignore viewpoints beyond those of political elites and obscure the possibility of more meaningful, and not always neat, exchanges.[51] Moreover, by unquestionably maintaining the state as 'the' voice of the nation, they overlook questions about the actual competence of political elites to define and police collective identities, and gloss over the possibility of richer and more complex outlooks to how nation-states are represented and communicated.

---

44   Mihelj & Jiménez-Martínez, 2021, 333.
45   Kalim & Janjua 2019, 69.
46   Liu 2006; Glukhov 2017; Yadlin-Segal 2017; Neog 2024.
47   Geis, Opitz & Pfeifer 2022; Ku 2022.
48   Zhang, Dumitrica & Jansz 2024; Mihelj 2023.
49   Geis et al. 2022; Kim & Melissen 2022; Ku 2022; Melissen 1999; Zaharna 2022.
50   e.g. Aguirre Azócar & Erlandsen 2018, 132; Lachelier & Mueller 2023, 98; Pamment 2014, 279.
51   For further critiques see Comor & Bean 2012.

4   States without the Nation: The Neglected Role of Citizens

Tensions between the state and 'home' are rarely addressed in studies on nation branding, public diplomacy or soft power. Works tend to optimistically depict the concentration of symbolic power in the hands of the state as a positive development that identifies and mobilises the 'essence' of a nation, and which facilitates mutually beneficial bonds. Emphasis is on collaboration and dialogue with domestic individuals and organisations, while political elites are portrayed as sharing similar goals to the inhabitants of a nation-state.[52] These works are therefore 'built on the premise or goal of a positive relationship between the state and publics',[53] depicting the former as homogeneous and harmonious, and with people acting in partnership with their governments as either 'citizen diplomats' or 'brand ambassadors.'[54]

Conflict and contestation are thus rarely acknowledged, with studies only marginally addressing dissent and disruption.[55] Moreover, when they do, studies uphold the centrality of the state, arguing for instance that national brands can deliberately be 'brandjacked' by non-state actors or other states,[56] or that the public can become a hindrance during episodes of disinformation, unrest or crisis.[57] These perspectives align with the responses of authorities, with for instance the French government relying on transnational state-sponsored broadcasters to 'correct' alternative accounts during the 2005 riots,[58] or Russian authorities supressing online dissent since the invasion of Ukraine.[59] A greater diversification of voices is therefore framed as a setback to manage or a threat to control.

When overlooking these issues, scholars in the field not only align with the viewpoint of states, but they also disregard non-state organisations and sole individuals as potentially equally relevant actors in the task of representing and communicating the nation. In Latin America for example, local activist groups played a key role in directing international attention to the human rights violations that states were committing during the 1970s and 1980s.[60] Crucially, these accusations refuted the slick and lustrous images that military

---

52   Yun 2022.
53   Zaharna & Uysal 2016, 111.
54   See Anholt 2007; Lachelier & Mueller 2023; Sharp 2001.
55   Pamment 2021.
56   Gilboa 2020, 331.
57   Manor, Jiménez-Martínez, & Dolea 2021.
58   Orgad 2012, 106.
59   Satariano & Hopkins 2022.
60   Keck & Sikkink 1997.

regimes, often with the help of international public relations agencies, tried to disseminate about their nation-states, such as when the dictatorship of Augusto Pinochet hired J. Walter Thompson to portray Chile as a righteous neoliberal paradise.[61] The representational interests and aims of people and states do not therefore necessarily align, and are sometimes even pitted against each other.[62]

The viewpoint I sketch here consequently aims to shed light on some of these strains. In the next two sections, I focus on two areas where the friction between states and citizens is particularly notorious. Although these areas are by no means the only ones where tensions exist, they have been especially salient in Latin America. The first one scrutinises collisions between the state and civil society, with a specific focus on recent spells of protests. The second looks at how, partly due to these frictions, governments seek to nominally engage ordinary individuals in processes that develop and circulate versions of national identity for overseas audiences. The examination of these fields has implications for current understandings of activities such as public diplomacy, nation branding and other soft power initiatives. It raises normative and empirical questions about the nature of these processes and the roles that citizens should have in them, especially in an expandingly cacophonic and fragmented communication environment.

5 Citizens Protesting: Obstacles or the 'Authentic' Nation

As previously mentioned, social movements have played a key role in the development of Latin American nation-states. Indigenous groups, activists, peasants, workers and students, among many others, have confronted the coercive and symbolic power of states by actively responding to official policies and narratives, and by sometimes formulating their own.[63] These confrontations are often conveyed through forms of 'contentious collective action',[64] such as protests, demonstrations, marches or gatherings. Whether peaceful or violent, these contentious actions are essentially acts of communication which seek to direct attention to a cause, strengthen collective solidarity and mobilise specific identities, especially among groups that either lack resources to channel their claims institutionally, perceive themselves far from the

---

61   Pryluka 2023.
62   Lossio Chávez 2014; Popkova 2020.
63   Chase-Dunn et al. 2017; Itzigsohn & vom Hau 2006; Radcliffe & Westwood 1996.
64   Tarrow 1996, 592.

centres of power, or are suspicious of the state.[65] Crucially, the success or failure of contentious collective action depends not only on what happens on the streets, but also on how these actions are articulated in and through different types of media.[66]

States have often considered these expressions of collective action as obstacles for national progress and have responded with diverse levels of coercive power.[67] Significantly, while the construction of Latin American nation-states was primarily an elite-driven process, a rhetoric of inclusion and diversity meant that national awareness successfully spread among the inhabitants of these territories, especially from the mid-20th century onwards.[68] It is thus unsurprising that, when engaging in contentious collective action, people have demanded different conditions of belonging *within* nation-states, rather than breaking away from them. This is a trend that continues until today. While movements such as the 2003 World Social Forum in Brazil had a largely transnational character, contemporary protests have been markedly national. They have been driven by domestic agendas, have sought to transform rather than reject the state and have been justified through explicit appeals to national identity, including the use of flags, national football t-shirts and other symbols.[69] The nation has therefore been not only a source of identity, but also a 'central battlefield' for social justice and human rights struggles.[70]

It is noteworthy that high profile protests such as the June Journeys in Brazil, the 2019 social upheaval in Chile, and the 2021 demonstrations in Colombia were communicated in and through the media as evidence that these countries had 'woken up'.[71] Crucially, these and previous episodes were not only domestically covered, but were staged for and witnessed by, overseas audiences. Drawing on the affordances of digital technologies, activists produced and disseminated their own accounts, challenging the narratives of authorities and national media.[72] At the same time, they sought to reach individuals and organisations based abroad, hoping that international pressure would have an impact on domestic politics.[73]

---

65   Stokes, 2020, 269; Wall, 2023, 3.
66   Cammaerts 2024.
67   Doran 2017, 184; Hobsbawm 2016, 423.
68   Chasteen 2003, xix; Miller 2006, 211.
69   Jiménez-Martínez 2020.
70   Gerbaudo 2017, 117.
71   Jiménez-Martínez & Dolea 2024, 48; Miño 2022a, 2776.
72   Jiménez-Martínez 2020; Scherman & Rivera 2021.
73   See Keck & Sikkink 1997; Weber 2004.

The visibility that foreign media occasionally give to protests means that episodes of social unrest tend to be interpreted as expressions of the 'authentic' nation. In many of these accounts, the state was depicted as treacherous to the nation, concerned more with defending the interests of political and economic elites rather than of citizens. That was the case in Brazil and Chile, where the 2013 and 2019 demonstrations were narrated in a largely celebratory manner, as surprising but ultimately welcome expressions of collective action that exposed the everyday struggles of a nation. Significantly, these demonstrations were described as events that unsettled official versions of collective identity, either by undermining the international reputation of a nation-state, or by unveiling a supposedly 'authentic' nation that had been concealed under the communication efforts of authorities.[74]

Interpretations like these were helped by the fact that protests occasionally had a direct impact on state attempts at cultivating and disseminating a specific version of national identity. The demonstrations in Brazil raised, for instance, significant doubts about the local appetite for hosting both the 2014 FIFA World Cup and 2016 Summer Olympics; the social upheaval in Chile led to a cancellation of the 2019 Asia-Pacific Economic Cooperation summit and the UN Climate Change Conference in Santiago; and, as discussed earlier, when tens of thousands of people took to the streets of Colombia in 2021, the country lost its hosting rights to Copa América and the nation branding campaign promoting it as 'the most welcoming place on earth' was cancelled.[75] These episodes of collective action were notorious for both the damage caused to public and private infrastructure, as well as the state violence against citizens, with cases of police brutality resulting in arbitrary arrests, sexual violence, injuries and death.[76] It is, however, noteworthy that diplomats as well as institutions managing national images remained silent or took a long time to address these occurrences. When authorities did speak to foreign audiences, they drew on platitudes about democracy, freedom of expression and assembly, or described protests as either foreign interventions or incidents unrepresentative of the national character.[77]

Episodes of collective action are consequently a dramatic example of the coercive and symbolic power struggles that happen within a nation-state. For local authorities, protests can be a threat to be contained or avoided, due to their potential of destabilising painstakingly crafted national reputations.

74   Jiménez-Martínez & Dolea 2024, 48–49.
75   Jiménez-Martínez & Dolea 2024, 40; Miño 2022b, 176.
76   Pineda Castro 2022; Somma, Bargsted, Disi Pavlic, & Medel 2021.
77   Jiménez-Martínez & Dolea 2024, 47; Nery & Coutinho 2014.

However, protests are – at least in democratic governments, as many claim to be in Latin America – an essential component of civic life that is nominally protected within the rights of freedom of expression as well as assembly.[78] Fantasies of a harmonious and unified national voice, upheld by public diplomacy, nation branding, and other soft power initiatives, therefore blow up when people and political elites are in discord, exposing the plurality of views that characterise social life and baring the sutures that keep the nation and the state together.

6   Citizens Participating: Partnership or Exploitation

Throughout their history, nation branding, public diplomacy and the overall field of diplomacy have been the prevalent domain of elites, with ordinary citizens playing only a limited role, if any at all, in these activities.[79] Political, social and technological developments, as well as the need to secure domestic support over government policies, have however prompted authorities to introduce 'bottom up' approaches that seek to include the inhabitants of a nation within these practices.[80] This has also been the case in Latin America, with calls for greater transparency, democratisation and further citizen involvement, especially in view of some of the previously discussed episodes of social unrest.[81]

During the past decade, Latin American states have proudly emphasised spells in which ordinary individuals played – at least nominally – an active role, as supposed partners in the overseas representation and communication of the nation. Three partnership modes involving different degrees of control and tension can be identified. In the first one, the inhabitants of a nation-state are invited to voice their opinion, in a highly delimited manner, about textual or visual outputs of future promotional initiatives. That was the case in Honduras and Argentina, where in 2015 and 2021 respectively, people were encouraged to vote online for the logo that most successfully encapsulated the nation as a brand.[82] While authorities justified these initiatives as ways to strengthen national pride and a sense of belonging, as well as make the national brand

---

78   Wall 2023, 2.
79   Kim & Melissen 2022; Popkova & Michaels 2022.
80   Geis et al. 2022.
81   Aguirre Azócar & Erlandsen 2018.
82   Quintana 2021; Redacción 2015.

more democratic,[83] contingent, short-term considerations were still relevant. In the case of Argentina, citizen participation was stressed by the government of the time as a means to criticise the initiatives of the previous administration, which belonged to a different political colour.[84]

The second mode opens space for people to be co-constructors of meaning. That was the case of Chile between 2016 and 2018, when, as part of the branding campaign 'Chile, I really love you', state officials organised a series of workshops across the country to identify geographical, cultural and social features considered nationally representative. These were subsequently voted in an online poll.[85] Likewise, a public-private initiative called 'It's Colombia, not Columbia' encouraged Colombians in 2013 to openly complain every time they found the name of their country misspelled on social media.[86] Although technological and legal frameworks for participation are clearly demarcated, in these cases citizens have a higher degree of autonomy: they can sustain, supplement and even occasionally criticise the narratives encouraged by authorities.

The third mode refers to a set of activities labelled as 'citizen diplomacy', in which ordinary individuals take a representational role in foreign affairs, sometimes on behalf of the nation.[87] Scholarship in Latin America has provided a varied set of examples for them, including feminist movements and educational NGOs in Mexico, spontaneous appeals for aid during floods in Peru and earthquakes in Chile, as well as lobbies opposing a free trade agreement between Colombia and the United States.[88] 'Citizen diplomacy' therefore covers initiatives that support and complement, but also undermine, the interests of the state. It is however unclear to what extent such openness, which captures the frictional nature of nation-states, is on purpose or is, instead, evidence of conceptual vagueness.

Although scholars and practitioners have celebrated many of the above cases due to the apparent challenge they represent to traditional models of diplomacy,[89] it is unclear to what extent they are effectively examples of 'bottom-up' participation. Notwithstanding the varying level of elite control across these modes, ideas and suggestions contributed by ordinary individuals

---

83   Llobet 2021.
84   Quintana 2021.
85   Miño & Austin 2022.
86   Gómez Carrillo 2018.
87   Lachelier & Mueller 2023; Sharp 2001.
88   Aguirre Azócar & Erlandsen 2018; Alejo 2020; Pría 2008; Trejos Rosero 2016.
89   e.g. Aguirre Azócar & Erlandsen 2018.

are cast within pre-existing schemas about what to show or conceal about a human community, and decisions about what the nation 'actually' is remain largely in the hands of the state. This constrained participation should not, however, be of any surprise. Latin American nation-states have been histori-cally characterised as 'top-down' affairs, with mass citizen involvement begin-ning only in the second half of the 20th century, due to changing economic models, urban migration, higher levels of literacy, and widespread communi-cation technologies.[90] While these transformations meant that elites could not ignore local populations anymore, those in power began approaching or-dinary people as mere resources to mobilise in support of political projects.[91]

The latter trend is arguably replicated in initiatives aiming to represent and communicate the nation. Earlier nation branding initiatives in the continent were predominantly elitist, restricted to a narrow group of state officials or foreign communication consultants. Some of these individuals, such as David Lightle or Simon Anholt – who advised the governments of Colombia, Chile and Mexico, among others – met with ordinary people to extract infor-mation about a supposedly timeless national essence.[92] Yet these meetings were not part of an exercise of ontological delineation and were arguably unconcerned with developing a solid collective identity. The aim was instead advancing specific, short-term, and often commercially driven promotional initiatives, such as the development of logos and slogans, marketing cam-paigns, and the hosting of mega events, in order to climb positions in rankings produced by these very same consultants.[93] Moreover, some of these activities took a disciplinary turn in places such as Peru or Colombia, where authorities drew on symbolic forms to teach individuals about their 'correct' identities, in the hopes of converting them into happy 'ambassadors' who embraced and replicated the narratives manufactured by the state.[94]

Although the modes outlined above demonstrate that citizen involvement has expanded, many of these activities comprise only a veneer of participa-tion, with people sporadically invited to take part in processes concerned with representing the nation. For authorities, the role of ordinary individuals has therefore consisted of providing raw material to inform public diplomacy and nation branding activities, as well as of being educated and regimented around what the 'authentic' national identity is. In face of the significant trans-

---

90   Chasteen 2003; Eakin 2017.

91   Hobsbawm 2016.

92   Aronczyk 2013; Ramos & Noya 2006.

93   Aronczyk 2013.

94   Lossio Chávez 2014; Miño 2022b.

formations outlined earlier on how nation-states are communicated, states have persisted in attempts at preserving a monopoly on symbolic power, determining budgets, outlining legal and institutional boundaries that facilitate or restrict communicational efforts, and having the final word on the strategies and messages that are implemented. People are only cast in secondary roles within the task of representing overseas the nation-states they inhabit and are often exploited and disciplined to grant legitimacy to decisions taken by a selected few.

7   Concluding Remarks

The above account sketches the gradual but profound transformation that the representation and communication of nation-states have experienced in recent decades. Although at the outset of modern nation-states, the construction and overseas dissemination of versions of national identity was a task primarily restricted to political elites, social, political and technological shifts – such as the development of digital media – have facilitated a greater number of individuals to potentially speak on behalf of the nation. As a result, the monopoly of the state as the main or sole representative of the voice of the nation has been severely destabilised, with actors outside the state cultivating and disseminating versions of collective identity that may challenge those manufactured by authorities.

Practitioners in public diplomacy, nation branding, and soft power have partly acknowledged these changes. Initiatives such as the online polls about promotional outputs conducted in Honduras and Argentina, focus groups asking Chileans to underline local features, or social media campaigns requesting foreigners to correctly spell Colombia's name, have attempted to incorporate, with varying degrees of involvement and success, the viewpoints of the inhabitants of these nation-states. Unlike the promises of many consultants advising Latin American governments,[95] implied in these efforts is an acceptance that states will never achieve complete control over the representation and communication of the nation, regardless of attempts at imposing stability, and developing a façade of unity. By stressing the need to incorporate ordinary individuals into these processes, this more participatory turn underscores the belief that in democratic governments – and those pretending to be so – people are, at least nominally, the ultimate locus of power.[96]

---

95   e.g. Anholt 2007.
96   Popkova & Michaels 2022.

Scholarship in the field has however trailed behind, generally trapped within a methodological statism that encourages and celebrates the concentration of symbolic power in the hands of the state, while claiming that relationships between the latter and citizens are based on harmonious bonds and mutual benefits. Broader theoretical outlooks are therefore necessary. Individuals and organisations outside the state should be approached as prominent agents in the task of communicating nation-states overseas, not simply as implementers of state policies, but as actors capable of disseminating equally, and occasionally more valid versions of national identity. Such perspective would line up with literature on everyday nationhood, which recognises the role of ordinary people in performing, interpreting and negotiating the nation,[97] as well as with studies in international relations that observe how domestic contestations can be played out beyond the boundaries of nation-states.[98]

Acknowledging the significance of people in representing and communicating the nation is an imperative matter. The cultivation and dissemination of versions of national identity is an inherently untidy process, although technological, economic and legal barriers associated with the mass media facilitated greater control in the hands of the state. This is no longer the case in a more fragmented and unstable digital environment. Ignoring ordinary individuals is therefore unwise, as their defiance of official symbols and narratives is potentially more visible, especially when contentious collective action is magnified in and through forms of media. State resources invested into strategic communication initiatives aiming to spread and manage national identities are therefore not only at risk of being wasted, but even backfiring. That does not, however, imply assuming that citizens are on an equal footing to the state in terms of resources and goals. Authorities continue to have access to a greater number of coercive, political, economic and symbolic assets when attempting to impose their versions of collective identity as the 'authentic' ones, in comparison with those available to ordinary individuals. At the same time, people occasionally show a stronger push for solidarity, cooperation and collective problem-solving that does not always match the more competitive, protective disposition of the state.[99]

Practice and research in public diplomacy, nation branding, soft power, as well as the broader field of diplomacy, should thus pose further empirical and normative questions about the role that ordinary citizens can and should have

---

97   Skey & Antonsich 2017.
98   Hintz 2018.
99   Zaharna 2022.

in the task of constructing, communicating and managing collective identities. Lingering queries include who has the right to define the nation, what the tensions between 'top-down' and 'bottom-up' public diplomacy and nation branding approaches are, how states police and manage official versions of national identity – and whether they have the capacity to effectively do so –, as well as in which circumstances people and states not only collide, but potentially line up. Practitioners and scholars should also reflect on how well-intentioned yet potentially shallow discourses and policies aspiring to determine supposedly timeless national values or increase citizen participation, may inadvertently conceal important socioeconomic inequalities, perpetuating the viewpoints of diplomats, civil servants and authorities while excluding historically marginalised groups.[100] Moreover, further discussions are needed regarding whether democratic ideals of participation and representativeness are aligned with a set of tasks that to date have prioritised the concentration of symbolic power in the hands of the state, accentuating the latter as the sole representative of the nation, while ignoring increasingly louder and often contradictory voices, such as those heard in the streets of Colombia in April 2021.

Acknowledgements

I would like to thank the book editors for their invitation to contribute, their continuous support throughout the process of research and writing, as well as their valuable suggestions on how to improve the text. I am also grateful to Sameera Durrani, Lee Edwards, Pablo Miño and Rhonda Zaharna for their valuable comments on earlier drafts of this chapter.

Bibliography

Aguirre Azócar, Daniel and Erlandsen, Matt. 'La Diplomacia Pública Digital en América Latina: Desafíos y Oportunidades'. *Revista Mexicana De Política Exterior*, 113 (mayo-agosto) (2018), 119–139.
Alejo, Antonio. 'Global Citizenship Education: The Case of Equipo Pueblo's Citizen Diplomacy Program in Mexico'. *Education, Citizenship and Social Justice*, 15(2) (2020), 181–193. DOI 10.1177/1746197919833381

---

100   Geis et al. 2022; Popkova & Michaels 2022.

Anderson, Benedict. *Imagined Communities: Reflections on the Origin and Spread of Nationalism* (London: Verso, 1991).

Anholt, Simon. *Competitive Identity: The New Brand Management for Nations, Cities and Regions* (Basingstoke: Palgrave Macmillan, 2007).

Aronczyk, Melissa. *Branding the Nation: The Global Business of National Identity* (Oxford: Oxford University Press, 2013).

Beck, Ulrich. *What is Globalization?* (Malden, MA: Polity, 2000).

Billig, Michael. *Banal Nationalism* (London: Sage, 1995).

Bull, Hedley. *The Anarchical Society: A Study of Order in World Politics.* (New York: Columbia University Press, 1977).

Calhoun, Craig. *Nationalism* (Buckingham: Open University Press, 1997).

Cammaerts, Bart. 'The Mediated Circulation of the United Kingdom's YouthStrike4-Climate Movement's Discourses and Actions'. *European Journal of Cultural Studies*, 27(1) (2024), 107–128. DOI 10.1177/13675494231165645

Cerda, Andrea. 'Promotion Before Nation Branding: Chile at the World Exhibitions'. In *Branding Latin America: Strategies, Aims, Resistance*, eds. Dunja Fehimović and Rebecca Ogden (Lanham, Maryland: Lexington, 2018), 35–57.

Chase-Dunn, Christopher, Morosin, Alessandro and Álvarez, Alexis. 'Movimientos Sociales y Regímenes Progresistas en América Latina: Revoluciones Mundiales y Desarrollo Periférico'. In *Movimientos Sociales en America Latina: Perspectivas, Tendencias y Casos*, eds. Paul Almeida & Allen Cordero Ulate (Buenos Aires: Consejo Latinoamericano de Ciencias Sociales, 2017), 29–46.

Chasteen, John Charles. 'Introduction: Beyond Imagined Communities'. In *Beyond Imagined Communities: Reading and Writing the Nation in Nineteenth-Century Latin America*, eds. Sara Castro-Klarén and John Charles Chasteen (Baltimore and London: The John Hopkins University Press, 2003), ix–xxv.

Comor, Edward and Bean, Hamilton. 'America's "Engagement" Delusion: Critiquing a Public Diplomacy Consensus'. *International Communication Gazette*, 74(3) (2012), 203–220. DOI 10.1177/1748048511432603

Deutsch, Karl. *Nationalism and Social Communication: An Inquiry into the Foundation of Nationality* (2nd ed.) (Cambridge, Massachusetts: MIT Press, 1966).

Doran, Marie Christine 'The Hidden Face of Violence in Latin America: Assessing the Criminalization of Protest in Comparative Perspective'. *Latin American Perspectives*, 44(5) (2017), 183–206. DOI 10.1177/0094582X17719258

Eakin, Marshall. *Becoming Brazilians: Race and National Identity in Twentieth-Century Brazil.* (Cambridge, UK: Cambridge University Press, 2017).

Fehimović, Dunja and Ogden, Rebecca, eds. *Branding Latin America: Strategies, Aims, Resistance.* (Lanham, MD.: Lexington Books, 2018).

García Canclini, Nestor. *Hybrid Cultures: Strategies for Entering and Leaving Modernity* (Minneapolis, Minn.: University of Minnesota Press, 1995).

Geis, Anna, Opitz, Christian and Pfeifer, Hanna. 'Recasting the Role of Citizens in Diplomacy and Foreign Policy: Preliminary Insights and a New Research Agenda'. *The Hague Journal of Diplomacy*, 10(4) (2022), 1–14. DOI 10.1163/1871191x-bja10136

Gerbaudo, Paolo. *The Mask and the Flag: Populism, Citizenism and Global Protest.* (London: Hurst & Company, 2017).

Gilboa, Eytan. 'Israel: Countering Brandjacking'. In *Routledge Handbook of Public Diplomacy*, eds. Nancy Snow and Nicholas Cull (New York: Routledge, 2020), 331–341.

Glukhov, Andrey. 'Construction of National Identity through a Social Network: A Case Study of Ethnic Networks of Immigrants to Russia from Central Asia'. *AI and Society*, 32(1) (2017), 101–108. DOI 10.1007/s00146-016-0644-9

Gómez Carrillo, Paula (2018). 'Covert Nation Branding and the Neoliberal Subject: The Case of "It's Colombia, NOT Columbia." In *Branding Latin America: Strategies, Aims, Resistance*, eds. Dunja Fehimović and Rebecca Ogden (Lanham, Maryland: Lexington, 2018), 95–116.

Haugevik, Kristin and Neumann, Cecile Basberg. 'Reputation Crisis Management and the State: Theorising Containment as Diplomatic Mode'. *European Journal of International Relations*, 27(3) (2021), 708–729. DOI 10.1177/13540661211008213

Hintz, Lisel. *Identity Politics Inside Out: National Identity Contestation and Foreign Policy in Turkey* (New York: Oxford University Press, 2018).

Hobsbawm, Eric. 'Nationalism and Nationality in Latin America'. In *Viva la Revolución: Eric Hobsbawm on Latin America*, ed. Leslie Bethell (London: Abacus, 2016), 417–432.

Itzigsohn, José and and vom Hau, Matthias. 'Unfinished Imagined Communities: States, Social Movements, and Nationalism in Latin America'. *Theory and Society*, 35(2) (2006), 193–212. DOI 10.1007/s11186-006-9001-1

Jiménez-Martínez, César. *Media and the Image of the Nation during Brazil's 2013 Protests* (Cham, Switzerland: Palgrave Macmillan, 2020).

Jiménez-Martínez, César. 'Imaged Communities: The Visual Construction, Contestation and Commercialisation of the Nation'. In *Research Handbook on Visual Politics*, eds. Darren Lilleker and Anastasia Veneti (Cheltenham, UK: Edward Elgar, 2023), 94–107.

Jiménez-Martínez, César and Dolea, Alina. 'Threats, Truths and Strategies: The Overlooked Relationship between Protests, Nation Branding and Public Diplomacy'. *Nations and Nationalism*, 30(1) (2024), 39–55. DOI 10.1111/nana.12980

Kalim, Salma and Janjua, Fauzia. '#WeareUnited, Cyber-nationalism during Times of a National Crisis: The Case of a Terrorist Attack on a School in Pakistan'. *Discourse and Communication*, 13(1) (2019), 68–94. DOI 10.1177/1750481318771448

Keck, Margaret and Sikkink, Kathryn. *Activists Beyond Borders: Advocacy Networks in International Politics* (Ithaca, NY: Cornell University Press, 1997).

Kim, HwaJung and Melissen, Jan. 'Engaging Home in International Diplomacy: Introduction'. *The Hague Journal of Diplomacy*, 17(4) (2022), 611–613. DOI 10.1163/
1871191x-bja10141

Ku, Minseon. 'Summit Diplomacy as Theatre of Sovereignty Contestation'. *The Hague Journal of Diplomacy*, 27(1) (2022), 628–642. DOI 10.1163/1871191x-bja10131

Lachelier, Paul and Mueller, Sherry Lee. 'Citizen Diplomacy'. In *A Research Agenda for Public Diplomacy*, ed. Eytan Gilboa. (Cheltenham, UK: Edward Elgar, 2023), 91–105.

Larraín, Jorge. *¿América Latina Moderna? Globalización e Identidad* (Santiago: LOM Ediciones, 2011).

Leddy-Owen, Charles. 'Bringing the State Back into the Sociology of Nationalism: The Persona Ficta Is Political'. *Sociology*, 54(6) (2020), 1088–1104. DOI 10.1177/00380 38520925730

Liu, Shih-Diing. 'China's Popular Nationalism on the Internet. Report on the 2005 Anti-Japan Network Struggles'. *Inter-Asia Cultural Studies*, 7(1) (2006), 144–155. DOI 10.1080/14649370500463802

Llobet, Marcos. 'La Marca Argentina ya Tiene su Nuevo Logo'. *La Agencia de Viajes Argentina*. 15 July 2021. https://argentina.ladevi.info/marca-pais/la-marca-pais-argentina-ya-tiene-su-nuevo-logo-n32329

Lomnitz, Claudio. 'Nationalism as a Practical System: Benedict Anderson's Theory of Nationalism from the Vantage Point of Spanish America'. In *The Other Mirror: Grand Theory through the Lens of Latin America*, eds. Miguel Angel Centeno and Fernando López-Alves (Princeton, N.J.: Princeton University Press, 2000), 329–359.

Lossio Chávez, Félix. 'La Necesaria Fantasía de la Marca Perú'. In *Perspectivas sobre el Nacionalismo en el Perú*, ed. Gonzalo Portocarrero (Lima: Red para el Desarrollo de las Ciencias Sociales en el Perú, 2014), 23–38.

Manor, Ilan, Jiménez-Martínez, César and Dolea, Alina. 'An Asset or a Hassle? The Public as a Problem for Public Diplomats'. *The Hague Journal of Diplomacy Blog*. 16 November 2021. https://www.universiteitleiden.nl/hjd/news/2021/blog-post–an -asset-or-a-hassle-the-public-as-a-problem-for-public-diplomats

Melissen, Jan. 'Introduction'. In *Innovation in Diplomatic Practice*, ed. Jan Melissen (Basingstoke, UK: Palgrave Macmillan, 1999), xiv–xxiii.

Mihelj, Sabina. *Media Nations: Communicating Belonging and Exclusion in the Modern World* (Basingstoke: Palgrave Macmillan, 2011).

Mihelj, Sabina. 'Platform Nations'. *Nations and Nationalism*, 29(1) (2023), 10–24. DOI 10.1111/nana.12912

Mihelj, Sabina and Jiménez-Martínez, César. 'Digital Nationalism: Understanding the Role of Digital Media in the Rise of 'New' Nationalism'. *Nations and Nationalism*, 27(2) (2021), 331–346. DOI 10.1111/nana.12685

Miller, Nicola. 'The Historiography of Nationalism and National Identity in Latin America'. *Nations and Nationalism*, 12(2) (2006), 201–221. DOI 10.1111/j.1469-8129.2006.00237.x

Miño, Pablo. 'Nation Branding as a Modern Expression of Colonialism in Latin America: A Focus on Chile, Colombia, and Peru'. *International Journal of Communication*, 16 (2022a), 2762–2780.

Miño, Pablo. *Nation Branding in Latin America: Global, Regional, and Local Representations Intertwined*. (Doctoral Thesis, University of North Carolina at Chapel Hill, 2022b).

Miño, Pablo and Austin, Lucinda. 'A Cocreational Approach to Nation Branding: The Case of Chile'. *Public Relations Inquiry*, 11(2) (2022), 293–313. DOI 10.1177/2046147x221081179

Mylonas, Harris and Tudor, Maya. 'Nationalism: What We Know and What We Still Need to Know'. *Annual Review of Political Science*, 24 (2021), 109–132. DOI 10.1146/annurev-polisci-041719- 101841

Neog, Krishanu Bhargav. 'Memes, National Identity and National Belonging: Visual "Nation-Talk" on Indian Social Media Pages'. *Television & New Media*, 25(2) (2024), 150–167. DOI 10.1177/15274764231180496

Nery, Natuza and Coutinho, Filipe. 'Protestos Fizeram Governo Mudar Discurso sobre Copa'. *Folha de São Paulo*. 9 February 2014. http://www1.folha.uol.com.br/poder/2014/02/1409525-protestos-fizeram-governo-mudar-discurso-sobre-copa.shtml

Orgad, Shani. *Media Representation and the Global Imagination* (Cambridge, UK: Polity, 2012).

Pamment, James. 'The Mediatization of Diplomacy'. *The Hague Journal of Diplomacy*, 9(3) (2014), 253–280. DOI 10.1163/1871191X-12341279

Pamment, James. 'Does Public Diplomacy Need a Theory of Disruption? The Role of Nonstate Actors in Counter-branding the Swedish COVID-19 Response'. *Journal of Public Diplomacy*, 1(1) (2021), 80–110. DOI 10.23045/jpd.2021.1.1.080

Pineda Castro, Laurent Lizeth. 'Las Protestas son el Temor a los Gobiernos Colombiano y Chileno en los Años 2020 a 2021'. *Estudios Socio-Jurídicos*, 25(1) (2022). DOI 10.12804/revistas.urosario.edu.co/sociojuridicos/a.12699

Popkova, Anna. 'Transnational Non-state Actors as "Alt Agents" of Public Diplomacy: Putin's Russia versus Open Russia'. *Place Branding and Public Diplomacy*, 16(1) (2020), 70–79. DOI 10.1057/s41254-019-00126-6

Popkova, Anna and Michaels, Jodi Hope. 'Who Represents the Domestic Voice? Diversity, Equity and Inclusion in Citizen Diplomacy'. *The Hague Journal of Diplomacy*, 18(1) (2022), 1–10. DOI 10.1163/1871191x-bja10135

Pría, Melba. 'Las Relaciones Internacionales del Siglo XXI: Hacia una Diplomacia Ciudadana'. *Revista de Relaciones de Internacionales de La UNAM*, 101–102(mayo-diciembre) (2008), 157–171.

Pryluka, Pablo. 'Advertising Pinochet: The Cold War Limits to a Neoliberal Crusade'. *The International History Review*, 45(2) (2023), 416–430. DOI 10.1080/07075332.2022 .2139283

Quintana, Daniela. 'Ahora se Puede Votar la Marca Argentina en el Exterior'. *Clarín*. 15 April 2021. https://www.clarin.com/arq/diseno/ahora-puede-votar-marca-argen tina-exterior_0_MFnpPmwV-.html?srsltid=AfmBOop17pylyua5bAqkOSesgxpF2Joa QjJylIZQcHSycbo4p61mE-6G

Radcliffe, Sarah and Westwood, Sallie. *Remaking the Nation: Place, Identity and Politics in Latin America* (London and New York: Routledge, 1996).

Ramos, Marisa and Noya, Javier. 'América Latina: Del Riesgo País a la Marca País y Más Allá'. *Real Instituto Elcano*, 7 (2006), 1–38.

Redacción. 'Gobierno de Honduras Define a Finalistas para Elegir la "Marca País."' *La Prensa*. 16 April 2015. https://www.laprensa.hn/honduras/gobierno-de-honduras-define-a-finalistas-para-elegir-la-marca-pais-MXLP831580

Satariano, Adam and Hopkins, Valerie. 'Russia, Blocked From the Global Internet, Plunges Into Digital Isolation'. *The New York Times*. 7 March 2022. https://www. nytimes.com/2022/03/07/technology/russia-ukraine-internet-isolation.html

Scherman, Andrés and Rivera, Sebastián. 'Social Media Use and Pathways to Protest Participation: Evidence From the 2019 Chilean Social Outburst'. *Social Media and Society*, 7(4) (2021). DOI 10.1177/20563051211059704

Schneider, Florian. *China's Digital Nationalism*. (Oxford: Oxford University Press, 2018).

Shahin, Saif. 'User-generated Nationalism: Interactions with Religion, Race, and Partisanship in Everyday Talk Online'. *Information, Communication & Society*, 24(13) (2021), 1854–1869. DOI 10.1080/1369118X.2020.1748088

Sharp, Paul. 'For Diplomacy: Representation and the Study of International Relations'. *International Studies Review*, 1(1) (1999), 33–57. DOI 10.1111/1521-9488.00140

Sharp, Paul. 'Making Sense of Citizen Diplomats: The People of Duluth, Minnesota, as International Actors'. *International Studies Perspectives*, 2(2) (2001), 131–150. DOI 10.1111/1528-3577.00045

Skey, Michael. 'Nationalism and Media'. *Nationalities Papers*, 50(5) (2022), 839–849. DOI 10.1017/nps.2021.102

Skey, Michael and Antonsich, Marco, eds. *Everyday Nationhood: Theorising Culture, Identity and Belonging after Banal Nationalism* (London: Palgrave Macmillan, 2017).

Somma, Nicolás, Bargsted, Matías, Disi Pavlic, Rodolfo and Medel, Rodrigo. 'No Water in the Oasis: The Chilean Spring of 2019–2020'. *Social Movement Studies*, 20(4) (2021), 495–502. DOI 10.1080/14742837.2020.1727737

Stokes, Susan. 'Are Protests Good or Bad for Democracy?' In *Protest and Dissent*, ed. Melissa Schwartzberg (New York: New York University Press, 2020), 269–284.

Tarrow, Sidney. 'The People's Two Rhythms: Charles Tilly and the Study of Contentious Politics. A Review Article'. *Comparative Studies in Society and History*, 38(3) (1996), 586–600. DOI 10.1017/s0010417500020065

Taylor, Philip. *Global Communications, International Affairs and the Media since 1945* (London: Routledge, 1997).

Thompson, John Brookshire. *The Media and Modernity: A Social Theory of the Media* (Cambridge, UK: Polity, 1995).

Trejos Rosero, Luis Fernando. 'Los Actores no Estatales en la Sociedad Internacional: Una Aproximación a la Diplomacia Ciudadana en Colombia'. *Investigación & Desarrollo*, 24(1) (2016), 76–94. DOI 10.14482/indes.24.1.8685

Wall, Illan. 'The Right to Protest'. *The International Journal of Human Rights* 28(8–9) (2023), 1378–1393. DOI 10.1080/13642987.2023.2262395

Weber, Clare. 'Women to Women: Dissident Citizen Diplomacy in Nicaragua'. In *Women's Activism and Globalization: Linking Local Struggles and Transnational Politics*, eds. Nancy Naples and Manisha Desai (London: Routledge, 2004), 44–81.

Yadlin-Segal, Aya. 'Constructing national identity online: The case study of #IranJeans on Twitter'. *International Journal of Communication*, (2017), 2760–2783.

Yun, Seong-Hun. 'Against the Current: Back to Public Diplomacy as Government Communication'. *International Journal of Communication*, (2022), 3047–3064.

Zaharna, Rhonda. *Boundary Spanners of Humanity: Three Logics of Communication and Public Diplomacy for Global Collaboration* (Oxford: Oxford University Press, 2022).

Zaharna, Rhonda and Uysal, Nur. 'Going for the jugular in public diplomacy: How adversarial publics using social media are challenging state legitimacy'. *Public Relations Review*, 42(1) (2016), 109–119. DOI 10.1016/j.pubrev.2015.07.006

Zhang, Xiaoyu, Dumitrica, Delia and Jansz, Jeroen. 'Mapping Chinese Digital Nationalism: A Literature Review'. *International Journal of Communication*, 18 (2024), 1891–1912.

CHAPTER 3

The Evolution of Domestic Public Diplomacy in Germany: Engaging the 'Public' at Home on Foreign and Security Policy Since 1990

Christian Opitz, Hanna Pfeifer, and Anna Geis

Summary[1]

This chapter traces the expansion of the domestic public diplomacy repertoire by German state actors since 1990. We use critical junctures in German foreign policy as snapshots of diplomats' and politicians' relationships to, constitution of, and inter-action with the public. We argue that new modes of engagement amount to the development of a more participatory form of domestic public diplomacy in Germany. Our contribution proceeds in three steps. First, we review recent debates on public diplomacy and find that the term 'public' has so far been under-theorised. We then offer a conceptualisation that makes use of diplomats' understanding of the public and briefly explain our methodological approach. The main body of the chapter comprises an account of five focal points that represent major crises for German foreign and security policy over the last three decades. These episodes not only reveal existing perceptions of the public but also open up the opportunity (or yield the necessity) to re-evaluate these perceptions. These crises provide a window of oppor-tunity to reconstitute publics and innovate interaction practices, including practices of 'new public diplomacy' directed towards the domestic population. In the conclu-sion, we reflect on the evolution of domestic public diplomacy in Germany and dis-cuss the conditions and broader implications of our findings.

Keywords

Public diplomacy – domestic engagement – German foreign and security policy – military conflicts – state-society relations – citizen participation

---

1 We extend our deep gratitude to the German Research Council (DFG) for their generous funding of the underlying research project.

1   Introduction[2]

Diplomacy has long been considered an elitist and state-centric institution. And yet citizens – whether domestic or foreign – are an indispensable part of diplomatic practice and foreign policy. Moving beyond established roles as consumers, objects, or protégés, citizens have recently also acted as subjects with agency in diplomacy and foreign policy.[3] Scholars and diplomatic practitioners alike have therefore suggested that the public's role in diplomatic practice may be changing.

The scholarship on public diplomacy (PD) has long stressed the relevance of *foreign* publics for achieving foreign policy goals. Over the last ten years, though, *domestic* publics have come under scrutiny, as well.[4] While the exact definition of PD is a matter of contestation, key contributors have reasoned that the domestic public may be just as instrumental in restricting or enabling the implementation and success of foreign policies as foreign publics are. Diplomatic engagements *both* at home *and* abroad can be conceptualised as two sides of one practice of PD.[5]

'Domestic public diplomacy' refers to instances in which 'the domestic public [...] is [...] treated as a target, partner, or interlocutor with which public diplomacy relationships are to be developed and conducted by representatives of the state in which they live'.[6] While some authors have reservations about the analytical value of the term, they acknowledge the emergence of domestically-oriented practices, 'undertaken by governments, their ministries of foreign affairs [...], and their diplomats'.[7]

In our chapter, we take this conceptual debate as a point of departure to examine what is actually meant by 'the public' within the domestic sphere of

2   We would like to thank Paul Beaumont and the participants of the panel 'Diplomatic Interactions: with Domestic Civil Society, with Other States' at the EISA Pan-European Conference on International Relations 2023, as well as the participants of the 'Riesigen Kolloquium (RiesiKo)' at Goethe University Frankfurt for helpful feedback on earlier versions of this article. We are also grateful to the editorial team for the professional support and critical guidance. In addition, we greatly appreciate the invaluable assistance by Meike Roth and David Weiß. Finally, we are indebted to the German Research Foundation (DFG) for funding the project 'Recasting the role of citizens in foreign and security policy? Democratic innovations and changing patterns of interaction between European executives and citizens' (project number 452986450, 2022–2025), from which this chapter emerged.
3   Popkova and Michaels 2022; Opitz, Pfeifer, and Geis 2022.
4   Huijgh 2012; Kim and Melissen 2022.
5   Huijgh 2019, 20.
6   Sharp 2016, 266.
7   Sharp 2016, 267.

diplomacy and foreign policy. We scrutinise how the public was repeatedly constituted, reconstituted, and modified in various important decisions of German foreign policy in recent decades. We explore the multifaceted dynamics between how state actors understand the public and how their practical engagement simultaneously constructs and reconstructs that same public. Through these interactions, state actors not only manifest and perform, but also reify a certain interpretation of the public. We understand this relationship as co-constitutive. Conceptualisations of *'who'* the public is inform decisions on *'how'* to engage it. Conversely, *modes* of interaction influence and modify existing notions of *the public* itself.

We can make use of this co-constitution methodologically, by understanding forms of 'public engagement' as providing insights into elites' conceptions of the public and, thus, as a device to reconstruct their understanding of the role of citizens in foreign and security policy. At the same time, we argue that the various ways of engaging the public should be understood as a repertoire of PD that expands over time. Like a growing inventory of performances, new modes of interaction are added without replacing existing ones. At the same time, established modes may lose importance, relatively speaking, without disappearing entirely and novel ones may be tried out without establishing themselves as a new standard.[8]

Our empirical analysis traces how the repertoire of German foreign policy elites and diplomats has expanded and how it has been coupled with the changing understanding of the domestic 'public'. We investigate decisive junctures in German foreign and security policy (FSP) over the last three decades as manifestations of a fundamental tension. This tension comprises, on the one hand, international partners' expectation that Germany contributes to military operations of various kinds; and, on the other, the ingrained reluctance of the German population to support the use of military means in foreign policy-making. German governments have not always considered it necessary to seriously engage the public or even to comprehensively explain or justify their decisions. But since the early 2010s, they have increasingly interacted with specific, smaller segments of the public ('mini-publics') in dialogical and participatory formats, thereby diversifying their repertoire of interaction. This evolution of PD within the domestic sphere reflects a change in how established elites understand the role of citizens in FSP.

This chapter attempts to make a conceptual and empirical contribution to the debate on (domestic) PD. We will not theorise about the reasons driving the expansion of interaction formats[9] or try to establish a causal relationship

---

8   Opitz, Pfeifer, and Geis 2024.
9   We have discussed some of the reasons in Opitz, Pfeifer, and Geis 2024.

between the changed views (or actual composition) of the public and the emergence of new forms of interaction. Rather, we follow a constitutive logic in using critical junctures for German FSP as illustrative snapshots to explore diplomats' and politicians' relationships to, constitution of, and interaction with the public. These moments reveal the prevailing understandings and standard handling of the public. From the actors' perspective, they also provide windows of opportunity to reconstitute publics and innovate interaction practices. This includes what could be called practices of 'new public diplomacy' directed towards the domestic population.[10]

Our chapter proceeds in three steps. First, we review recent developments in the research on public diplomacy and highlight that the term 'public' has so far been under-theorised (2). We then offer a conceptualisation that makes use of diplomats' understanding of the public and briefly explain our methodological approach (3). In the analytical core of the chapter (4), we reconstruct five focal points that represent major crises for German FSP over the last three decades. The conclusion reflects on the evolution of domestic PD in Germany and discusses the conditions and broader implications of our findings (5).

2　Shifting Boundaries of Public Diplomacy Research and the 'Domestic Turn'

Public diplomacy (PD) is a rather young area of academic inquiry which began to evolve in the early 2000s. Despite its considerable growth, the theoretical and analytical underpinnings of this research area are arguably still rather weak.[11] One of the persisting desiderata concerns the actual definition of PD. Conceptually, it has to be distinguished from the negatively connotated notion of propaganda, on the one hand, and broader concepts like political communication or legitimation, on the other. It important to note that 'public diplomacy' is not merely an academic term but a concept used by practitioners. Its introduction in the US was normatively driven, based on the claim that talking to people, rather than to states, in a direct, open, and strategic manner – as opposed to using propaganda that resorts to misinformation and lies – was the 'right and fair thing to do'.[12]

10　Melissen 2005.

11　Melissen 2018, 200; Gilboa 2023, 1; Pamment, Fjällhed, and Smedberg 2024, 51–55; Gregory 2016, 4. For methodological challenges, see Ayhan and Sevin 2022.

12　Sharp 2016, 266.

Most existing academic conceptualisations of PD share the approach that they see third populations as the target audience. Public diplomacy is then understood as 'a communication process states, nonstate actors, and organizations employ to influence the policies of a foreign government by influencing its citizens',[13] or as 'the processes by which international actors advance their ends abroad through engagement of publics'.[14] More holistic understandings of PD define it broadly as 'diplomatic engagement with people',[15] leaving it open where the public is located with whom diplomats interact.

It is only over the last couple of years that the domestic dimension of PD has explicitly been addressed. Rejecting the notion that diplomacy was solely associated with the 'international', Ellen Huijgh[16] proposed an integrative approach to PD. She claimed that engagement at home and abroad had to be considered as 'stepping stones on a continuum of public participation (including traditional and new practices implemented at varying speeds) that is central to international policymaking and conduct'.[17] While this does not imply that 'traditional' public diplomacy aimed at foreign societies is no longer relevant, the domestic dimension is to be considered in its own right. By studying both dimensions, cross-connections between the two spheres become visible.

But the domestic side of PD has also gained relevance in diplomatic practice. A variety of processes in different countries now reveal 'a distinct pattern towards more inward-directed conversations on external relations issues and the impact of international and global challenges on the domestic sphere'.[18] In the political environment after World War II, PD was primarily designed to be one-sided dissemination of information directed at foreign publics.[19] During the ideological confrontation between Western states and the Soviet Union, the aim was to influence public opinion in the countries of the opposing side as well as the 'Third World'. Admittedly, the state communicating to the domestic audience about foreign policy has always been part of diplomacy.[20] Yet, for a long time, diplomatic professionals did not see themselves as responsible for this type of 'public relations' work. They perceived it as 'mundane' and therefore happily left it to others.[21]

---

13   Gilboa 2015, 1297.
14   Snow and Cull 2020, xi.
15   Melissen 2018, 199.
16   Huijgh 2012, 360.
17   Huijgh 2019, 20.
18   Kim and Melissen 2022, 611.
19   Parker 2016.
20   Gregory 2016, 6.
21   Huijgh 2019, 15–16.

But this has changed with the perception of the domestic public and its relevance for foreign policy.[22] Several recent studies illustrate a growing trend among states to turn their diplomatic attention and practices towards their own societies.[23] They do so in a variety of forms and formats, depending on the respective geographic and cultural context. The domestic public may be the explicit addressee of PD, as observed in Brazil.[24] Alternatively, it can be an indirect audience that is more or less convinced by, and can thus become a supporter of or an obstacle to PD, as exemplified by Chinese PD for investment in Africa.[25] In other instances, such as in Turkey under Erdoğan, the domestic public can be the actual target audience of a form of PD that ostensibly addresses a foreign population.[26]

Thus, whether or not PD addresses the domestic public may be less of a conceptual than an empirical question. Not all governments will see the need to address their own populations directly and openly, and with strategic intent at all times. For Germany, too, we will show that the public was not always constructed as a relevant addressee in this policy area – sometimes not at all, sometimes only in the form of smaller sub-publics.

For the purpose of this chapter, we define *domestic public diplomacy* as state-driven communication relations which are directed at the domestic society to secure political legitimacy for FSP decisions. This implies that domestic populations are no longer seen as obvious (tacit or outspoken) supporters of their government's FSP. Only then does diplomatic interaction with the public at home become necessary in the first place. Governments may perceive the need to reach out to domestic publics as more or less urgent or not relevant at all.[27] Where there is an impulse to engage in domestic PD, we often find that FSP has been politicised or become an arena for populists.[28]

Our proposed understanding is, then, also in line with broader conceptualisations of *diplomacy* as 'relations between groups, rather than within groups, and ways of conducting them effectively', or 'a boundary-spanning practice, which operates as an instrument or servant of foreign policy'.[29] In our context, the two groups between whom a bridge needs to be built are, on the one hand, the broader German population and, on the other, Germany's

---

22   Fitzpatrick 2010.
23   Yang 2020; Zhang 2022.
24   Pestana 2020.
25   Rawnsley 2020.
26   Çevik 2020.
27   Fitzpatrick 2010.
28   Hagmann, Hegemann, and Neal 2018; Destradi, Plagemann, and Taş 2022.
29   Sharp 2016, 275.

international partners and foreign policy elites, whose expectations often align. Such a balancing act can be 'successful' for state actors when PD creates the necessary public support for a given FSP decision. But it is just as likely to 'fail'. The population may withhold support, place restrictions on diplomats' room to manoeuvre, or even try to impose its preferences on state policy.

We delimit PD from the broader concept of *political communication* in terms of its more specific content, national FSP, and its distinct speakers – diplomatic actors who communicate to and with domestic society. The purpose of this communication is essentially to acquire and maintain legitimacy. It serves to create acceptance and justify decisions to, for example, gain support for a national contribution to a military mission abroad.[30]

However, PD is also more than the mere *legitimation* of FSP decisions after the fact, manifested in more or less successful speech acts. Diplomacy can be described as 'the handling of the Other',[31] and how exactly the public as one such 'Other' is handled has evolved over time. As Jan Melissen[32] wrote more than a decade ago, '[...] public diplomacy today is increasingly based on listening to "the other", that it is about dialogue rather than monologue, and is not just aimed at short-term policy objectives but also at long-term relationship-building'. Public diplomacy has always been used as a one-off tactical form of communication but it has also become a means of 'facilitating dialogue'.[33] The two approaches coexist and represent two poles of a spectrum of diplomatic practice which varies in the degree of public activation and participation.[34] The repertoire of interaction has expanded accordingly, from largely monological to include more dialogical formats.[35]

---

30   Steg 2010, 341; Huijgh 2019, 20.

31   Neumann 2020, 22.

32   Melissen 2011, 10.

33   Sharp 2016, 268.

34   Huijgh 2019, 56–57. In Huijgh's conceptualisation of PD, the various forms of engagement are placed on a continuum based on the degree of activation and participation of the public. At one end of this spectrum lies the 'old' yet still relevant monological informational approach, where state actors primarily disseminate information and explain foreign policy, but public involvement is minimal. At the opposite, more participatory end, the population (or a part of it) is actively empowered to be an equal partner in decision-making processes. Intermediate forms of engagement, such as information gathering, discussion, or consultation, exist between these two poles. The universe of these diverse activities constitutes the communication repertoire to which state actors can resort in PD.

35   Our conception is relatively agnostic towards the regime type of the state practicing PD. It may well be that the quantity or quality of this type of communication is particularly high in participatory-oriented systems as argued by Huijgh 2019, 12. But such differences

3   Who Constitutes 'the Public' in Public Diplomacy and How Can We Study Them?

3.1   *Changing Understandings of the Public*

The term 'public' is obviously central for the eponymous research field of (domestic) PD. But, rather surprisingly, this notion is barely conceptualised in academic debates.[36] 'Who are the public in public diplomacy? Are they the people of a country and, if so, must it be all of them or can it be some of them?'[37] There are 'diverse communities at home' and 'these "own" citizens are less of a homogenous mass than the term suggests'.[38]

Only a small number of works have tried to address this question. Among them are Kathy Fitzpatrick's[39] notion of a 'strategic public' or those parts of society that could 'enhance or constrain a nation's ability to accomplish its mission'. Similarly, Lisa Tam and Jeong-Nam Nim[40] advocate a focus on '*prioritized* publics', given that PD cannot possibly address the entirety of a population. Finally, Andreas Pacher[41] also thinks of the public in terms of strategic segments, outlining six ideal types based on their strategic importance and power. These 'partial publics' can be foreign or domestic, governmental or non-state, more or less powerful. As important as these works are, they focus on which publics *ought* to be targeted by PD, rather than *empirically* investigating the actual practices of domestic PD and the underlying understanding of what constitutes the public.

As shown by research on diplomacy more broadly, what the public means to diplomats is subject to change over time.[42] Initially, the term 'public' was limited to 'educated men', subsequently extended to include all national citi-

---

are gradual, not categorical. It is theoretically possible and empirically observable that non-democratic regimes use PD for gaining support among their respective publics, China being a case in point as shown by Yang 2020. In these contexts, the question of where to draw the boundaries between PD and propaganda is particularly relevant, yet not always clear. We understand propaganda as a strictly one-sided form of state communication which seeks to persuade without leaving room for reflection and deliberation, at times relying on fabricated or incorrect information; see Melissen 2005, 16–19.

36   Fitzpatrick 2023, 146.
37   Sharp 2009.
38   Huijgh 2019, 35–36. Several passages suggest that Huijgh (e.g., 2019, 11) largely equates domestic publics with civil society groups. This reduction indicates a certain normative bias in her understanding of the 'public'.
39   Fitzpatrick 2012, 424.
40   Tam and Nim 2019, 28.
41   Pacher 2018, 287–291.
42   la Cour 2018.

zens, and ultimately took on a global perspective. For public diplomacy in particular, it has been pointed out that domestic publics have been targeted for a long time, suggesting that diplomatic practice predates the comparatively recent scholarly attention it has received.[43] That said, we still lack longitudinal studies of how practices of domestic PD and understandings of the public have evolved over time.[44]

3.2   *Methodological Approach to the German Case*

In this chapter, we provide the first empirical case study in this field. We seek to determine what German diplomats and foreign policymakers perceive as the public that is relevant to FSP. We do this by studying how domestic publics have been addressed by state PD initiatives at different points in history. This analysis of the communicative engagement between diplomatic actors and their publics over the past three decades will allow us to infer prevailing understandings of 'the public' at given points in time and in specific political contexts.

We examine potential critical junctures not because we assume that any 'big decisions' in FSP at the time gave rise or are causally connected to changes in elites' perceptions of the public. Rather, these are moments when existing understandings are most visibly articulated. At these junctures, decision-makers and diplomats are required to engage in some form of interaction with the public, thus revealing, through the mode of interaction, who is being addressed as 'the public'. How, by what means, and in what formats this public is addressed provides further clues about its structure and characteristics, as well as the role it is assigned in FSP matters.

Methodologically, our study is anchored in qualitative longitudinal research, which aims 'to trace continuity and change in a social phenomenon' over longer periods of time.[45] We investigate Germany's longer-term domestic PD strategies in response to important junctures. Given the particularly contentious question of military engagement and armed conflict in the German context, we chose five such instances over the last 30 years as our focal points.[46] These distinct junctures render the latent gap between the preferen-

---

43   Cull 2023, 110.

44   Manor, Jiménez-Martínez, and Dolea 2021.

45   Gulmez and Ates 2022, 217.

46   Although outside the scope of our study, there had already been various focal points with considerable conflict between decision-makers and large parts of the population in the Federal Republic of Germany (West Germany) before reunification. Early cases such as rearmament under Konrad Adenauer in the 1950s or the NATO 'double-track decision' in the early 1980s would also lend themselves to an in-depth analysis of state PD at home.

ces of decision-makers and those of the population on FSP particularly viru-
lent – thus highlighting the legitimising function of domestic state PD. Our
diachronic analysis provides chronologically ordered 'snapshots' of German
PD practices which reveal important developments in their distinct characteristics. The guiding question is whether changes can be observed in the understanding of 'the public', and if so, what these changes are and how they manifest in modes of diplomatic interaction.

We chose the German case because the specific relations between FSP
elites and the public have consistently been described as complex and have
sometimes been experienced as challenging by policymakers. As Kai Oppermann[47] puts it, there is a notorious 'mismatch between the foreign policy
views of decision-makers and the general public' in this country. Traditionally,
the German population is portrayed as reluctant to face the 'realities' of Germany's position as a middle power in a globalised world. But beyond this over-
simplified assessment, it remains unclear who 'the public' in German FSP actually is.[48]

Our analysis encompasses five focal points that can be considered as 'crises'
for German foreign policy:[49] the Gulf War (1991), the Kosovo War (1999), the
Iraq War (2002–2003), the debate on being 'at war' in Afghanistan (2009), and
the Russian invasion of Ukraine (2022).[50] These focal points primarily revolve
around decisions of the political leadership to deploy military and other specialised staff abroad, or not. In addition, they include serious international
conflicts that required Germany to adopt a position, such as the Russian invasion of Ukraine, and crises unique to Germany, including the bombing of Afghan civilians in Kunduz. Due to space constraints, this selection is not ex-
haustive but intentionally chosen to cover episodes in German FSP that carry
significant political weight and that are distributed over the past 30 years since
the country's reunification.[51] This long-term view allows us to observe the
evolution of 'the public' as constructed in German PD, primarily by consulting
secondary literature focusing on key events.

---

47   Oppermann 2019, 487.
48   Jacobi 2018.
49   Stern 2003.
50   For a similar analysis of public diplomacy in response to major 'crises', see Manfredi-
      Sánchez and Smith 2023.
51   For instance, Germany's abstention in the UNSC's vote on the Libya resolution in 1973 or
      the question of sending weapons to the Peshmerga in Iraq in 2014 could be other impor-
      tant focal points.

4   Crises for German Public Diplomacy over the Past Three Decades

In the following snapshots, we trace the expansion of the German PD repertoire in unified Germany from the early 1990s to the 2020s. We show that
diplomats used to treat the domestic public as external to FSP decisions. The
tacit and passive support of a majority was considered sufficient. Over time,
broader monological engagement with the general public or specific segments
of the population became more common. While the mode of interaction continued to be monological, the first dialogical 'experiments' began to take place
vis-à-vis dissenting sections of coalition parties. This was an early precursor of
what would later become a broader and deeper engagement of lay citizens in
various formats of participation. For the time being, the citizens dialogue series in preparation of Germany's first National Security Strategy constitutes
the climax of this latest expansion of Germany's PD repertoire to more inclusive, dialogical, lay citizen-centred formats of interaction.

4.1   *The 1991 Gulf War: Widespread Protest as Non-public, Supportive*
         Majority as Relevant Public

4.1.1   Context and FSP Decision

In August 1990, Iraqi troops under Saddam Hussein invaded Kuwait. When
sanctions and negotiations proved unsuccessful, an international alliance led
by the United States commenced military air and ground operations against
Iraqi troops in mid-January 1991. At the time, Germany was in the midst of a
challenging phase of rapid transition towards unification and, therefore,
rather unprepared for the question of whether to participate in the alliance.

Germany had not yet resolved important constitutional questions at this
point, notably the permissibility of deploying the *Bundeswehr* in an 'out-of-
area' mission at all.[52] Decision-makers' standard interpretation of the Basic
Law until then had been that deployments outside NATO territory were pro-
hibited. As a result, the focus of discussions among political actors in Germany
was the constitutional legality of a possible participation in the Gulf War.

Eventually, the government under the centre-right CDU's Chancellor Helmut Kohl decided not to actively participate in the military operation. Germany nevertheless acted as a major deployment base and supported the allied
troops logistically and financially.[53] In addition, Israel received German anti-
aircraft missiles to defend against Iraqi attacks, and air forces were stationed
in NATO member Turkey in case of an Iraqi attack.

---

52   Oldhaver 2000, 132–138.
53   Schwab-Trapp 2002, 87.

Among the German public, the Gulf War led to significant political mobilisation and polarisation. In the run-up to the expiration of a UN ultimatum
given to Saddam Hussein, almost every major city saw rallies, human chains,
and vigils. On the eve of the war, around 250,000 people demonstrated under
the slogan 'No War in the Gulf – No Blood for Oil', primarily opposing the
international intervention led by the United States and criticising what they
perceived as a 'militarisation of thought' in Germany.[54]

The protests continued even after the outbreak of the Gulf War. At the end
of January, over 200,000 people took part in a large-scale demonstration in
Bonn, demanding an immediate end to the military operation. The peace
movement also initiated numerous actions such as temporary work stoppages
at Germany's major car factories and the cancellation of the seasonal carnival
festivities.[55] Over the course of the war, however, the intensity and frequency
of these peace demonstrations faded noticeably.

4.1.2   Constitution and Engagement of Publics: From Ignoring Mass
Protests to Enjoying the Support of a Silent Majority

During the Gulf War, in view of the intense 'state of collective agitation',[56] the
German government kept an astonishingly low profile from a communicative
perspective. Public statements concerning the possible deployment of German soldiers abroad were conspicuously sparse. Observers denounced the
decision-makers' passive approach as 'indecisiveness',[57] criticising Defence
Minister Gerhard Stoltenberg in particular. The latter acted mainly behind
the scenes, within closed circles of political leaders, while remaining in a
state of 'speechlessness'[58] toward the public. Communication of FSP decisions
to the domestic population was minimal.

Despite disagreement within the governing coalition regarding military
deployment, leading decision-makers were united on how to approach the
large-scale public protests. They viewed them with scepticism and ultimately
rejected them outright. Peace demonstrators were accused of hypocrisy, as
they opposed military intervention, while ignoring Hussein's human rights
violations and invasion of Kuwait. The rallies were seen as explicitly or implicitly anti-American, which contradicted the political elites' commitment to
maintaining a strong transatlantic partnership. In sum, the political leader-

---

54   Oldhaver 2000, 181–182; Schwab-Trapp 2002, 95–98.
55   Schwab-Trapp 2002, 98.
56   Schwab-Trapp 2002, 108.
57   Oldhaver 2000, 200.
58   Oldhaver 2000, 242.

ship saw the protesting masses as a 'non-public' rather than a domestic 'Other' that needed to be managed.

From the perspective of the policymakers, the 'relevant' public was the silent majority, which was perceived as supporting their decisions and whose views were reflected in the polls as aggregated 'public opinion'. Initially, most Germans had called for measures to prevent the war shortly before its outbreak. However, sentiments shifted when the intervention was launched, with the majority subsequently in favour of allied military action. Public opinion generally reflected the government's criticism of the protests as inappropriate or excessive. Nevertheless, opinion polls showed that three quarters of the population opposed any participation of the *Bundeswehr*.[59] This opposition foreshadowed a split between the elite and the masses on FSP matters, thus driving a new conceptualisation 'the public' and its engagement.

4.2   *The 1999 Kosovo War: Media Appearances and Ambiguous Party Communication*

4.2.1   Context and FSP Decision

The military conflict in Kosovo escalated in spring 1998, initiated by the Kosovo Liberation Army's fight for the independence of the province. Serbian President Slobodan Milošević sought to suppress this separatist movement with military force. The United States pushed within NATO for the so-called 'activation order' in autumn 1998, which would authorise NATO to launch air strikes against designated targets if negotiations with Milošević were to fail. However, the activation order required the consensus of all NATO members, including Germany.

On 12 October 1998, the German government under Chancellor Kohl consented to the order, after it had decided to participate in possible air strikes against Serbia with around a dozen *Tornado* combat reconnaissance aircrafts. After a final mediation attempt failed, NATO launched its first air strikes on 24 March 1999 – with the involvement of German *Tornados*. This marked the first time since the Second World War that German soldiers had taken part in an active military combat mission.

During this period, German decision-makers were yet again navigating a volatile time of transition. Elections to the *Bundestag* at the end of September, in which the conflict in Kosovo played no more than a peripheral role,[60] resulted in a victory for the opposition: the social democratic SPD with Gerhard

---

59   Oldhaver 2000, 203–211.

60   Kutz 2014, 182.

Schröder as Chancellor-elect and The Greens led by Joschka Fischer who was the designated Foreign Minister. Although the outgoing government had suffered an electoral defeat, it provisionally remained in office, as the newly elected *Bundestag* had not yet convened.

The cabinet's decision to support the NATO activation order had been coordinated with the incoming leadership. Decision-makers had also agreed to convene an extraordinary session of the *Bundestag* to decide on Germany's participation in a possible NATO military operation in Kosovo. An overwhelming majority of 500 members of parliament approved this motion, reflecting large cross-party consensus.[61] This was at odds with what used to be a central principle of Germany's FSP: that a deployment of the *Bundeswehr* abroad must be based on a mandate from the UN Security Council (UNSC), which, in the case of Kosovo, was lacking.[62]

4.2.2   Constitution and Engagement of Publics: Monological Communication for the Media Public, Dialogical Engagement of Rebelling Party Segment

As this turning point in national FSP unfolded, decision-makers ensured that this time it was accompanied by media communication towards the German population. On the first day of the air strikes, Chancellor Schröder gave a televised speech, in which he justified the military operation as necessary to prevent a humanitarian catastrophe in Kosovo.

Defence Minister Rudolf Scharping was particularly engaged in communication activities, holding daily press conferences to provide updates on the NATO operation and answer journalists' questions. Compared to other NATO partners, these media appearances were unique. The argumentation Scharping used to justify Germany's participation clearly drew on historical humanitarian interventions, invoking analogies to Nazi crimes.[63] This emotionally charged narrative was met with criticism,[64] but underscored the political lead-

---

61   Friedrich 2005, 56.

62   For the SPD and especially large parts of The Greens, this change of attitude within a very short time could be characterised as radical. It can only be explained by the course of the Bosnian War and especially the Srebrenica genocide of 1995. The latter triggered an intense debate about 'humanitarian interventions' and Germany's responsibility to combat and prevent such mass crimes, especially in its own neighbourhood. The participation in the Kosovo intervention should be seen in the light of this prior experience with Bosnia.

63   Stahl 2008, 263–266.

64   Kutz 2014, 94.

ership's commitment to securing public approval for its decisions.[65] They primarily engaged with a media public, aiming to influence opinion via television and newspapers.

At the beginning of the NATO operation, polls had indicated broad support for the air strikes, even accepting potential German military casualties.[66] As Milošević's resistance prolonged the conflict, calls for deploying ground troops intensified among NATO partners. The German political leadership, however, publicly ruled out participation in any ground offensive, motivated by concerns over the dwindling legitimacy of the war.[67] At this point, a growing number of civilian casualties had already eroded public support.[68]

The prolonged military escalation placed the government under additional pressure. Chancellor Schröder managed to commit his party to the official government line. In contrast, The Greens faced serious internal divisions. Amidst massive anti-war protests, their party congress highlighted these tensions, with the left wing demanding an immediate end to the war and the withdrawal of German forces, and the party leadership proposing only a temporary suspension of the bombing to facilitate diplomatic negotiations.

Foreign Minister Fischer delivered what became a famous speech to the delegates, despite being physically attacked prior to speaking. He emphatically argued against the left wing's resolution, linking peace to the prevention of atrocities and invoking historical imperatives: 'I stand on two principles, never again war, never again Auschwitz, never again genocide, never again fascism! The two go together for me.' Observers spoke of his performance as 'the fight of his political life'.[69]

Although Fischer addressed the Green delegates, a wider political party public acted as an overhearing audience. He sought support beyond his party, which he could then leverage in internal debates. The Greens, thus, became the central forum for the state's communication activities aiming at justifying German FSP decisions[70] or a specialised 'mini-public', effectively acting as 'the discourse machine of the Federal Republic of Germany'.[71] This contributed to enlarging the German PD repertoire of interaction with

---

65   Schwab-Trapp 2002, 292.
66   Maull 2000, 64–65; Friedrich 2005, 87–88.
67   Friedrich 2005, 114.
68   Kutz 2014, 184–185.
69   Lantis 2022, 33.
70   Lantis 2022, 32.
71   Schwab-Trapp 2002, 154.

the public towards a more dialogical, albeit contentious, mode of engagement – a trend which would be taken up some decades later (see section 4e).

4.3 The 2002–2003 *Iraq War: Public Diplomacy during Election Campaigns*

4.3.1 Context and FSP Decision

After the Al-Qaeda attacks of 11 September 2001 and the subsequent invasion of Afghanistan in October 2001, the United States identified Iraq as a potential target for a military operation by spring 2002. The German government under Chancellor Schröder adopted a cautious stance. While recognising the bellicose rhetoric of the US administration as a strategic tactic to apply pressure on Saddam Hussein to stop the alleged production of weapons of mass destruction, the leadership remained sceptical about the merits of a military intervention. Instead, it called for diplomatic means and further international weapons inspections. Schröder still managed to avoid direct confrontation with the United States, largely trying to keep the issue off the government agenda.[72]

But in early August 2002, Schröder shifted his approach. He publicly declared a 'double no', stating that Germany would neither participate in a military intervention against Iraq nor support such action, with or without a UNSC's mandate. This emphatic rejection coincided with the lead-up to the parliamentary elections at the end of September 2002, in which the SPD was trailing far behind the CDU in the polls.[73] Schröder's firm stance against a possible war in Iraq was obviously aimed at rallying support to help his party catch up by election day.

4.3.2 Constitution and Engagement of Publics: Monological Communication with the Electorate

Public opposition to military intervention in Iraq was widespread among the German population. President George W. Bush's visit in early 2002 was accompanied by significant public protest against a US Iraq policy perceived as warmongering. Opinion polls showed that a clear majority opposed a war and over 80 per cent rejected Germany's participation.[74]

Schröder and the SPD leveraged this by making a possible German contribution to military action against Iraq one of the central issues of their election campaign. They framed their categorical rejection as exercising national sov-

---

72   Mader 2017, 134.

73   Geis 2013, 254.

74   Geis 2013, 259–260.

ereignty, rejecting the notion of a US-led invasion.[75] The CDU criticised this rhetoric as anti-American and lacking solidarity. Although the opposition was not unreservedly pro-war, preferring conditions such as a UNSC's mandate, their position seemed ambiguous and uncertain compared to Schröder's unequivocal 'no'.[76]

In the end, in coalition with The Greens, the SPD narrowly won the elections, allowing Schröder to remain in office. Given the close outcome, it is plausible that the partisan issue of Iraq ultimately tipped the balance in favour of the incumbents.[77] The Schröder government subsequently stuck to its 'no', despite the intensive efforts of the United States to secure a UNSC's resolution to approve a military intervention. This stance was bolstered by widespread domestic demonstrations against the imminent war, including a massive protest in Berlin in February 2003 which drew 500,000 people.

The German government's decision regarding (non-)participation in the US-led Iraq War was underpinned by intensive PD at home, which was uniquely intertwined with a closely contested national election. The strategic choice to make the rejection of military intervention a central campaign issue demonstrates that the decision-makers understood the public primarily as the electorate – more precisely, as the *party-affiliated voting constituency* which was to be mobilised. Within the polarising context of the campaign, the question of the Iraq War was perceived and communicated along party lines. As a result, the discourse surrounding this decision exhibited a distinctly more party-political orientation than that of previous foreign missions.

4.4 *The 2009 Afghanistan War: The Kunduz Air Strike and the Question of Being or Not Being at War*

4.4.1   Context and FSP Decision

The German 'no' to the Iraq War must be contextualised within its longstanding participation in Afghanistan, which had begun shortly after the attacks of 9/11. Chancellor Schröder had pledged 'unconditional solidarity' with the United States, aiming to affirm that Germany was a reliable ally. The political leadership advocated for participation in the US-led military mission, *Operation Enduring Freedom* (OEF), which the *Bundestag* authorised in November 2001. The latter also mandated the *Bundeswehr* to participate in the *International Security Assistance Force* (ISAF), initially framed as a 'stabilisation operation'. Over time, the ISAF changed significantly in terms of its territorial scope and military character, evolving into a series of counter-

75   Stahl 2008, 271–275.
76   Mader 2017, 134–135.
77   Schoen 2004.

insurgency operations that resulted in increased casualties among civilians and soldiers, including German troops.[78] With up to 5,350 soldiers, this became the biggest *Bundeswehr* mission to date.

The German political elite largely avoided the term 'war' to describe this mission until it reached a crucial turning point, the so-called 'Kunduz air strike' in 2009. German Army Colonel Georg Klein ordered an air strike on two fuel tankers, resulting in many civilian deaths. This crisis intensified the German public debate on the character of the Afghanistan mission – and brought another segment of 'the public' to the forefront: the military, its representatives, and those who felt solidarity with the soldiers engaged in combat operations in Afghanistan.

4.4.2 Constitution and Engagement of Publics: Monological Communication with Aggrieved Military Actors

During the first years of Germany's military engagement in Afghanistan, a large majority in the *Bundestag* had maintained an optimistic view, emphasising the normative goals of spreading democracy and human rights to the war-torn country. Increasingly, however, the vague concept of 'stabilisation' dominated parliamentary discussions, subtly replacing the earlier, more idealistic goals.[79] Meanwhile, the extent and scope of the German deployment was increased significantly, but the 'stabilisation rhetoric' persisted even as actual counter-insurgency realities were unfolding on the ground.

The military operations in Afghanistan, governed by separate mandates for OEF and ISAF, were subject to regular parliamentary renewal and scrunity. Over the years, these mandates were met with differing degrees of criticism and opposition. Speakers carefully tried to avoid any impression that Germany was involved in a 'war'. Opinion polls consistently showed high approval for a *Bundeswehr* deployment as long as it was framed as 'humanitarian'. However, support dropped massively when missions were perceived as combat operations.[80] Consequently, politicians crafted narratives that de-emphasised or even concealed the 'military' character of deployments, catering to both domestic and international expectations.[81]

The political discourse on Germany's involvement in Afghanistan only gradually changed in 2008/2009.[82] Representatives of the military were a

---

78   Noetzel 2011.
79   Müller and Wolff 2011, 215.
80   Jacobi, Hellmann, and Nieke 2011, 177–179.
81   Hilpert 2014, 109.
82   Geis 2021.

key driver of this development. They pointed out that the *Bundeswehr* was involved in actual combat operations. Soldiers lamented that their 'war-like' experiences were not understood at home and complained about a lack of recognition of their difficult mission on the part of both the political leadership and the broader German population.

This disconnect became more pronounced as the *Bundeswehr* began to suffer casualties. The death of larger numbers of soldiers in combat was a new experience for post-war Germany. The use of the term 'fallen soldiers' by Defence Minister Franz Josef Jung (CDU) at a funeral ceremony in October 2008 marked a notable shift in rhetoric from rather neutral language ('killed') to terms historically associated with war time.[83]

This change was well received by both the German media and the soldiers.[84] Around 2009/2010, Defence Minister Karl-Theodor zu Guttenberg and Chancellor Angela Merkel would begin speaking of 'war-like circumstances' in Afghanistan, even using the more explicit term 'war'.[85] Slowly, the political leadership was adopting the subjective perspective of German soldiers who were *experiencing* combat situations that *might* be *perceived* as 'war', distinguishing between international legal terminology and colloquial language during the funeral speeches. By using an empathetic tone, political leaders sought to express gratitude, addressing a specialised public of soldiers with a message of acknowledgement from a state that had itself placed them in harm's way.

The 'Kunduz air strike' of 4 September 2009 further transformed the debate. The air strike, which resulted in numerous civilian casualties, was subject to intense scrutiny. Described by *Der Spiegel*[86] as the 'bloodiest military operation of the German military since the end of the Second World War', it raised pressing questions as to what the *Bundeswehr* was actually *doing* in Afghanistan. A subsequent inquiry by the *Bundestag* yielded divergent perspectives on whether Colonel Klein's decision to order the air strike constituted a justifiable action to protect German soldiers from attack or grave misconduct. Defence Minister Jung, who had initially denied that there were any civilian casualties, eventually resigned.

The 'Kunduz affair' became a game-changer for the wider public.[87] It catapulted the issue of the 'war' from discussions among experts to the heart of the

---

83   Nieke 2016.
84   Dörfler-Dierken 2010, 140.
85   Schroeder and Zapfe 2015, 186–187.
86   Demmer et al. 2010
87   Noetzel 2011, 408.

German security debate. The combination of military incidents, combat experiences, changed rules of engagement, and the diminishing prospects of 'success led to intense political contestation over the characterisation of Germany's involvement as being 'at war'. While previously, only the demands of a specialised public of military actors for political recognition had to be satisfied, now the general public became a critical mass that warranted new modes of rhetorical interaction. Political elites adapted their previously insincere, evasive, and hypocritical discourse on Germany's participation in combat missions in Afghanistan accordingly.

4.5   *The Russian War on Ukraine and Germany's National Security Strategy 2022: Participatory Public Diplomacy and the* Zeitenwende

4.5.1   Context and FSP Decision

Germany's experience in Afghanistan certainly constituted an important reality check for a public that, from the perspective of German decision-makers and allied governments alike, was all too reluctant to acknowledge the need to address ramifications of global (in)security. During the 2010s, Foreign Minister Frank-Walter Steinmeier (SPD) had already made various attempts to 'bridge the gap' between the perceived need for Germany to play a 'more active' international role, on the one hand, and a population with a deeply ingrained culture of restraint, on the other. But it was not until the Russian war of aggression against Ukraine, starting in February 2022, that the reality of war required Germany to both adapt its security policy and find new ways of addressing the public.

Russia's full-scale invasion had two specific consequences for German FSP and PD. First, Chancellor Olaf Scholz (SPD) announced the *Zeitenwende*, a rupture in German FSP which involved the country entering a new era with new military necessities. This shift required a special fund of EUR 100 billion for the *Bundeswehr* and, within just a few months, a move away from long-standing principles such as '*Wandel durch Handel*' (transformation through trade).[88] Large parts of the German population signalled their support for the delivery of heavy weapons to Ukraine, putting the topic of security, with its many facets, being on everyone's lips and minds.

Second, this development led to political elites redressing the role that they had assigned to the general public when they wrote Germany's first National Security Strategy – a process which had coincidentally been planned for 2022

---

88   Blumenau 2022.

as well.[89] Traditionally, the drafting process would have involved representatives from various federal ministries, with the Foreign Office taking the lead,
and might have included limited consultations with closed groups of external
FSP experts. However, the crisis in Ukraine rendered this conventional approach inside the 'Berlin bubble' inadequate. In the eyes of the political leadership, it seemed unthinkable to keep the heated and growing discussion
about security challenges and threats behind closed doors.

4.5.2   Constitution and Engagement of Publics: Dialogical Deliberation
           with a Representative 'Mini-public'
In response to the evolving situation, the Foreign Office introduced a significant participatory framework.[90] This consisted of three parts, starting with
seven citizen dialogues held in summer 2022 in various regions of Germany.
Each dialogue involved 50 'ordinary' citizens who were randomly selected,
ensuring demographic representation of the national population. These were
followed by two 'Open Situation Rooms' at the Foreign Office, in which participants from the previous dialogues and foreign policy experts jointly discussed security-related scenarios and formulated policy recommendations.
The series culminated in a concluding event in Erfurt, held in September,
at which selected citizens debated their ideas with Foreign Minister Annal-
ena Baerbock (The Greens).

The citizen dialogues formed the core of the participatory framework. Each
dialogue included approximately two hours of small-group discussions, following a predefined, multi-stage structure. Participants first listed perceived
security threats, then discussed overarching goals or values jeopardised by
these threats, and finally, ranked these goals in order of priority. They also
explored tensions and convergences among the goals and identified potential
obstacles to achieving them. The dialogues concluded with participants presenting their group findings in front of the plenary. Subsequently, discussions
ensued, sometimes involving diplomats from the Foreign Office and representatives from other ministries, and at times, even Minister Baerbock herself
who participated in almost half of the events.

The participatory framework implemented for the National Security Strategy in summer 2022 was remarkable due to its extensive scope, the substantial

---

89   In contrast to the other empirical cases in this paper, for this process, we can draw on
     first-hand empirical data, consisting of interviews, participatory observations, and priv-
     ileged knowledge through our expert involvement in strategy drafting and other policy
     processes.
90   Opitz, Pfeifer, and Geis 2024.

resources invested, and the involvement of high-ranking political representatives. This initiative represented an important milestone in the Foreign Office's ongoing learning process, crowning efforts initiated in 2014 to reshape the relationship between citizens and political elites in FSP.[91] At the time, Foreign Minister Steinmeier launched the 'Review 2014' process, which was designed to foster dialogue between diplomats and citizens through various participatory formats. Since then, certain participatory events have occurred regularly, most notably the 'Citizen Workshop on Foreign Policy', the Foreign Office's participatory flagship event.[92]

In conclusion, due the exceptionally vigorous public debate on FSP matters triggered by the Russian invasion of Ukraine, when drafting Germany's first-ever National Security Strategy, the Foreign Office decided to address and involve a 'mini-public' composed of randomly selected citizens.[93] Conducted within predefined boundaries, this participatory framework was an experiment engaging a small, yet demographically representative segment of the public in an innovative way. This set-up lent itself to a 'controlled politicisation' of the strategy-making process, allowing for a new mode of PD interaction to be tested without risking too much.[94] The mini-public was constructed not only as a participant in drafting political guidelines, but was also seen as an important pillar of a democratic FSP.

5   Conclusion

This chapter explored the evolving meaning of 'the public' in German domestic public diplomacy (PD), as manifested in interactions between diplomats and political elites, on the one hand, and national citizens, on the other, in the context of foreign and security policy (FSP). We traced the trajectory of this evolution from the initial dismissal of the public as a relevant factor in decision-making, to more monological forms of engagement, and ultimately to sophisticated dialogical interactions tested with a representative mini-public. Table 3.1 illustrates how the German state actors' understanding of and engagement with 'the public' at home has transformed across the five selected focal points over the past three decades.

---

91   Geis and Pfeifer 2017.
92   Geis, Opitz, and Pfeifer 2022.
93   Smith and Setälä 2018.
94   Opitz, Pfeifer, and Geis 2024.

TABLE 3.1 Characteristics of domestic public diplomacy by state actors in German foreign and security policy

Focal point	Gulf War (1991)	Kosovo War (1999)	Iraq War (2002–2003)	Afghanistan ('Kunduz air strike', 2009)	National Security Strategy (2022)
Public(s)	Mass protesters as non-audience	Silent majority as tacit supporters	Media public as passive audience	Rebelling party wing	Anti-war masses as electorate	Military members as aggrieved actors	Representative mini-public
Mode of engagement	Non-engagement	Passive through polls	Monological through media communication	Dialogical through emotional struggle and deliberation	Monological through staged party competition	Monological through speeches and dialogical through parliamentary inquiry	Dialogical through participatory deliberation

Our analysis reveals that German domestic PD has come to include more dialogical formats over time. However, we do not think of this progression as a teleological development, which would inevitably lead to an ever-deeper engagement of an ever-broader public. Rather, we understand it as an *expansion of a repertoire* of state domestic PD. This 'toolbox' now also encompasses more inclusive, participatory modes of interaction with the public. Yet, it also contains older forms of interaction, which continue to be relevant and in use.

However, once dialogical forms of PD are 'on the table', a return to policy-making in exclusive circles is hard to sell. When citizens have positive experiences of these new formats (e.g. collaborating with diplomats and fellow citizens with different viewpoints, being valued by the state), they may ask for more of the same, as studies on other policy fields have shown.[95] Inclusive PD can contribute to a politicisation of FSP and increase citizens' demand to have a say. In the longer run, this may actually contribute to a changed perception of the public and its role in FSP.

However, we caution against equating the expanded repertoire of domestic PD with a democratisation of FSP in Germany (or elsewhere). First, we do not yet have reliable evidence on the extent to which the novel participatory formats have a tangible effect on policy, or indeed whether they have an impact at all. For example, even the most participatory series of dialogues for the National Security Strategy was not explicitly mentioned in the final strategy document.

Second, these increased communication activities do not seem to be overly successful at conveying their messages to the broader public: 51 per cent of citizens in Germany still feel (very) poorly informed about the military operations in which the *Bundeswehr* is involved and 47 per cent would like better and more detailed information.[96] Again, the participatory framework for the Security Strategy received barely any media attention and raised little awareness among the general population.

Third, the ability of the expanded PD repertoire to make the FSP discourse more inclusive remains questionable. The recent participatory formats that invested heavily into representative recruitment were largely boycotted by supporters of far-right parties. Thus, alienated groups continue to be at risk of no longer behind part of 'the public', both in terms of the understanding and engagement by state actors.[97]

---

95   E.g. Krick 2023, 473.
96   Graf 2022, 8.
97   See also Popkova and Michaels 2022.

Our analysis underlines the need to differentiate 'the public' and keep pace with the diversity of empirical practices of domestic PD. Today more than ever, a 'public' consists of a multitude of 'sub-publics', each potentially reacting differently to the offers made by PD. This conclusion opens important and exciting avenues for future research. Using a synchronous analytical perspective, future studies could provide a more in-depth analysis of how PD on one specific FSP issue is practiced in different places and formats at the same time. This may involve multi-sited studies within a single country or a comparison of different countries.[98] Such efforts would not only expand our knowledge on the repertoires of domestic PD, they would also shed light on the connection between the characteristics of a given sub-public and the forms and modes used by PD to address that specific sub-public. In addition, a more comparative approach would help to address the question of whether and to what extent domestic state PD differs from country to country.

Finally, an important development, that we could only briefly address here, is the increasing digitalisation of domestic PD. Recent studies have demonstrated how the 'digital disruption' is reshaping diplomatic practices at home.[99] Future research could explore how 'the public' is understood and constructed in digital contexts, including the interplay between online and offline activities and perceptions.[100] Such an approach would broaden our understanding of the contemporary PD repertoire employed by state actors and illuminate the dynamics of public engagement in the digital era.

Bibliography

Ayhan, Kadir Jun, and Efe Sevin. 'Moving public diplomacy research forward: methodological approaches'. *Place Branding and Public Diplomacy* 18 (3) (2022), 201–203. DOI 10.1057/s41254-022-00263-5.

Blumenau, Bernhard. 'Breaking with Convention? *Zeitenwende* and the Traditional Pillars of German Foreign Policy'. *International Affairs* 98 (6) (2022), 1895–1913. DOI 10.1093/ia/iiac166.

Çevik, Senem B. 'Turkey's Public Diplomacy in Flux. From Proactive to Reactive Communication'. In *Routledge Handbook of Public Diplomacy*, eds. Nancy Snow and Nicholas J. Cull (New York, NY: Routledge, 2020, 2nd Edition), 350–359.

---

98   Geis, Opitz, and Pfeifer 2022.
99   Manor 2024.
100   Manor and Yarchi 2023.

Cull, Nicholas J. 'History'. In *A Research Agenda for Public Diplomacy*, ed. Eytan Gilboa (Cheltenham: Edward Elgar, 2023), 109–124.

Destradi, Sandra, Johannes Plagemann, and Hakkı Taş. 'Populism and the Politicisation of Foreign Policy'. *The British Journal of Politics and International Relations* 24 (3) (2022), 475–492. DOI 10.1177/13691481221075944.

Dörfler-Dierken, Angelika. 'Identitätspolitik der Bundeswehr'. In *Identität, Selbstverständnis, Berufsbild: Implikationen der neuen Einsatzrealität für die Bundeswehr*, eds. Angelika Dörfler-Dierken, and Gerhard Kümmel (Wiesbaden: vs Verlag für Sozialwissenschaften, 2010), 137–160.

Demmer, Ulrike, Markus Feldenkirchen, Ullrich Fichtner, Matthias Gebauer, John Goetz, Hauke Goos, Jochen-Martin Gutsch, Susanne Koelbl, Shoib Najafizada, Christoph Schwennicke, and Holger Stark. 'Ein deutsches Verbrechen'. *Der Spiegel*, 31 January 2010.

Fitzpatrick, Kathy R. 'US Public Diplomacy's Neglected Domestic Mandate'. *CPD Perspectives on Public Diplomacy*, no. 3 (Los Angeles: Figueroa Press, 2010).

Fitzpatrick, Kathy R. 'Defining Strategic Publics in Networked World: Public Diplomacy's Challenge at Home and Abroad'. *The Hague Journal of Diplomacy* 7 (4) (2012), 421–440. DOI 10.1163/1871191X-12341236.

Fitzpatrick, Kathy R. 'Public Relations'. In *A Research Agenda for Public Diplomacy*, ed. Eytan Gilboa (Cheltenham: Edward Elgar, 2023), 141–156.

Friedrich, Roland. *Die deutsche Außenpolitik Im Kosovo-Konflikt* (Wiesbaden: vs Verlag für Sozialwissenschaften, 2005).

Geis, Anna. 'Burdens of the Past, Shadows of the Future: The Use of Military Force as a Challenge for the German "Civilian Power"'. In *The Militant Face of Democracy: Liberal Forces for Good*, eds. Anna Geis, Harald Müller, and Niklas Schörnig (Cambridge: Cambridge University Press, 2013), 231–268.

Geis, Anna. 'The Ambivalence of (Not) Being in a "War": The "Civilian Power" Germany and the "Stabilization Operation" in Afghanistan'. In *Concepts at Work: On the Linguistic Infrastructure of World Politics*, ed. Piki Ish-Shalom (Michigan: Michigan University Press, 2021), 65–90.

Geis, Anna, Christian Opitz, and Hanna Pfeifer. 'Recasting the Role of Citizens in Diplomacy and Foreign Policy: Preliminary Insights and a New Research Agenda'. *The Hague Journal of Diplomacy* 17 (4) (2022), 614–627. DOI 10.1163/1871191x-bja10136.

Geis, Anna, and Hanna Pfeifer. 'Deutsche Verantwortung in der „Mitte der Gesellschaft" aushandeln? Über Politisierung und Entpolitisierung der deutschen Außenpolitik'. *Politische Vierteljahresschrift* Sonderheft 52 (2017), 218–243. DOI 10.5771/9783845271934-219.

Gilboa, Eytan. 'Public Diplomacy'. In *The International Encyclopedia of Political Communication*, ed. Gianpietro Mazzoleni (New York, NY: Wiley-Blackwell, 2015), 1297–1306.

Gilboa, Eytan. 'Moving to a New Phase in Public Diplomacy Research'. In *A Research Agenda for Public Diplomacy*, ed. Eytan Gilboa (Cheltenham: Edward Elgar, 2023), 1–23.

Graf, Timo. *Zeitenwende im sicherheits- und verteidigungspolitischen Meinungsbild: Ergebnisse der ZMSBw-Bevölkerungsbefragung 2022* (Potsdam: Zentrum für Militärgeschichte und Sozialwissenschaften der Bundeswehr, 2022).

Gregory, Bruce. 'Mapping Boundaries in Diplomacy's Public Dimension'. *The Hague Journal of Diplomacy* 11 (1) (2016), 1–25. DOI 10.1163/1871191X-12341317.

Gulmez, Seckin Baris, and Miray Ates. 'Bringing History Back in: A Qualitative Longitudinal Approach to Public Diplomacy'. *Place Branding and Public Diplomacy* 18 (3) (2022), 216–227. DOI 10.1057/s41254-021-00228-0.

Hagmann, Jonas, Hendrik Hegemann, and Andrew Neal. 'The Politicisation of Security: Controversy, Mobilisation, Arena Shifting'. *European Review of International Studies* 5 (3) (2018), 3–29. DPO 10.3224/eris.v5i3.01.

Hilpert, Carolin. *Strategic Cultural Change and the Challenge for Security Policy: Germany and the Bundeswehr's Deployment to Afghanistan* (Basingstoke: Palgrave Macmillan, 2014).

Huijgh, Ellen. 'Public Diplomacy in Flux: Introducing the Domestic Dimension'. *The Hague Journal of Diplomacy* 7 (4) (2012), 359–367. DOI 10.1163/1871191X-12341240.

Huijgh, Ellen. *Public Diplomacy at Home: Domestic Dimensions* (Leiden: Brill, 2019).

Jacobi, Daniel. 'Die Öffentlichkeit der Sicherheit und die Sicherheit der Öffentlichkeit'. In *Das Weißbuch 2016 und die Herausforderungen von Strategiebildung: Zwischen Notwendigkeit und Möglichkeit*, eds. Daniel Jacobi and Gunther Hellmann (Wiesbaden: Springer VS, 2018), 223–246.

Jacobi, Daniel, Gunther Hellmann, and Sebastian Nieke. 'Deutschlands Verteidigung am Hindukusch: Ein Fall misslingender Sicherheitskommunikation'. *Zeitschrift für Außen- und Sicherheitspolitik* 4 (Suppl 1) (2011), 171–196. DOI 10.1007/s12399-011-0207-6.

Kim, HwaJung, and Jan Melissen. 'Engaging Home in International Diplomacy: Introduction'. *The Hague Journal of Diplomacy* 17 (4) (2022), 611–613. DOI 10.1163/1871 191x-bja10141.

Krick, Eva. 'Beteiligungsprofis in der Demokratie. Zur Professionalisierung und Kommerzialisierung einer Wachstumsbranche'. *Leviathan* 51 (3) (2023), 454–483. DOI 10.5771/0340-0425-2023-3-454.

Kutz, Magnus-Sebastian. *Öffentlichkeitsarbeit in Kriegen: Legitimation von Kosovo-, Afghanistan- und Irakkrieg in Deutschland und den USA* (Wiesbaden: Springer VS, 2014).

la Cour, Christina. 'The Evolution of the "Public" in Diplomacy'. *Place Branding and Public Diplomacy* 14 (1) (2018), 22–35. DOI 10.1057/s41254-017-0093-3.

Lantis, Jeffrey. 'The Moral Imperative of Force: The Evolution of German Strategic Culture in Kosovo'. *Comparative Strategy* 21 (1) (2022), 21–46. DOI 10.1080/0149 59302317350864.

Mader, Matthias. *Öffentliche Meinung zu Auslandseinsätzen der Bundeswehr: zwischen Antimilitarismus und transatlantischer Orientierung* (Wiesbaden: Springer VS, 2017).

Manfredi-Sánchez, Juan-Luis, and Nicholas Ross Smith. 'Public Diplomacy in an Age of Perpetual Crisis: Assessing the EU's Strategic Narratives through Six Crises'. *Journal of Communication Management* 27 (2) (2023), 241–258. DOI 10.1108/JCOM -04-2022-0037.

Manor, Ilan. 'Domestic Digital Diplomacy: Digital Disruption at the Macro and Micro Levels'. *The Hague Journal of Diplomacy* 19 (1) (2024), 145–183. DOI 10.1163/1871191x-bja10173.

Manor, Ilan, César Jiménez-Martínez, and Alina Dolea. 'An Asset or a Hassle? The Public as a Problem for Public Diplomats'. *The Hague Diplomacy Blog*, 16 November 2021. https://www.universiteitleiden.nl/hjd/news/2021/blog-post–an-asset-or -a-hassle-the-public-as-a-problem-for-public-diplomats.

Manor, Ilan, and Moran Yarchi. 'From the Global to the Local and Back Again: MFAs' Digital Communications During COVID-19'. *International Journal of Communication* 17 (2023), 860–881.

Maull, Hanns W. 'Germany and the Use of Force: Still a "Civilian Power"?' *Survival: Global Politics and Strategy* 42 (2) (2000), 56–80. DOI 10.1093/survival/42.2.56.

Melissen, Jan. 'The New Public Diplomacy: Between Theory and Practice'. In *The New Public Diplomacy: Soft Power in International Relations*, ed. Jan Melissen (London: Palgrave Macmillan UK, 2005), 3–27.

Melissen, Jan. 'Beyond the New Public Diplomacy'. *Clingendael Paper No. 3* (The Hague: Clingendael, 2011).

Melissen, Jan. 'Public Diplomacy'. In *Diplomacy in a Globalizing World*, eds. Pauline Kerr and Geoffrey Wiseman (New York, NY: Oxford University Press, 2018, 2nd Edition), 199–218.

Müller, Harald, and Jonas Wolff. 'Demokratischer Krieg am Hindukusch? Eine kritische Analyse der Bundestagsdebatten zur deutschen Afghanistanpolitik 2001-2011'. In *Zehn Jahre Deutschland in Afghanistan*, eds. Klaus Brummer and Stefan Fröhlich (Wiesbaden: VS Verlag für Sozialwissenschaften, 2011), 197–221.

Neumann, Iver B. *Diplomatic Tenses: A Social Evolutionary Perspective on Diplomacy* (Manchester: Manchester University Press, 2020).

Nieke, Sebastian. 'Gefallene Helfer: Das Soldatengedenken der Bundesrepublik zwischen militärischer Zurückhaltung und professionsethischer Würdigung der Bundeswehr'. *Zeitschrift für Außen- und Sicherheitspolitik* 9 (1) (2016), 79–100. DOI 10.1007/s12399-015-0545-x.

Noetzel, Timo. 'The German Politics of War: Kunduz and the War in Afghanistan'. *International Affairs* 87 (2) (2011), 397–417. DOI 10.1111/j.1468-2346.2011.00979.x.

Oldhaver, Mathias. *Öffentliche Meinung in der Sicherheitspolitik: Untersuchung am Beispiel der Debatte über einen Einsatz der Bundeswehr im Golfkrieg* (Baden-Baden: Nomos, 2000).

Opitz, Christian, Hanna Pfeifer, and Anna Geis. 'Engaging with Public Opinion at the Micro-Level: Citizen Dialogue and Participation in German Foreign Policy'. *Foreign Policy Analysis* 18 (1) (2022). DOI 10.1093/fpa/orab033.

Opitz, Christian, Hanna Pfeifer, and Anna Geis. 'Kontrollierte Politisierung: Bürgerdialoge im Rahmen der Entwicklung der ersten Nationalen Sicherheitsstrategie in Deutschland'. *Politische Vierteljahresschrift* (2024). DOI 10.1007/s11615-024-00548-9

Oppermann, Kai. 'Between a Rock and a Hard Place? Navigating Domestic and International Expectations on German Foreign Policy'. *German Politics* 28 (3) (2019), 482–498. DOI 10.1080/09644008.2018.1481208.

Pacher, Andreas. 'Strategic Publics in Public Diplomacy: A Typology and a Heuristic Device for Multiple Publics'. *The Hague Journal of Diplomacy* 13 (3) (2018), 272–296. DOI 10.1163/1871191X-13020004.

Pamment, James, Alicia Fjällhed, and Martina Smedberg. 'The "Logics" of Public Diplomacy: In Search of What Unites a Multidisciplinary Research Field'. *The Hague Journal of Diplomacy* 19 (1) (2024), 49–83. DOI 10.1163/1871191x-bja10161.

Parker, Jason C. *Hearts, Minds, Voices: US Cold War Public Diplomacy and the Formation of the Third World* (Oxford: Oxford University Press, 2016).

Pestana, Augusto. 'The Brazilian Approach to Public Diplomacy'. In *Routledge Handbook of Public Diplomacy*, eds. Nancy Snow and Nicholas J. Cull (New York, NY: Routledge, 2020, 2nd Edition), 342–349.

Popkova, Anna, and Jodi Hope Michaels. 'Who Represents the Domestic Voice? Diversity, Equity and Inclusion in Citizen Diplomacy'. *The Hague Journal of Diplomacy* 17 (4) (2022), 669–678. DOI 10.1163/1871191x-bja10135.

Rawnsley, Gary D. 'Communicating Confidence: China's Public Diplomacy'. In *Routledge Handbook of Public Diplomacy*, eds. Nancy Snow and Nicholas J. Cull (New York, NY: Routledge, 2020, 2nd Edition), 284–300.

Schoen, Harald. 'Der Kanzler, zwei Sommerthemen und ein Foto-Finish: Priming-Effekte bei der Bundestagswahl 2002'. In *Die Bundestagswahl 2002: Analysen der Wahlergebnisse und des Wahlkampfes*, eds. Frank Brettschneider, Jan Deth, and Edeltraud Roller (Wiesbaden: vs Verlag für Sozialwissenschaften, 2004), 23–50.

Schroeder, Robin, and Martin Zapfe. '"War-like Circumstances": Germany's Unforeseen Combat Mission in Afghanistan and Its Strategic Narratives'. In *Strategic Narratives, Public Opinion and War Winning Domestic Support for the Afghan*

War, eds. Beatrice De Graaf, George Dimitriu, and Jens Ringsmose (London: Routledge, 2015), 177–198.

Schwab-Trapp, Michael. *Kriegsdiskurse: Die politische Kultur des Krieges im Wandel 1991–1999* (Wiesbaden: Springer Fachmedien, 2002).

Sharp, Paul. *Diplomatic Theory of International Relations* (Cambridge: Cambridge University Press, 2009).

Sharp, Paul. 'Domestic Public Diplomacy, Domestic Diplomacy, and Domestic Foreign Policy'. In *The Transformation of Foreign Policy: Drawing and Managing Boundaries from Antiquity to the Present*, eds. Gunther Hellmann, Andreas Fahrmeir, and Milo Vec (Oxford: Oxford University Press, 2016), 263–283.

Smith, Graham, and Maija Setälä. 'Mini-Publics and Deliberative Democracy'. In *The Oxford Handbook of Deliberative Democracy*, eds. André Bächtiger, John S. Dryzek, Jane Mansbridge, and Mark Warren (Oxford: Oxford University Press, 2018), 299–314.

Snow, Nancy, and Nicholas J. Cull. 'Preface and Introduction'. In *Routledge Handbook of Public Diplomacy*, eds. Nancy Snow and Nicholas J. Cull (New York, NY: Routledge, 2020, 2nd Edition), x–xiv.

Stahl, Bernhard. 'Nationale Geschichte(n) für den Krieg – Der deutsche und französische Diskurs im Kosovo-Krieg und in der Irak-Krise'. *Zeitschrift für Vergleichende Politikwissenschaft* 2 (2) (2008), 257–286. DOI 10.1007/s12286-008-0016-z.

Steg, Thomas. 'Nach außen wirken, nach innen überzeugen: Besonderheiten in der Kommunikation von Außenpolitik'. *Zeitschrift für Außen- und Sicherheitspolitik* 3 (3) (2010), 337–356. DOI 10.1007/s12399-010-0141-z.

Stern, Eric K. 'Crisis Studies and Foreign Policy Analysis: Insights, Synergies, and Challenges'. *International Studies Review* 5 (2) (2003), 183–202. DOI 10.1111/1521-9488.5020016.

Tam, Lisa, and Jeong-Nam Nim. 'Who Are Publics in Public Diplomacy? Proposing a Taxonomy of Foreign Publics as an Intersection between Symbolic Environment and Behavioral Experiences'. *Place Branding and Public Diplomacy* 15 (1) (2019), 28–37. DOI 10.1057/s41254-018-0104-z.

Yang, Yifan. 'Looking Inward: How Does Chinese Public Diplomacy Work at Home?' *The British Journal of Politics and International Relations* 22 (3) (2020), 369–386. DOI 10.1177/1369148120917583.

Zhang, Yun. 'The Disintegration of State-Society Relations and Its Moderating Effects on Japanese Diplomacy towards China'. *The Hague Journal of Diplomacy* 17 (4) (2022), 643–653. DOI 10.1163/1871191x-bja10137.

CHAPTER 4

Home Diplomacy Across Borders: Consular and Diaspora Diplomacy in France

Christian Lequesne

Summary

It would be a mistake to consider home diplomacy as only the development of dip-lomats' relations with citizens within the borders of the national territory. Home diplomacy is also extra-territorialized and requires that the diplomat develop rela-tions with national citizens living abroad. For this reason, any research programme on home diplomacy that overlooks the relationship between the diplomat abroad and the diasporas from the home country would be incomplete, as this chapter based on the French case aims to demonstrate. The chapter is divided into three sections. It begins by explaining why French diplomatic practice favours consular protection of citizens living abroad. In the second section, it analyses the consequen-ces for diplomatic practices of the export of national electoral politics to the diaspora through the right to vote. Finally, it explains why state historicity makes the shift of French diplomacy from consular diplomacy to diaspora diplomacy based on partner-ships with diasporic citizens difficult.

Keywords

citizenship abroad – consular diplomacy – diaspora diplomacy – diaspora vote – extra-territoriality of politics – public diplomacy

1 Introduction

New research on engaging home in diplomacy has not yet included in its scope the practices of national diplomats towards their national citizens liv-ing abroad, or diasporas. However, if one diplomatic practice leads diplomats to engage home, it is the development of various relations with diasporas when posted abroad. The intensity of this daily work with national citizens forming diasporas has dramatically increased in the last 50 years due to the development of migrations, not only South–North but also South–South and North–North.

As a consequence, diplomatic studies has an increased interest in the consequences of migrations for diplomacy. It leads researchers to envisage a greater conceptualization of consular diplomacy, which can be defined as the extra-territorial protection of citizens by the country of origin, but also of diaspora diplomacy, a wider concept that reflects the way national diplomats use their diasporas to shape decisions and build influence abroad.

This chapter is the result of research that I carried out between 2018 and 2023 to understand how diplomats posted in French consulates and embassies take diasporic citizens into account in their daily practice. This research, which resulted in a book currently available in French,[1] was conducted in five countries where the French diaspora is represented (Germany, Israel, Ivory Coast, Japan and the United Kingdom). It enabled me to analyse the conditions under which representatives of the French state develop practices abroad vis-à-vis their own national citizens. To proceed, the chapter is divided into three sections. I begin by explaining why French diplomatic practice favours consular protection of the diaspora. In the second section, I analyse the export of national electoral politics to the diaspora through the right to vote and its consequences for diplomatic practices. Finally, I explain the difficulty French diplomacy faces in moving from consular diplomacy to diaspora diplomacy.

2   French Consular Diplomacy Engages Home

Sixty years after the signature of the Vienna Convention on consular relations,[2] we observe a growing consularization of diplomacy resulting from the dramatic increase of migration flows and, in consequence, growing transnational complexity.[3] Consular diplomacy can be defined as the public policy of a state consisting in organizing abroad relations with two sets of individuals. The first is one's own citizens, who need travel documents to go overseas, and protection and help while they travel abroad: extradition, emergency assistance, and repatriation. The second group includes foreign citizens who need visas, illegal migrants, and overseas workers.[4]

---

1 Lequesne 2024.
2 United Nations 1963.
3 Melissen and Fernandez 2011.
4 https://www.diplomacy.edu/course/consular/.

2.1   *Origin of French Consular Diplomacy*

In France, taking care of French citizens abroad (the French diaspora) is an established part of the diplomatic practice of the Ministry of Europe and Foreign Affairs (MEFA), which has provided a wide range of protective rights since the 16th century.[5] There are few rights granted to national citizens living in France that are not symmetrically granted to their compatriots living abroad, including delivery of documents, education of children, but also welfare benefits. There are three variables that explain such generous protection, as I have analysed in my recent book.[6]

The first variable is France's colonial history, which long ago led the French state to grant French nationals in former colonies (but not the indigenous peoples living in those colonies) the same rights as they would have in France.[7] This assimilation to the national territory explains why the French state has never used the term diaspora in its official discourse. Ambassadors and consuls still used the term 'French colony' in telegrams to Paris in the 1970s.[8] The second variable is linked to France's inclusive conception of citizenship.[9] France has never recognized particularism or specific community rights in the granting of citizenship. Regardless of where a French citizen comes from or lives, he or she is considered to have the same universal rights. The French system of citizenship does not, for example, grant specific and limited rights to overseas citizens, as India and the UK do for overseas nationals.[10] The third and final variable is the strong legitimacy of the welfare state in France, which generates social redistribution and offers symmetric services beyond the country's borders. French citizens living abroad can benefit from redistributive social policies if they prove to the French state that their income is under a certain threshold. It is worth pointing out that only legal citizenship (nationality), and not fiscal citizenship, is taken into account in providing social benefit. It is perfectly possible to benefit from redistributive social policies if you are a French citizen living abroad without paying taxes in France.

5   Bartolomei et al. 2016.

6   Lequesne 2024.

7   Lambert 2009.

8   Letter of the French General Consul in Pondicherry to the Department, 16 June 1977, archives of the French Ministry of European and Foreign Affairs, La Courneuve.

9   Weil 2008.

10   Kumar Banerjee 2019; Benson 2023.

2.2 *Effects on Administrative Organization*

The protective consular diplomacy has an effect on the administrative organization. With 206 consular posts in 2023, France has one of the largest networks of consulates in the world compared with the number of citizens living abroad. To compare with other EU member states, Italy and the UK have slightly smaller consular networks, but with a migrant population almost double that of France: 5.6 million for Italy and 4.2 million for the UK, compared with 2.5 million for France.[11] In the case of France, there are also 501 honorary consulates led by volunteer consuls, 301 of whom are French citizens and 200 of whom are nationals of the country in which they work. In 2020, special credits for the programme dedicated to consular diplomacy and French living abroad amounted to 136 million euros.[12] It is a generous level of funding, even if it remains a relatively modest percentage (2.5 per cent) in relation to the total expenditures of the French MEFA.

Diplomatic institutions cannot be studied only as organizations. They are also sites where diplomatic practices take place, as Iver Neumann, Merje Kuus and Frederik Jerris have analysed in their work.[13] From a site perspective, a French consulate, and more specifically its public reception areas, receives two types of population on a daily basis: on the one hand, citizens of the country of residence where visas are requested to travel to France, and on the other hand, citizens of the country of origin – the French – who find in the consulate the equivalent of a town hall. The ethnographic research I conducted led me to observe different French consulates and honorary consulates in the five countries mentioned in the introduction. I spent time as an observatory participant in the public reception areas of diplomatic sites, which can be considered as a transnational equivalent of French town halls. They have office hours, appointments and counters for welcoming French citizens. Honorary consuls, who are non-professional diplomats acting on a voluntary basis, reinforce this day-to-day diplomacy. In a building that is her private property, the French Honorary Consul in Netanya, Israel, collects applications to renew identity papers, life certificates for pensioners and applications for social benefits and forwards them to the Consulate General in Tel Aviv. The atmosphere in the waiting room of Netanya's Honorary Consulate is reminiscent of the town hall in a small French town, with conversations carried out in French

---

11   French Ministry of European and Foreign Affairs 2021.
12   French Ministry of European and Foreign Affairs 2021.
13   Neumann 2012; Kuus 2013; Jerris 2023.

between citizens in the queue, beneath the symbolic portrait of the President of the Republic.[14]

2.3   *Diplomats Engaging Home*

It is clear from these practices that French diplomats, in their day-to-day dealings with French citizens, are engaging home in diplomacy. What does this mean in more concrete terms?

Firstly, diplomats issue national documents, notably identity papers. Any French citizen living abroad can have a passport or a national identity card issued under the same conditions as in France. The consulates collect the biometric data, and some consulates have the same technical resources as the prefectures in France to produce the documents.

Secondly, diplomats instruct French citizens in how to apply for social welfare. Consulates intervene in health issues. They direct French nationals to French-speaking referral doctors in the event of illness, or (in Africa) to medical dispensaries subsidized by the French state. During the Covid-19 crisis, consulates were particularly active in ensuring that French nationals abroad could be vaccinated in countries where it was difficult to access vaccines. More specifically, French nationals living abroad (outside the European Union) are eligible for social benefits if they meet certain criteria, such as low income, single status or disability. In the 2010s, the MEFA allocated some 15 million euros a year to social assistance. Due to the Covid-19 crisis, the allocation has reached exceptional levels, amounting to 19 million euros in 2020 and 31 million euros in 2021. In addition, consulates attribute 100 million euros a year for school grants to help French citizens abroad pay tuition fees for their children in French international schools.[15] This extraterritorial projection of welfare distribution has no real equivalent in the Western world. Its distinguishing feature is that it is based not just on regulatory policies, as is the case for Mexican consulates, which ensure that their nationals working in the United States benefit from legal employment contracts, but on redistribution.[16] We are very far indeed from Adler-Nissen and Tsinovoi's observation that 'the state no longer sees the population only as an object for pastoral protection'.[17] The French national living abroad has not become the client of a neoliberal consular diplomacy, because the historicity of the French state offers resistance to the neoliberal art of governing. By

---

14   Lequesne 2024.
15   French Ministry of European and Foreign Affairs 2022.
16   Delano Alonso 2018.
17   Tsinovoi and Adler Nissen 2018, 230.

historicity, I mean the capacity of the state to apprehend legitimate action in the present and in the future only in reference to what has been built over the long term in the past.[18]

Thirdly, diplomats organize elections because, as we will see in detail in the next section, French citizens living abroad can vote in all elections on the same basis as their fellow French citizens, with no other condition than French nationality.

Finally, in countries that are not safe, either because of high criminality or due to a state of civil war, consulates organize security policies based on volunteer heads of blocks (*chefs d'îlots*) who are responsible for warning fellow citizens and evacuating them rapidly in the event of imminent danger. Equivalent practices do not exist in the same way for citizens living in France, as national and local police forces are supposed to ensure the security of citizens. Mass repatriations can be organized by the consulates with the support of the national air forces. Between 10 and 18 November 2004, for instance, 8,334 French citizens were rapatriated from Abidjan airport to escape the climate of civil war that was arising in Ivory Coast.

In the past, French consulates offered even more extensive services. For reasons of budget rationalization, these were reduced in the 2010s. Up to 2019, consular services included, for instance, notarial services, which have now been discontinued. French citizens abroad are now advised to contact a notary in France for their patrimonial affairs. Similarly, prior to 2015, some consulates had employment and vocational training desks that provided support to French nationals wishing to work in the country of residence. This latter function has gradually been transferred by the consulates to the associative sector made up of French nationals living abroad, which nevertheless continue to receive subsidies from the MEFA.

This impressive list of services shows that consular protection, available to all French citizens abroad, is particularly well established. It goes hand in hand with the idea that the benefits of citizenship must not be lost when one crosses the country's borders. French diplomats are used to exercising this protection, which they consider to be a routine duty. Consular protection is also a political interest for diplomats. It is a way to maintain relations with French citizens abroad by making them dependent on the state's resources and policies. School grants are the best example of this. They are available not only to very low-income families in Africa, but also to middle-

---

18   Lefort 1952.

class families living, for instance, in the United States (New York, San Francisco), where fees for French schools are as expensive as they are for American private schools. The link of dependence can therefore be broad in terms of social groupings.

2.4   Consular Diplomacy and Electoral Politics

French consular diplomacy also has the particular characteristic of being controlled by a range of citizens' representatives who are supposed to exercise citizen control over consular activities. This results in the politicization of consular diplomacy.

There are 442 consular counsellors, elected in each consular district by the French citizens living abroad to defend their interests with the consular administration. There are also 90 counsellors of the Assembly of French Nationals Abroad (AFE), a consultative body that the diplomatic administration consults before deciding on consular policies. As a general rule, the consular advisers and the members of the AFE spend a great deal of time ensuring that distributive policies continue to be attributed to French nationals by the consulates. Often affiliated to one of the two major associations of French people living abroad, the right-wing *Union des Français de l'Etranger* or the left-wing *Français du Monde*, elected representatives all agree that consular services must not be diminished. They, along with politicians (senators and deputies) specifically elected to represent French living abroad, as is the case in only thirteen countries of the world,[19] contribute to maintaining the status quo in distribution and in consular services in general. Any reduction in services (such as the notary's office) or in financial aid by the state of origin is subject to an appeal to consult similar to those made to prefects in the national territory.

France has an active consular diplomacy whose main actors are emigrant citizens but who also include elected representatives. Abroad, we observe a near-replication of the classic triangular administration–representatives–citizens' relation that shapes the making of public policies at home. French consular diplomacy means, then, looking for close policy symmetry with the decision-making of the state at home.

---

19   Collyer 2014.

3   Practising Home Politics Abroad

France has chosen not to deprive French nationals living abroad of national politics by allowing them the right to vote in all national elections since 1979, but also the right to elect specific members of parliament who represent French nationals living abroad. Within the European Union, a specific system of parliamentary representation for citizens living abroad only exists in four other member states: Croatia, Italy, Portugal and Romania.

The lower house, the National Assembly, has eleven deputies elected by direct universal suffrage, while the upper house, the Senate, has twelve representatives elected by indirect suffrage by the representatives of the French diaspora.

3.1   *The Right to Vote in National Elections*

According to political theory, granting the diaspora the right to vote in their country of origin reveals the shifting nature of the link between citizenship and territory. The German political scientist Rainer Bauböck speaks of an 'expansive citizenship' that is increasingly granting non-national residents (immigrants) as well as non-resident nationals (emigrants) the right to vote.[20] Giving voting rights to diasporas also marks an official recognition of emigrant status by the state of origin, as is frequently demanded by international organizations. In June 2011, the Venice Commission of the Council of Europe concluded a report on out-of-country voting with the following recommendation:

> Although the introduction of the right to vote for citizens who live abroad is not required by the principles of the European electoral heritage, the European Commission for Democracy through Law suggests that states, in view of citizens' European mobility, and in accordance with the particular situation of certain states, adopt a positive approach to the right to vote of citizens living abroad, since this right fosters the development of national and European citizenship.[21]

In contrast to other EU countries such as Romania, the impact of the diaspora vote is rarely decisive for the final outcome of a national election in France, since citizens abroad only represent 7–8 per cent of the total electorate. Moreover, the abstention rate is generally high (61 per cent in the 2022 presidential election and 79 per cent in the 2022 parliamentary election). Nevertheless,

---

20   Bauböck 2005.
21   Council of Europe 2011.

candidates in national elections do not neglect significant French communities living abroad, as they can provide support at the margins. Not only populist leaders, such as President Recep Tayyip Erdoğan in Turkey or Prime Minister Narendra Modi in India, understand that they can capitalize on the voting potential of diasporas.[22] French President Emmanuel Macron considered during the two presidential elections in 2017 and 2022 that it was necessary to address the large French communities in London, New York and Geneva because they were very supportive of his liberal and pro-EU programme.[23] For their part, the left-wing candidates travelled to the Maghreb and Africa during the electoral campaigns, where former migrant workers returning from France with a French passport gave them their support. Far-right candidate Marine Le Pen, meanwhile, never neglects to meet with the Franco-Lebanese Christian Maronites in Lebanon, who favour her programme to reduce the rights of Muslims in French society.

3.2   *Diplomats and the Election Process*

Similar to what municipal staff would do in France, diplomats are involved in the organization of national elections at consulates. The first task of a diplomat is to maintain the electoral roll. This is a delicate operation because emigration is no longer limited to the model of permanent settlement. There is temporary mobility, such as that of students, as well as emigrants marked by comings and goings, which makes it difficult to keep the electoral lists up to date. In 2019, a single electoral register was introduced, leading the consular administration to reform its IT application for managing the electoral rolls of French citizens living abroad. This put an end to the possibility for French citizens living abroad to be registered both on the electoral roll of a consulate and on that of a municipality in France.

For all elections by direct universal suffrage, the consulates organize polling stations that can be visited in person. In the case of elections for senators, who are elected by indirect voting, eligible voters (counsellors and delegates of French nationals living abroad) who do not wish to travel to Paris can hand-deliver a sealed envelope with their vote to the head of the diplomatic or consular post in their constituency. Lastly, since 2012 electronic voting has been authorized for legislative elections, which is a right that citizens living in France do not have. In this case, diaspora voters use a secure platform that operates under the supervision of the state agency *Agence Nationale de Sécurité des Services d'Information* (ANSSI). Although there is no tangible evidence

---

22   Szulecki et al. 2021.
23   Kernagellen and Pellen 2019.

of the impact of electronic voting on voter turnout, it saves members of the diaspora from having to travel in some cases several hours to get to a polling station. In Ivory Coast, a French citizen living in Korhogo or Bouaké would have to travel several hours by car to get to the only polling station in the capital, Abidjan.[24] However, electronic voting has never been authorized for the presidential election. Representatives of the AFE and expatriate associations have asked for this on several occasions in the run-up to the presidential elections, but without success. In his first speech to AFE counsellors on 2 October 2017, Macron declared: 'If we are not able to organize ourselves for the next elections to have a voting system that is impervious to any attack, that is not France.'[25] However, the rejection of electronic voting was renewed for the 2022 presidential election in the face of strong reservations by the Ministry of the Interior and ANSSI about the risk of cyber-attacks. A massive diversion of votes as the result of online hacking would entail the complete annulment of the presidential election by the Constitutional Council, a risk that the Ministry of the Interior is hardly prepared to assume.

The possibility for the diaspora to use electronic voting on the internet, which currently is not authorized for those voting in France, is an interesting exception. In this case, the diaspora is granted more advanced rights than citizens living inside French territory enjoy. It is relevant to note that territorial citizens do not make an issue of the privileged right of their extra-territorial compatriots, even though there are demands for reform in favour of electronic voting in France. Territorial French citizens always constitute a reference for the claims of the French living abroad, but not the other way round.

3.3   *Extra-Territorial Practices of Politics*

The election of specific representatives of French living abroad to the National Assembly and the Senate raises the question of how national politics is practised in an extra-territorial context. Campaigning for the election of deputies, as analysed by Cédric Pellen in the 1st constituency abroad (United States and Canada) and Etienne Smith in the 9th constituency abroad (North Africa and West Africa), reveals specific characteristics of campaigning compared to the national territory.[26] Firstly, it is impossible for any candidate to cover physically the whole of his or her constituency during an election campaign, as these constituencies often represent several countries with long distances be-

---

24   Interview, French Consulate General, Abidjan, 28 October 2019.
25   Macron 2017.
26   Pellen 2013; Smith 2020.

tween them. Much of the campaigning activity is limited to meetings organized in large cities and on the internet. Politics through the internet is a
factor that explains the success of liberal candidates from Macron's party, as
the liberal middle-class electorate more readily accepts the use of new technologies. In 2017, ten out of eleven French MPs came from the ranks of LREM-
Renaissance; in 2022, nine out of eleven belonged to the same presidential
majority. Anne Genetet, elected for LREM-Renaissance in 2017 and 2022
in the 11th constituency (50 countries, including Russia and China), stresses
that it is, however, necessary to rely on local relays (AFE's elected representatives and consular counsellors) to invite citizens to join video-conference
meetings.[27]

Secondly, it is more difficult to ensure that an election is properly conducted – a task entrusted to diplomatic and consular posts – in an extra-
territorial context because constraints specific to the country of residence
play a role. For example, citizens who vote electronically are dependent on
the telephone networks of the country of residence, which ensure the trans-
mission of an SMS password required for voting. As a result of malfunctions,
voters in several African and South American countries did not receive their
passwords in time for the 2022 legislative elections. This had legal consequences for the validity of the election. In January 2023, the Constitutional Council
annulled the election of MP Karim Ben Cheïckh in the 9th constituency
(Maghreb and West Africa) and MP Eléonore Caroit in the 2nd constituency
(Latin America and the Caribbean). They were re-elected afterwards in by-
elections. Similarly, it is harder for the state to control for cronyism abroad
than it is at home. In February 2023, the Constitutional Council annulled the
election of deputy Meyer Habib in the 3rd constituency (Israel, Turkey, Southern Europe) because his supporters in Israel had set up a telephone platform
enabling voters to cast their votes online using their login and password.[28]
Supported by the right-wing part of the diaspora, Habib claimed that French
diplomats were plotting against the French diaspora of Israel, with the Consulate General in Tel Aviv pointing out his dubious practices during the
election.

Thirdly, campaigns for the election of French citizens living abroad are
marked by forms of political autochthony. This is first and foremost linked
to the profile of the candidates themselves. The vast majority of candidates
elected to the National Assembly and Senate are living abroad and not in
France. Political autochthony can also be measured by the topics that drive

---

27   Interview with Anne Genetet, National Assembly, Paris, 27 September 2018.
28   Lequesne 2024.

the campaign addressed to citizens.[29] They include a number of issues specific to the diaspora, such as the quality of education in French schools abroad, social benefits and the French tax regime for non-residents. Political autochthony finally results from the penetration of the politics of countries of residence in the electoral campaign. In 2017, Leila Haïchi was thus deprived of the LREM-Renaissance nomination for candidacy in the 9th constituency (Maghreb, West Africa) after being strongly suspected by French voters in Morocco of sympathy for the Polisario Front, and therefore Algeria. It was another presidential majority candidate, M'jid El Guerrab, clearly supported by the Moroccan government, who went on to win the election.[30] In 2017 and 2022, Meyer Habib also used his close ties with Benyamin Netanyahu to attract the votes of the large number of Franco-Israeli citizens who support the Likud policy in Israel. France's parliamentary representation abroad thus consists in citizen debates importing the politics of countries of residence into the national political game.

3.4 Parliamentary Work as Usual

Once elected, the deputies and senators of the French living abroad take part in parliamentary work in the same way as their elected colleagues of territorial France. They sit on the standing committees of both chambers, with, unsurprisingly, an over-representation in the Foreign Affairs Committee. Alexandre Holroyd, French MP for the United Kingdom, Ireland and several Northern European countries, devoted much of his parliamentary work between 2017 and 2020 to the issue of Brexit at the National Assembly. In 2018, he was the rapporteur for the bill authorizing the French government to issue a specific law in preparation for Brexit. He was also co-rapporteur for the information mission on the future partnership between the European Union and the United Kingdom. Frédéric Petit, MP for Central and Eastern Europe, was responsible in 2022 for an evaluation mission on the enlargement of the European Union to the Western Balkans. Meyer Habib devoted numerous speeches to the fight against anti-Semitism and the Israeli–Arab conflict. The number of reports, questions to the government and parliamentary missions serves to legitimize the MPS' and senators' re-election in the same way as for elected representatives from the national territory. These are the elements of the political records that will be promoted to potential voters at the next election.

---

29   Smith 2020.
30   Smith 2020.

3.5   *The Diplomat and the Member of Parliament*

As a servant of the state, the diplomat is in constant contact with the politician. Paradoxically, diplomatic studies have given little thought to the exact nature of the diplomat–politician nexus, as Geoffrey Wiseman pointed out in a recent publication.[31] Traditionally, the interlocutors of French diplomats are the members of the executive: the President of the Republic, the ministers in Paris and their private offices. But there are also the parliamentarians elected by the French living abroad who contribute to controlling and challenging the power of diplomats.

The tension between the diplomat and the parliamentarian makes it possible to verify three analytical hypotheses. The first is the permanent compromise that diplomats must build with societal actors in the conduct of diplomacy. The deputy or senator representing the French living abroad is contributing to making diplomacy more politicized in the sense of exercising control but also speaking publicly about the administrative actions that impact French citizens. Ambassadors and consuls are accountable to the MPs representing French citizens living abroad, who question and write to ministers and directors of central administrations in Paris to ask for solutions to problems, such as the capacity of a French school to welcome new students or the efficiency of the appointment process at a consulate. Because they have a political clientele among the citizens of the French diaspora, on whom they depend for their re-election, the deputies and senators of the French living abroad bring interest representation practices close to national politics into diplomatic work. French diplomats have been, however, less accustomed than other civil servants to dealing with interest groups in the formulation and implementation of public policies, even if they have to respond to more and more claims coming from their own citizens.[32] In France, the existence of a specific parliamentary representation for the diaspora means that diplomats have to accept the development of practices that have more to do with domestic politics than with diplomacy. This domestication of the work decreases the specificity of diplomacy by bringing diplomats into line with the practices of other civil servants working in France. This clearly contributed to the unease felt by French diplomats when their corps was integrated into that of the generic category of state administrators following the 2022 general reform of the French senior civil service.[33]

---

31   Wiseman 2022.

32   Kim and Melissen 2022a.

33   Official Journal of the French Republic 2022.

The right of French citizens living abroad to take part in national elections and the existence of specific representatives in parliament have clearly brought diplomatic work closer to the relations with citizens carried out at home. The result has been the export of French party politics to the extra-territorial space. Diplomats have had to leave their comfort zone of defending the diplomatic interests of their state abroad to deal with lobbying practices on the part of French political and social actors who behave according to the references of domestic politics rather than foreign policy.

4 The Difficult Shift from Consular Diplomacy to Diaspora Diplomacy

4.1 *Enhancing Influence through Public Diplomacy*
The French state has an established tradition of public diplomacy, notably through its long-established network of cultural institutes and French schools abroad.[34] However, for a long time, French policy-makers did not feel the need to elaborate a strategic approach to public diplomacy, as it seemed obvious to them that a power such as France had an influence on societies around the world.[35] From the 2010s onwards, the decline of the French language and cultural influence changed the attitude towards public diplomacy within the French MEFA. Senior diplomats considered that the French state needed to develop a more strategic reflection about its influence as a soft power.[36] A directorate for diplomacy of *influence* (the French prefer this term to public diplomacy) was created within the directorate general for globalization. In 2022, Foreign Minister Jean-Yves Le Drian published a 'roadmap for influence' that set out six strategic priorities: the French language in the service of mul-tilingualism, the attractiveness of higher education and scientific research, the revival of cultural and creative industries, the international influence of the media, support for think tanks and strengthening France's attractiveness in international organizations.[37]

While strategic documents on public diplomacy or soft power strategies in countries other than France include explicit references to diasporas, the 2022 'roadmap for influence' does not say a single word about it. This absence is in itself an indicator of a genuine difficulty for the French state to consider its diaspora not only as a group of national citizens to be protected, but also as

---

34   Lequesne 2021.
35   Charillon 2022, 270.
36   Lequesne 2020.
37   Le Drian 2022.

social partners to be utilized for enhancing diplomatic influence in the country of residence. In my view, exercising protection or researching influence marks the conceptual difference between consular diplomacy on the one hand and diaspora diplomacy on the other hand. Following the definition given by Ho and McConnell, diaspora diplomacy consists in states of origin enrolling 'their diasporas to lobby for the national interest, facilitate bilateral mediation, or as a resource for information gathering by intelligence agencies'.[38] The move from consular to diaspora diplomacy requires a change in the practice of the state. Such a change is not just a technical issue, because the historical legacy of the state has encouraged diplomats (and civil servants in general) to develop, over the long term, a vertical supervision of social actors rather than horizontal partnerships. I call this long-term process the regalian historicity of the French state.

4.2   *The Regalian State against Diaspora Diplomacy*

As far as economic issues are concerned, embassies, consulates and state agencies operating abroad, such as Business France, naturally rely on private actors such as chambers of commerce and industry or diasporic entrepreneurs who are endorsed by the state in official organizations, such as 'foreign trade counsellors' (*conseillers du commerce extérieur*). Similarly, major French companies operating abroad are involved in some forms of state sponsorship consisting in subsidizing cultural and sporting events or even the 14 July celebrations organized at the embassies. In these cases, French diplomacy builds a relationship with collective actors and not with individual citizens to be used for their personal success and networks. Secondly, French diplomacy finds it difficult to instrumentalize successful diasporic actors into a strategy of influence, since the latter do not necessarily intend to return to France. French official discourse still reflects a territorialized conception of economic success. This second problem is well exemplified by the relationship between French diplomacy and French high-tech entrepreneurs based in Silicon Valley. While several EU member states' consulates in San Francisco are ensuring that as much national investment as possible is going to Silicon Valley, a strategic goal of French diplomacy remains the return of successful French entrepreneurs to France.[39] However, very few French entrepreneurs who have succeeded in Silicon Valley will return to France, because they will not find in their country of origin an equivalent ecosystem combining business creation, university research and financing by venture capital funds. In practice, the French Consul-

---

38   Ho and McConnell 2019, 241.
39   Interview, French Consulate General in San Francisco, 18 April 2023 (Zoom).

ate General in San Francisco is caught between an economic reality that clearly fixes French entrepreneurs in the US and the French government's recurrent economic policy focusing on the return of successful expatriates to home.

This is not to say that there is no movement inside French diplomacy to use the successes of French citizens abroad as a resource. The 'School Plan' set up in the 2000s by the French Embassy in the UK to build new French schools in London is one such example. In 2007, the cultural counsellor at the French Embassy in the UK relied heavily on French diasporic actors to strengthen France's influence. During this period of 'Cool Britannia', the French diaspora in London included businessmen and financiers who earned huge bonuses in the City. Some of them were in a position to make donations of over £500,000 in return for tax exemption in the UK. Moreover, they had networks that French diplomats could use to find a location for a new school in London, a challenge in a city where the square metre price is one of the most expensive in the world. The cultural counsellor decided – in agreement with the educational agency AEFE in charge of French schools abroad – to set up a UK charitable trust to finance a new French school. The board of directors includes French diaspora members who could be influential donors. The French Education Charitable Trust (FECT) provided the budget for the new school, which opened its doors in the Wembley district in September 2015. It had a direct impact on citizens as it made possible an increase in the number of places available to children by 21 per cent compared with 2007.[40] In this case, the liberal tradition of the country of residence, the United Kingdom, accustomed to subsidizing projects through private fundraising, explains the relative ease with which the French diplomats moved in this direction, as it was more easily accepted as legitimate by French citizens forming the UK diaspora.

But such changes showing a move from consular diplomacy to diaspora diplomacy create debates inside the French MEFA. It is still not self-evident to French diplomats in general because the historicity of the French state, despite neoliberal practices gaining in strength in Europe from the 1980s onwards, legitimizes the protective practices of the regalian state. Consuls continue to concentrate mostly on protection duties. 'Building influence on French people abroad is not what I was trained to do',[41] explained a French consul in an EU capital. Another consul in a Balkan country, who has long experience of consular work, said that he would like to meet with more French nationals in order to build influence in the country of residence, but that this

---

40   Lequesne 2024.
41   Interview with a consul in an EU capital, 30 March 2022.

is not within his remit.[42] General consuls still receive little strategic instruction from the MEFA's directorates in charge of consular diplomacy about including the diaspora in influence work.

The political mobilization of the MPs representing French people living abroad, as well as the AFE counsellors and consular counsellors, also makes it more difficult to shift from consular diplomacy to diaspora diplomacy. Their advocacy is largely focused on perpetuating protection and generous welfare policies as this is expected by citizens at home, whatever political party they belong to. From this perspective, France's diplomacy differs from that of other countries such as Mexico or India, where consuls are in charge of developing influence towards the country of residence based on partnerships with successful nationals living abroad.[43] If the practice of French diplomats is changing, it is doing so at a slow pace. The 2023 report of the General Estates on Diplomacy, which includes the self-reflections of the MEFA staff after the contested civil service reform of 2022, is enlightening on this issue. Most of the report's recommendations focus on the improvement of regalian practices by French diplomats representing the state's interest. Only one section in the report calls for 'creating a reflex for working together with civil society',[44] without specifying in detail the synergies to be developed with non-state actors.

My ethnographic work on French diplomatic practices does not allow me to confirm a neoliberal shift of diplomacy with regard to the treatment of the diaspora. Some researchers would see the French example as a blessing in disguise, considering that a too liberal approach by MEFA's to diasporas runs the risk of a breach of equality in favour of the richest or best-known diasporic actors, as exemplified by the leading role of French bankers in the non-profit trusts set up in London. Here the debate becomes normative. The contribution of citizens who possess economic capital may also be considered a constituent of democracy. When the parents of the French School in San Francisco donate $600,000 to the annual gala, they are exercising a social responsibility that helps France to consolidate its public diplomacy in the US to the benefit of all French citizens.[45] Their donations are transformed into a collective good for French diplomacy. But this argument, to be legitimized, requires a change in the normative representation of the legitimate role of the state. In this case, the diplomat is no longer simply the

---

42   Interview with a consul in a West Balkan country, 26 November 2021.
43   Rana 2019; Delano Alonso 2018.
44   Etats Généraux de la Diplomatie 2023, 101.
45   Interview, French Consulate General in San Francisco, 18 April 2023 (Zoom).

representative of the regalian state abroad protecting national citizens, but the state coordinator of national resources abroad working in partnership with national citizens, who become what Riva Kastoryano calls 'private ambassadors'.[46] This conception is still hardly accepted by the French diplomats. The legacy of the regalian state introduces a clear limit on the ability of diplomats to aggregate individual citizens in their diplomatic deals, even if liberal trends in this direction exist, as the example of London shows.

5   Conclusion

The diplomat has often been described as the mediator of cultural alterity operating outside the borders.[47] Diplomats like to present themselves as strangers inside the state, accomplishing very different tasks than other civil servants. Diplomatic studies have too often forgotten that 'diplomatic practitioners have a role to fulfil at home', as this book project rightly stresses.[48] But it would be far too restrictive to consider that home diplomacy only concerns the development of diplomats' relations with citizens within the borders of the national territory, such as the creation of citizens' panels or better information on national parliaments.[49] Home diplomacy is also extra-territorialized and requires that the diplomat develop relations with national citizens living abroad. For this reason, any research programme on engaging home in diplomacy that overlooks the relationship between the diplomat abroad and the diasporas from the home country will be incomplete, as this chapter based on the French case study (but it could be other countries as well) aims to demonstrate.

In France, the reproduction of home practices by diplomats towards the diaspora can be observed, as the extra-territorial citizen has many similar rights as the territorial citizen, such as the right to vote and the right to ask for welfare benefits. Studying home diplomacy includes understanding how diplomats build relations with national citizens abroad with constant reference to home practices. French consular diplomacy reproduces abroad the welfare practices of the French state at home, such as providing scholarships to pupils to study in French schools. Taking into account the historicity of the state is therefore a crucial variable in the analysis of consular and diaspora

---

46   Kastoryano 2022, 253
47   Sofer 1997.
48   Kim and Melissen 2022b.
49   Geis, Opitz and Pfeifer 2022.

diplomacy.[50] The reluctance of the French diplomat to shift from consular diplomacy to diaspora diplomacy, according to the definitions given above, reflects a situation where the French regalian state continues to fuel a certain unease about developing private partnerships with diasporic actors.

A research programme on engaging home in diplomacy cannot limit itself to a functional approach identifying new domestic constraints for diplomats. Explanations must be found in questioning the essence of the state that exports its practices beyond its borders. For this reason, studying the relations between diasporas and diplomats representing the state of origin is absolutely crucial to understanding home's engagement with diplomacy.

Bibliography

Bartolomei, Arnaud, Mathieu Grenet, Fabrice Jesné and Jörg Ulbert. *La chancellerie consulaire française, XVIe–XXe siècle: attributions, organisation, agents, usagers* (Mélanges de l'École française de Rome–Italie et Méditerranée, 2016.

Bauböck, Rainer. 2005. 'Expansive Citizenship: Voting beyond Territory and Membership'. *Political Science and Politics* 38 (4)(2005), 683–687.

Benson, Michaela. 'Hong Kongers and the Coloniality of British Citizenship from Decolonisation to Global Britain'. *Current Sociology* 71 (5) (2023), 743–761.

Charillon, Frédéric. *Guerres d'influence. Les Etats à la conquête des esprits* (Paris: Odile Jacob, 2022).

Collyer, Michael. 'Inside Out? Directly Elected "Special Representation" of Emigrants in National Legislatures and the Role of Popular Sovereignty'. *Political Geography* 41 (2014), 64–73.

Council of Europe. *Report on Out-of-Country Voting*. Venice Commission, 16 June 2011.

Delano Alonso, Alexandra. *Mexico and Its Diaspora in the United States: Policies of Emigration since 1848* (Cambridge: Cambridge University Press, 2018).

Etats Généraux de la Diplomatie. *Pour un réarmement de la diplomatie française?* Report, Paris, March 2023.

French Ministry of European and Foreign Affairs. *Rapport au Gouvernement sur la situation des Français établis hors de France*. Paris, 2021.

French Ministry of European and Foreign Affairs. *Rapport au Gouvernement sur la situation des Français établis hors de France*. Paris, 2022.

---

50   Hobson 1998.

Geis, Anna, Christian Opitz and Hanna Pfeifer. 'Recasting the Role of Citizens in Diplomacy and Foreign Policy: Preliminary Insights and a New Research Agenda'. *The Hague Journal of Diplomacy* 17 (4) (2022), 614–627.

Ho, Elaine L. E. and Fiona McConnell. 'Conceptualizing "Diaspora Diplomacy": Territory and Populations betwixt the Domestic and Foreign'. *Progress in Human Geography*, 43 (2) (2019), 235–255.

Hobson, John M. 'The Historical Sociology of the State and the State of Historical Sociology in International Relations'. *Review of International Political Economy* 5 (2) (1998), 284–320.

Jerris, Frederik B. *Compound Diplomacy: Everyday Spatiality in the Diplomatic Frontlines in Lomé*. Thesis for the Master in International Relations, Sciences Po, 2023.

Kastoryano, Riva. 'Transnationalism: Theory and Experience'. In *Contested Concepts in Migration Studies*, eds. R. Zapata-Barrero, D. Jacobs and R. Kastory (London: Routledge, 2022), 243–258.

Kernagellen, Tudi and Cédric Pellen. 'En Marche Français expatriés! L'émergence d'un nouvel acteur politique parmi les Français de l'étranger'. *Revue internationale de politique comparée* 26 (2–3) (2019), 159–186.

Kim, HwaJung and Jan Melissen, eds. 'Engaging Home in Diplomacy'. Special issue, *The Hague Journal of Diplomacy* 17 (4) (2022a).

Kim, HwaJung and Jan Melissen. 'The Diplomatic Elite, the People at Home and Democratic Renewal'. Blog, University of Leiden, 2022b.

Kumar Banerjee, Ananya. 'Contested and Cemented Borders: Understanding the Implications of Overseas Indian Citizenship'. *New Global Studies* 13 (3) (2019), 365–380.

Kuus, Merje. *Geopolitics and Expertise: Knowledge and Authority in European Diplomacy* (Hoboken: Wiley-Blackwell, 2013).

Lambert, David. *Notables des colonies. Une élite de circonstance en Tunisie et au Maroc (1881–1939)* (Rennes: Presses universitaires de Rennes, 2009).

Le Drian, Jean-Yves. *Feuille de route de l'Influence*. Report. Paris, 2022.

Lefort, Claude. 'Sociétés sans histoire et historicité'. *Cahiers internationaux de sociologie* 12 (1952), 91–114.

Lequesne, Christian. *Ethnographie du Quai d'Orsay. Les pratiques des diplomates français* (Paris: CNRS Editions, 2020).

Lequesne, Christian, ed. *La puissance par l'image. Les Etats et leur diplomatie publique* (Paris: Presses de Sciences Po, 2021).

Lequesne, Christian. *Le diplomate et les Français de l'Etranger. Comprendre les pratiques de l'Etat envers sa diaspora* (Paris: Presses de Sciences Po, 2024). English version in 2026.

Macron, Emmanuel. Speech to the Assemblée des Français de l'étranger. Paris, 2 October 2017.

Melissen, Jan and Ana Mar Fernandez, eds. *Consular Affairs and Diplomacy* (The Hague: Martinus Nijhoff, 2011).

Neumann, Iver B. *At Home with the Diplomats: Inside a European Foreign Ministry* (Ithaca, NY: Cornell University Press, 2012).

Official Journal of the French Republic. *Décret n° 2022–561 portant application au ministère de l'Europe et des affaires étrangères de la réforme de la haute fonction publique.* 17 April 2022.

Pellen, Cédric. 'A la conquête de l'Amérique. La campagne des élections législatives dans la 1ère circonscription des français de l'étranger'. *Revue française de science politique* 6 (2013), 1137–1162.

Rana, Kishan. 'India's Diaspora Diplomacy'. *The Hague Journal of Diplomacy* 4 (3) (2019), 361–372.

Smith, Etienne. 'Voter au loin. Dynamiques électorales transnationales dans la neuvième circonscription des Français de l'étranger'. *Les Etudes du CERI* 249 (2020).

Sofer, Sasson. 'The Diplomat as a Stranger'. *Diplomacy and Statecraft.* 8 (3) (1997), 179–186.

Szulecki, Kacper et al. 'To Vote or Not to Vote? Migrant Electoral (Dis)engagement in an Enlarged Europe'. *Migration Studies* 9 (3) (2021), 989–1010.

Tsinovoi, Alexei and Rebecca Adler Nissen. 'Inversion of the Duty of Care: Diplomacy and the Protection of Citizens Abroad, from Pastoral Care to Neoliberal Governmentality'. *The Hague Journal of Diplomacy* 13 (2) (2018), 211–232.

United Nations. Vienna Convention on Consular Relations. 1963.

Weil, Patrick. *How to Be French: Nationality in the Making since 1789* (Durham, NC: Duke University Press, 2008).

Wiseman, Geoffrey. 'Expertise and Politics in Ministries of Foreign Affairs: The Politician–Diplomat Nexus'. In *Ministries of Foreign Affairs in the World: Actors of State Diplomacy*, ed. Christian Lequesne (The Hague: Brill, 2022), 119–149.

CHAPTER 5

Social Legitimacy, State–Society Relations and Non-State Actor Diplomacy in Japan

Toshiya Takahashi

Summary

This chapter aims to examine the limitations of Japanese non-state actor diplomacy from the viewpoint of its social legitimacy and explore ways to overcome them. There has been some involvement by Japanese non-state actors in foreign affairs, but their activities have not been well developed. Their limitations come from their weak social legitimacy deriving from the characteristic of Japanese civil society in which the national government plays the leading role in social services. Even in the period of globalization, two impediments to their social legitimacy stand out. The first is the continuing hierarchical relationship between the state and society. This relationship has been respected by Japanese people through their obedience to the state in foreign affairs as well as domestic matters. Secondly, as a discursive impediment, the national security discourse has begun to influence Japan's diplomacy in the face of increasing security challenges from China and North Korea. Thus, Japanese people's reliance on the national government in diplomacy has been strengthened. The weak social legitimacy of Japanese non-state actors appears to be a limitation to their independent decision-making from government, open debate, the reflection of public interest and proposals of alternative policy to government, none of which have reached the level of public engagement. The key to increasing non-state actors' social legitimacy is external: the enmeshment of Japanese non-state actors in global networks with the support of the national government offers a solution to this ossified domestic problem.

Keywords

non-state actor – diplomacy – public engagement – social legitimacy – Japanese civil society – non-profit organization – national security – state–society relationship

© TOSHIYA TAKAHASHI, 2026 | DOI:10.1163/9789004738324_007

1   Introduction

The increasing role of non-state actors in foreign relations has been broadly
pointed out and celebrated by the liberal literature on international relations,
especially in the fields of global governance, finance and business, environment, United Nations (UN) activities and nuclear disarmament.[1] The liberal
literature espouses the view that the role of non-state actors will increase in
international fields in accordance with domestic progress in the greater provision by civil society of necessary services, information and knowledge, and
communities for the domestic public.[2] Diplomacy is changing. A 'level diplomatic playing field, mainly consisting of state actors, can no longer be taken
for granted'.[3] The role of non-state actors in diplomacy has expanded in Western countries and other regions. Non-state actors who represent changing
political, economic, social or environmental need to have the capability to
provide alternatives to traditional diplomacy.[4] However, this liberal expectation is not necessarily observed in Japan. The number of Japanese non-
governmental organizations (NGOs) has increased since the late 1990s and
their role has become important especially in the provision of social welfare
and services in Japan's ageing society. But the expansion of their role to global
fields is still limited and their influence in diplomacy remains marginal. Their
relationship with Japanese society has not been deepened and the group of
Japanese diplomatic actors is not becoming diversified.

Why do Japanese non-state actors still only have a marginal influence on
diplomacy? The limited role of Japanese non-state actors in diplomacy is a
result of their underdeveloped 'legitimacy in society'. The authority of the
national government is unchallengeable in Japanese society despite the increasing importance of non-state actors' roles in diplomatic channels and networks. This chapter approaches the question from the viewpoint of their weak
social legitimacy, which comes from the characteristics of Japanese civil society and cultural and discursive impediments. Legitimacy is 'the normative
belief by an actor that a rule or institution ought to be obeyed'.[5] Social legiti-

---

1   On global governance, see, for example, Marchetti 2016; Erman and Uhlin 2010; Hall and
    Biersteker 2002. On global business and finance, see, for example, Schnabel 2002; Higgott,
    Underhill and Bieler 2000. On the environment, see for example, Moss 2020; Newell 2000.
    On UN activities, see, for example, Lüdert 2023. On nuclear disarmament, see, for example,
    Kissling 2008.
2   Lester Salamon points out the increasing importance of the non-profit sector in four emerg-
    ing crises of the welfare state, development, the environment and socialism. Salamon 1994.
3   Melissen 2018, 203.
4   Kelley 2014, chaps. 1–2.
5   Hurd 1999, 381.

macy refers to whether members of society accept a rule or institution in a normative sense. For non-state diplomatic actors, it asks how and to what extent their activities are accepted and supported by society.[6] In diplomacy, they are expected to have the capability to reflect various public interests and voices which traditional diplomacy fails to capture. Though their activities are observed in foreign affairs to some extent, Japanese non-state actor diplomacy has not sufficiently reached 'public or civil engagement' due to their weak social legitimacy.[7] Public engagement is defined here as involving members of the public in decisions that impact them.[8] It also has a normative dimension in solving 'problems that affect people's lives'.[9]

The chapter describes the historical and social constraints on Japanese non-state actors stemming from the characteristics of Japanese civil society, cultural and discursive impediments to their development, and limitations on their activities in the realm of public engagement. First, the chapter focuses on the social legitimacy of the Japanese non-profit sector in general and reveals its weakness, which is based on the characteristics of Japanese civil society. As a general category to cover non-state actors, the Japanese non-profit sector (i.e. NPOs) as a whole is the focus here. Second, the chapter examines cultural and discursive impediments to the social legitimacy of Japanese diplomatic non-state actors. It focuses on the continuing hierarchical state–society relationship and the increasing influence of national security discourse. Third, it examines the activities of six types of Japanese non-state diplomatic actors and points to their limitations in terms of public engagement. Finally, it explores the potential for Japanese non-state actors' diplomacy from the viewpoint of their capabilities and social legitimacy.

2 The Social Legitimacy of the Japanese Non-profit Sector and Japanese Civil Society

Japan's non-profit sector has a history of contributing to local communities, but its activities are limited in scope, and it lacks broad social legitimacy.[10]

---

6   A similar definition is found in: Dellmuth and Tallberg 2015, 454.

7   The term public engagement is used in various fields such as university education, local government, the arts and the academic community for the inclusion of people in their decision-making.

8   For example: National Center for State Courts n.d..

9   The government of New Brunswick n.d..

10   For a positive evaluation of the development of the Japanese non-profit sector, see Alagappa 2004; Vinken et al. 2010.

Small local voluntary groups, such as *Chōnai kai* (neighbourhood associations), traditionally play a key role in a neighbourhood's or community's daily life, but public interest in the non-profit sector did not arise until the 1990s. When the Cold War ended, so too did the political and ideological confrontation between the Liberal Democratic Party (LDP) and the Japan Socialist Party (JSP), and the creation of NPOs became a focus in Japanese politics irrespective of ideological differences. In addition, the importance of voluntary groups at the grassroots level was gradually focused on from the 1980s to the 1990s under the influence of Japanese liberal discourse. Those moves were prompted by the 1995 Great Hanshin earthquake, in which many victims were helped by volunteer groups, whose social importance became broadly recognized. In turn, the social empowerment of volunteer groups by granting them a legal status became a focus, and the 1998 NPO law was enacted. The law was intended to encourage the creation of NPOs and to strengthen their foundation by lowering the hurdles to obtain legal status, and for some NPOs, tax-free donations from the public were introduced.[11] Prior to the introduction of the NPO law, the civil code of Japan, which was enacted in 1896, was the only law that could approve legal status for NPOs, but its requirements for such status were onerous. The procedure for an NPO to obtain legal status was not stipulated in the civil code itself and it was only granted by administrative consideration. It was often said that it was nearly impossible for small and medium-sized volunteer groups to be approved.[12] Thus, under the 1998 NPO law, the number of Japanese NPOs increased.[13] While the expansion in the number of NPOs in the United States occurred in the 1980s,[14] the same happened in Japan in the period from the late 1990s to the 2010s.

This legal solution helped the Japanese non-profit sector raise its social profile, but the effect was limited due to its relatively weak capability level in relation to government. The 1998 NPO law and its successive revisions succeeded in promoting the creation of NPOs at the grassroots level, but the main purpose of the law was to provide a legal status for them rather than to improve their capabilities. Robert Pekkanen points to the dual structure of Japanese NPOs, in which the majority are small local groups and only a few are large, professional ones.[15] The majority of Japanese NPOs continue to have only weak capability. According to a 1997 comparative survey of NPOs in Japan, South Korea and Germany, Japanese NPOs faced the greatest limits on

---

11   Kumashiro 2003, 4–5.
12   e.g. Kumashiro 2003, 4.
13   Sakamoto 2017, 9.
14   Putnam 2000, 60–61.
15   Pekkanen 2006, 1.

their influence and had the worst records in terms of modifying or thwarting government policy.[16] In relation to the government, they consider that while the relationship is cooperative, the government is also their most important source of information.[17] Under these conditions, their independent capability is limited. '[The] state powerfully shapes' them, and as a result their level of professionalization is low.[18] Since the enactment of the 1998 NPO law, Japanese NPOs have increased their presence in Japanese society, but they continue to suffer from insufficient capability and a lack of professionalism, and there are only a limited number of large NPOs such as those found in Western countries.[19]

The weak capability of Japanese NPOs is related to the characteristics of Japanese civil society. The origin of the idea of civil society can be traced back to early modern European political thought, including the works of Hooker, Locke, Hegel and others.[20] The term fell into disuse in the mid-nineteenth century, but in the 1970s, it reappeared in Western discourse to refer to 'resurgent social forces' challenging totalitarian regimes in Eastern and Central Europe.[21] While there are various definitions of the term in academic works, civil society is defined here as a realm or field which bridges private groups and the state in the public interest, not NPOs themselves. It is 'the space of uncoerced human associations' and 'the set of relational networks'.[22] It has 'a dual role' in 'connecting citizens to and protecting them from government'.[23] The question of whether Japan has its own 'civil-society tradition' has been debated among academic works. There have been numerous cases in Japan's history in which the Japanese government exercised overwhelming authority and power over its people's activities and the latter simply obeyed or were even 'satisfied' with the status quo. Even today, Japanese volunteer activities are often subordinated to the authority and power of the Japanese government rather than being independent of it.[24] One study asserts that vol-

---

16 Tsujinaka and Che Jiyon 2002, 73, 76.

17 Mori and Adachi 2002, 124, 126–127.

18 Pekkanen 2006, 7–8.

19 For example, Ushiro and Sakamoto positively evaluate the development of Japanese non-profit organizations especially in their gradual independence from the government, but the gap in capability among them is a continuing problem. Ushiro and Sakamoto 2019, 255–265.

20 Hall and Trentmann 2005, 2–3; Hann 1996, 1.

21 Pharr 2003, xiii.

22 Walzer 1995, 5, cited in Deakin 2001, 4.

23 McVeigh 1998, 47.

24 e.g. Pekkanen 2006, 7.

untarism and civil society in the Western sense, both of which are more or less related to Christianity, are not found in the Japanese or other Asian traditions.[25] Another study espouses the view that, even before its modernization, Japan had 'a long tradition of philanthropy' in which Buddhism, Confucianism and Shintoism played leading roles.[26] Those observations need more extensive examinations, however. A public sphere did exist in Japanese villages and towns prior to the period of modernization, for example common agricultural fields, village festivals and funerals. Japanese villages and towns created common goods for their own use, and collective activities were organized by selected leaders of a village or town.[27] Thus, while a Western model of civil society is difficult to find in Japan, voluntarism and the public sphere, which are elements of civil society, did exist in the past in Japan.

There are two distinctive characteristics of Japanese civil society, which can be called 'tradition'. Firstly, the influence of quasi-government organizations on the Japanese public sector continues to be salient. The number of NPOs has been increasing since the 1998 NPO law, but their social presence in the Japanese public sector remains secondary to the quasi-government organizations, most of which were established before the 1998 law and are closely linked to the government. These groups, referred to as *Tokushu hōjin* (government-affiliated cooperation) and *Kōeki hōjin* (public interest incorporated associations or foundations), were created under the authority of the national or local government. Though the private sector was involved in their establishment, it was driven 'from above' and was not necessarily based on public needs. They were created for specified public purposes, such as providing administrative services under government control and finance, coordinating private bodies or companies in a specified field, or conducting research on environmental, economic or social issues. Their relationship with the national government is different from that of government and non-profit groups in the US: in the latter, non-profit organizations contract with the government to provide public services on an independent contractor basis, but in the former, they are de facto affiliated bodies of the government or maintain a special relationship with it. '[W]hile private in form', they 'are in reality extended arms of governmental agencies'.[28] The official purpose of these quasi-government organizations is to provide public services, but in reality they represent the expansion of administrative control and contribute to maintaining the strength of Japa-

---

25   Osborne 2003, 9, 11.
26   Amenomori 1997,190–191, 195–213.
27   e.g. Tsuruta n.d..
28   Amenomori 1997, 213.

nese bureaucracy as it overlaps with the private sector. They have also been criticized by the Japanese public for contributing to the *Amakudari* system (a second carrier system for national and local bureaucrats after their retirement) by providing 'executive seats' for retired high-ranking public officers, or for consuming excessive tax funds due to inefficient management or unnecessary works. There are also many local *Tokushu hōjin* and *Kōeki hōjin* in Japan's prefectures and cities, where their authority remains strong because they are closely associated with local government.[29]

Secondly, the Japanese idea of civil society (the Japanese term is *Shimin shakai*) has often been linked to post-war Japanese leftist and liberal political discourse, and this politically distorted image remains prevalent in Japanese society today. Political scientist Hajime Shinohara asserts that the idea of civil society is not rooted in Japan, but rather civil society is an imported idea.[30] The term was used in the Western sense starting in the 1990s by Japanese liberal academics and policymakers to refer to a new approach to democracy, but its Japanese translation *Shimin shakai* or *Shimin* (civilian) was used earlier. According to Keishi Saeki, the use of the term *Shimin undō* (civilian movement) started in the 1950s and was applied to the movement to oppose the US–Japan Security Treaty beginning in 1959 (*Anpo tōsō*), becoming a keyword for moderate leftists and liberals.[31] After that, it gradually became a keyword for leftist activists and Japanese Marxist scholarship as well. From the 1960s, political movements by leftist university students such as *Anpo tōsō* and the anti-Vietnam War movement were referred to as *Shimin undō*. *Shimin undō* also took the form of the peace movement, the environment movement, the anti-nuclear movement, and the human rights movement under the influence of Western political currents.[32] It was developed in Japanese society as narrow leftist and liberal political activities in opposition to the conservative national government, and their image as 'anti-establishment' or 'anti-American movements' became strong.[33] The main characteristic of those movements is a 'confrontational style' in relation to the national government.[34] and marked by narrow-mindedness and a tendency towards factional conflict. As a result, *Shimin shakai* (civil society) sounds leftist-inclined and its public image is of grassroots-level activities by leftist-led groups, though it has become more

29 Ushiro and Sakamoto 2019, 97–112.
30 Shinohara 2004, 93.
31 Saeki 1997, 47–48.
32 Amenomori 1997, 193.
33 Ibid.
34 Ibid.

politically nuanced over time. Because of this historical background, Japanese society's political support for civil society has been limited.

As mentioned, what distinguishes Japanese civil society from Western ones is the continuing strong influence of government-affiliated bodies on the Japanese public sphere and the distorted social identification of civil society with leftist activism. In this civil society, Japanese people rely on quasi-governmental organizations for public services and do not seek to replace them with private ones. The state plays a distinctive role in Japanese civil society through its high capability to provide public services. Even in Western countries, civil society has been developed more or less with the support of the state,[35] and so the non-profit sector's lack of independence from the state does not necessarily preclude the presence of civil society. However, the powerful influence of quasi-governmental organizations makes the 'non-state and non-profit' in Japanese civil society weak and immature. Stephen P. Osborne goes so far as to say that Japanese civil society 'is dependent upon the state for its legitimacy'.[36] At the same time, the social identification of civil society with leftist activism has had a negative effect on its development. Japanese society's perception of the 'non-state and non-profit' sector is often distorted by this ideological lens, leading to limited trust in civil society. The two limitations in the above, that is, the influence of quasi-government organizations on the public sector and the leftist-inclined image of Japanese civil society, mean that society does not recognize the important role they play.

3   Impediments to the Social Legitimacy of Japanese Non-State Diplomatic Actors

3.1   *People's Obedience to the Hierarchical Relationship between State and Society*

Even in the era of new diplomacy, in which non-state actors are expected to play a significant role, their development has been insufficient in Japanese society due to two impediments, both of which continue to justify the supremacy of the national government in diplomacy and will be difficult to overcome. Firstly, Japan's hierarchical state–society relationship is a cultural impediment to the social legitimacy of Japanese non-state actors in diplomacy.[37] It

---

35   Szücs 1988, 295, cited in Schwartz 2003, 2.

36   Osborne 2003, 10.

37   Many works on Japanese society have pointed out the hierarchical state–society relationship from different perspectives. See, for example, Aida 1984, 204–212; Sugimoto 2021, 232–236; Nakane 1970, 102; Matsumoto 1978, 38.

means that the national government continues to maintain its absolute political and social influence over society and that this state–society relationship is 'ossified'. With the exception of the big business sector, Japan's hierarchical state–society relationship has not changed despite liberal attempts to reform the Japanese administrative system into a more efficient or democratic one under the Hashimoto (1996–1998), Koizumi (2001–2006) and Democratic Party of Japan governments (2009–2012). Despite these attempted reforms, however, Japanese people's demands for a large and strong government are being strengthened in the face of increasing needs for social welfare, economic growth and security.[38] In addition, the hierarchical state–society relationship is embedded in Japan. Before Japan's modernization, Japan was not necessarily a centralized country. In the ancient and medieval eras, the authority of Japanese politics was not centralized, and the *Tenno* (Japanese emperor) was not necessarily an absolute power. Political power was regionally divided among political clans, temples, warrior groups and cities, the most powerful of which created a government but whose influence did not necessarily cover the whole of Japan. From the beginning of the Edo period (1603–1867), the Tokugawa Bakufu, the warrior government, centralized governance, but plenty of room was left to each *Han* (local warrior government appointed by the *Tokugawa Bakufu*) to make decisions and to govern.[39] A fully fledged centralized national government emerged during the Meiji period (1868–1912) and played a leading role in the modernization of Japan and the creation of an administrative hierarchy, at the top of which is the national government and whose lesser tiers are local ones. While Japanese modernization from above began by following Western models, the hierarchical state–society relationship became embedded through modernization, industrialization, militarization and planned economic growth.

This persistent hierarchy cannot be fully explained by the history of Japanese modernization, however. 'Having legitimacy implies that there is some form of normative, uncovered consent or recognition of authority on the part of the regulated or governed'.[40] The hierarchical state–society relationship is supported by Japanese society's attitude towards state authority. Some studies point out that the Japanese population's obedience to the national govern-

---

38   On the increasing demand for the role of the Japanese government in social welfare, see
      Iwata 2012, 250.
39   In contrast to this chapter's view, cultural elements behind the pre-Meiji Confucian
      legacy of hierarchical bureaucracy or Japanese ritual or subordinate attitudes to national
      bureaucracy are sometime pointed out. See McVeigh 1998, 71, 102–117.
40   Hall and Biersteker 2002, 5.

ment does not rely on coercive power from the latter. It is neither statism nor an ideology, but the outcome of Japanese social attitudes. It has been described, for example, as friendly authoritarianism,[41] command without coercion, and a no-use-in-complaining mentality.[42] In addition, it has a moral dimension that goes beyond the calculation of costs. Robert Smith notes that the Japanese state continues to influence the public realm by assuming moral leadership or moral authority,[43] thus maintaining indirect control over Japanese people by its legitimacy.[44] This moral dimension is difficult to overcome because it is beyond cost calculations. The Japanese public's obedience and lack of will to change have been observed at many important points in its history. Osamu Kuno argues that Japanese people are receptive to the national government and that both war (the Pacific War) and post-war liberal and democratic reform came from above, not from the grassroots level.[45] Kuno's description of the state–society relationship accurately reflects the reality today, with one scholar asserting that in the post-war period, Japanese bureaucracy became stronger and had fewer rivals than in the pre-war period.[46]

The majority of Japanese people believe that the national interest should be prioritized over individual interest. According to a 2022–2023 national survey on Japanese social consciousness, 54.4 per cent of those surveyed gave a higher priority to the national interest, compared with 38.6. per cent to individual interest.[47] The percentage among older generations was even higher (e.g. 63.7 per cent among those over 70), while less than half of those surveyed among younger cohorts shared that view (e.g. 42.0 per cent of those aged 18–29), with the majority (54.6 per cent) prioritizing individual interest.[48] Japanese affection for the state also remains strong. In the same survey, 51.2 per cent said their affection for the state is stronger than that of others, and only 10.3 per cent said it was not. This tendency is almost unchanged from the 1977 survey.[49] Of those surveyed, 82.1 per cent agreed that affection for the state should be nurtured among the Japanese people, while 16.8 per cent disagreed. At the same time, some surveys show the jarring coexistence of Japanese dissatisfaction with the national government and obedience to it. According to one survey, less than 30 per cent of those surveyed said they

---

41   Sugimoto 2021, 332.
42   McVeigh 1998, 105.
43   Smith 1983, 129–130.
44   e.g. Smith 1983, 38; Haley 1991, 7, 13–14.
45   Kuno 1976, 106–107.
46   Johnson 1975.
47   Cabinet Public Relations Office of Japan 2023.
48   Ibid.
49   Ibid.

trusted political parties and the Diet, and about 30 per cent said they trusted the national government and the mass media.[50] The same dissatisfaction was found in another survey that also pointed to Japanese obedience. About 70 per cent of those surveyed expressed dissatisfaction with Japanese politics and about 20 per cent or less felt that their will was not reflected in Japanese politics, but, surprisingly, only around 20 per cent expected this to change.[51] Such surveys show that Japanese society continues to support the state's legitimacy though it is not necessarily satisfied with national policy. Japanese people's approach is to 'wait and see' and it is difficult to find strong motivation to change.

As the opinion surveys showed, obedience to the national government is a well-observed behaviour in Japanese people's politico-social life. Practical considerations reinforce people's adjustment to the national government or similar authority. In reality, the national government and its affiliated bodies do have greater capability than private ones in specialized areas. The best and the brightest among the Japanese working population are expected to work for the national government or its related institutions, though some change has been observed in the Tokyo area, where leading Western consulting firms attract the brightest talents today. In addition, the legitimacy of Japanese think tanks and private institutions is determined by their closeness to the national government; institutions that are close to the government produce better quality work. Especially in local areas, people rely on the national budget for infrastructure, social welfare, education and so forth.[52] Society is highly unlikely to bring change to the politico-social system, as Japan's history shows. Sannosuke Matsumoto deplores the fact that, in Japan, 'the political system was not a means that emerged out of the daily lives of the people in response to their social needs. It was adopted from among existing forms of government (in Western countries) in answer to the needs of the state in its external rela-

---

50 Genron NPO 2019.

51 Fujii 2020; NHK Broadcasting Culture Research Institute 2017.

52 The hierarchical state–society relationship is supported by benefits that the national government provides for the citizen. The distribution of the national budget to local ones is important for local governments. On average, only about 40 per cent of local government revenue comes from its own taxation and the rest is from the national government or bonds which require its permission. In addition, the construction of new or high-priced infrastructure in local prefectures and cities normally requires funds from the national budget and entails budget competitions among them. One ability of local prefectural governors and city-mayors lies in whether they have strong connections with the national government for their competition over national subsidies. Naturally, Japanese people accept the authority of the national government as the most financially strong supporter.

tionships.'[53] Japanese modernization and post-war democratization were instituted from 'above' and involved a process of Japanese adoption of foreign
ideas and practices. The Japanese idea of civil society was a product of this
adaptation and was introduced as part of the hierarchical state–society relationship. As the mechanism to bring politico-social ideas and systems to Japanese society, the national government occupied the prominent place in Japan's history.

3.2 *National Security Discourse from the 2010s*

The increasing influence of national security discourse is also an impediment
to the establishment of social legitimacy by Japanese non-state diplomatic
actors. Japan's changing security environment from the end of the 1990s, including the power shift from Japan to China and North Korea's increasing
nuclear arsenal, has justified the exclusive role of the national government
in the provision of national security. The post-war Japanese debate on diplomacy was characterized by liberal discourse, and Japanese society has supported the pacifist principles in the 1947 constitution, though the US–Japan
alliance has been maintained to ensure Japan's security. Given the public's
pacifist sentiments, post-war Japan pursued its foreign policy mainly through
non-military means. Anti-nuclear weapons sentiment among the public was
strong and encouraged the Diet's resolution on three non-nuclear principles
in 1971, which prohibit the state from having, producing or importing nuclear
weapons. The liberal discourse in the 1980s and 1990s espoused Japan's *Kokusai Kōken* (international contribution) as financial support for developing
countries and international organizations while also allowing non-military
or non-combatant activities by the Self-Defense Forces in UN peacekeeping
operations and multinational security cooperation under the condition of
ceasefire.

The emergence of the national security discourse has changed the post-war
liberal one, and 'national security' has become the keyword in Japan's foreign
policy institutions since the 2010s. National security concerns in Japan were
obviously observed well before the introduction of the term, but an attempt to
institutionalize a national security apparatus in the national government
began in the 2000s. The first Shinzo Abe government (2006–2007) attempted
to establish a National Security Council (NSC) using the United States' NSC as
a model. At the time, there were increasing Chinese and North Korean security challenges around Japanese territory and territorial waters and Japan

---

53   Matsumoto 1978, 33.

needed a new approach to its security. North Korea conducted a test of the *Nodong*-1 missile in the Sea of Japan in 1993 and started nuclear development with the announcement of its withdrawal from the International Atomic Energy Agency in 1994, and it has continued to conduct missile tests ever since. The intrusions of North Korean spy boats into Japan's territorial waters in 1999 and 2001 shocked the Japanese public, especially when it was revealed that such intrusions had occurred frequently and involved abductions of Japanese individuals in the 1970s and 1980s. Meanwhile, China began to enlarge its naval force and activities around Japan from the second half of the 1990s. It conducted oceanographic research around Japan in the latter half of the 1990s, and People's Liberation Army naval passages in Japan's international straits were reported from the 2000s. China also began to modernize its forces, and its first aircraft carrier was commissioned in 2012. The presence of Chinese official vessels around the Senkaku/Diaoyu islands, whose sovereignty is disputed between Japan and China, since the beginning of the 1970s considerably increased after a 2010 incident in which a Chinese fishing boat rammed two Japanese Coast Guard vessels. To meet these new security challenges, the defence of Japan's territory became a top issue in its security policy and the term national security became known to the public. The second Abe government (2012–2020) introduced the NSC and National Security Strategy, and the Fumio Kishida government (2021–2024) enacted the Economic Security Promotion Act and implemented this policy.

Behind the institutional change, the increasing influence of the national security discourse on Japanese society can be seen. It began to appear in Japanese society from the 2000s, especially from proponents of Japanese neo-conservatism (JNC), defence experts and pro-defence lawmakers. The late Prime Minister Shinzo Abe and the journalist Yoshiko Sakurai were JNC opinion leaders in the 2000s and 2010s. The JNC arose in the late 1990s and began to influence Japanese society and politics through its nationalistic language. Its political campaign was initiated by some religious groups and limited rightist journals and books, but it then entered national-level politics and formed a group in the LDP, and it gained political clout and a greater voice under the second Abe government, though the majority of Japanese people did not share its views. It espouses a nationalist conservativism which praises ideas and practices of pre-war Japan and seeks the revision of history, though its proponents were born in post-war democratic Japan and do not really understand pre-war Japan. In security policy, it espouses anti-China and anti-leftist views while maintaining a pro-US–Japan alliance stance. JNC proponents appeal to the Japanese public's nationalistic emotions and warn of emerging national crises in an attempt to attract supporters, manipulating their limited knowledge of the past. Meanwhile, the role of defence experts and pro-defence lawmakers in Japan's security discourse has increased since the 2000s, when Chinese and North Korean security challenges became broadly perceived. The mass media also relies on their expertise in news programmes and publications on security matters. Defence is needed to meet security challenges, but in the Japanese discourse the security debate has been narrowed to national defence. Japanese people now equate security with it, which means that the national government is the only defender of their security.

JNC and defence experts' nationalistic calls for the defence of Japan's territory, while emotionally distorted, have gained currency in the public debate, especially in the face of the Chinese coastguard's increasing presence in waters around the Senkaku/Diaoyu islands. The need to defend Japanese territory is clear even to ordinary people, and it is easy to reach an emotionally driven consensus on the importance of the national government as the guarantor of national security. Since the second Abe government, the LDP has attempted to raise the issue of diplomacy and national security as one of the key agendas in its election campaigns, and Japanese voters have come to believe in their importance in national elections, though they put more priority on welfare and economic policy. On security policy, the Diet has nearly reached a consensus on the need to strengthen Japan's military capability, though how an increasing defence budget can be ensured is not clear. Nonetheless, the national security discourse has narrowed Japanese people's view of security and the capability of the national government has been prioritized.

With such cultural and discursive impediments, enhancing the social legitimacy of Japanese non-state diplomatic actors is obviously a difficult task. It requires a 'partial' transition or shift of authority from the national government to non-state actors, but Japanese people's continuing respect for and obedience to the hierarchical state–society relationship are difficult to overcome. The Japanese public is reluctant to challenge traditional diplomacy in which the national government is the key player. In addition, the national security discourse has enhanced the social legitimacy of the national government as the central player in diplomacy, and Japanese national unity in foreign relations has been strengthened. Bernard Eccleston has pointed to the contrast between the Japanese propensity for collective action for the good of the nation and the approach of Western countries, for example in the case of the two oil shocks of the 1970s, which Japan survived and overcame with a domestic consensus.[54] In contrast to the pre-war pe-

---

54   Eccleston 1989, 5.

riod, different opinions and approaches are now allowed in Japan, but Japanese people continue to prefer unity in diplomacy.

4   Public Engagement and Japanese Non-state Actors' Activities in Foreign Affairs

The social legitimacy of Japanese non-state diplomatic actors is limited by the characteristics of Japanese civil society, and its development faces the cultural and discursive impediments set out above. This section examines, from the viewpoint of public engagement, how those limitations can be observed in their activities. Public engagement in diplomacy involves more than nominal participation by non-state actors in diplomatic meetings or government hearings. It is an ideal and a purposive idea to alter the routine course of traditional state-to-state diplomacy by reflecting the diversity of public interests more closely, believing in non-state actors' capacity to correct disfunctions or malfunctions of traditional diplomacy. It requires the reflection of public interest and the substantive engagement of non-state actors in foreign policy processes or their independent influence on foreign policy. It should ensure that ordinary people's views are accounted for in the decision-making process; non-state actors should reflect ordinary people's view and such actors' activities should be accountable to ordinary people.

The following four conditions, which are related to the quality of participation in diplomacy and the capacity of non-state actors, should be considered necessary for public engagement. Firstly, non-state actors' independent decision-making from government has to be ensured (Condition A). 'Private, independent from the state' is the bottom line for non-state actors.[55] In diplomacy, government influences on them may increase, but their greater engagement with government may have possibilities of the lack of independence and the distortion of their activities.[56] Secondly, their decisions and activities must be open to public debate (Condition B). The 'democratic qualities' of non-state actors are important for their legitimacy.[57] Transparency not only to their members but also to the public is the key element of their representation as a diplomatic actor.[58] Thirdly, their decisions and activities should reflect the public interest to some extent (Condition C). People's perception of holding

---

55   United Nations 2003, 16.

56   Lamb 2018, 17.

57   See Erman and Uhlin 2010.

58   Van Rooy 2004, 70–76.

common interests with non-state actors enhances their credibility.[59] Fourthly, non-state actors' public engagement in diplomacy should be effective enough to present alternatives to the national government's policy if necessary (Condition D). The rationale of non-state actor diplomacy lies in their ability both to cope with new diplomatic issues and to introduce such issues.[60] They should have the capacity to present alternatives to national policy, not just support the government. Public engagement requires them to play a substantive role as a diplomatic actor, and their participation in diplomacy should not be 'tokenism' as a part of traditional diplomacy.[61]

While Japanese non-state actors can be found in several areas of foreign affairs, six types of Japanese non-state actors are identified here: the business sector; development NGOs; think tanks and track-two diplomacy groups; peace and disarmament groups and academics; sister cities; and country-to-country friendship associations. Firstly, the Japanese business sector represents a non-state actor in foreign affairs through its three umbrella business organizations, which are supposed to represent the voices of Japanese companies. These groups comprise Keidanren (The Japanese Business Federation), which is the most influential umbrella organization for Japanese big business; the Japan Association of Corporate Executives, which is a personal committee of Japanese big business CEOs; and the Japan Chamber of Commerce and Industry, which is mainly composed of Japanese small and medium-sized enterprises. As representatives of the Japanese business sector, they are engaged in business relations with their foreign counterparts and often express their views on Japanese foreign economic relations in the form of policy proposals and in press conferences. In addition to these three, further business associations have been formed to pursue specific bilateral business relations. For example, the Japan–China Economic Association, which is composed of companies which conduct business in China, plays a role in promoting friendship within their business environment. Such pro-China business associations, which were created by the business sector and pro-China lawmakers, worked to maintain relations between Japan and China before diplomatic normalization in 1972 and, after it, to promote trade.

As to the business sector, Conditions A and D would be met, but Conditions B and C are still difficult to observe. The decision-making of the three business organizations is independent of the national government because they are

---

59   On NGOs, see Gourevitch and Lake 2012, 14–15.
60   Kelley 2014, 1, 4.
61   On tokenism, see Arnstein 1969, 217.

private bodies, and their policy proposals as alternatives to national government policy have been observed, though the cases are limited. In espousing
the importance of economic ties between Japan and China, some Japanese
business groups were engaged in unofficial trade schemes before the 1972 diplomatic normalization, which was an alternative to the government's policy of
non-recognition of China. After China announced an embargo on Japanese
fishery products to counter Japan's release of 'treated water' from the Fukushima Daiichi nuclear plant into the Pacific Ocean, Keidanren quickly announced that it would send a delegation to China in early 2024 to mitigate
the tension between the two countries and end the embargo.

However, social recognition and openness in public debate (Condition B)
and the reflection of public interest (Condition C) are both lacking. The decision-making of the three umbrella organizations is not open to the public. It is
conducted by selected leaders from large companies. Even the selection of the
president is not an open process in any of the three organizations: members
are not involved in the decision-making, and it is conducted behind closed
doors. Their governance is maintained by informal groups in which personal
relationships among CEOs is a crucial mechanism. The unofficial trade between Japan and China before 1972 reflected the pro-China sentiments of
some business groups but was not open to public debate. Japan's technical
assistance to China during the 1970s and 1980s, which was led by Nippon
Steel, reflected Japanese people's pro-China sentiments, but this was not
open to public debate either. As to Condition C, the business sector may partly
reflect the public 'economic' interest because its business conditions directly
influence households, but this economic interest is essentially from the employers' viewpoint and has limitations in reflecting the public interest directly.
Those limitations in Condition B and C come from the groups' origins: the
three business organizations were created to coordinate between the national
government and the business sector. Keidanren and the Japan Association of
Corporate Executives were founded during the occupation period (1945–
1952), and the Japanese Chamber of Commerce, which was established in pre-
war Japan, was reformed in the post-war period.

Secondly, Japanese development NGOs conduct their foreign activities
using their own funds or Japan's official development assistance (ODA)
money, and some of them advocate development policy proposals. Post-
war Japan started providing economic assistance as part of its war compensation to Southeast Asia and South Asia in 1954, and since then it has espoused economic assistance and ODA as a pillar of Japan's foreign policy.
The Japan International Cooperation Agency (JICA) was established in 1974
to strengthen the management and content of Japan's economic assistance

and ODA to developing countries. From the end of the 1980s, *Kokusai Koken* (international cooperation) became an agenda in Japan's international affairs both for the national government and for Japanese NGOs, but Japanese ODA was criticized by its recipients and by Japanese leftist activists and academics for the way it was used. They questioned ODA's focus on the development of infrastructure such as bridges, roads and ports and its ignorance of residents' actual needs. In the face of the recipient countries' dissatisfaction, the Japanese government decided to expand its cooperation with Japanese NGOs and began to support their projects within Japan's ODA. In 1989, the Japanese government introduced a budget for its cooperation with Japanese NGOs by subsidizing small-scale projects, though the scale of the budget was small. In the late 1990s, the Ministry of Foreign Affairs (MOFA) began to embark on partnerships with Japanese NGOs, universities and local governments, though in limited development fields.[62] The number of Japanese development NGOs increased and reached more than 400 in the 2020s.[63] There are three types of development NGOs in Japan: field-based (*Genba-gata*), advocacy and network NGOs.[64] Field-based NGOs have their own bases or counterparts in recipient countries and provide financial and technical support for them, but the majority of this type are very small in scale, similar to small volunteer groups. They often have only one or two permanent employees (they are sometimes referred to as *Hitori* (one-person) NGOs). Advocacy NGOs are interested in ODA policy and advocate for its revision and improvement. They are located mainly in Tokyo and Osaka. Network NGOs support small Japanese NGOs on the local level by providing information on NGO policy, management and financial support. NGOs of this type began to appear in the early 2000s and number around 21.[65]

The capability level of Japanese NGOs is still weak despite the institutionalization of cooperation between them and the government. They maintain independent decision-making from the national government (Condition A) and some of them are active in criticizing Japan's development policy and attempting to change it by suggesting alternative policies (Condition D), but Conditions B and C depend on the political background of each NGO. Their openness to public debate is not necessarily strong. Some NGOs are willing to consider open debate, but others are not. Japanese NGOs' activities are often

---

62   The House of Councilors of Japan 1998.
63   Ministry of Foreign Affairs of Japan n.d..
64   JICA Institute for Development 2005, 259.
65   JANIC n.d..

sectorial and organized in small groups. Large development NGOs are, in many cases, based on religious or political groups, which are not necessarily open to the general public. Development itself may be of interest to the Japanese public in a general sense, but whether Japanese NGOs' activities are always attentive to it is a different matter. In the case of Condition D, the influence of Japanese NGOs on Japan's foreign policy is limited by their capability constraints. Japanese NGOs have their own development projects, but their financial foundation is usually weak unless they are supported by large religious or political bodies. Because Japan lacks a strong tradition of philanthropy and charity, they have to support themselves financially or, if they meet the necessary conditions, through ODA funding. The national government and JICA have enhanced their cooperation with Japanese NGOs, as already mentioned, but this has not strengthened Japanese NGOs. They can represent the public interest in development to some extent and advocate for it, but most of them have only a limited ability to maintain their daily activities.

Thirdly, some Japanese think tanks and track-two diplomacy groups could be considered non-state actors, though their number is limited and the large and influential ones are under the control of the national government. The Japan Institute of International Affairs (JIIA), which was founded in 1959 by ex-Prime Minister Shigeru Yoshida, is the leading think tank in Japan's foreign affairs. It is now a public-interest incorporated foundation but is a de facto affiliated body of MOFA. Its director is appointed from among retired top diplomats in MOFA. The National Institute for Defense Studies (NIDS) is de facto the only think tank in defence studies in Japan, but it is an administrative institute under the Ministry of Defense. The JICA Institute (JICA Ogata Sadako Research Institute for Peace and Development) is Japan's leading think tank in development policy but is a branch of JICA, an affiliated body of the Japanese national government for development policy. Other think tanks, such as the Tokyo Foundation or the Canon Institute for Global Studies, are not specifically focused on foreign and security policy. Track-two diplomacy groups, meanwhile, which originated in the late 1980s, have some academics as key members and hold conferences periodically to generate public interest in foreign affairs. The Japan International Forum, Genron NPO, New Diplomacy Initiative and API are examples. Among them, Genron NPO is engaged in track-two diplomacy with China and South Korea.

In the case of Japanese think tanks in foreign affairs, independence from the state may be absent or weak. Independent decision-making from the national government is difficult to ensure (Condition A) because, as mentioned above, the top three think tanks, that is, JIIA, NIDS and the JICA Institute, are

under the influence of the national government institutionally. They are posi-
tioned to promote the national government's foreign and defence policy, not
to suggest alternatives (Condition D). JIIA, as a de facto affiliated body of
MOFA, conducts research on foreign affairs, but the content is based on priorities set by MOFA. Debate in the three institutes is not open to the public and
the reflection of public interest is institutionally difficult unless the national
government orders it (Conditions B and C). Other non-government-affiliated
think tanks such as the Tokyo Foundation maintain independent decision-
making (Condition A), but most of them are reluctant to present alternatives
to national government policy because they need government money or networks for their research and business. What they can do is conduct research in
line with national government policy (Condition D). They, as private bodies,
are in a free position in public debate, but they are not necessarily receptive to
open debate and the reflection of public interest because of the importance of
their networks with government (Conditions B and C). The track-two diplomacy groups maintain independent decision-making (Condition A), but their
capability is limited in providing effective alternatives to Japanese society
(Condition D). Their activities can reflect the public interest through their
open meetings with their members and raise it in international conferences
in which they participate (Conditions B and C), but their effectiveness is a
different matter. They are institutionally weak and often led by one or two
charismatic leaders (and so may be referred to as a 'Hitori (one-person)
think tank'). Finding independent sources of financing is often difficult in
Japan. Ordinary people do not often make donations, so support from the
business sector or the government is needed. For most of them, it is preferable
to promote track-two diplomacy in line with national government policy instead of suggesting alternatives. Most of them do not push the national government to change its policy because they need to maintain a good relationship with it for their survival.

The fourth type is peace and disarmament groups and academics. While
they engage in peace and disarmament issues as independent actors and advocate for their importance domestically and globally, some of them collaborate with the national government in attending international conferences and
expressing Japanese views on the issues. The peace movement has been
deeply rooted in Japanese society since the end of the Pacific War. Japan experienced the horrors of Hiroshima and Nagasaki, and peace and nuclear disarmament are key diplomatic principles of the Japanese government, though
it relies on US nuclear deterrence for security. At the societal level, there is
strong support for nuclear disarmament policy, and the peace movement is
led by political groups or activists. The peace movement and non-nuclear

advocacy originated in the 1950s.[66] *Gensuikyō* (the Japan Council Against Atomic and Hydrogen Bomb) was created in 1955 as a protest against the US nuclear test in Bikini Atoll in 1954, in which 23 Japanese fishermen were exposed to radiation. At the outset, the council included different political groups, from conservatives to leftists, but it was soon divided. The JSP formed another association called *Gensuikin* (the Japan National Conference Against Atomic and Hydrogen Bomb), while *Gensuikyō* came under the leadership of the Japan Communist Party. After that, the peace and disarmament movement became the key focus for Japanese leftist political activities. At the same time, non-ideological groups advocating for peace and nuclear disarmament were also created. For example, Nihon Hidankyo, a group of those who experienced nuclear bombing in Hiroshima or Nagasaki, was established in 1956 (awarded Nobel Peace Prize in 2024). Hiroshima for Global Peace was launched in 2012 at the initiative of the Hiroshima prefecture office, and it maintains a close relationship with the national government. Some participation in diplomacy on the part of Japanese academics and disarmament NGOs in diplomacy has been observed. Representatives of peace groups such as Peace Boat and academics from the Japan Association of Disarmament Studies have been invited by MOFA to join international conferences on peace and disarmament as well as the revision of the Non-Proliferation Treaty.

In terms of public engagement, peace and nuclear disarmament groups as diplomatic actors have limitations in terms of independent decision-making (Condition A), openness and the reflection of public interest (Conditions B and C), and effectiveness of alternative policy provision (Condition D). Their social legitimacy has not been fully developed. Leftist peace and disarmament groups and academics are independent of the national government but they do not have much influence on foreign policy and diplomacy. The national government, almost always led by the LDP, tends to disregard leftist policy proposals though it generally agrees on the importance of peace and nuclear disarmament. In addition, debates within leftist groups are not open to the general public and tend to be sectorial because they are often affiliated bodies of Japanese leftist parties. They are guided by leftist parties and their activities are for leftist political agendas. Against this political background, they are able to appeal to public pacifist sentiments, but there is little reflection of balanced public interest in their policy proposals. At the same time, political groups and academics interested in disarmament who are close to

---

66   Fujiwara 2014, 90, 97.

the LDP are invited to government-led international conferences or to become members of government-sponsored committees, but their independent decision-making and their reflection of public interest are weak as a result. The government–non-state actor relationship in this case can be described as 'tokenism'. The national government chooses groups or academics who share its views to demonstrate cooperation between the state and society to international audiences, though the content of the policy is often decided by the former beforehand. A case of Japanese government-led councils is illustrative. There are many government-led councils under ministries and local governments whose role is to justify the state's policies to the public. The councils are 'formally' set up to listen to professional opinions and voices on specified policy, but actually their government secretaries, who are government officials, decide the drafts of policy beforehand and substantive debate in the councils is avoided. Thus, those affinity groups and academics are not in a position to provide alternatives to foreign policy.

The fifth type of non-state actor is local prefectures, cities and towns that participate in the Japanese sister-city programme. They are engaged in locally based foreign exchanges to foster friendship with their foreign counterpart states, provinces or cities. Though it is conducted by local government, the programme naturally involves ordinary citizens in each local prefecture, city or town. The sister-city programme, which was started as a US initiative in Japan in the post-war period, is administered in Japan by the Council of Local Authorities for International Relations (CLAIR), which is an affiliated body of some ministries of the national government: the Ministry of Education, Culture, Sports, Science and Technology, MOFA, and the Ministry of Internal Affairs and Communications. The first Japanese sister-city agreement was between Nagasaki city and St Paul (US) in 1955. Its original purpose was to reconcile the peoples of the two countries and promote friendship between them at the grassroots level. Because most Japanese local prefectures, cities and towns only have limited international contact, the sister-city programme is crucial for their reaching over 1,800 as of July 2023.

The sister-city programme has limitations and weaknesses in all four conditions. Local governments in the sister-city programme are obviously not in a position of independent decision-making from the national government (Condition A). As mentioned, the programme itself is directed by CLAIR, which is affiliated with the national government, though each local government can choose its sister cities. Not all local governments are necessarily free to conduct the programme because it is situated at the lower rank of the hierarchy of Japan's administration. Local governments seek international exchanges within the framework of the sister-city programme administered by

CLAIR, which suggests they cannot present policy alternatives to the national government (Condition D). As for Conditions B and C, the sister-city programme is open to local people and they can participate in its activities, but it is a local government policy and its openness and reflection of public interest are conditioned because local government determines the content. The purpose of the programme is mainly to promote international exchange at the local level, though in some cases other motivations may be in play, such as business exchange, community revitalization or technological cooperation.[67] The programme avoids politically controversial issues. For example, in the case of sister cities in Japan and South Korea, there is an implicit understanding that they will not address national-level issues and only seek local-level friendship, avoiding inter-state confrontations.[68] The programme supports Japan's foreign policy by establishing friendships, but its influence on foreign policy change is minimal at best.

Finally, some country-to-country friendship associations are non-state diplomatic actors which are based on local communities. There are many country-to-country associations in Japan, including the Japan–America Society and the Japan–China Friendship Association, and locally based ones are found in many local prefectures and cities. Their purpose is simply to promote or maintain friendship with a specified country through people-to-people exchange and local voluntary gatherings. Most of them are small voluntary groups composed of local people and cannot be defined as non-state actors, but some country-to-country friendship associations in Tokyo are engaged in public diplomacy. For example, some Japanese–Chinese people-to-people exchange associations support Japan's China diplomacy, and the Japan–China Friendship Association, in partnership with the Chinese government, is engaged in student exchanges and mutual visits.

The decision-making of the country-to-country friendship associations is independent of the national government (Condition A), but, as seen in the above, most of them have no capability to propose alternatives to national government policy (Condition D). They only seek grassroots-level friendship with a specified country, not policy debate, and in some cases the motivation for seeking friendship with foreign countries becomes unclear. For example, in local areas, prefecture governors, mayors and local top business CEOs are normally appointed as president and board members. Local members are sometimes motivated to participate in the associations simply in pursuit of

---

67   Menju 2018, 196–204.
68   Ibid.,148.

local prestige. As members, they are able to meet with foreign diplomats, officials, politicians and other local 'elites'. As a result, their in-group activities are
often attended only by the local Japanese, neglecting the original purpose of
maintaining international friendships. In this case, open debate and the reflection of public interest are distorted in favour of their in-group members'
prestige and interests (Conditions B and C).

5   The Steps to Japanese Non-state Actors' Diplomacy

What should be done to enhance Japanese non-state actor diplomacy? None
of the six types has succeeded in reaching the level of public engagement in
their foreign activities. While the business sector and development NGOs
maintain independent decision-making and partially have the capability to
propose alternative policy to the national government, they are not necessarily open to public debate and their reflection of the public interest is limited.
The other types have difficulty meeting any conditions of public engagement.
Those weak conditions in public engagement suggest a marginal relationship
with ordinary Japanese people and their limited capability, reflecting their
weak social legitimacy. How can these limitations be resolved? The marginal
relationship may stem mainly from their organizational culture. As seen in the
above, the main organizational foundations of the Japanese non-profit and
non-state sector are leftist parties and activists, religious groups and govern-
ment-related bodies. They are sectorial in their origin. Changing their organizational culture to be more open to the public would not be easy to the extent
that their capability rests on sectorial support.

At the same time, it may be possible to improve that capability, which
might subsequently influence the organizational culture. The capability of
non-state diplomatic actors comes from two sources. One is domestic, such
as financial support from government or society, and the other is transnational, such as networks with foreign counterparts. As already mentioned,
there are limitations to domestic sources in Japan. Under the hierarchical
state–society relationship, there are few domestic motivations to influence
diplomacy, and this inertia has ossified a domestic problem in Japan. For ordinary Japanese people, foreign affairs are still far removed from their daily
lives due to language barriers, and there is (as yet) weak social recognition of
non-state actor diplomacy. In contrast, transnational networks may help to
improve Japanese non-state actors' capability from a different standpoint by
providing information, ideas, shared practices, knowledge and human resour-

ces for their use.[69] This capability may attract public interest and change the organizational culture through increasing contacts with the general public.

In this network-capability approach, two steps are necessary given the hierarchical state–society relationship in which the social legitimacy of the national government is strong. Firstly, the diffusion of ideas and practices of non-state actor diplomacy into Japanese society is needed to initiate change. History shows that changes to Japanese systems have originated from 'international' sources. Japan began its modernization initiative only after the arrival of US Black Ships, which forced Japan to open up to foreign countries in the middle of the nineteenth century. The democratization of Japan was initiated by US occupation forces and the Japanese government followed it. Similarly, an external hand is necessary for the diffusion of non-state actor diplomacy into Japan. Academics and journalists can play a role here. Secondly, the role of the national government in establishing a framework for non-state actor diplomacy should be considered. An example can be found in the ABAC (APEC Business Advisory Council), an official council under APEC. It was established by APEC leaders in 1995 and is composed of representatives of the business community of APEC member countries. It holds a series of annual meetings separate from APEC's government-to-government meetings. The Support Council for ABAC Japan (SCABAC-J), whose leaders are selected presidents of large Japanese companies, attends the annual meetings and proposes its own vision. It has established a network with its counterparts and contributes to Japan's APEC policy under the ABAC framework. The Japanese government and the SCABAC-J are independent within APEC, and the latter decides actions from its standpoint. The extent of SCABAC-J's activities is dependent upon its leaders, but state–society cooperation is realized with their independent stance. The ABAC case suggests a Japanese approach to enhancing non-state actor diplomacy via the enmeshment of non-state actors in transnational networks within an inter-state framework. The national government is expected to create the framework in which Japanese non-state diplomatic actor can develop their capability with foreign counterparts. This method may seem to be state-centric at the first stage, but it is a practical approach for Japan, where the social legitimacy of the national government remains strong.

---

69   There are numerous works on the positive roles of networks in global governance and non-state actors. See, for example, Reinicke 1999–2000, 44–57.

6   Conclusion

While Japanese non-state actors can be seen to engage in foreign affairs activities, they have not achieved a level of public engagement, and this underdevelopment is unlikely to change soon, due in part to their weak capability and social legitimacy. This reflects the characteristics of Japanese civil society in which the national government has more capability in providing public services to Japanese people and the hierarchical state–society relationship continues to be supported by the public. Moreover, a national security discourse has emerged as a reaction to the security challenges posed by China and North Korea, so that it positions the national government as the country's most reliable security guarantor. Japanese people's reliance on the national government is increasing in the face of their expanding needs for social welfare in an ageing society, and their expectation of its capability in diplomacy is intact.

Improving the capability of Japanese non-state diplomatic actors is not easy because it requires the enhancement of their social legitimacy. One path to overcoming this problem is their enmeshment in transnational networks, which could improve their capability through interactions with foreign counterparts. From a practical standpoint, this should be pursued in such a way that Japanese conditions, in which there is a hierarchical state–society relationship and a strong influence of the Japanese government on civil society, are took into account. The role of national government should be considered positive under the continuing hierarchical state–society relationship. A government initiative to establish a framework for the enmeshment of non-state actors in transnational networks would be indispensable to enhancing their diplomatic role. This change is not yet at hand, but social, political and economic needs are evolving very slowly to become more diverse, which will eventually require a transformation of Japanese diplomacy.

Bibliography

Aida, Yūji. *Nihon teki keni no ronri* [The logic of Japanese authority] (Tokyo: PHP, 1984).

Alagappa, Muthiah. *Civil Society and Political Change in Asia: Expanding and Contracting Democratic Space* (Stanford: Stanford University Press, 2004).

Amenomori, Takayoshi. 'Japan'. In *Defining the Non-Profit Sector: A Cross-National Analysis*, eds. Lester M. Salamon and Helmut K. Anheier (Manchester: Manchester University Press, 1997), 188–214.

Arnstein, Sherry R. 'A Ladder of Citizen Participation'. *AIP Journal*, July 1969, 216–224.

Cabinet Public Relations Office of Japan. *Shakai ishiki ni kansuru yoron chōsa no gaiyō* [The summary of public opinion survey on social consciousness], March 2023. https://survey.gov-online.go.jp/index-sha.html.https://survey.gov-online.go.jp/index-sha.html.

Deakin, Nicholas. *In Search of Civil Society* (Basingstoke and New York: Palgrave, 2001).

Dellmuth, Lisa M. and Jonas Tallberg. 'The Social Legitimacy of International Organisations: Interest Representation, Institutional Performance, and Confidence Extrapolation in the United Nations'. *Review of International Studies* 41 (2015), 451–475.

Eccleston, Bernard. *State and Society in Post-War Japan* (Cambridge: Polity Press, 1989).

Erman, Eva and Anders Uhlin. *Legitimacy Beyond the State? Re-examining the Democratic Credentials of Transnational Actors* (London: Palgrave Macmillan, 2010).

Fujii, Kai. *Kokumin no seiji ni taisuru ishiki chōsa to kenkyū* [Survey and research on japanese public consciousness of politics], Liquitous, 18 August 2020. https://liqu itous.com/lisearch/2020081801.

Fujiwara, Osamu. 'Nihon no heiwa undō: shisō, kozō, kinō' [Japanese pacifist movement: Its thought, structure, and function]. *Kokusai seij* 175 (March 2014), 84–99.

Genron NPO. *Nihon no seitō ya kokkai o shinrai dekinai to kangaeru kokumin ga rokuwari koeru* [Those who do not trust Japanese political parties and the Diet exceeded 60%], 12 July 2019.https://www.genron-npo.net/politics/archives/7292 .html.

Gourevitch, Peter A. and David A. Lake. 'Beyond Virtue: Evaluating and Enhancing the Credibility of Non-governmental Organizations'. In *The Credibility of Transnational NGOs: When Virtue Is Not Enough*, eds. Peter A. Gourevitch, David A. Lake and Janice Gross Stein (Cambridge: Cambridge University Press, 2012), 3–34.

Haley, John O. *Authority without Power: Law and the Japanese Paradox* (New York: Oxford University Press, 1991).

Hall, John A. and Frank Trentmann, eds. *Civil Society: A Reader in History, Theory and Global Politics* (Basingstoke and New York: Palgrave Macmillan, 2005).

Hall, Rodney Bruce and Thomas J. Biersteker, eds. *The Emergence of Private Authority in Global Governance* (Cambridge: Cambridge University Press, 2002).

Hann, Chris. 'Introduction: Political Society and Civil Anthropology'. In *Civil Society: Challenging Western Models*, eds. Chris Hann and Elizabeth Dunn (Abingdon and New York: Routledge, 1996), 1–26.

Higgott, Richard A., Geoffrey R.D. Underhill and Andreas Bieler, eds. *Non-state Actors and Authority in the Global System* (Abingdon and New York: Routledge, 2000).

Hurd, Ian. 'Legitimacy and Authority in International Politics'. *International Organization* 53 (2) (Spring 1999), 379–408.

Iwata, Noriko. 'Kokumin ga seifu ni kitaisuru shakai hoshō' [Social welfare which the Japanese people expect from the government]. *Kikan shakai hoshō kenkyū* [Social welfare research quarterly] 48 (3) (December 2012), 250–251.

JANIC. *Kokusai kyōryoku NGO no nettowākingu nitsuiteno chōsakenkyū*, p. 26. https://www.mofa.go.jp/mofaj/gaiko/oda/shimin/oda_ngo/shien/ngo_nw/index.html.

Johnson, Chalmers. 'Japan: Who Governs? An Essay on Official Bureaucracy'. *Journal of Japanese Studies* 2 (1) (Autumn 1975), 1–28.

Kelley, John R. *Agency Change: Diplomatic Action Beyond the State* (Lanham, MD: Rowman & Littlefield, 2014).

Kissling, Claudia. *Civil Society and Nuclear Non-proliferation: How Do States Respond?* (Abingdon: Routledge, 2008).

Kumashiro, Akihiko. *Shin, Nihon no NPO hō* [New Japan's NPO law] (Tokyo: Gyōsei, 2003).

Kuno, Osamu. Keni Shugi Kokka no Nakade [In An Authoritarian State] (Tokyo:Chikuma Shobo, 1976).

Lamb, Brian. 'Non-profit PR as the Voice of Civil Society?'. In *Communicating Causes: Strategic Public Relations for the Non-profit Sector*, by Nicky Garsten and Ian Bruce (Abingdon: Routledge, 2018), 13–26.

Lüdert, Jan. *Non-state Actors at the United Nations: Contesting Sovereignty* (Abingdon: Routledge, 2023).

Marchetti, Raffaele. *Global Strategic Engagement: States and Non-State Actors in Global Governance* (Lanham, MD: Lexington Books, 2016).

JICA Institute for Development. *Non fōmaru kyōiku no kakujyū ni mukete* [For the expansion of non-formal education programme] (Tokyo: JICA, 2005).

Matsumoto, Sannosuke. 'The Roots of Political Disillusionment: "Public" and "Private" in Japan'. In *Authority and the Individual in Japan: Citizen Protest in Historical Perspective*, ed. J. Victor Koschmann (Tokyo: University of Tokyo Press, 1978), 31–51.

Melissen, Jan. 'Public Diplomacy'. In *Diplomacy in a Globalizing World: Theories and Practices*, second edition, ed. Pauline Kerr and Geoffrey Wiseman (New York and Oxford: Oxford University Press, 2018), 199–218.

McVeigh, Brian J. *The Nature of the Japanese State: Rationality and Rituality* (Abingdon and New York: Routledge, 1998).

Menju, Toshihiro. *Shimai toshi no chōsen* [Sister-city's challenges] (Tokyo: Akashi-shoten, 2018).

Ministry of Foreign Affairs of Japan. ODA, *Kokusai kyōryokyu to NGO* [International cooperation and NGO]. https://www.mofa.go.jp/mofaj/gaiko/oda/shimin/oda_ngo.htm.

Mori, Yūki and Kenki Adachi. 'Dantai-gyōsei kankei: Seifu to shakai no seshoku men' [Organization-administration relationship: contact between the government and society]. In *Gendai nihon no shimin shakai, rieki dantai* [Civil society and interest groups of contemporary Japan], ed. Yutaka Tsujinaka (Tokyo: Bokutaku-sha, 2002), 119–138.

Moss, Jeremy, ed. *Climate Justice and Non-state Actors* (Abingdon: Routledge, 2020).

Nakane, Chie. *Japanese Society* (Berkeley: University of California Press, 1970).

National Center for State Courts. What Is Public Engagement?. https://www.ncsc.org/consulting-and-research/areas-of-expertise/communications,-civics-and-disinformation/community-engagement/toolkit/why-to-use/the-promise-of-public-engagement/what-is-public-engagement.

Newell, Peter. *Climate for Change: Non-state Actors and the Global Politics of the Greenhouse* (Cambridge: Cambridge University Press, 2000).

NHK Broadcasting Culture Research Institute, *Jyūhassai Senkyo, Yūkensha no ishiki to tōhyō kōdō* [Voting rights lowered to 18 year old: consciousness and voting behavior of the new voters], 2 April 2017.https://www.nhk.or.jp/bunken/research/yoron/20170401_8.html.

Osborne, Stephen P. 'The Voluntary and Non-profit Sector in Contemporary Japan: Emerging Roles and Organizational Challenges in a Changing Society'. In *The Voluntary and Non-Profit Sector in Japan: The Challenge of Change*, ed. Stephen P. Osborne (London and New York: Routledge, 2003), 7–22.

Pekkanen, Robert. *Japan's Dual Civil Society* (Stanford: Stanford University Press, 2006).

Pharr, Susan J. 'Preface'. In *The State of Civil Society in Japan*, eds. Frank J. Schwartz and Susan J. Pharr (Cambridge: Cambridge University Press, 2003), xiii–xviii.

Putnam, Robert D. *Bowling Alone: The Collapse and Revival of American Community* (New York: Simon & Schuster Paperbacks, 2000).

Reinicke, Wolfgang H. 'The Other World Wide Web: Global Public Policy Networks'. *Foreign Policy* 117 (Winter 1999–2000), 44–57.

Saeki, Keishi. *Shimin towa dareka: Sengo minshushugi o toinaosu* [Who are citizens? Rethinking post-war Japanese democracy] (Tokyo: PHP, 1997).

Sakamoto, Haruya, ed. *Shimin Shakai Ron* [A study on civil society] (Kyoto: Hōritsu bunka sha, 2017).

Salamon, Lester M. 'The Rise of the Nonprofit Sector'. *Foreign Affairs* 73 (4) (July/August 1994), 115–118.

Schnabel, Albrecht, ed. *Civil Society and Global Finance* (Abingdon: Routledge, 2002).

Schwartz, Frank J. 'Introduction: Recognizing Civil Society in Japan'. In *The State of Civil Society in Japan*, eds. Frank J. Schwartz and Susan J. Pharr (Cambridge: Cambridge University Press, 2003), 1–19.

Szücs, Jenö. 'Three Historical Regions in Europe'. In *Civil Society and the State: New European Perspectives*, ed. John Keane (London: Verso, 1988).

The government of New Brunswick. Economic and Social Inclusion Corporation. https://www2.gnb.ca/content/gnb/en/departments/esic/overview/content/what_ispublicengagement.html.

The House of Councilors of Japan. The Minutes of the Diet, The Committee of Labor and Social Policy, 3 February 1998.https://kokkai.ndl.go.jp/#/detail?minId=1142152 85X00419980203¤t=1.

Tsujinaka, Yutaka and Che Jjyon, 'Gaikan: Shimin shakai no seijika to eikyōryoku' [Overview: politicization and influence of civil society]. In *Gendai nihon no shimin shakai, rieki dantai* [Civil society and interest groups of contemporary Japan], ed. Yutaka Tsujinaka (Tokyo: Bokutaku-sha, 2002).

Tsuruta, Tadasu. 'Village Commons in Japan from the Moral Economy Perspective:A Note on the Right to Subsistence of the Disadvantaged Villagers,' Digital Library of the Commons. https://dlc.dlib.indiana.edu/dlc/bitstream/handle/10535/8985/TSU RUTA_0194.pdf?sequence=1&isAllowed=y.

United Nations. *Handbook on Non-profit Institutions in the System of National Accounts* (New York: United Nations, 2003).

Ushiro, Fusao and Haruya Sakamoto. *Gendai nihon no shimin shakai: sādo-sectā chōsa niyoru jitsushō bunseki* [Civil society in contemporary Japan: empirical analysis based on research on the third sector] (Kyoto: Hōritsu bunka-sha, 2019).

Van Rooy, Allison. *The Global Legitimacy Game: Civil Society, Globalization, and Protest* (Basingstoke: Palgrave Macmillan, 2004).

Vinken, Henk, Yuko Nishimura, Bruce L.J. White and Masayuki Deguchi, eds. *Civic Engagement in Contemporary Japan: Established and Emerging Repertories* (New York: Springer, 2010).

Walzer, Michael, ed. *Toward a Global Civil Society* (Providence, MA and Oxford: Berghahn Books, 1995).

CHAPTER 6

Internal Societisation of Diplomacy

The Disintegration of State-Society Relations and Its Moderating Effects on Japanese Diplomacy toward China

Yun Zhang

Summary

Scholars are increasingly considering the societal dimension of diplomacy. However, existing literature focuses primarily on the external societisation of diplomacy (e.g. public diplomacy). I turn to the internal societisation of diplomacy – a political community-building process between the state and society – by exploring an empirical case study of Japan's diplomacy towards China. Despite the seemingly high convergence of the Japanese state and societal perception of the so-called 'China menace', related policies do not similarly converge. I argue that this can be primarily attributed to the absence of political community between the Japanese state and society. Normative Japanese societal interests contrast with the 'national security first' rationale of mainstream conservative Japanese politicians. Despite not being able to impact foreign policy directly, society can influence politics (e.g. withdraw support). The 'China threat' cannot change the very nature of the disintegration of the state–society relationship in Japan, which moderates Japan's diplomacy towards China.

Keywords

internal societisation of diplomacy – political community – China – Japan – disintegration – state – society

1   Introduction

Kenneth Waltz argued that there are three levels of international politics, namely, the human, the state, and the international levels.[1] The mainstream

---

1   Waltz 1959.

discourse of international relations studies has emphasised the third level, arguing that the international system mainly determines the foreign behaviours of states. Most scholarship on diplomacy, whether historical or contemporary, has applied the governmental elite-based perspective; for example, existing literature applies this perspective to political leaders,[2] bureaucratic politics,[3] and diplomatic negotiations.[4] In other words, the role of society in diplomacy has been implicitly assumed to be limited if not totally irrelevant and, as argued in the introduction of this book, dominant International Relations (IR) theories have not yet incorporated this perspective. With the rise of democratisation and globalisation in recent decades, the role of society in diplomacy has attracted increasing attention in both academic and policy circles; for example, interest has grown in public diplomacy,[5] city diplomacy,6 and civil society advocacy diplomacy.[7]

This article argues that there are two types of societisation of diplomacy, namely, internal and external societisation. The re-orientation of research on diplomacy to the societal dimension seems to be more focused on the external societisation of diplomacy, which sheds light mainly on the impacts of societal actors across borders on diplomatic relations, including transnational corporations, NGOs, and various forms of societal contacts. In contrast, the internal dimension of the societisation of diplomacy has not yet received sufficient academic and practical attention. Briefly, the internal societisation of diplomacy could be defined as a political community-building process characterised by diplomatic policy deliberation between the state and society in a domestic context. Despite not being able to make direct decisions on foreign policy, society still has intangible power to influence political dynamics; for instance, social actors can punish even very powerful politicians by withdrawing support or even expelling them from politics.

Further, significant diplomatic policies must be filtered through the scrutiny of domestic society. However, does domestic society really have leverage on state elites in the context of diplomatic decisions? How do domestic state–society political processes impact a state's diplomacy with another country? This article takes up these questions to fill the gap in existing schol-

---

2 Rosecrance and Stein 1993; Rosenau 1997; Jervis 1976; Jervis, Lebow and Stein 1985.
3 Milner 1997; Allison 1971; Kaufmann 1996; McCormi 1969; Rowman 2012; Rosenau 1969.
4 Kamau, Chasek and O'Connor 2018.
5 Melissen 2018; Huijgh 2019.
6 Marchetti 2021.
7 Gotz 2011.

arship around the internal societisation of diplomacy through an empirical case study on Japan's diplomacy toward China.

2   The Roots of the Internal Societisation of Japanese Diplomacy toward China

There are several reasons why Sino–Japanese diplomacy is an ideal case for developing theoretical insights into the internal societisation of diplomacy. On the one hand, Sino-Japanese diplomacy has been conceived as being driven predominantly by elites. Mao Zedong and Zhou Enlai on the Chinese side and Tanaka Kakuei and Ohira Masayoshi are widely regarded and remembered as the key political leaders in the normalisation of bilateral relations in 1972.[8] Immediately after realising détente with the United States, Mao Zedong decided to normalise relations with Japan, America's most prominent security ally in Asia, to advance China's grand strategy of allying with the US to contain the Soviet Union.[9] Similarly, Japan was eager to normalise its relationship with its most prominent neighbour. The carefully selected and capable officials in both countries have been considered as the primary managers of their important diplomatic relationship. On the other hand, People's Diplomacy has been highly praised as a striking feature in Sino–Japanese diplomacy. During the Sino–Japanese confrontation period before 1972, many Japanese civil organisations and individuals actively echoed the Chinese government's call for people-to-people diplomacy with the goal of gradually developing a favourable societal environment for the breakthrough of official diplomatic ties.

Meanwhile, since 1972, high social and economic interdependence has been regarded as a major stabilising factor in Sino-Japanese diplomacy. Since 2007, China has been Japan's biggest trading partner. In 2019, their bilateral trade volume reached USD 340.7 billion, accounting for almost 21.3 per cent of Japan's total external trade volume (the share for Japan-US trade was 15.4 per cent).[10] In 2025, Japan was China's third biggest trading partner and third biggest investor, with more than 30,000 Japanese companies in China.[11] This is reflected by the fact that there were 1097 direct flights connecting air-

---

8   Zhang 2017.

9   Dayong 2014.

10   Japan External Trade Organization 2019.

11   Ministry of Foreign Ministry of Japan 2025, 2.

ports in the two countries every week in 2019[12] and that there are 382 sister-province or sister-city pairings between China and Japan.[13] Such an intense connectedness is rarely seen in global bilateral relationships.[14] In a sense, the external societisation of Sino–Japanese diplomacy has contributed significantly to the nations' stable bilateral ties.

However, Sino–Japanese relations have been extremely turbulent, especially since 2010. The nations' bilateral relations have been troubled by territorial disputes, historical issues, and security dilemmas. Notably, Japan's diplomacy toward China has been conventionally interpreted as relatively hawkish and nationalistic; however, this conventional intellectual understanding has changed in the past decade owing to the rise of increasingly rightist politics and, relatedly, conservative social trends amidst Japan's low economic growth. China's rapid rise has stirred nationalism in Japan, and rightist Japanese politicians are considered to have successfully mobilised this anti-China nationalist sentiment for their political gain.[15] Some attempts have been made to explain their relationship deterioration by applying a realist lens; specifically, this perspective suggests that China's rise changed the dynamics of its power struggle with Japan and worsened the nations' relationship.[16] Recent Japanese economic security legislation seems to prove that economic and social interdependence is not an asset but a liability in working to stabilise China-Japan relations.

In this context, previous explanations of the external societisation of Sino–Japanese diplomacy have begun to lose their intellectual legitimacy. In the 2010s, the Japanese government and the majority of media outlets increasingly depicted China as a threat to Japanese national security and regional stability. In its 2022 Japanese National Security Strategy, Japan situated China as 'present[ing] an unprecedented and the greatest strategic challenge in ensuring the peace and security of Japan and the peace and stability of the international community'.[17] As many as 90 per cent of Japanese respondents said that they disliked China. A recent poll in 2023 showed that 92.2 per cent of

---

12   Nihon Keizai Shimbun 2020.

13   www.clair.or.jp/j/exchange/shimai/countries/detail/13

14   Zhang 2017.

15   There is some literature investigating the domestic sources of Japan's security policy and its implications on Sino-Japanese relations, including Sheila A. Smith's *Rivals: Japanese Domestic Politics and a Rising China* (New York: Columbia University Press, 2015) and Amy Catalina, *Electoral Reform and National Security in Japan: From Pork to Foreign Policy* (Cambridge: Cambridge University Press, 2017).

16   Bush 2010.

17   National Security of Japan, 2022, 7.

Japanese respondents disliked China, and 62.9 per cent of Chinese respondents disliked Japan.[18] Despite this seemingly high convergence of the Japanese state and societal perception of the 'China menace', we do not see an equivalent convergence of policy tendencies. A dramatic increase in the defence budget to address the so-called 'China challenge' supported by many political elites has not yet been realised.[19] Related constitutional revisions have been stalled due to societal reluctance. In a sense, Japanese society seems to be preventing more hawkish and hostile policies towards China. What may account for the seemingly contradictory divergence in policy and convergence in perception? How should we explain this puzzle in Japan's politics–diplomacy nexus in the second decade of this century?

I argue that this contradiction can be primarily attributed to the absence of political community between the Japanese state and society. According to Grazia Sebastian, a political community should be based on the foundations of a shared belief system;[20] therefore, a political community is formed when mainstream political elites and citizens share a common belief and value system. Political communication plays an important role in this process; specifically, it can evoke understanding in society. Additionally, a sense of commonality between the state and society is essential in the formation of a political community. Two central societal norms are deeply rooted in post-war Japan: Anti-war pacifism and civil liberty protection. Although Japanese society has mainly accepted depictions of China as a threat to Japan's national security, these societal norms and interests are at odds with the national security-first political norms of mainstream conservative Japanese politicians. Thus, Japanese political elites have largely failed to convince society that a more hostile approach to diplomacy is needed to address the so-called 'China threat'. This article presents three empirical cases to support these arguments.

3   The 2012 *Diaoyu/Senkaku* Nationalisation Case

Former Tokyo Governor Shintaro Ishihara has been an iconic hawkish anti-China nationalist in the Japanese political arena for decades. In 2012, he was regarded as the main architect of Japanese anti-Chinese sentiment because he

---

18   Genron NPO 2023.

19   Despite Prime Minister Fumio Kishida's pledge to increase the defence budget to 2% of the Japanese GDP by 2027, the source of this budget remains undetermined.

20   Sebastian 1948.

floated the idea of purchasing the disputed *Diaoyu/Senkaku* Islands located between the two nations;[21] ultimately, this proposal triggered the most damaging shock to Sino–Japanese diplomacy since the normalisation of ties in 1972. It would be natural to question how a local government governor could influence foreign policy at the national level. In reality, Ishihara has been a long-standing national Diet member known for supporting nationalism since before he was elected Tokyo Governor. Notably, the prime minister during this time, Yoshihiko Noda, consulted with Ishihara on the nationalisation of the islands. The Japanese national government justified its decision to nationalise the islands by arguing that it was seeking to avoid an unexpected and potentially uncontrollable situation that may result from Ishihara purchasing the islands. However, China rejected this explanation and even situated the national government's nationalisation of the islands as a joint conspiracy between the national government and Ishihara. On 26 October 2012, Vice Foreign Minister Zhang Zhijun summarised China's official recognition of the nationalisation of the islands as a joint conspiracy of the Noda government and right-wing political forces. He further warned that China would respond strongly and remove hindrances and obstacles to peaceful development if its bottom line was challenged.[22] Ultimately, these events triggered the worst diplomatic confrontation between China and Japan to date.

Ishihara proposed purchasing the islands two years after the Fishing Boat Collision Incident occurred in September 2010. A Chinese finishing boat collided with a Japanese Coast Guard patrol boat in disputed waters near the Diaoyu/Senkaku Islands. The Japanese authority detained the captain, which sparked a major diplomatic backlash between China and Japan. This event profoundly worsened Sino–Japanese relations and, relatedly, the nations' mutual perceptions of each other. Meanwhile, Japanese domestic politics had been in the process of profoundly evolving in the aftermath of the historical landslide success of the historical opposition party, the Democratic Party of Japan (DPJ), in the 2009 general election, which made the long-standing ruling party, the Liberal Democratic Party (LDP), the opposition. The decision to release the Chinese captain led to criticisms that the DPJ government had a weak approach to diplomacy toward China. Accordingly, the DPJ faced domestic pressure to be tougher on China and was, therefore, increasingly losing flexibility in its China policies. The 2010 incident created a sense of crisis in

---

21   For more on the Diaoyu/Senkaku dispute, see Erica Downs and Phillip Saunders, 'Legitimacy and the Limits of Nationalism: China and the Diaoyu Islands,' *International Security*, 23 (3) (Winter 1998/99), 114–146.

22   Embassy of the People's Republic of China in Japan 2012.

Japanese society in terms of both the DPJ's governance and Sino–Japanese relations. Indeed, the 2012 Lower House election intensified the political salience of the Diaoyu/Senkaku issue – this territorial dispute was highly politicised in the context of turbulent Japanese domestic politics.

Ishihara accurately identified anxieties in Japan around China and tried to exploit Sino–Japanese diplomacy accordingly for his political agenda. On 16 April 2012, Ishihara announced his plan to use public money to purchase the Senkaku Islands in a speech at the Heritage Foundation in Washington, DC. He stated that if the Japanese national government was unwilling or unable to defend the Senkaku Islands, the Tokyo Metropolitan government would do so.[23] Within a short period, the Tokyo metropolitan government managed to solicit donations to fund the purchase, collecting nearly JPY 1.5 billion. This imposed huge pressure on the national government. Three months later, Prime Minister Yoshihiko Noda finally announced a plan to nationalise the islands on 7 July 2012. After the nationalisation, a series of unprecedented large-scale anti-Japanese demonstrations took place in many Chinese cities. Sino–Japanese relations fell to their lowest point since 1972.

Ishihara resigned as the governor of Tokyo on 25 October 2012 and announced his intention to compete in the upcoming Diet general elections. On 13 November 2012, he founded a new highly conservative political party, *Taiyo no To* (the Sun Party). The party's manifesto called for a fight against Chinese hegemony to prevent the islands from becoming a second Tibet. A week later, Ishihara merged his party with an Osaka-based populist party, *Nippon Ishin no Kai* (the Japan Restoration Party) and became the new party's co-leader. On 20 November 2012, Ishihara publicly stated that Japan should 'simulate' the possession of nuclear arms to deter Beijing. He called for a drastic increase in the defence budget and the immediate revision of the constitution. Ishihara seemed to successfully mobilise political and public attention towards China by skilfully converging nationalism and political opportunism. Accordingly, China's policies became a significant issue in the Lower House elections campaigns in December 2012.

However, Ishihara's seemingly successful mobilisation of anti-China nationalism did not translate to broader public support for his political career. On the one hand, the Japanese cabinet office's survey showed that the Japanese affinity towards China dropped to a record low in 2012. On the other hand, the public did not widely support Ishihara's hawkish stance towards China. In the press conference before the general election in 2012, he was

---

23   'Tokyo to buy disputed islands, says Governor Ishihara 2012.

publicly questioned on whether he felt responsible for the chaos between China and Japan. He blamed the LDP for failing to defend Japanese territory and argued that China was responsible for the deterioration of Sino–Japanese diplomatic relations. Although Ishihara was elected as a parliament member, his nationalist ideology did not seem to appeal to the broader public. Indeed, his hawkish policy proposals towards China increased public fears of a war between China and Japan. Ironically, the more he tried to appeal to Japanese nationalism, the more fear intensified in Japanese society. He even argued for abandoning Japan's peace constitution on the grounds that Japan would not be able to retaliate if it was attacked by China, hinting at a possible military conflict between the nations. In early 2013, Ishihara actively promoted his idea of abandoning the constitution. However, Japanese society was uneasy about this idea; indeed, the LDP's vice president, Masahiko Komura, severely criticised Ishihara, stating that he was not qualified to serve as a politician.[24]

In December 2014, Ishihara lost the 47th General Election to the House of Representatives and quit politics. His failure may be attributed to a variety of reasons, including his discriminatory remarks regarding women and the opportunistic decision to suddenly abandon his role as Governor of Tokyo to run for national office. However, his war-like stance towards China was a significant reason for his failure. While Ishihara successfully evoked strong negative social sentiments towards China, he failed to translate these sentiments into an anti-China social movement in Japan. Ironically, left-wing parties gained more seats in the 2014 election – in the Lower House, *Komeito*, a Bundist Party in a coalition with the ruling LDP, increased its seats from 31 to 35, and the Japanese Communist Party increased its seats from 8 to 21.

Meanwhile, the Party for the Next Generation, the extreme right-wing party headed by Ishihara, lost 17 seats (its number of seats declined from 19 to 2). Japanese society punished the extreme rightist political forces by withdrawing support, pulling the break on the political tendency for a more hawkish Japanese policy toward China. Notably, this societal marginalisation of extreme nationalism disincentivises Japanese politicians from overplaying the China card to appeal to the public. Like Ishihara, another nationalist politician and former SDF general, Toshio Tabogami, lost an election mainly due to his hawkish attitude toward China.

We did not witness large-scale anti-Chinese demonstrations or a boycott of Chinese goods in Japan. Furthermore, the Japanese public became increasingly concerned with potential conflict and even war with China due to Ishi-

---

24   Nihon Keizai Shimbun 2013.

hara's extreme nationalistic tendency. For the Japanese public, Ishihara's election increased the risk of a possible war with China – a future entirely unacceptable for a pacifist Japan. While Ishihara might have mobilised Japanese society's concerns and nationalism, he fatally failed to understand the essence of Japanese pacifism, that is, the refusal to display military power to imply its potential use. The Japanese media reported that Ishihara had told Prime Minister Yoshihiko Noda that a war with China would have been acceptable. As the individual responsible for mobilising the Japan Self-Defence Forces (SFD) if a war erupted, Noda was highly concerned about Ishihara's radicalism.[25]

4   National Security Legislation of 2015 and Internal Societalisation

4.1   *The 2014 Cabinet Decision: A Turning Point*
The Diaoyu Crisis in 2012 served as an important pretext for changes in Japanese security policy; conservative politicians frequently quoted the crisis as a serious security concern in light of China's increasingly assertive stance. Below, I consider two cases of national security-related legislation in 2015 and state-society interactions relevant to Japan's diplomacy towards China.

On 1 July 2014, the Shinzo Abe government made a Cabinet Decision on basic policies for developing new security legislation, which re-interpreted the right of collective self-defence as consistent with the constitution.[26] For decades, the Japanese government held the view that exercising such a right was unconstitutional; thus, the reinterpretation marked a major turning point in Japan's national defence policy. The reinterpretation was assertedly pushed primarily to address the so-called 'China threat'. Around this time, the Japanese government and media had been increasingly describing China as an assertive – even aggressive – power, particularly in the East China Sea and South China Sea. A Chinese Foreign Ministry spokesman, Hong Lei, commented:

> Recently, Japan's ruling authority has been stirring up troubles on historical issues, taking unprecedented measures in the military and security field, and bringing great changes to Japan's military and security policies. We are opposed to Japan's pursuit of its domestic political goal by deliberately making up the so-called 'China threat'. We urge the Japanese side to earnestly respect the legitimate security concerns

---

25   Yamaguchi and Nakakita 2014.
26   Prime Minister's Office of Japan 2014.

of its Asian neighbours and prudently deal with relevant issues. It must not undermine China's sovereignty and security interests, nor shall it harm regional peace and stability.[27]

Due to the Japanese military's wartime invasions and atrocities, East Asian countries, particularly China and Korea, have consistently been attentive to the linkage between Japanese attitudes toward Japan's militaristic history and its defence posture. For instance, during his state visit to the Republic of Korea, President Xi Jinping reportedly shared concerns about Japan's historical revisionism and security policy changes with President Park Geun-hye.[28]

4.2   Abe's Proactive Pacifism and International Diplomacy

Meanwhile, Prime Minister Abe actively promoted Proactive Pacifism after the Cabinet granted the right to collective self-defence. In his visit to Australia in 2014, Abe told the Australian Parliament that Japan and Australia should 'join up in a scrum, just like in rugby, to nurture a regional and world order and to safeguard peace'.[29] In his speech, he also floated the idea of Indo–Pacific partnerships, which later led to the revival of the Quadrilateral Security Dialogue (QSD) between the United States, Japan, India, and Australia regarding multilateral mechanisms. Although Abe did not explicitly mention China, his message was an invitation to join the anti-China campaign. Although the Japanese public has historically had an unfavourable perception of China, it seemed relatively unsupportive of Abe's reinterpretation of the Constitution. An opinion poll conducted by *Nikkei Shimbun* (an ideologically neutral newspaper) in May 2014 showed that 51 per cent of respondents opposed the change in constitutional interpretation to approve the exercise of the right of collective self-defence.[30]

4.3   Comprehensive National Security Legislation of 2015

After the Cabinet decision in 2014, the Abe government's next ambition was to update Japan's comprehensive national security laws in accordance with the right to collective self-defence. This unprecedented change to national security legislation in post-war Japanese history involved modifying ten laws

---

27   MFA.

28   Nikkei Shimbun 2014.

29   Prime Minister of Japan and his Cabinet, Remarks by Prime Minister Abe to the Australian Parliament 2014.

30   Nihon Keizai Shimbun 2014.

related to the SDF and Ministry of Defence and two laws related to peacekeeping operations (PKO). The most controversial of this sprawling national security-related legislation was that the SDF could support the Japanese allies when an armed attack happened. This was directly linked to the constitutional reinterpretation in the previous year. On 4 June 2015, the ruling LDP printed 1 million flyers calling for the Japanese public to support the security legislation to address China's military assertiveness. In stark contrast, on the same day, all three invited Japanese constitutional experts told the House of Representatives Constitutional Research Committee that the new security bills enabling the use of the right of collective self-defence were unconstitutional. More ironically, one expert was even invited by the ruling LDP, which was eager to mobilise public understanding and support of the new security bills. More than 80 per cent of constitutional scholars in Japan shared the view that the national security legislation based on the reinterpretation of the constitution was unconstitutional. However, because the ruling LDP held the majority in Parliament, the security legislation was finally passed on 19 September 2015.

Nevertheless, this seeming legislative victory did not indicate public support. Each opposition party countered the legislation for different reasons. Meanwhile, the *Nihion Keizai Shinbum* public opinion survey showed that 55 per cent of respondents opposed the legislation while only 27 per cent supported it; further, more than 80 per cent of respondents believed that the government's explanation of the bills was insufficient. In 2015, The Japanese public strongly opposed the Abe government's revision of security-related bills assertedly designed to more effectively deal with the 'China threat', with large-scale protests emerging outside of the Diet building. Societal opposition initially derived from societal fears of the increasing likelihood of Japan being dragged into the wars of its allies (particularly the US). Broadly, the China threat and enhanced US-Japanese deterrence toward China were not enough to convince Japanese society of the necessity of the national security bills.

Furthermore, the state secrets law in the legislation led to societal fears of punishment for criticising politicians. Related concerns regarding civil liberties and the freedom of the press were a major reason the public opposed the legislation. Along these lines, *Komeito*, a minor ally party with a strong pacifist orientation in the LDP-led coalition government, insisted on imposing conditions on the national security legislation. In the end, the government failed to fully embrace the right to collective self-defence, and the 2014 Cabinet decision became subject to three conditions; specifically, the right to collective self-defence is only valid when:

1. Japan is facing an imminent and illegitimate act of aggression;

2.   there are no other means to counter the threat, and
3.   the force used for self-defence is limited to the minimum necessary
      level.

Therefore, the right to collective defence is minimal and conditional. Broadly, the conditions listed above have been summarised as 'criteria for the use of force authorisation, restrictions on the development of power projection capabilities, and limits to the types of overseas military operations that can be sanctioned'.[31]

4.4   *Internal Societisation and Foreign Policy Decisions*

Interestingly, in the process of the debate on the 2015 national security legislation, both the opposition leaders and the Japanese general public did not dispute the 'China threat' against the government; instead, they disputed the constitutionality of the legislation. In this state–society political interaction, insufficient societal legitimacy served as a *de facto* restraint on Japanese politicians' efforts to implement more hawkish policy toward China. Japanese society seemed concerned that the government was trying to use the 'China threat' to justify national security bills and an uncontrollable China policy.

Most Japanese people perceive Abe as a two-faced politician who combines strong leadership with strong right-wing political ideology. The degree of public trust in Abe reflected by the ballot box has been largely due to public expectation that Abe will be a strong leader rather than support for his rightist agenda. Notably, the public has displayed alarmist sentiments towards Abe's potential abuse of his leadership powers. During his first premiership from 2007–2008, Abe learned the bitter lesson of losing public support as a result of overly pushing his rightist agenda. He also experienced harsh public backlash after visiting the Yasukuni Shrine honouring Class A war criminals on 26 December 2013 – this was the first time a serving prime minister had made an official visit to the shrine in 7 years (the last visit had been made by Prime Minister Junichiro Koizumi in 2006). As expected, the Chinese Ministry of Foreign Affairs immediately lodged a strongly-worded protest against Abe's visit. More surprisingly, the US Embassy in Japan also issued an unprecedented warning, stating, 'the United States is disappointed that Japan's leadership has taken an action that will exacerbate tensions with Japan's neighbours'.[32] This direct criticism triggered a sense of urgency and crisis among the Japanese public about the potential loss of US security protection in a Japan-China conflict. Along these lines, a January 2014 poll indicated that 52 per cent

---

31   Solis 2023, 196.
32   Statement on Prime Minister Abe's December 26 Visit to Yasukuni Shrine 2013.

of respondents thought that the visit had damaged Japan's international reputation.

Meanwhile, another poll showed that 84 per cent of Japanese respondents now felt uneasy about Japan's alliance with the US.[33] However, another poll revealed that 76 per cent of respondents believed that Abe should actively work to improve relations with China.[34] Some politicians wisely sensed these societal concerns and began to engage China more actively. For example, the Governor of Tokyo, Yoichi Masuzoe, visited China on 26 April 2014 – this was the first time a Tokyo governor had paid an official visit to China in more than a decade; Masuzoe's anti-Chinese predecessor, Ishihara, largely blocked exchanges with Beijing (Tokyo's sister city).[35] A *Nikkei* poll in late September 2014 showed that almost half of the respondents supported a Sino–Japanese summit meeting as soon as possible – this support rate was 8 points higher than that in August.[36] Against this background of societal demand, Abe started to moderate his China policy by resuming diplomatic channels. He sent his National Security Advisor, Shotaro Yachi, to Beijing. Yachi and his Chinese counterpart, State Councillor Yang Jie Chi, reached a principled agreement on handling and improving bilateral relations.

Specifically, this agreement comprised the following four points. First, the two sides affirmed that they would follow the principles and spirit of the four political documents between China and Japan and continue to develop a strategic relationship of mutual benefit. Second, in the spirit of 'facing history squarely and looking forward to the future', the two sides agreed to work to overcome political obstacles in their bilateral relations. Third, the two sides acknowledged that they hold different positions on the Diaoyu Islands and some waters in the East China Sea and agreed to prevent the situation from escalating through dialogue, consultation, and crisis management mechanisms. Fourth, the two sides agreed to gradually resume political, diplomatic, and security dialogues through various multilateral and bilateral channels and work to build mutual political trust.[37] This agreement paved the way for a Sino–Japanese summit in November 2014 on the sidelines of the Asia-Pacific Economic Cooperation (APEC) in Beijing. At the APEC, Abe proved to be more of a pragmatic conservatism than a blind nationalist, and this pragmatism has since been a constant element of his extended premiership.

---

33   Nikkei Shimbun 2014.
34   TV Asahi 2014.
35   Kyodo News Agency 2014.
36   Nikkei Shimbun 2014.
37   Embassy of the People's Republic of China in Japan 2014.

The same situation emerged after Abe strongly pushed the national security legislation mentioned above. After the constitutional reinterpretation of the right to collective defence, it was expected that Abe would amend the constitution accordingly. Japanese society was highly suspicious of this possible scenario. In a July 2016 Nikkei poll, only 38 per cent of respondents replied that they supported amending the constitution during Abe's tenure, while 49 per cent stated that they opposed it.[38] Meanwhile, the World Value Survey revealed the strong social norm of resistance to war in Japan: more than 60 percent of respondents replied that they opposed wars, even just and necessary ones, and only 15 per cent of respondents stated that they would be willing to fight for Japan if a war happened; further, among all countries surveyed, Japan had the lowest rates of war approval.[39] Ultimately, Abe's pragmatism – not his rightist tendency – made his China policy acceptable to the Japanese public and secured his premiership over the long term.

5   Three Strategic Documents from 2022

5.1   *Public Opinion and Japan-China Relations*
On 16 December 2022, the Kishida government released three strategic documents: the National Security Strategy (NSS), the National Defence Strategy (NDS), and the Defence Buildup Program. This was the first major revision of the NSS since it was first issued almost a decade ago. The most striking change in the 2022 NSS is the definition of China as 'the great strategic challenge' for Japan and the international community.[40] In contrast, the 2013 NSS described China as 'an issue of concern'. The documents also recognised Japan's counterstrike capabilities, which had previously been consistently denied by the government. Notably, these counterstrike capabilities were widely interpreted as aimed at China. The 2022 NSS also pledged to increase Japan's defence budget to realise both the fundamental reinforcement of defence capabilities and complementary initiatives, reaching 2 per cent of Japan's current GDP.[41] At the same time, Japanese public opinion toward Japan-China relations became more pessimistic, and they figured such relations were of less importance than previously. Since the mid-2000s, both sides have been assertedly working to improve bilateral ties. A 2013 poll by the Genron NPO (specifically

---

38   www.nikkei.com/article/DGXLZO05207340V20C16A7PE8000/ 2014.

39   www.worldvaluessurvey.org/wvs.jsp

40   National Security Strategy of Japan 2022.

41   National Security Strategy of Japan 2022.

focused on this bilateral relationship) demonstrated how badly the nations view each other.

Among Chinese respondents, 92.8 per cent viewed Japan unfavourably; meanwhile, 90.1 per cent of Japanese respondents held the same view of China. However, 72.3 per cent of the Chinese respondents and 74.1 per cent of Japanese respondents felt that Sino–Japanese relations were important;[42] indeed, more than 50 per cent of respondents from both countries stated that Sino–Japanese relations were more important than their relations with the US.[43] Ten years later, the 2023 poll showed that 62.9 per cent of Chinese respondents disliked Japan and 92.2 per cent of Japanese respondents disliked China; meanwhile, 60.2 per cent of Chinese respondents and 65.1 per cent of Japanese respondents replied that Sino–Japanese relations were important. Only 5.7 per cent of Japanese respondents replied that they viewed China as the most important country. Similarly, only 15 per cent of Chinese respondents replied that they viewed Japan as the most important country.

Further, 76 per cent of Japanese respondents perceived China as a threat, and 79.9 per cent did not want to visit China.[44] A poll conducted by Yomiuri Shimbun showed that 71 per cent supported enhanced defence capabilities, and 50 per cent supported the three strategic documents issued in 2024,[45] with 91 per cent recognising China as a threat to Japan.[46] Notably, mass demonstrations did not occur to protest the 2015 security legislation, the Kishida cabinet's major revisions to Japan's strategic and defence postures in 2022, or Japan's promise to purchase hundreds of long-range missiles from the US and even develop its production facilities. However, despite the high convergence of state and societal perceptions of China as a threat to Japan, Japan's diplomatic approach to China is still rooted in the desire to build a stable bilateral relationship.

5.2   Strategic Documents and Defence Policies

Prime Minister Kishida repeatedly mentioned the significance of peace and security in the Taiwan Strait and said that Japan would not tolerate changes to the status quo through force; this triggered fears of Japan's possible military involvement in a potential Taiwan crisis. Further, Kishida's response to the

---

42   Genron NPO 2013.
43   Genron NPO 2013, 13.
44   Genron NPO 2013.
45   www.yomiuri.co.jp/election/yoron-chosa/20240407-OYT1T50069/ 2024.
46   www.yomiuri.co.jp/election/yoron-chosa/20240407-OYT1T50069/ 2024.

Ukraine crisis – comprising robust economic sanctions against and condemnation of Russia – was swift and unprecedented, ending his predecessor's diplomatic relationship with Russia. It is useful to note that Kishida repeatedly mentioned that Ukraine might become East Asia: by connecting European and Asian security, Kishida situated China's harmful unilateral behaviours on its regional order.

In part due to the US encouragement, a trilateral cooperation mechanism between the US, Japan, and South Korea was established in 2022. On the sidelines of the East Asia Summit in Phnom Penh in November 2022, the leaders of the three countries promised to address the common challenges in the region, including the Taiwan issue and Chinese economic coercion.[47] The first Japan-US–Philippines summit was held in the US in 2024, and the nations' joint statement at the summit explicitly criticised China.[48]

However, Japan has also reassured China. Regarding Taiwan, Kishida told President Xi in San Francisco that Japan had not changed its position on the Taiwan question and that it remained aligned with the Japan-China Joint Statement.[49] In 2023, the problem of the contaminated water used to cool down melted fuel at the Fukushima Nuclear Plant emerged after the Japanese government decided to drain it into the ocean. The triple disaster of an earthquake, tsunami, and Fukushima Nuclear Plant meltdown led to the mass accumulation of contaminated water. A Chinese Foreign Ministry spokesman accused Japan of treating the ocean as its private sewer.

Interestingly, Japanese society has also questioned the Japanese government's decision in this matter. One societal academic organisation even compiled a report of more than 200 pages on the contaminated water, exposing the TEPCO's failure to address the problem.[50] Japan and China agreed to find ways to resolve the contaminated water issue at the Fukushima Nuclear Plant through constructive dialogue. At the San Francisco summit, both leaders agreed to promote a mutually beneficial relationship based on common strategic interests. The two leaders confirmed the broad path of building constructive and stable Japan-China relations to carve out a new era.[51]

---

47   'The Spirit of Camp David: Joint Statement of Japan, the Republic of Korea, and the United States' 2023.

48   Joint Vision Statement from the Leaders of Japan, the Philippines, and the United States' 2024.

49   Renmin Ribao 2023.

50   Research Group for Geological and Hydrogeological Issues of Fukushima Daiichi Nuclear Power Station 2021.

51   Japan-China Summit Meeting 2023.

In terms of Japan's counterstrike capabilities, which would enable it to deviate from its pacifist path, the 2022 NSS defines Japan's use of counterstrike capabilities as follows:

> Counterstrike capabilities fall within the purview of Japan's Constitution and international law; they do not change Japan's exclusively defence-oriented policy; and, they will be used only when the abovementioned Three New Conditions are fulfilled. Needless to say, preemptive strikes, namely striking first at a stage when no armed attack has occurred, remain impermissible.[52]

In this sense, the newly approved counterstrike capabilities are subject to the restrictions of the use of force overseas; namely, such force can only be implemented if Japan's survival is at stake, no other responses are possible, and it can only be implemented to the minimum necessary degree. It remains uncertain whether Japan may further loosen these restrictions and become a more typical military power in the future. While legally speaking, this change is possible, politically, societal restraints suggest that such developments will be incremental at best.

5.3   *Domestic Challenges and Societal Constraints*

'No war pacifism' remains a tremendously powerful societal restraint on Japan's security policy and diplomacy toward China. Japanese society seems to be much more receptive to and supportive of a stronger military, as public opinion surveys have shown. However, one survey showed that most respondents believe the current size of the SDF should be maintained, with nearly 70 per cent reporting that the SDF should not increase its activities overseas.[53] Along these lines, most Japanese people still primarily treat the SDF as a disaster relief force rather than a fighting army. A *Yomiuri Shimbun* public opinion survey conducted in June 2022 showed that only 15 per cent of respondents supported increasing defence expenditures by more than 2 per cent, while 32 per cent supported increases of 1–2 per cent. In contrast, 37 per cent stated that the status quo should be maintained, and 9 per cent believed that defence expenditures should be reduced.[54]

The SDF has been facing a recruitment shortage for years. The irony is that the more the government stresses the deteriorating security environment, the

---

52   Cabinet Secretariat 2022, 19.
53   Ministry of Defence 2023.
54   www.yomiuri.co.jp/election/sangiin/20220627-OYT1T50010/ 2022.

less young Japanese people want to join the SDF.[55] The essence of Japanese pacifism – non-involvement in war – remains intact. Along these lines, Japanese people logically want stable Sino–Japanese relations despite negative societal sentiments towards China. Is Japanese society genuinely ready for the costs of a great power rivalry in Asia? Is it ready to fight? I do not believe it is.

Today, Japan faces the profound problem of a declining population and is experiencing a demographic crisis. The Japanese fertility rate fell to a record low of 1.26 in 2022, declining for the seventh straight year.[56] The number of deaths was 1,568,961 in 2022. Meanwhile, the number of newborns in 2023 hit a record low of 770,747.[57] According to the latest government data, the number of Japanese nationals dropped by 837,000, reaching its lowest level in the 12 months ending October 2023.[58] The share of older adults (people over 65 years old) in the total population has reached a record high of 29.1 per cent.[59] Japan's ageing population is making it increasingly challenging to recruit new SDF members. Although the maximum age to join the SDF has been increased from 27 to 33,[60] the SDF remains unpopular among Japanese youth.

Furthermore, in a strong job market, the SDF must compete with civilian sectors to recruit young people. The ratio between candidates and job opportunities in Japan was 100 to 127 in January 2024,[61] causing the prime minister to warn that Japan was on 'the brink of being unable to maintain social functions'.[62] Young graduates will likely be reluctant to join the military, given the possible risk of military conflict and other employment opportunities. Furthermore, the SDF does not enjoy significant social respect compared to forces in other countries, such as the US and China, where forces enjoy benefits such as priority lanes in airports, special hotel rates, and no-toll fees. Therefore, there are limited incentives for Japanese youth to join the SDF – it is not a financially attractive or socially desirable choice.

In the fiscal year of 2021, there were more than 13,000 newly recruited SDF officers; however, these same 5,700 officers quit the SDF before the end of their terms.[63] The annual turnover rate in the SDF was 43 per cent in 2021,

---

55   www.tokyo-np.co.jp/article/268883.
56   Otake 2022.
57   Otake 2022; Japan Times
58   Financial Times 2024.
59   Financial Times 2024.
60   www.mod.go.jp/gsdf/jieikanbosyu/news/index.html.
61   Japan Institute for Labour Policy and Training.
62   Financial Times 2024.
63   www.tokyo-np.co.jp/article/253084 2023.

almost 1.7 times that of a decade ago. In the 2022 fiscal year, the SDF authorised force numbered 247,154 officers (the actual force comprised 227,843 officers), consisting of 150,500 in the Ground SDF (actual 137,024), 45,293 in the Maritime SDF (actual 43,106), 46,994 in the Air SDF (actual 43,694), and 4,367 in the Joint Staff Office (actual 4,019) divisions.[64] If the SDF wants to reach its targets, it needs to expand its current size by 7 per cent. In February 2019, Abe stated in the Lower House that 60 per cent of Japanese local governments did not cooperate to facilitate SDF recruitment, pointing out that only 36 per cent of local governments offered the personal information of the qualified candidates for joining the SDF. Abe further mentioned that this atmosphere would be vastly altered with the amendment of the constitution.[65] However, his remarks triggered severe criticism and concerns surrounding privacy rights violations due to the constitutional amendment.

Japanese political elites must grapple with the dilemma that, ironically, the biggest obstacle to transforming Japan into a normal country remains Japanese society. Although the polls indicate support for an active defence posture and a general dislike of China, the Japanese public finds it difficult to mobilise.[66] Japanese society's immobility is rooted in its deeply embedded pacifist refusal of war. Although Japan's pacifism has been repeatedly criticised as passive pacifism or *Ikkoku Heiwa Shyugi* (one country pacifism), Japanese society seems to be comfortable with its style of pacifism, which, as noted above, is characterised by a refusal of war and affirmation of personal freedom. The Japanese government's call for a 'proactive pacifism' is restrained by these strong societal norms.

This societal restraint also comes from Japanese academia, which has resisted the government's efforts to develop military technologies. Due to the scientific community's remorse over its past cooperation with Japanese war efforts, *Nihon Gakujyutsu Kaigi* (Science Council of Japan, SCJ), a major Japanese academic organisation established in 1949, stated in 1967 that it would never engage in scientific research for war or military purposes.[67] With the reinterpretation of the collective defence right and the introduction of the National Security Technology Research Promotion, Japanese academics began to worry about the emergence of military research in universities. In

64   www.mod.go.jp/j/profile/mod_sdf/kousei/.
65   Nihon Keizai Shimbun 2019.
66   George 1988, 237.
67   Science Council of Japan, www.scj.go.jp/ja/member/iinkai/anzenhosyo/pdf23/170204-youshi2.pdf.

response, the Science Council of Japan issued the Statement on Research for Military Security on 24 March 2017:[68]

> Past experience demonstrates that scientific research is often restricted or mobilised especially by political powers. Therefore, autonomy of re-search, especially the unrestricted publication of research results, must be guaranteed. However, for military security research, there exist con-cerns that government intervention in the activities of researchers might become stronger in regards to the direction of the research and the preservation of confidentiality during project periods and there-after.[69]

This statement shows that the Japanese academic circle remains firmly com-mitted to pacifism. Accordingly, the Japanese intellectual community remains unwilling to accept the government's national security-first logic. Human se-curity, which involves many dimensions of societal diplomacy, is clearly more compatible with the prevailing Japanese intellectual environment.[70]

A total of 109 individuals applied for funding from the National Security Technology Research Promotion initiative in the fiscal year of 2015, but this number dropped to 44 in 2016. The number of applications from universities in 2015 was 58, but this dropped to 23 in 2016. After the introduction of this funding program, many professors in Japanese universities organised a vari-ety of opposition movements to warn of the dangers of scientific research for military activities. In particular, their work to emphasise why it was impor-tant for scholars to refuse to engage in military research to the parents of current and future university students proved effective. In the end, universi-ties and faculty members recognised that applying for this funding would damage their reputations. National and local news reports on these opposi-tion movements also dramatically raised awareness of them in Japanese society. In sum, this funding program was perceived as a dangerous anti-pacifist initiative.[71] Accordingly, although the Japanese government warned the Japanese public of security dangers in East Asia during the Ukraine con-flict, we have not yet seen a dramatic increase in the number of applicants for this funding. In 2021, 2022, and 2023, 91, 102, and 119 researchers and 12, 11,

---

68   Science Council of Japan, www.scj.go.jp/ja/info/kohyo/pdf/kohyo-23-s243-en.pdf.
69   Science Council of Japan, www.scj.go.jp/ja/info/kohyo/pdf/kohyo-23-s243-en.pdf.
70   Daisaku 2017.
71   Ikeguchi 2017, 5–8.

and 23 universities applied for funding, respectively.[72] Many scholars remain deeply alarmed by the push for military technology research.[73]

The nuclear issue is another potentially contentious problem shaping Japan's diplomacy toward China. Abe called for debate around NATO-style nuclear sharing[74] against the background of increasing Japanese criticism of China's development of its nuclear arsenal. China immediately rebuked Abe's remarks, situating them as at odds with Japan's three non-nuclear principles[75] and as inconsistent with the obligations of a signatory member of the NPT.[76] Further, after Abe mentioned nuclear sharing, the ruling LDP Security Investigation Committee initiated a study session in March 2022. Three experts on nuclear sharing were invited to guide in this closed session; reportedly, they concluded that nuclear sharing would not have any real benefits and was not suitable for Japan. One of the three experts, Professor Yoko Iwama, also clearly warned in her book that introducing NATO-like sharing would not only require further work to ensure harmonisation with the NPT regime but also make the management of the US-Japan alliance more difficult.[77] Finally, the LDP Security Investigation Committee decided not to proceed with the idea of nuclear sharing.[78]

Meanwhile, the Japanese business circle also offers little support to the defence economy because many major Japanese enterprises worry that active involvement in the defence sector may damage their reputation. Additionally, unlike in the US, the defence sector in Japan does not produce many employment opportunities. The defence sector is also not well represented in the Japanese electoral politics. No political representatives in the Japanese Diet strongly support the defence sector – historically, prominent defence-related Diet members have not witnessed attractive career paths. For instance, Shigeru Ishibashi, the former Director of the Defence Agency and General Secretary of the ruling LDP, failed to be elected as the prime minister. Along these lines, the influence of the *Boeizoku* (defence-related Diet member group) in Japan's electoral politics has also been limited.

---

72   www.mod.go.jp/atla/funding/kadai.html

73   Ikeguchi 2017.

74   www3.nhk.or.jp/news/html/20220303/k10013511741000.html.

75   The Three Non-Nuclear Principles of not possessing, not producing, and not permitting the introduction of nuclear weapons were first introduced by *former* Prime Minister Eisaku Sato at the Budget Committee in the House of Representatives on 11 December 1967.

76   www.asahi.com/articles/ASQ2X7D98Q2XUHBI04W.html 2022.

77   Iwama 2023.

78   www.tokyo-np.co.jp/article/165962.

Local Japanese societies also serve as a powerful force in checking overly assertive security postures and overly hawkish policies towards China. It seems rational to argue that local societies would be more politically conservative and easily influenced by the central government on security and diplomatic issues. For instance, the Niigata Municipal Government was forced to halt a plan to sell city land to the Chinese Consulate General after locals opposed the deal following the 2010 Fishing Boat Collison Incident.[79] However, the societal dislike of China has not translated into a nationalistic movement supportive of the central government's security-related actions. Local Japanese societies are naturally suspicious that the central government may sacrifice local interests to pursue so-called 'national' interests in the name of national security. Notably, local newspapers in Japan are primarily considered left-leaning. Indeed, Matumoto highlighted how a local newspaper in Akita identified mistakes in materials provided by Japan's Ministry of Defence regarding the possible deployment of an Aegis Ashore land-based missile interception system as a shield against high-tech projectiles.[80] This system was said to be designed to deal with missile attacks from North Korea; however, it is widely believed that it was also aimed to address potential missile attacks from China. Local societies are fundamentally concerned about becoming the target of such attacks. Due to strong local opposition, the Japanese government scrapped the plan.[81]

Therefore, we are witnessing ambiguity in Japanese diplomacy toward China. On the one hand, the Kishida government formally identified China as Japan's 'unprecedented greatest strategic challenge'. On the other hand, when Kishida met with Xi in San Francisco on the sidelines of the APEC Summit in November 2023, he called for the comprehensive promotion of a 'Mutually Beneficial Relationship Based on Common Strategic Interests.'[82] The Chinese side also agreed with the Japanese wording of the broad goal of building constructive and stable Japan-China relations to carve out a new era in bilateral relations.[83] Chinese Ambassador to Japan Wu Jianghao affirmed the reported reintroduction of the wording 'comprehensively promoting Japan-China strategic mutual beneficial relations' in the 2024 Japan's Diplomatic

---

79   Matsutani 2010.
80   Matsumoto 2021, 13–51.
81   Teramoto 2020.
82   www.mfa.gov.cn/web/gjhdq_676201/gj_676203/yz_676205/1206_676836/xgxw_676842/
      202311/t20231117_11182335.shtml 2023.
83   www.mfa.gov.cn/web/gjhdq_676201/gj_676203/yz_676205/1206_676836/xgxw_676842/
      202311/t20231117_11182335.shtml 2023.

Blue Book.[84] This was the first such description in the most authoritative Japanese document on Japan-China relations in five years[85] and is a reassuring signal not only for China but also for Japanese society, as uncontrollable growing tensions with China may lead to conflict.

The Kishida government understood the concerns of Japanese society well. The section 'Reinforcing the Social Base' in Japan's latest National Security Strategy reads:

> Japan will consistently engage in efforts to deepen the understanding of and cooperation on national security among the people of Japan and organisations, inside and outside the Government, including local municipalities and corporate enterprises. Japan will also pay respect to other countries and their citizens, and foster love for its own country and homeland. In addition, Japan will further promote efforts to ensure that activities of the members of SDF and JCG, police officers, and others who dedicate themselves to hazardous duties for the peace and security of Japan be appropriately appreciated across its society. Furthermore, measures will be taken to ensure understanding and cooperation of residents living near security-related facilities, which form the basis for the activities of these personnel.[86]

6   Conclusion

Existing studies on how society impacts foreign policy are limited. Indeed, society has been traditionally perceived as relatively irrelevant to foreign policymaking, particularly in the field of high politics, such as security policy. This article introduces the theoretical concept of the internal societisation of diplomacy to identify the linkage between the state and society. In particular, it explores this concept through a study of Japanese diplomacy toward China. Several theoretical and empirical conclusions can be drawn from the above analysis.

First, the internal societisation of diplomacy is rooted in the construction of a political community through political integration. The advancement of the political integration of the state and society – and, in turn, their political

---

84   Embassy of the People's Republic of China in Japan, www.jp.china-embassy.gov.cn/sgkxnew/202403/t20240329_11273610.htm 2024.

85   www.nikkei.com/article/DGXZQOUA217310R20C24A3000000/ 2024.

86   National Security Strategy 2022, 34.

community – is positively related to the coherence of diplomacy. Notably, Karl Deutsch described political integration as a dynamic process[87] and highlighted the role of political appeal in the political community. The Japanese case analysed above shows that the Japanese government has not yet convinced Japanese society to support a rearmament program in response to the 'China threat' (even though most Japanese people perceive China as a potential threat) and related amendments to Japan's pacifist Constitution. Generally, Japanese society has been concerned with the excessive military commitments and burdens pushed by reckless and irresponsible politicians. Such 'disintegrative conditions'[88] (as conceptualised by Deutsch) prevent political integration in Japan.

Second, during the process of political integration, political elites need to echo general societal norms regarding diplomacy and international relations to ensure their political survival. As the analysis shows, any ambitious politician in Japan needs to develop a diplomatic approach to China that balances a resolute stance toward China's assertiveness with nuanced pragmatism. Otherwise, societal fears that failed diplomacy may spark a war with China and erode civil liberties and freedoms may prevent the politician from gaining societal support. Ishihara's failed attempts to gain support by stirring anti-Chinese sentiment and calling for a hostile policy toward China proved counter-productive to political ambitions. Meanwhile, Abe's Yasukuni visit showed that an extreme hawkish attitude toward China may cause Japanese society to worry about the loss of peace. Abe understood this sentiment and accordingly adjusted his China policy by pragmatically seeking to stabilise bilateral relations. Against this background, Abe could not firmly push the constitutional amendments – he had to take societal concerns seriously to prevent voters from punishing the ruling LDP in the next election, hurting his popularity in the party. Faced with the choice between extending his office and making a rapid constitutional amendment, Abe took the approach of a realistic pragmatist and chose the former. More broadly, the hawkishness of other conservative politicians has contributed to their electoral defeats. Future politicians should accordingly avoid such extreme diplomatic stances and instead balance desires to assertively deal with China against desires to stabilise Japan's relations with China.

Third, political communications regarding diplomacy designed to appeal to the public (as highlighted by Deutsch) should be based on pragmatic rather

---

87   Deutsch 1957, 70.
88   Deutsch 1957, 59.

than radical ideologies, as society may meet the latter with suspicion and concerns. Societal understanding is vital for sustainable diplomacy. Despite being a compelling politician, Abe could only realise his political agenda at the expense of his popularity. Although the Japanese public recognised the 'China threat', it was deeply disturbed that Abe's potentially reckless actions may trigger a war or damage civil liberties if legal restraints were fully lifted. In contrast, Abe's pragmatic diplomatic stance and domestic political communications regarding China after 2014 solidified his political standing as a sophisticated diplomatic politician. They partially contributed to his long tenure as prime minister. Along these same lines, Prime Minister Kishida also understood that a more active and assertive security posture requires societal support. Although he actively promotes the so-called 'China challenge theory' internationally, Kishida has pursued a pragmatic approach to Japan's relationship with China.

In sum, the so-called 'China threat' is not enough to change the very nature of the disintegration of the state–society relationship in Japan, which moderates Japan's diplomacy towards China. In light of the current situation, future Japanese diplomacy towards China will likely be characterised by a mixture of rhetorical hawkishness (combined with a desire to enhance capabilities) and pragmatism.

Acknowledgements

This research was supported by JSPS-Kakenhi 21KK0229

Bibliography

Allison, Graham. *Essence of Decision: Explaining the Cuban Missile Crisis* (Boston: Little, Brown and Company, 1971).

Acquisition, Technology, and Logistics Agency, www.mod.go.jp/atla/funding/kadai.html

Bush, Richard C. *The Perils of Proximity: China–Japan Security Relations* (Washington, DC: The Brookings Institution, 2010).

Daisaku, Higashi. *Nigenno Anzen Hosho to Hewakochiku* (Human Security and Peace Making) (Tokyo: Nihon Hyoronsha, 2017).

Dayong, Niu. 'The Consideration and Trial of Strength over the Issue of Japan in the Period of the Thawing of Relationship between China and the United States.' *American Studies* 5 (2014).

Deutsch, Karl. *Political Community and the North American Area: International Organization in the Light of Historical Experience* (Princeton and New Jersey: Princeton University Press, 1957). Embassy of the People's Republic of China in Japan, jp. china-embassy.gov.cn/ztnew/dydnew/zhongfanglichangnew/201210/t20121027_94 74697.htmEmbassy of the People's Republic of China in Japan. www.jp.china-embassy.gov.cn/sgkxnew/202403/t20240329_11273610.htm www.nikkei.com/article/DGXZQOUA217310R20C24A3000000/embassy.gov.cn/jpn/zrdt_1/201411/t20141107_10433663.htm

Financial Times, 13 April 2024.

Genron NPO. *The 9th Japan–China Joint Public Opinion Survey*, October 2023.https://www.genron-npo.net/world/archives/16585-2.html www.jp.china-embassy.gov.cn/sgkxnew/202403/t20240329_11273610.htm

George, Aurelia. 'Japan and the United States: Dependent Ally or Equal Partner?' In *Dynamic and Immobilist: Politics in Japan* eds A.A. Stockwin and Alan Rix, Aurelia George, James Horne, Daiichi Ito and Martin Collick. (Science Council of Japan, 1988).

Gotz, Norbert. *Deliberative Diplomacy: The Nordic Approach to Global Governance and Societal Representation at the United Nations* (Dordrecht: Republic of Letters Publishing BV, 2011).

Huijgh, Ellen. *Public Diplomacy at Home: Domestic Dimensions* (Leiden: Brill Nijhoff University Press, 2019).

Ikeguchi, Satoru. *Kagakusya to Gunjikenkyu* (Scientists and the Military Research) (Tokyo: Iwanami, 2017).

Iwama, Yoko. *Kakukyoyu no Genjitsu: NATO no Keiken to Nihon* (Tokyo: Shinyama Sha, 2023).

Japan External Trade Organization, *Japan-China Trade 2019*, www.jetro.go.jp/biz/area reports/2020/7a3c80fbbd73f456.html

Japan Institute for Labour Policy and Training, www.jil.go.jp/kokunai/statistics/shuyo/0210.html www.tokyo-np.co.jp/article/253084

Japan-China Summit Meeting, Renmin Ribao (People's Daily, overseas version), 16 November 2023.

Jervis, Robert. *Perception and Misperception in International Politics* (New Jersey: Princeton University Press, 1976).

Jervis, Robert, Lebow, Richard Ned and Stein, Janice Gross. *Psychology and Deterrence* (Baltimore and London: The Johns Hopkins University Press, 1985).

Kamau, Macharia, Chasek, Pamela and O'Connor, David. *Transforming Multilateral Diplomacy: The Inside Story of the Sustainable Goals* (London and New York: Routledge, 2018).

Kaufmann, Jonah. *Conference Diplomacy: An Introductory Analysis* (London: Macmillan Press LTD, 1996).

Kyodo News Agency, 26 April 2014.

Marchetti, Raffaele. *City Diplomacy: From City-states to Global Cities* (Michigan: University of Michigan, 2021).

Matsumoto, Hajimu. *Chiho Media no Gyakushu* (The Counter-strike of the Local Media) (Tokyo: Chikuma, 2021).

Matsutani, Minoru. 'Niigata halts plan to sell plot for consulate amid outcry'. Japan Times. 20 November 2010. www.japantimes.co.jp/news/2010/11/20/national/nii gata-halts-plan-to-sell-plot-for-consulate-amid-outcry/

McCormic, James M. 'The Domestic Sources of American Foreign Policy: Insights and Evidence' In *Linkage Politics*, ed. James Rosenau (Toronto: The Free Press, 1969).

Melissen, Jan. 'Public Diplomacy.' In *Diplomacy in a Globalizing World: Theories and Practices*, eds. Pauline Kerr and Geoffrey Wiseman, eds. (New York: Oxford University Press, 2018).

MFA, http://www.fmprc.gov.cn/mfa_eng/xwfw_665399/s2510_665401/t1170401.shtml

Milner, Helen V. *Interests, Institutions, and Information: Domestic Politics and International Relations* (Princeton, NJ: Princeton University Press, 1997).

Ministry of Defence, www.mod.go.jp/gsdf/jieikanbosyu/news/index.html

Ministry of Defence, www.clearing.mod.go.jp/hakusho_data/2023/html/ns076000.html

Ministry of Foreign Affairs, People's Republic of China, www.mfa.gov.cn/web/gjhdq_676201/gj_676203/yz_676205/1206_676836/xgxw_676842/202311/t20231117_11182335.shtml

Ministry of Foreign Ministry of Japan. 'Chinese Economy and Japan-China Economic Relations' www.mofa.go.jp/mofaj/files/000007735.pdf.

National Security of Japan, December 2022.https://www.cas.go.jp/jp/siryou/221216an zenhoshou/nss-e.pdf

NHK, www3.nhk.or.jp/news/html/20220303/k10013511741000.html

Nihon Keizai Shimbun, 24 April 2020.

Nihon Keizai Shimbun, 5 April 2013.

Nikkei Shimbun, 4 July 2014.

Nihon Keizai Shimbun, 26 May 2014.

Nikkei Shimbun, 2 February 2014.

Nikkei Shimbun, 29 September 2014

Nihon Keizai Shimbun, 13 February 2019.

Otake, Tomoko. 'Japan's fertility rate matches record low as it drops for seventh consecutive year.' Japan Times. 02 June 2023 www.japantimes.co.jp/news/2023/06/02/national/2022-birthrate-record-low/.

Prime Minister's Office of Japan, http://www.kantei.go.jp/jp/96_abe/statement/2014/0701kaiken.html

Prime Minister of Japan and his Cabinet. 'Remarks by Prime Minister Abe to the Australian Parliament'. 8 July 2014. http://japan.kantei.go.jp/96_abe/statement/201407/0708article1.html

Renmin Ribao (People's Daily, overseas version). 18 November 2023.

Research Group for Geological and Hydrogeological Issues of Fukushima Daiichi Nuclear Power Station, *Geological and Hydrogeological Issues of Fukushima Daiichi Nuclear Power Station*, The Association for the Geological for the Geological Collaboration in Japan. July 2021.

Rosecrance, Richard and Stein, Arthur A. *The Domestic Bases and Grand Strategy* (Ithaca and London: Cornell University Press, 1993).

Rosenau, James. N. *Along the Domestic Foreign Frontier Exploring Governance in a Turbulent World* (Cambridge, Cambridge University Press, 1997).

Science Council of Japan. 'Statement on Research for Military Security'. 24 March 2017. www.scj.go.jp/ja/info/kohyo/pdf/kohyo-23-s243-en.pdf

Sebastian, Grazia. *Political Community* (Chicago: University of Chicago Press, 1948).

Solis, Mireya. *Japan's Quiet Leadership, Reshaping the Indo-Pacific* (Washington DC: Brookings Institution Press, 2023).

Teramoto, Jdaizo. 'Japan gives up plan to deploy Aegis system at Akita GSDF site'. 7 May 2020. www.asahi.com/ajw/articles/13355944

The White House. 'The Spirit of Camp David: Joint Statement of Japan, the Republic of Korea, and the United States.' 18 August 2023. www.whitehouse.gov/briefing-room/statements-releases/2023/08/18/the-spirit-of-camp-david-joint-statement-of-japan-the-republic-of-korea-and-the-united-states/

The White House, www.whitehouse.gov/briefing-room/statements-releases/2024/04/11/joint-vision-statement-from-the-leaders-of-japan-the-philippines-and-the-united-states/

'Tokyo to buy disputed islands, says Governor Ishihara'. BBC. 17 October 2012. https://www.bbc.com/news/world-asia-17747934

TV Asahi, www.tv-asahi.co.jp/hst_archive/poll/201401/index.html

US Embassy in Japan. '*Statement on Prime Minister Abe's December 26 Visit to Yasukuni Shrine*'. December 26 2013. http://japan.usembassy.gov/e/p/tp-20131226-01.html

Waltz, Kenneth. *Man, State, and War* (New York: Columbia University Press, 1959). www.clair.or.jp/j/exchange/shimai/countries/detail/13 www.nikkei.com/article/DGXLZO05207340V20C16A7PE8000/ www.worldvaluessurvey.org/wvs.jsp www.yomiuri.co.jp/election/sangiin/20220627-OYT1T50010/ www.tokyo-np.co.jp/article/268883 www.asahi.com/articles/ASQ2X7D98Q2XUHBI04W.html www.yomiuri.co.jp/election/yoron-chosa/20240407-OYT1T50069/ www.mod.go.jp/j/profile/mod_sdf/kousei/ www.tokyo-np.co.jp/article/165962

Yamaguchi, Jiro and Nakakita, Koji. *Minshyutou Senken towa Nan Dattanoka?* (What was the DPJ Government?), (Tokyo: Iwanami, 2014).

Zhang, Yun. *Sino-Japanese Relations in a US-China-Japan Trilateral Context: The Origins of Misperception* (New York: Palgrave Macmillan, 2017). was the DPJ Government?), (Tokyo: Iwanami, 2014).

Zhang, Yun. *Sino-Japanese Relations in a US-China-Japan Trilateral Context: The Origins of Misperception* (New York: Palgrave Macmillan, 2017).

CHAPTER 7

Diplomacy and People: Contrasting Cases of the Two Koreas' People-Empowerment Approaches to Diplomacy

HwaJung Kim

Summary

This chapter aims for a better understanding of domestic-public engagement in contemporary diplomacy. By comparing two contrasting cases of domestic-public engagement in diplomacy, namely the *Arirang* Mass Games of North Korea (an authoritarian country) and the Participatory Diplomacy Center of South Korea (a democratic country), the chapter seeks to answer the question: what makes for the distinctive characteristics of citizen participation in diplomacy in these two very different political contexts? To that end, a conceptual framework was developed by employing Empower Theory, and the two cases were analysed in terms of self-efficacy, knowledge, and competence. It was found that, while knowledge predetermines each country's diplomatic performance, self-efficacy and competence define that country's distinctive characteristics, according to the liberal or illiberal context. North Korea's highly effective performance, driven by the state's power *over* people, intensifies the government-people isomorphism, which, in turn, results in people's disengagement from the country's foreign policy or global issues. This suggests that an engaged citizenry of an illiberal state can be seen as a means of coercion to force the general public's sacrifice for the country's survival. Contrastingly, South Korea's evolution of a diplomatic system enhancing the state's "power *with/from* people" facilitates the government/people alignment, which further facilitates people's engagement with, and support for, the country's foreign policy and global issues. This implies that the existence of an engaged citizenry of a liberal country might mean that the general public should be informed and empowered through autonomous citizen participation.

Keywords

Citizen participation in diplomacy – people-empowerment approach to diplomacy – North Korea's *Arirang* Mass Games – South Korea's Participatory Diplomacy Center

1 Introduction

The recent critical re-visitation of the practices of diplomatic engagement with the ordinary people of the home country has examined many empirical cases in various contexts. South Korea (i.e., the Republic of Korea, ROK)'s establishment of the Participatory Diplomacy Center in 2018 reflects how democratic advancement and the first presidential impeachment in history (as initiated by public protests due to political scandals in 2016) can shape new dynamics in various fields of public policy, including diplomacy, in terms of citizens' aspirations and eagerness for participation. This is the first attempt to institutionalise citizen participation in the country's diplomatic practices and foreign-policy decision-making process. South Korea's case tells us that a higher degree of democracy may push public participation forward, since a democratic mode of governance allows for the involvement of a variety of actors and organizations in the public realm. But is democracy the prerequisite for people's engagement in diplomacy? Not necessarily.

North Korea (i.e., the Democratic People's Republic of Korea, DPRK), one of the most authoritarian countries in the world, has already shown citizen participation in diplomacy, such as through the Arirang Mass Games since the early 2000s – which are among the most spectacular gymnastics and performing arts events in the world, having been listed in the Guinness Book of Records (2007) and enshrined as Intangible Cultural Heritage of Humanity by UNESCO (2014). In terms of the total number of participants and their effectiveness as a diplomatic performance, the Arirang Mass Games must be considered to be one of the best diplomatic practices in terms of the number of the engaged people and their aspirations for being part of a national performance. In fact, North Korea's Games enable us to understand why and how an authoritarian country can conduct more effective public-engagement-driven diplomacy than many other, democratic countries.[1] It raises the critical issue of socio-political context, which is to say, of whether an authoritarian or dem-

---

1 Arirang Mass Games are often seen as domestic affairs to educate the mass public, which comes from lopsided views on North Korea. The Games clearly have dual purposes: targeting a domestic audience for propaganda education as well as sending diplomatic messages to an international audience by broadcasting the event and accepting foreign visitors in order to project who they are and what they stand for, similar to mega sporting events. This study concentrates on how the Mass Games have transformed ordinary individuals into agents of diplomacy.

ocratic governance system can more significantly affect diplomacy's public
dimension when allowing ordinary individuals to become involved.

This chapter aims to answer the question of what makes for the distinctive
characteristics of domestic-public engagement as pursued in the different political contexts of the two Koreas in order to more clearly perceive, through
the lens of people empowerment, the phenomenon of citizen participation in
foreign affairs and international relations. In so doing, it also examines the
different national role conceptions prevailing in the relevant two types of governance system, democracy and non-democracy, under which leaders seek to
gain legitimacy. This approach, in turn, will allow us to contribute to our
knowledge of citizen participation in diplomacy and, on that basis perhaps,
to identify future trends in diplomatic practice taking into account domestic
state-society dynamics.

In the following Section 2, the research surrounding existing literatures
related to the topic, Empower Theory, power dynamics, and people empowerment is reviewed to provide a conceptual framework within which the factors driving the mechanism of citizen participation in diplomacy can be better
understood. In Section 3, to examine the phenomenon, this chapter conducts
an analysis of North Korea's Arirang Mass Games and South Korea's Participatory Diplomacy Center by comparing and contrasting the two cases in their
respective dimensions. The final Section 4 unfolds the present findings in
order to galvanise our understandings of the different political contexts' differing characteristics and what they mean for a citizenry engaged in diplomatic affairs.

2   People Empowerment Process for Diplomacy at Home

The logic of the two-level game between diplomacy and domestic politics,
argued by Putnam,[2] laid the foundation for the foreign policy decision-
making process and further developed into the balance of domestic against
international concerns,[3] and is regarded as conventional wisdom in diplomatic studies. However, it does not clearly elucidate the power dynamics between the domestic public and policy decision makers (mostly high officials,
diplomats, ministers, and heads of state) at home because of its preconcep-
tions, concerning agents as rational actors, based on game theory. The two-
level game lacks in explaining how emotional factors affect foreign policy be-

---

2   Putnam 1988.
3   Evans, Jacobson, and Putnam 1993.

haviour. The concept of "new" public diplomacy, developed by Melissen,[4] contributes to the "public" dimension of diplomacy to a certain degree, but it still posits an outward-looking diplomacy that has *foreign* publics as its primary subjects.

Traditional diplomacy focusing on diplomat-to-diplomat interactions in political and state contexts has evolved over time, migrating towards new fields, formats, and actors, such as unattached diplomats in civil society diplomacy.[5] The emergence of individuals as diplomatic agents requires new approaches by which nuanced understandings of contemporary diplomacy can be gained. Significantly in this regard, Gregory defines public diplomacy as "an instrument used by states, associations of states, and some sub-state and non-state actors to understand cultures, attitudes, and behaviour; build and manage relationships; and influence thoughts and mobilise actions to advance their interests and values".[6] This definition may facilitate an understanding of why and how human relations became relevant to the practice of diplomacy.

The necessity of a holistic mode of public engagement based on the domestic-international nexus in the extensive realm of public diplomacy, as argued by Huijgh,[7] often fails to explain the emotional dimensions of diplomacy, largely due to the traditional assumptions about public diplomacy, which properly is network-based, as "public affairs", with its vertical relation between ministries of foreign affairs (MFAs) and the domestic public. Noteworthy in this regard are South Koreans' 2008 protests against US beef imports due to Bovine Spongiform Encephalopathy (BSE), the so-called "mad cow disease" affecting US cattle, which aggravated the anti-American sentiment that had already harmed Korea-US bilateral relations under the Free Trade Agreement.[8]

This event shows how domestic public emotion can play a significant role in diplomacy by challenging a nation-state's power and authority over the foreign policy decision-making process. The recent academic discourse of realists, by positing emotion as an essential element of rationality, presents a new perspective on rational choice assumptions or public rationality.[9] In fact, by examining emotion in a broader context, this discourse helps to clarify

---

4 Melissen 2005; 2011.
5 Anton 2023; Ang et al., 2015.
6 Gregory 2015, 3.
7 Huijgh 2013.
8 Yonhap 2008.
9 Mearsheimer and Rosato 2023.

citizen participation in diplomacy as a wider process of power relations among members of society. Meanwhile, the application of emotion in public diplomacy, as Graham's study suggests,[10] emphasises both cognition and emotion from a constructivist view, but it does not necessarily relate to the social dimensions of diplomacy. Then, what can explain the emerging phenomenon extending beyond the new public diplomacy conception?

It turns out that domestic engagement in diplomatic practices can be interpreted in terms of various concepts, such as the new dialogue format used by foreign ministries in communicating with citizens, the general public's participation in international dialogue, the "societization" of diplomacy, municipal twinning relationships, citizen diplomacy, grassroots diplomacy, and social diplomacy.[11] There is a thread that connects these various concepts and practices to diplomacy. Diplomacy now deals with social interactions in the home country, seen as a social practice[12] in dealing with cognition and emotion, which makes the study more relevant to the notion of empowerment entailing social relations through power dynamics. Indeed, recent studies answered the question of why the smallest units of society matter in diplomacy and illuminated the higher degree of democracy that contributes to people's engagement. This provides us with political implications about the rise of participatory democracy and its high correlation with citizen participation in diplomacy. However, there is an exception. An authoritarian country such as North Korea has also shown excellent skills in mobilising people, organising and upscaling international events through citizen participation, providing engaged citizens with privileged treatment, and achieving the country's diplomatic goals thereby. It is imperative to look through the lens of empowerment in analysing the domestic dimension of diplomacy and to discover the distinctive characteristics of liberal versus illiberal state systems.

The present study explored the explanatory value of Empower Theory through a pilot study involving interviews conducted in 2021 on participatory diplomacy in South Korea.[13] The practitioners emphasised that initiatives of the People Diplomacy Center in the beginning, by providing a platform from which people's voices could be heard, signalled the power transition from

---

10   Graham's 2014.

11   Kim and Melissen 2022.

12   Faizullaev 2022.

13   I conducted face-to-face in-depth interviews with one director general at MOFA, six director-level officers at MOFA, and one congressman at the National Assembly, with anonymity guaranteed, from January to November 2021 as part of a co-research project with Jan Melissen (Principle Investigator).

government to citizens. In a similar vein, a documentary film, *A State of Mind*, explains that those youth performers who had been selected as the main performers of the Arirang Mass Games were able to get special treatment and rewards from the government, which enhanced their self-confidence and increased their family's solidarity and loyalty to the country in return. This power dimension is rarely studied in terms of diplomacy's public dimension or governance. But empowerment of the powerless, regardless of the mode of governance, is the common denominator of the phenomenon of participatory diplomacy.[14] Also, it provides some explanatory power in terms of the psychological aspects of people's behaviours as agents of diplomacy.

Such psychological theory as it relates to empowerment enabled the current study to delve into the cognitive dimensions of both rational choice and emotion as applied to diplomacy and to fill the literature gap regarding domestic state-society power dynamics. Cattaneo and Chapman developed the Empowerment Process Model (EPM) as an iterative process instrumental to Empower Theory.[15] EPM, incorporating both individual and broad levels of social relations into the mechanisms of power dynamics, enables us to understand how, for example, individuals relative to bureaucratic authorities gain power and dominance as well as how the empowerment process of each individual who wants to increase their influence in a certain social context is facilitated. The EPM is based on such characteristics of empowerment as mastery, participation, promotion of the social good, goal achievement, and a nomological network, gathering lawful evidence for construct validation, in which to achieve prosocial action, such as empathy for others, and social justice values. According to the EPM, any level of human interaction, from interpersonal relationships to the relationship between a person and a system, is affected by an increase of one's power as well as an increase of one's influence, which process entails constant interaction between an individual and a society.

---

14   The distinction between governance and diplomacy has been extensively studied by prominent scholars in diplomacy studies. Governance can be understood at both international and domestic levels. In this study, it needs to be focused on "governance at the domestic level" as both cases are more relevant to domestic-public's participation in institutionalised diplomacy activities. The study follows Boas' definition, "governance is concerned with the regime which constitutes the set of fundamental rules for the organization of the public realm, and not with government... Governance clearly embraces government institutions, but it also subsumes informal, non-governmental institutions operating within the public realm (cited in Weiss 2000, 800)."

15   Cattaneo and Chapman 2010.

Empowerment can be defined as "an iterative process in which a person who lacks power sets a personally meaningful goal-oriented [*sic*] toward increasing power, takes action toward that goal, and observes and reflects on the impact of this action, drawing on his or her evolving self-efficacy, knowledge, and competence related to the goal".[16] Although this chapter agrees with this definition, there is a need to take the characteristics of diplomacy into consideration, since citizen engagement in diplomacy has already occurred on the ground; thus, herein, an attempt is made to modify the EPM by taking it as the foundation of the present analysis of people empowerment in the realm of diplomacy.

Cattaneo and Chapman's conception of the EPM has three, intersecting layers: the first layer at the core comprises self-efficacy (the motivation hub), knowledge (understanding of context), and competence (skills), which are the primary ways that individuals gain mastery over their affairs; the second layer in the middle has three dimensions – meaningful, power-oriented GOALS, ACTIONS toward goal achievement, and IMPACT of actions (emphasis original) – which make it possible for a person to change their social influence through human interactions; the third layer, called social context, subsumes the first and second layers, providing a structure for participation, influencing the entire process in either a facilitative or constraining way, and forwarding goal achievement and the social good. The whole process is nonlinear and far more interactive among the three layers and their respective elements; thus, the realization of empowerment evolves over time and reflects any type of transformation occurring in a given societal context.

As illustrated in Figure 7.1, this chapter applies the EPM to diplomacy, treating ordinary citizens as the domestic public. From the perspective of public policy, "social context", the first, all-subsuming layer, is already given to an individual in the form of the sovereign state's political system ("democratic" or "authoritarian"). Accordingly, this layer of the EPM predetermines the other two. The second layer, "diplomatic practice" as led by MFAs, central governments, or heads of state, includes the components "goals", "actions" and "impacts". At this stage, different national role conceptions can be held by different types of governments as a means of legitimization.[17] As role theory is rooted in social psychology and micro-sociology, the social behaviour of individuals, such as national leaders and foreign policy elites, and national identity determined by the ego and the alter, must be considered in the policy

16   Cattaneo and Chapman 2010, 647.

17   Cantir and Kaarbo 2012, 8.

formulation process of a state's behaviour.[18] In addition, foreign perceptions and public opinion, both domestically and globally, are also considered major determinants of a country's appropriate role through the foreign policy decision-making process, which is a constant process of interaction between international expectations and domestic constraints.[19] The third layer, the "people empowerment process" (including the components "self-efficacy", "knowledge", and "competence") is a result of both the "social context" (a "democratic" or "authoritarian" political system – the first layer) and "diplomatic practice" ("goals", "actions", and "impacts" – the second layer).

As again illustrated in Figure 7.1, there are two main sequence scenarios possible: 1) the path "*without* the people", taken, in the manner of conventional diplomacy, to maximise national interests, or 2) a path via the "people empowerment process", as practised as part of the contemporary diplomatic affairs of certain countries. Considering that "diplomacy is an instrument of statecraft",[20] it could be insisted that both of these scenarios emphasise the power and influence of diplomacy for various types of desired outcomes in terms of foreign policy effectiveness, which completes the conceptual framework for domestic people empowerment in diplomacy. From this perspective, after incorporating power dynamics discourses[21] into this framework, the result of the first scenario (without public engagement) can be associated with a state's diplomatic "power *without* people" (statecraft diplomacy unrelated to people); and the latter scenario (with domestic-public engagement) will have

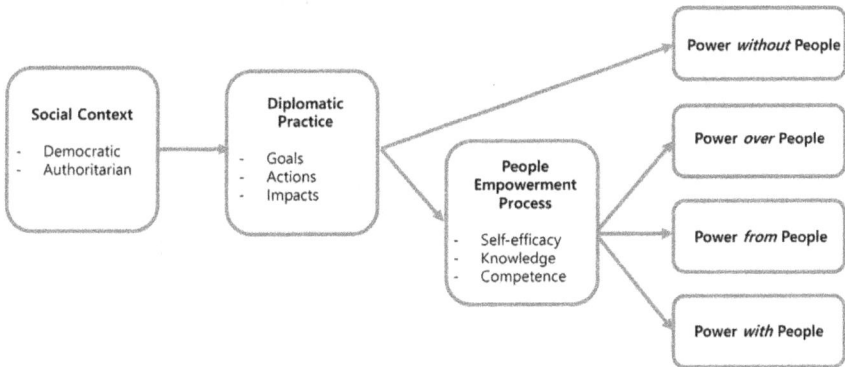

FIGURE 7.1   Conceptual framework for (domestic) people empowerment in diplomacy with desired outcomes

---

18   Grossman 2005, 335–337.
19   Kim 2020, 598.
20   Freeman 2023, 41.
21   Riger 1993; Blanchard, Carlos, and Randolph 1999.

three types of desired outcomes: 1) a state's diplomatic "power *over* people" (dominance, hierarchical relationships between a state and people), 2) a state's diplomatic "power *from* people" (a state's ability to conduct diplomacy reflecting an increase of influence of people through a bottom-up process), or 3) a state's diplomatic "power *with* people" (a state's ability to conduct diplomacy by sharing "power *with* people" based on mutual trust, requiring a delicate balance of responsibility and freedom). In the following section, this framework will be tested by comparing two contrasting cases: North Korea's Arirang Mass Games, a success story for an authoritarian country that captured global attention, and South Korea's Participatory Diplomacy Center, an equally successful case for a democratic country that made the institutionalization[22] of citizen participation in diplomacy possible.

3   Comparative Case Study: North Korea versus South Korea

3.1   *North Korea's Arirang Mass Games*
The only country still divided by the imperial forces of the Cold War in the 20th century is Korea. North Korea's state behaviour with Stalinist communist ideology, utilising nuclear threats as diplomatic tools,[23] became one of the biggest challenges to world peace. Investigating North Korea's citizen engagement in diplomacy provides added value to this chapter, as the country's ordinary people have heretofore been hidden under secrecy due to the monopoly on coercive power enjoyed by their leaders in the "modern theater state", a phrase that best describes contemporary North Korea.[24] North Korea is an authoritarian country categorised as "Not Free" by Freedom House, having received a score of 0 out of 40 in the index of Political Rights and just 3 out of 60 in that of Civil Liberties in that organization's 2023 report.[25] North Korea is led by a dynastic totalitarian dictatorship with the one-party political structure of *Rodongdang* (the Workers' Party of Korea or WPK); it utilises a political ideology known as *Juche* (self-reliance), the deification of the Kim family, the *Songbun* system (the socio-political classification of the populace, which will

---

22   The term *institutionalization* connotes the process of an institutions' creation of social knowledge and (to some extent) predictable social behaviours as well as their provision of stability and meaning to those behaviours through cognitive, normative, and regulative structures and activities, as argued by Wolf (2005, 185); therefore, it can be understood as "institutionalized frameworks in public administration."
23   Buzo 2021.
24   Kwon and Chung 2012, 45.
25   Freedomhouse.org 2023a.

be further explained in the following section), and forced labour to achieve its political agenda.[26] The cult of the Kims, namely Great Leader Kim Il-sung (1948–1994), Dear Leader Kim Jung-il (1994–2011, the founder's son), and Supreme Leader Kim Jung-un (2012–current, the founder's grandson), has sustained the country's survival as a communist country over the last 70 years and enabled each leader to pursue "power *without* people". Nevertheless, through diplomatic channels, North Korea has featured its ordinary citizens in schemes conceived to demonstrate itself to be a socialist paradise, released positive images of their wholesome or modern lifestyle, or showcased the country's great achievements, such as nuclear weapons at a military parade, with large crowds of people enthusiastically participating. In both cases of with and without people empowerment, North Korea's political ideology as a socialist country has determined the country's foreign policy behaviours.

The Arirang Mass Games or the Arirang Festival, including Mass Gymnastics and Artistic Performance,[27] operated by the Cultural Bureau of the Propaganda and Agitation Department (PAD, a department of the Central Committee of *Rodongdang*), is a large-scale gymnastics display accompanied by music, dance, and acrobatics that represents the country's successful diplomatic performance in showing huge numbers of citizens engaged in one single event, ran from 2002 until 2013. The Mass Games, referred to as one of the most spectacular forms of socialist-realist cultural expression, include nationalistic contents and themes, Western musical and theatrical concepts, and typically, 100,000 nationals as participants.[28] They show how the domestic public can be mobilised by the PAD for the purpose of national events.

The Arirang Mass Games enabled North Korea to achieve its goal (to project an image of the country as a utopian paradise), action (citizen participation in diplomacy projection), and impact (global attention), all contributing to the country's promotion of its cultural products to foreign publics. Firstly, the storytelling of North Korea as a utopian paradise was vividly shown in the lyrics of songs and dances as well as in written messages, both on "living screens",[29] whereby schoolchildren operated large flipbooks, and electronic screens to announce the progress of the Mass Games and display the title of the song ("Arirang"). The Arirang Mass Games, rooted in Kim Il-sung's Mass Games in 1946 which copied Stalinist displays, was the cultural model not only

---

26   Kim 2022, 13.
27   Jeon 2011.
28   Burnett 2013.
29   Living screens refer to changing screens made up of actual human beings, according to
      the paper held by the participants.

for Kim Jong-il (the actual Arirang performances in 2002, 2005, and thereafter annually since 2007), but also for Kim Jong-un, who took power in late 2011. Describing the country as utopian paradise became a consistent message to both domestic and international audiences.

Secondly, the Arirang Mass Games brought about a great amount of citizen participation in conducting mass gymnastics and performances. They took place in the 150,000-seat May Day Stadium in Pyongyang, and at least 16,240 schoolchildren in seating areas were involved in forming the living screens by holding 200-page flipbooks to show one page for each picture of the performance.[30] The total number of annual participants, including the children, was estimated to be up to 100,000 citizens.[31] The diplomacy projection of the Arirang Mass Games became a successful state-led action of citizen engagement.

Lastly, its impact went viral globally and captured global attention. The Arirang Mass Games was recognised by the Guinness Book of Records as the world's largest collective gymnastics and art performance in 2007.[32] In addition, North Korea's "Arirang" song was listed as an Intangible Cultural Heritage of Humanity by UNESCO in 2014, being recognised for its authenticity and creativity, even after South Korea's "Arirang" had already been listed in 2012.[33] The reason for this was the fact that "Arirang", one of the most significant Korean folk songs, developed in a bifurcated fashion, showing unique aspects of both North and South, after the division of the Korean peninsula in 1953.

Overall, the Arirang Mass Games has mainly dealt with the significance of the country's collective survival at the expense of the individual life, by showcasing anti-Japanese struggles during the colonial period of the Chosun Dynasty in the early 20th century, the divided Korea due to conflicts of imperial powers resulting from two great world wars, the greatness of the leaders (described as immortal, god-like figures), and the achievements of socialism.[34]

Table 7.1 provides an overview of the Arirang Mass Games that took place on September 12, 2012, as based on the observations of one of the leading scholars in East Asian Studies, Rudiger Frank,[35] and the author's interpretations about characteristics and intended meanings with regard to children's

---

30   Frank 2013.
31   Burnett 2013.
32   Guinness Book of Records 2007.
33   The reason for this was the fact that "Arirang," one of the most significant Korean folk songs, developed in bifurcated fashion, showing unique aspects of the North and South, respectively, after the division of the Korean peninsula in 1953.
34   Frank 2013.
35   Frank 2013, 8–9.

TABLE 7.1   The Arirang Mass Games: characteristics and intended meanings (by the author)

Overview	Characteristics	Intended meanings
Introduction	Political succession of the three leaders	To emphasise a new leader's biological lineage from the founder
Prologue: Arirang	Anti-Japanese colonialism during the era of imperialism	To showcase the historical genesis
Act 1: Arirang Nation (*arirang minjok*)	The succession of the power to the second leader	To deliver political symbolism through leaders' charisma
	The communist world's first hereditary transfer of power	To justify political authority
Act 2: Military First Arirang (*songun arirang*)	A successful transition to the military first policy	To convince formative moral and political slogans
		To target both the domestic population and the international community as important audiences
Act 3: Arirang of Happiness (*heangbogui arirang*)	Justification of the third leader's political authority and power	To deliver political slogans and diplomatic messages
		To confirm the continuation of the legacy politics
Act 4: Arirang of Unification (*tongil arirang*)	Unified yearning for national unification	To promote political symbolism, authority, and charismatic leadership
Act 5: Arirang of Friendship (*chinson arirang*)	The country's foreign policy directions	To show future aspirations for the country
Epilogue: Restoration as powerful and prosperous Arirang (*kansong puhung arirang*)	The country's ultimate goals to achieve in the forthcoming years	To strengthen the country's legacy politics

athletic labour and ordinary citizens' dramatic labour.[36] The year 2012 marked the one-hundredth anniversary of Kim Il-sung's birth and political succession. The "Introduction" played as the epilogue of the Games and praised the leaders of the country, including Great Leader Kim Il-sung, Dear Leader Kim Jung-il, and Supreme Leader Kim Jung-un. This was the first glorification of Kim Jung-un, as he had come to power only in late 2011 after the death of his father, Kim Jung-il. The following section, "Prologue: Arirang", told the story of the founder of the nation, Kim Il-sung, who left home to avenge what had been perpetrated against his loved ones by the Japanese during the colonial period. "Act 1: Arirang Nation", portrayed Kim Il-sung's autobiography, describing him as the "emerging sun", and the "one star" who saved the unfortunate country from Japan, and praised Kim Jung-il's great victory in the form of the military first policy. "Act 2: Military First Arirang", focused on a song of adoration for Kim Jong-il's death in honour of his tireless efforts and journeys to provide the best for his people. "Act 3: Arirang of Happiness", emphasised the "single-minded unity, invincible military power, [and] industrial revolution" of the new century and praised new Kim Jong-un. "Act 4: Arirang of Unification", showed the unified yearning for national unification as the ultimate goal of the WPK, and deplored the Arirang nation's division due to foreign imperial forces. "Act 5: Arirang of Friendship", projected means of enhancing the deep-rooted Korea-China friendship and emphasised the necessity of resisting US aggression and aid to South Korea. "Epilogue: Restoration as powerful and prosperous Arirang", presented North Korea's future-oriented outlook and optimism regarding its pursuit of independence, peace, and friendship on the Korean peninsula. The goals and actions of North Korea's diplomacy respecting the Mass Games can be summarised as follows: 1) political authority and symbolism, 2) charismatic leadership, and 3) power succession and legacy politics, this latter marking the country as the communist world's first hereditary transfer of power, and all three of them serving its national role conception.

3.1.1 Self-efficacy

The *Songbun* system can be a driving force for the self-efficacy of an engaged citizenry in the context of the Arirang Mass Games, because the high degree of rigidity of the system supported by the one-party politics contributed to the high degree of loyalty on the part of the people to the leader and country. The top pyramid of the *Songbun* system demands self-sacrifice of the people in the

---

36 Kwon and Chung 2012, 45–52.

middle and at the bottom of the pyramid in maintaining their current status. A monitoring mechanism among classes strengthens the ordinary citizens' "motivation" for nationalistic behaviours, making the whole political system, a dictatorship with legal supremacy over other political parties and people, even more closely interconnected based on social class.[37] This coercive mechanism results in what is, in effect, a passive motivation of North Koreans to be a part of national events in order to maintain their own social status.

Constitutional reforms in 1992 and 2016 upgraded the mass public (called *Inmin*) to emphasise the country as a people's democratic dictatorship; but the 2016 reform strengthened state control *over* people "by purging antisocialists and traitors and facilitat[ing] an incentive mechanism between high officials and their supporting groups within the *Rondongdang*; thus, *Inmin* showed loyal, chauvinistic, and dedicated behaviours toward the Kim family".[38]

In addition, being a cultural actor is highly prestigious in North Korean society, especially after Kim Jung-il's cultural policy promotion of *Gunjunghwa*, "obliging the public to become involved in the process of literary and arts creation" in the 1980s.[39] During his era, the invention of the *seed* theory, which put more effort into cultural affairs to enhance legacy politics[40], transformed North Korean cultural policy into an even more unique nature. North Korean artists or filmmakers who are awarded the title of Inmin tend to be socially well treated as part of a meritorious class.[41] This approach makes the country's national events even more effective and state-centric, specifically by bringing more people into the events (effective mobilization) and intensifying the compulsory participatory system of ordinary citizens' involvement in the Arirang Mass Games to project the country as a socialist paradise to global audiences. This also amplifies emotional uprising from the bottom, which can be politicised by the authority and power. On the other hand, a cultural actor becomes a subject of punishment due to leadership changes, which makes the compulsory participatory system of the PAD more dependent on the leader. For example, the *Unhasu* Band, created during the Kim Jung-il era, was ill-treated by Kim Jung Un, and then a new "girl group", *Moranbong* Band, was created to honour the Kim Jung-un regime.[42]

---

37   Kim 2022, 20.

38   Kim 2022, 19.

39   Kim 2022, 18.

40   Kwon and Chung 2012, 48.

41   Information Center on North Korea n.a.

42   Kim 2019.

Also, the Arirang Mass Games are part of the education of schoolchildren. They must attend the Mass Games either as a performer or an audience member. A training course on the country's history and political ideology, for example, is mandatory. This educational aspect of the Mass Games makes the event even more compulsory. Therefore, a motivation hub for taking part in the Mass Games is deeply rooted in the rewards and punishment control of the country's social class system and education as well as in the leader's preferred policy, which ultimately stresses the deification of the Kim family, laying the foundation for a feudal political system with its congruency between government and people.

3.1.2   Knowledge

The Arirang Mass Games provide both the domestic and foreign publics with knowledge on North Korea's political system, and function as propagandistic measures, policy advocacy for socialist values and ideas, and finally, consolidation of the hierarchical power of the Kim family and ruling class. The Mass Games consist of three sections: card sections, collective gymnastics, and artistic dance with an appropriate catchphrase crafted to make North Korea a socialist superpower and promote nationalism.[43]

In line with communist and socialist ideas, the performance of the Arirang Mass Games made the individual feel less important – even going so far as to take self-sacrifice for granted – compared with the state.[44] Along with the multi-part *Art Film Nation and Destiny*, which was extended from 10 to 100 series, the Mass Games became even more politicised in 2002 for the purpose of re-legitimising Leader Kim Jong-il as the successor of the country.[45] The Mass Games had first been introduced in 2002 to celebrate Kim Il-sung's 90th birthday (describing him as an immortal god-like figure), his son Kim Jong-Il's 60th birthday, as well as the 70th anniversary of the establishment of *Rodongdang*. In these ways, the year 2002 facilitated nationalist measures through various media outlets to affirm the legitimacy of the political system to the people.

In accordance with their national purpose, the Mass Games delivered a clear political message about the country's leader and its history, helping to lay the foundation of North Koreans' basic understandings about the totalitarian characteristics of their country, not only domestic but also global audiences. For that purpose, the deification of the Kim family, and the partisan strug-

---

43   Kang 2017, 158.
44   Park 2020.
45   Kang 2017.

gle against the Japanese during the colonial era were especially emphasised. This Arirang Mass Games relegated the individual to the status of a small part of a great machine, not unlike the mass gymnastics and propaganda performed and delivered under such totalitarian systems as Stalin's, Hitler's or Mao's.[46] The North Korean-style of communism, the beauty of the Joseon Dynasty, the great productivity of collective farms, the justification of military politics, and the hope for a unified Korea: all of these were focused on. Such utopian-rhetorical storytelling is largely based on disinformation and manipulation to enhance the nationalism of the domestic public. As a consequence, the Mass Games transformed the country's ideological crisis in the face of the collapse of the Soviet Union and its allies into a new formation of collectivism based on legacy politics in response to the fundamental problems of nationalism and reconstructed the national identity of North Korea thereby.[47] North Korean nationalism, based on a future-oriented paradox, represents North Korea as the promised utopian society yet to come.[48]

As mentioned above, the Arirang Mass Games served as an education programme. Training schoolchildren as participants in the Mass Games, a coercive mechanism to engage the youth in a national event, became an important way for the PAD to educate them about the basic qualities of a communist citizen, as cultural expression functions as knowledge reproduction of socialist utopian ideals and ideology. It reminds us that the PAD takes a significant role in ideology production, distribution and consumption in accordance with the leader's interpretation of the country's ideology.[49] The Arirang Mass Games, in effect, coerced the general public's sacrifice for the country's survival by showcasing the anti-Japanese struggles, the divided Korea, the greatness of the leaders, and the achievements of socialism (Table 7.1).

3.1.3 Competence

Training schoolchildren through participation in the Arirang Mass Games was dedicated to knowledge reproduction no less than excellence in the performing arts. The Arirang Mass Games were performed a total of 900 times over the course of 10 years (2002, 2005, 2006, 2013). As more than 100,000 people participated in the Games on a large scale each time, the Mass Games became more than a public performance with trained citizen-actors, schoolchildren, women, and soldiers, recognised by the international

---

46   Frank 2013.
47   Jeon 2011.
48   Burnett 2013.
49   Kang 2017, 142.

community.[50] In fact, the Games achieved more goals and beneficial effects than did the existing gymnastics aiming at communist class education for youth and students.[51] This educational aspect also contributed to the high competence of the participants and the legitimization of the three Kims' authority and political power, giving extensive societal impact through the instrumentality of the Mass Games.

According to Kim Jong-il's statement about his philosophy on mass gymnastics (1987), schoolchildren who participate in mass gymnastics can develop exceptionally fit, powerful bodies, a high level of organization, discipline, and collectivism; furthermore, they can make every effort to subordinate all of their thoughts and actions to the collective thereby, since they are made aware that one mistake could ruin the whole performance. This state-centric mode of the Arirang Mass Games can be more naturally justified for the purpose of education than for that of raising individual competence. Rather, it suppresses individuality and puts more value on the group.[52] In fact, while the government-people isomorphism, significantly reducing individualism, pluralism, or diversity, has been intensified through citizen participation in the Mass Games, the domestic public tends to disengage with the country's foreign policy or global issues due to the psychological impact of brainwashing, such as the PAD's power over people through disseminating propagandistic public information and controlling over the society.[53]

Although the existing gymnastics games were conducted under the guidance of the National Sports Committee, the Arirang Mass Games has been administered and managed by the Cultural Bureau of the PAD after the Cabinet reforms in 1998, which implies that North Korea considers the Mass Games as propaganda or incitement.[54] The central role of culture in North Korea, focusing on communist values, reflected the status of collective gymnastics, which guarantees creative, artistic, and collective functions as an important propaganda tool for teenagers and students.[55]

In particular, Kim Jong-il expanded the audience for the performance and made efforts to attract people by combining group gymnastics with art performances to reinforce collective ideological culture and its salutary effects.[56]

---

50   Kwon and Chung 2012.
51   Kang 2017, 161.
52   Frank 2013.
53   Medicott 2005.
54   Kang 2017, 161.
55   Gordon 2004.
56   Jeon 2010.

More than 100,000 teenagers nationwide became eager to be part of the Mass Games, due largely to the material reward mechanism that delivered a colour tv in recognition of participation. Thereby too, the political effects were taken into account. The core significance of the Arirang Mass Games is believed to have been their strategic purpose of mobilising people, stirring up political agitation and securing public support by stressing the necessary sacrifices of the people.[57]

Participating schoolchildren, between the ages of six and fourteen, must train for six to twelve hours per day for a period of six to twelve months; thus, they cannot study any other subjects properly and suffer from harsh trainings and corporal punishments.[58] For these reasons, the Arirang Mass Games have been accused of child abuse by the international community. The PAD's radical and result-oriented Kim family policy impositions have resulted in a negative image for the country, notwithstanding the success of the Mass Games with their display of highly developed skills and overall competence. The criticism also touches upon human rights violations in the country – forced labour and women and girls at risk in particular[59]. Thus, the degree of competence must be assessed in the given social context of participatory mechanisms, either democracy or nondemocracy.

3.2   *South Korea's Participatory Diplomacy Center*

South Korea modernised its diplomatic system during the administration of President Kim Young-sam (1993-97), the first civilian government after 32 years of authoritarianism. The Kim government also introduced innovative reforms in public administration to achieve the goal of small and efficient governance.[60] There were substantial precedents that made for the changes: a nationwide pro-democracy movement in 1987 and the successful hosting of a mega-sporting event, the Seoul Olympics, in 1988. This was the impetus for the Kim Young-sam administration's announcement of a "New Korea" to be aligned with the liberally democratic world in terms of internationalization and globalization.[61] Since then, South Korea's social and political context has been transformed from "power *without* people" to "power *with/from* people", and from the "*state-centric* approach" to the "decentralised mode of governance approach" to diplomacy. South Korea, consequently, is ranked as a

---

57   Kang 2017, 168.
58   rfa news 2013.
59   Human Rights Watch 2022.
60   Kim 2023.
61   Kim 2023, 297.

"Free" country according to the Freedom House Index[62], receiving 83 of 100 total points: 33 out of 40 in terms of political rights; 50 out of 60 in civil liberties.

The establishment of the Participatory Diplomacy Center in 2018 (original name: People Diplomacy Center) as part of the public diplomacy (PD) efforts of the Ministry of Foreign Affairs (MOFA) of South Korea, can be seen as an exemplary outcome of the democratic transformation that had occurred over the course of 30 years and that had resulted in a new dynamic of diplomatic practice known as *people-centric* diplomacy. The more specific rationale behind the establishment of the people-centric Participatory Diplomacy Center was the Moon Jae-in government's hopes to mitigate the previous Park Geun-hye administration's political mistakes – notably, the consensus on uneven negotiation results with Japan regarding the issue of "comfort women" and the overall lack of foreign policy breakthroughs. In fact, the domestic public had not been satisfied with the Japan-Korean Comfort Women Agreement of 2015, which led to the Moon administration's call for more participatory democracy.[63] Accordingly, the Participatory Diplomacy Center was instituted as part of a shift toward more inward-looking diplomacy by enhancing communication with the domestic public, encouraging citizen participation in foreign affairs, and utilising digital infrastructure. As the concept of integrative diplomacy emerged, referring to the blurred distinction between traditional diplomacy and public diplomacy, elites and decision-makers looked at the Center as an extensive use of public diplomacy.[64] Therefore, the role of the Center was initially overlapped with public diplomacy.

The Participatory Diplomacy Center can be considered to be the success of the movement advocating for the institutionalisation of citizen participation in diplomacy. In terms of the "second layer" of the EPM as applied to diplomacy, namely "diplomatic practice", comprises three elements of goals, actions, and impacts based on the first layer of social context, either democratic or authoritarian. As a young democracy since the early 1990s, after the end of the authoritarian regimes, South Korea has become an active adapter of neoliberal economy and democratization. The national role conceptions of the country have been largely defined by each administration's presidential pledges, visions, or missions due to the five-year single-term presidency. As the impeachment of President Park became the birthplace of the Moon administration, people's aspirations for better communication with the govern-

---

62   Freedomhouse.org 2023b.

63   Lee 2018.

64   Kim 2017.

ment laid the groundwork for President Moon's political visions to restore trust between the government and the people. With the Center's establishment, South Korea achieved its "goal" (to be consistent with PD strategies, the PD Act, and its Master Plan for PD (2017-2021) – for more on which, see below), its "action" (people participation in international affairs), and its "impact" (realization of deliberative democracy in diplomacy).

First, in terms of "goal", the Participatory Diplomacy Center is well aligned with the overarching concept of PD and the related strategies and plans. Even before the establishment of the Center, South Korea's citizen participation was two-fold: 1) Korea Foundation (KF) initiatives on public diplomacy and implementation of public engagement programmes, and 2) the MOFA's campaigning in the early 2010s. The KF is a leading organization in the realm of PD. The term *Public Diplomacy* first appeared in the title of its annual report of 2007, "Public Diplomacy and the Korea Foundation: Past, Present and Future".[65] When the MOFA established a PD Division in 2013, it implemented and executed various public engagement programmes to raise people's awareness about the importance of PD and to enhance the country's soft power. The PD Division also initiated the pre-stage of citizen participation in diplomacy with the help of institutional structures, practices, and resources. PD strategies, the PD Act, and the five-year Master Plan made goal alignment between the MOFA/KF and the Participatory Diplomacy Center possible. As for the terminology, *Shimioegyo* [citizen diplomacy] is scarcely used in Korean academia, practice, and media, but *Min'ganoegyo* [private diplomacy] is often used to describe "people-to-people" diplomacy, so-called P2P diplomacy, in a broader sense, an old term since the Korean Council on Foreign Relations was established by current and former diplomats in 1971, while recognising civil society as one of the actors in diplomacy along with such private sectors as enterprises, non-profit organizations, experts or individual citizens. For these reasons, public diplomacy was first widely understood as people's diplomacy.[66]

Second, in terms of "action", actual citizen participation in diplomacy started when projects called "You Do, I Do PD!" opened the door for citizens to take part in diplomacy, which previously had been considered to be a realm only for accredited officials in closed circles. In the beginning, the project took the form of a Public Relations (PR) campaign calling for people's attention and participation regardless of age, gender, education, or occupation. This brought about both opportunities to sketch out a mechanism of PD under MOFA hier-

---

65   News Focus 2007.
66   KF 2010.

archies and challenges in the forms of uncertainties and risks incurred in the process of public engagement. One issue to consider is whether public engagement can be consistent regardless of continually changing national role conceptions due to government changes. For instance, the Pak administration's middle-power diplomacy, the Moon administration's diplomacy for the people, and the Yoon administration's global pivotal state.[67] The answer is yes. Consistent policy measures related to citizen participation have been sought since the implementation of public diplomacy, as seen in the goal and action analysis.

Third and finally, in terms of "impact", the successful implementation and operation of the Participatory Diplomacy Center has shown the effects of people's perceptual changes, for example, an increased understanding of the utility of people-to-people (P2P) links. In order words, people had come to acknowledge themselves as legitimate PD actors initiating, constructing, and expanding P2P links, as well as benefitting from extensive networks with foreign publics. Indeed, public and participatory diplomacy can overlap. For instance, the application of public diplomacy by the Moon administration is an example of participatory diplomacy in embryo form, as it emphasises the importance of public participation and enhanced civic capacity. In practice, participatory diplomacy has developed over time, even though its central animating idea is still contested as to whether a new concept is necessary while existing programmes and events serve similar purposes or whether nonprofessional citizens can be the subject of diplomacy.[68] The increasing civic capacity of South Koreans has pushed participatory diplomacy forward to claim its own territory, beyond the diplomatic foreign/domestic divide, thus extending the role of citizens in enhancing the effectiveness of diplomacy in reflecting the opinions of citizens through public discussion.

Table 7.2 provides an overview of the Participatory Diplomacy Center and its characteristics: three purposes (communication with people, citizen participation, digital infrastructure), six programmes (Sympathy Factory, Open Campus, Design Group for Participatory Diplomacy, Foreign Policy Suggestions, People Engagement Programme, Foreign Policy Suggestions through Mobile App), and detailed explanations. The first two programmes, Sympathy Factory and Open Campus, are designed to strengthen communication with people and provide participants with information on foreign policies, current issues, and the tendencies of international politics as well as to enable them to express their opinions. While Sympathy Factory is aimed at members of the

67   Kim 2023.
68   Kim 2018.

TABLE 7.2   The Participatory Diplomacy Center: characteristics (by the author)

Purpose	Programmes	Details
Communication with People	Sympathy Factory (monthly event)	Participants are informed about foreign policies, current issues, and tendencies of international politics and express opinions.
	Open Campus	Same as Sympathy Factory, through collaboration with Seoul Citizen University of the Metropolitan Seoul Government and foreign embassies
Citizen Participation	Design Group for Participatory Diplomacy	A design group comprising selected citizens interested in foreign policy who plan and promote events and activities, bridging the government/people gap
	Foreign Policy Suggestions	The main feature is an interactive process between the MOFA and citizens to project their suggested ideas onto actual policies. An annual contest as part of the programme has been held since 2019.
	People Engagement Programme	The main feature is an interactive process between the MOFA and people. Since 2019, an annual project based on a deliberative democracy model has been held to realise deliberative democracy in diplomacy.
Digital Infrastructure	Foreign Policy Suggestions through Mobile App	Making the participatory mechanisms more effective by developing mobile apps as a new component of diplomacy's digital infrastructure

general public who visit the Participatory Diplomacy Center, Open Campus targets a specific audience by collaborating with Seoul Citizen University of the Metropolitan Seoul Government and foreign embassies. The next three programmes, Design Group for Participatory Diplomacy, Foreign Policy Suggestions, and People Engagement Programme, have significant and distinctive roles to play regarding citizen participation. Design Group for Participatory Diplomacy allows a group of selected citizens to plan and promote events and activities to make people more relevant to state-led foreign policy and enable the mass public to have enhanced awareness of diplomatic issues. Foreign Policy Suggestions and People Engagement Programme are the main features of the Center's activities in terms of the interactive process between the MOFA and the domestic public. Foreign Policy Suggestions is an interactive contest that has taken place annually since 2019 to reflect citizens' suggested ideas in actual policies. People Engagement Programme has aimed to realise deliberative democracy in diplomacy by conducting, since 2019, an annual project based on a model of deliberative democracy. The last programme, Foreign Policy Suggestions through Mobile App, is designed to make the participatory mechanisms more effective by developing mobile apps as a new component of diplomacy's digital infrastructure.

3.2.1   Self-Efficacy

Public dissatisfaction with representative democracy has generated a strong motivation for citizens to be a part of foreign policy and international affairs. Negative public opinion regarding the 2015 Japan-Korea Comfort Women Agreement, perceived as unfair and absurd by most Korean citizens, not to mention hurtful, was one of the causes of the public uprising, known as the "candlelight protest" to impeach President Park Geun-hye in late 2016, an oft-referred to the success of participatory democracy.[69] This led in turn to scrutiny of the rise of civic power in the country. The people-centred policy of the subsequent Moon Jae-in administration (2017-2021) mirrored the aims of the MOFA and affiliated agencies, and heavily influenced the establishment of the Participatory Diplomacy Center in 2018, which has been expanded by the current Yoon Seok-yeol government (2022-current). The emphasis on *people* was reflected in the Center's original name, the People Diplomacy Center, which subsequently was changed to the present name due to confusion and disagreement over what "people diplomacy" actually meant and how programmes and events were to be organised accordingly. Regardless, this exper-

---

69   Lee 2018.

imental approach facilitated public involvement in foreign affairs, ensuring an engaged citizenry as an important constituent of diplomacy, which enabled autonomous participation based on active, voluntary and proactive motivations in support of diversity and individualism.

According to the Master Plan for PD (2017–2021), there are four areas of public participation: 1) Next Generation, promoting PD projects concerned with major diplomatic initiatives and occasions, which projects young people plan and participate in for the purpose of youth employment and support for international youth exchanges; 2) Multicultural Families, providing support for the operation of PD programmes led by multicultural families and expanding the inclusion of multicultural children in projects of central ministries and local governments; 3) Overseas Koreans, extending support for the PD activities of overseas Koreans and the establishment of PD education for them; 4) People and Domestic Public, involving training of PD professionals and development of PD curricula for the people, as well as step-by-step implementation of PD education in universities, and reviews of public engagement in PD based on mid- and long-term research. Thereby, the concept of public participation is quite broadly covered in the Master Plan, as the first three of those areas (Next Generation, Multicultural Families, Overseas Koreans) were derived by grouping the projects already carried out by various ministries into the concept of PD. The final area (People and Domestic Public) is regarded by the MOFA and the KF (an organization affiliated with the MOFA) as the main avenue by which the domestic public can become involved in diplomacy.

With the development of PD, South Koreans have been able to raise their self-efficacy for diplomatic practices through citizen engagement programmes administered by the MOFA or the KF, such as Public Diplomacy Week events (146,604 participants, from 2018 to 2020), KF Public Diplomacy Academy projects (83 cases and 14,602 participants, from 2018 to 2020), and Support for Public Diplomacy Projects of Citizens (63 cases and 894 participants) (KF 2021). As for other, longer-term programmes, Global Challengers sent 362 personnel to 63 locations in 20 countries from 2011 to 2020, and Youth Exchanges and Global Networking involved 5,580 people from 1992 to 2020. KF's public participation focuses on giving citizens more chances to take part in PD practice. The increasing numbers serve to show how significantly the democratic values of a liberal country can affect the mode of diplomatic practices in constructing a new, integrated dynamics of citizen participation, such as is seen in the Participatory Diplomacy Center's Foreign Policy Suggestions and People Engagement Programme. In particular, the People Engagement Programme, conducted since 2019, is an unprecedented foreign policy approach to deliberative discussion; indeed, it is considered to be an archetype of a programme that can inspire, motivate and encourage active participation on the of the domestic public. By incorporating deliberative democracy into participatory diplomacy, South Korea seeks the formulation of a government/people alignment whereby the MOFA can facilitate people's engagement in and support for the country's foreign policy directions. Although the Participatory Diplomacy Center's total number of participants and outcomes are quite limited relative to those of other long-term PD projects, its initiatives for people-centric diplomacy effectively enhance ordinary citizen's self-efficacy with regards to foreign policy and its practices.

3.2.2   Knowledge

South Korea's soft-power PD based on democratic values[70] helped to lay the foundation for the Participatory Diplomacy Center. In fact, it is important to acknowledge PD as the Center's overarching concept that has pushed citizen participation in diplomacy forward.

South Korea's PD conception included, from the beginning, the domestic public as an actor. The PD Act of 2016 defines public diplomacy as "diplomacy activities through the State [that enhance] foreign national's [*sic*] understanding of and confidence in the Republic of Korea directly or in cooperation with local governments or the private sector through culture, knowledge, policies, etc." (Article 2). The private sector includes individual citizens; therefore, the domestic public becomes not only a subject of diplomacy but also a diplomatic actor. Based on this definition, the operation of the Center maximises democratic values while seeking public buy-in regarding the MOFA's strategies, policy advocacy per se, and consensus-building, all in order not to repeat the same mistake as represented by the 2015 Japan-Korea Comfort Women Agreement. However, there is a concern about the risk of the politicization of diplomacy. Nonetheless, PD and the Center have an educational aspect, the purpose of which is to make the mass public more conscious of their status as global citizens, to get them involved in global issues by raising public awareness, and to enhance their knowledge of their country and the world.

According to the MOFA, participatory diplomacy involves an integrated effort to concentrate citizens' diplomatic capabilities by strengthening communication with them and engaging them in foreign policy decisions.[71] The Participatory Diplomacy Center conducts its main programmes to enhance two-way communication between the MOFA and people and to strengthen citizen participation in diplomacy and the foreign policy decision-making

---

70   Kim 2023.
71   MOFA 2023.

process, largely through the upgrading of digital platforms (Table 7.2). Foreign policy Suggestions and People Engagement Programmes are the main features of the Center, since they project citizens' opinions onto actual foreign policies, which process realises an interactive mechanism of deliberative democracy in diplomacy.

The Center pursues the goal of listening to people through two-way communication, and reflects people's perspectives on foreign policy by giving them genuine authority, leading to shared power between the MOFA and the people. South Korea's ability to exert "power *with* people" might be predicted on that basis, even though the Center's projects thus far only partially demonstrate this. The Participatory Diplomacy Center implies, by its existence, that in the context of a liberal country, the general public must be informed and empowered through autonomous citizen participation in diplomacy. However, there are still areas for improvement in that people can gain only limited knowledge about real diplomacy by being informed about selectively chosen topics by elites and diplomats, surrounding more apolitical and less sensitive issues.

3.2.3   Competence

Although it is too soon to assess the participants' level of competence, it has been discovered that as civic capacity improves, so too do the Participatory Diplomacy Center's programmes and activities that take deliberative democracy into account when formulating diplomatic agendas. In the beginning, the Participatory Diplomacy Center faced tremendous difficulties due to the lack of practical or academic conceptions of people-centred diplomacy. Rather than searching for a grand definition, the Center found its meaning in "togetherness". Since its establishment, there has been criticism from the National Assembly, particularly from an oversight group consisting of minority-party politicians. Also, monitoring from the Ministry of Finance intensified due to overlapping programmes with the Ministry of Culture. Nonetheless, the Center went through the transitionary period of changing its location from the MOFA to the Korea National Diplomacy Academy in order to raise its accessibility and provide public space for citizens. Although the Center had been founded by the MOFA's PD Division, this period transformed the Center into an independent and depoliticised actor.

The Center's two main programmes – Foreign Policy Suggestions, People Engagement Programme – serve to demonstrate its integrated mechanism of citizen participation. First, the successes of the annual Foreign Policy Suggestions contest are as follows: 1) a mobile application, produced in 2018; 2) indicating the place of birth on passports only for those who consented, in 2019; 3) integrating scattered SNS accounts and different channel names from You-Tube, Facebook, etc., into one name, "KOREAZ (meaning A to Z about Korea)", in 2020; 4) hosting a youth quiz contest, "Youth Golden Bell of Diplomacy", in 2021; 5) making digital contents for KOREAZ on the topic, "Wise Life in Korea". The Foreign Policy Suggestions contest enables people to raise their voices, and the Center exerts its leadership in turning their suggestions into reality through collaborative efforts with various partnering organizations and actors.

Second, the People Engagement Programme, having been in operation since 2019, is a prime example of a citizen consultation mechanism owing to its new approach to developing the fundamental idea of "deliberative discussion" for promotion of the public's active participation. There are five steps in the process of deliberative discussion: 1) selection of participants by utilising both sampling through the Random Digit Dialing methodology and, in rare cases, voluntary participation, with the target of a maximum of 300 people; 2) participants in the sample group are provided with pre-information, usually a booklet, about a specific topic; 3) participants attend a lecture related to the topic; 4) ten representatives of the sample group discuss the topic more than 20 times; 5) surveys are conducted (both before and after the lecture and discussion).

This programme has produced meaningful outcomes, such as protection of overseas citizens by the Consular Assistance Act of 2019, which means that overseas Koreans can receive more systematic consular assistance based on the law concerning criminal proceedings, criminal damage, death, minor and patient, missing, and critical situations, actively promoting global issues, particularly as concern the environment, for the 2021 P4G Summit, in 2020, engaging in diplomacy vis-à-vis Latin America and the Caribbean in 2021, and participating in diplomacy to strengthen cooperation with five central Asian countries on the occasion of the 30th anniversary of diplomatic relations in 2022. The topic of a given year is chosen based on a survey.

It turns out that the alignment of goals and objectives among governmental actors and the public was what made it possible for the MOFA to implement a state policy of citizen participation. The factors that proved key to success were strategic planning, coordination, systematic operation, and collaborative innovation. Innovation came with taking risks – including the uncertainties surrounding citizen engagement with the foreign policy decision-making process. However, innovation seems to have brought about a positive impact on the country's formulation of public participation and citizen consultation in diplomacy.

In addition, exogenous factors, such as COVID-19 and the rise of the nation's status in world politics, have accelerated the development of citizen participation from 2021. This is a new phase in terms of the enhancement of "people diplomacy" capabilities, expansion of PD, and strengthening of cooperation with various actors such as local governments, universities, and experts. Taking public opinion into account is one of the main drivers of the government's emphasis on people-centred diplomacy and communication for the realization of "PD with People". Another main driver has been self-awareness of the country's improved standing, in world politics, to advanced-country status. This turned into the alter ego that shaped the national role conceptions of the country, as President Yoon envisioned South Korea as a global pivotal state with a broader commitment to a liberal world order, which made the country move beyond middle powerism. This transformation has contributed to the generation of a virtuous cycle of national confidence, global responsibility, and global citizenry with people empowerment, which process raises public interest in citizen consultation in diplomacy. The autonomy and willingness of the people have accelerated their degree of civic participation in a bottom-up process. Therefore, the key concerns of this new phase should be dealt with properly in order to secure essential principles and standards for citizen participation in diplomacy.

The development of South Korea's diplomatic system includes efforts to increase the state's diplomatic "power *with/from* people" by establishing a government/people alignment that encourages support for the nation's foreign policy and global issues. This innovative mechanism came with governmental change; thus, the main driver was the new Moon administration's desire to avoid mistakes made by the previous, Park administration. And certainly, investing in the Participatory Diplomacy Center was an urgent matter, because rebuilding trust between the government and people was the Moon administration's foremost concern. The outcomes of the Center over the last three years show the possibility of public engagement in foreign policy decision-making processes in terms of appropriate topics, scopes of discussion, interaction methods, and reflection on the results of citizen consultations. In addition, successful participatory programmes also have been carried out by the PD Division of the MOFA and the KF, with a focus on the autonomy and willingness of the people to be a part of a bottom-up process. Exemplary programmes are the MOFA's initiatives for the "United Against Racism" campaign in collaboration with UNESCO Korea and the KF's "Public Participation", which provides various opportunities for citizens to become active practitioners rather than just passive participants.

However, one lesson learned by the Participatory Diplomacy Center concerns the possibility of politicisation, which, in turn, might prove detrimental to the actual survival of the country and people. It turned out that, given the case of the Shin Kori nuclear power plant's ad hoc committee's overturning of the previous government's nuclear policy, it was nearly impossible to maintain the initial purpose of the Center, which was to bring diplomatic issues to public debate, because high security or politically controversial issues could disturb the policy decision-making process and widen the gap between political parties. Nevertheless, the Center found a way to optimise a process of implementing citizen consultation in diplomacy without provoking public arousal: its solution was a carefully designed Public Engagement Programme called "Deliberative Discussion". Also, due to the MOFA's gradual-adaptation-based and process-oriented approach to policy implementation, it could be claimed that South Korea's competence in diplomacy has had little impact thus far. For example, there remains a lack of any methodological approach to enhance the soft power of the country through participatory diplomacy; there have been relatively few policy advocacy activities vis-à-vis major countries; efforts toward digital content promotion have been limited; about the Center's PR and marketing have been relatively ineffective; and finally, there is still the necessity of developing strategies to implement two-way communication and expanding programmes based on the degree of people's understanding about citizen participation in diplomacy.

4   Conclusion and Implications

In conclusion, this chapter has addressed some of the consequences of the domestic public's participation in diplomacy within the context of the given political system, whether liberal or illiberal, which context predetermines a state's behaviour towards its people. In so doing, it has proposed an Empower Theory-based conceptual framework of (domestic) people empowerment in diplomacy for a better understanding of the phenomenon of public engagement in foreign affairs. North Korea (an authoritarian country) and South Korea (a democratic country) were chosen as contrasting cases of different political systems. The Arirang Mass Games of North Korea (2002-2013), brought in about 100,000 people annually and listed in the Guinness Book of Records (2007) and by UNESCO (2014), and South Korea's Participatory Diplomacy Center (2018-current), the first innovative institutionalization of domestic-citizen engagement in MFAs, which includes approximately 2,500 participants annually, were used as successful examples demonstrating the application of the conceptual framework and revealing what makes for the distinctive characteristics in diplomacy and public participation in the two different political contexts, according to the analytical dimensions of "self-efficacy", "knowledge", and "competence".

First, "self-efficacy", referring to a motivation hub that strengthens expectancies and beliefs, shows differences between the two countries. North Koreans' passive motivation can be interpreted as the result of the coercive mechanism of schoolchildren training and participation that sustains the social classifications of the *Sungbun* system at the foundation of the feudal political system reigned over by the Kim family. On the other hand, South Korea tends to display active, voluntary-based, and proactive motivations amplifying the diversity and individualism of its society, which in turn makes autonomous participation possible. By the number of annual participants and the events' results, North Korea's Arirang Mass Games are much more effective than South Korea's Participatory Diplomacy Center, because it produces a high degree of self-efficacy on a much larger scale through a compulsory participatory system, and thus exerts a greater impact on (North Korea's) diplomatic practice – showcasing the country as a socialist paradise to global audiences, while its international reputation is highly related to nuclear provocations. As for South Korea, despite the minimal impact of the Participatory Diplomacy Center in terms of the total number of participants and outcomes, South Koreans have demonstrated heightened civic power when requesting that the government establish such an organization and operate it based on democratic values. This case shows that implementation of deliberative democracy can be possible even in the foreign policy making process, where statecraft puts the emphasis on the pursuit of national interest.

Second, "knowledge", indicating an understanding of a social/political context wherein a country is grounded, reveals an important commonality of the contrasting cases: knowledge in the process of empowering people greatly affects both countries, because public participation can be utilised as politicization of diplomacy, policy advocacy, and knowledge reproduction regardless of a liberal/illiberal political system. This dimension also makes for differences between the two Koreas, in that knowledge is significantly affected by the ideological norms and values embedded in their respective national politics and culture, in which altered forms, it shapes the goals and objectives of their foreign policies. In the case of North Korea, participating in the Mass Games was an important part of the education program of the PAD, which sought to teach the young generation socialist values and ideas and to raise nationalism to the point that the self is eliminated, taking self-sacrifice for granted for the

Kim family's regime and state survival. Therefore, the Arirang Mass Games functioned as a nurturing ground for schoolchildren as socialists, intensifying North Korea's leaders' power *over* people, and eventually reinforcing the deification of the Kim family. In the meantime, South Korea's Participatory Diplomacy Center's main purpose is to cultivate people's understanding of the country's foreign policy direction and consensus building on a specific diplomatic agenda, which in turn educates the mass public as conscious global citizens keen to contribute to global issues through public awareness. South Korea's intended outcome for the Center's establishment is listening to citizens, realising two-way communications, and projecting those opinions onto foreign policy by giving actual power to people, which gives rise to power sharing between the MOFA and the citizenry. As a result, South Korea's diplomatic "power *with* people" can be anticipated, although the Center's programmes have shown only partial achievements thus far, limited to selectively chosen topics, more apolitical and less sensitive, to be dealt with by the domestic public, rather than having a public discussion to get citizens to engage in high-political issue areas.

Third and finally, "competence", meaning skills, uncovers a vivid contrast between the two cases. North Korea's state power *over* people through the intensification of government/people isomorphism determines people's high competence in making the Games even more successful as one of the world's most spectacular aesthetic and artistic performance displays. However, notwithstanding the high competence of the participants, the extreme, hyper-result-oriented and cruelly imposed policies of the Kim family in training those participants have brought charges of child abuse by international audiences and turned the Games into an actual hazard for the country's image. Simply put, what made the Games successful actually became a negative for North Korea and the Kim regime. On the contrary, South Korea's approach to diplomatic "power *with/from* people" brought about the formation of government/people alignment. It is too early to evaluate the competence level of participants, but it has been found that a rise of civic capacity contributes to participants' competence as well as the development of the Center's programmes and activities that implement the mechanism of deliberative democracy in pursuing diplomatic agendas. Compared with the case of North Korea, South Korea's competence in diplomacy can be said to have had only a minimal impact, due to the MOFA's gradual-adaptation-based, process-oriented approach to policy implementation.

Based on these findings, this chapter argues that diplomacy is an instrument of statecraft entailing power dynamics operating through interactions not only between a state and a foreign state/people but also between a state and the domestic public; further, it reveals that people empowerment in diplomacy, a form of social interaction, has become one of the driving forces for statecraft diplomacy, foreign policy, and international politics, regardless of a country's political system. Meanwhile, the country's political system greatly defines a country's diplomatic performance and characteristics of public participation, as predetermined by the dimension of knowledge, and reveals new dynamics of diplomatic practice. As for the other two dimensions, self-efficacy and competence, North Korea's state-centric diplomacy conducted by the PAD shows highly effective performance in mobilising people through intensification of the government/people isomorphism to better exert the state's power over them; however, this intensification unintentionally results in people's disengagement from the country's foreign policy or global issues. By contrast, South Korea's evolution of its diplomatic system and attempts to enhance the state's diplomatic "power *with/from* people" through formulating the government/people alignment, facilitates people's engagement and support for the country's foreign policy and global issues. Therefore, the meaning of an *engaged citizenry* in diplomacy differs depending on the political context: an "engaged citizenry" of an illiberal state can be seen simply as a means of coercion to force the general public's sacrifice for the country's survival, whereas that of a liberal state actually might reflect an imperative to inform and empower the general public through autonomous citizen participation.

In this light, it may be concluded that one of the main drivers of participatory diplomacy discussed herein can be considered to be the "aspirations" of a state (top-down imposed) or its people (bottom-up rising) for individuals' accredited roles as members of society, which roles increase their sense of belonging, and underline the significance of the psychological aspects of both foreign policy and national role conceptions. Another main driver of participatory diplomacy is related to "knowledge" or the degree of understanding of a social/political context that can determine the desired outcome, such as socialist values associated with a state's diplomatic power *over* people, which intensify the dominance of the state, or democratic values associated with a state's diplomatic power *with* people, which enhance mutual state/people trust. Knowledge also drives various forms of diplomatic practice, such as politicization, policy advocacy, and knowledge reproduction, as mentioned above. The purpose of this chapter was to highlight how public participation, as a diplomatic practice, can be interpreted differently within a different political system, not to suggest that one political system is more effective than the other in that regard. Further work is critical in order to understand the complexity of domestic-society dynamics according to a form of government in today's more turbulent and challenging diplomatic environment.

Acknowledgement

This work was supported by the Ministry of Education of the Republic of Korea and the National Research Foundation of Korea (NRF-2021S1A5B5A16078325).

Bibliography

Ang, Ien, Yudhishthir R. Isar, and Phillip Mar, 'Cultural Diplomacy: beyond the National Interest?' *International Journal of Cultural Policy* 21 (4) (2015), 365–381.

Anton, Anca. 'Profiling a Niche Actor of Civil Society Diplomacy: the Unattached Diplomat'. *Journal of Communication Management* 27 (2) (2023), 191–206.

Blanchard, Kenneth H., John P. Carlos, and W. Alan Randolph. *The 3 Keys to Empowerment: Release the Power within People for Astonishing Results* (Oklaland: Berrett-Koehler Publishers, 1999).

Burnett, Lisa. 'Let Morning Shine over Pyeongyang: The Future-Oriented Nationalism of North Korea's "Arirang" Mass Games'. *Asian Music* 44 (1) (2013), 3–32.

Buzo, Adrian. (ed.) *Routledge Handbook of Contemporary North Korea* (New York: Routledge, 2021).

Cattaneo, Lauren Bennett, and Aliya R. Chapman. 'The Process of Empowerment: A Model for Use in Research and Practice'. *American Psychologist* 65 (7) (2010), 646–659.

Evans, Peter B., Jacobson, Harold K., and Robert D. Putnam (eds.). *Double-Edged Diplomacy: International Bargaining and Domestic Politics* (Berkeley, Los Angeles, London: University of California Press, 1993).

Faizullaev, Alisher. 'The Social and Relational in Diplomacy'. In *Diplomacy for Professionals and Everyone*, Diplomatic Studies Series, volume 20, ed. Jan Melissen (Leiden, Netherlands: Brill, 2022), 165–187.

Frank, Rudiger. 'The Arirang Mass Games of North Korea'. *The Asia-Pacific Journal* 11 (46) (December 2013), 1–46.

Freedomhouse.org. 'Freedom in the World 2023. Overview of North Korea'. (2023a). https://freedomhouse.org/country/north-korea/freedom-world/2023.

Freedomhouse.org. 'Freedom in the World 2023. Overview of South Korea'. (2023b). https://freedomhouse.org/country/south-korea/freedom-world/2023.

Freeman, Chas W. 'A Diplomatic Taxonomy for the New World Disorder'. In *The Palgrave Handbook of Diplomatic Reform and Innovation*, eds. Paul Webster Hare, Juan Luis Manfredi-Sanchez, and Kenneth Weisbrode (New York: Palgrave Macmillan, 2023), 41–58.

Gordon, Daniel. *A State of Mind* [Film]. (VeryMuchSo Productions, 2004).

Graham, Sarah Ellen. 'Emotion and Public Diplomacy: Dispositions in International Communications, Dialogue, and Persuasion'. *International Studies Review* 16 (2014), 522–539.

Gregory, Bruce. 'Mapping Boundaries in Diplomacy's Public Dimension'. *The Hague Journal of Diplomacy* (2015), 1–25.

Grossman, Michael. 'Role Theory and Foreign Policy Change: The Transformation of Russian Foreign Policy in the 1990s'. *International Politics* 42 (2005), 334–351.

Guinness World Records. 'Largest Gymnastic Display'. August 14, 2007. Accessed January 17, 2024. https://www.guinnessworldrecords.com/world-records/largest-gymnastic-display.

Huigh, Ellen. 'Changing Tunes for Public Diplomacy: Exploring the Domestic Dimension'. *Exchange: The Journal of Public Diplomacy* 2 (1) (2013), 62–73.

Human Rights Watch. 'North Korea Events of 2022'. May 23, 2022. Accessed January 17, 2024. https://www.hrw.org/world-report/2023/country-chapters/north-korea

Jeon, Young-Sun. 'Arirang as the Cultural Code of the 21st Century North Korea'. *Korean Humanities* 2 (1) (March 2016), 45–75.

Jeon, Young-Sun. 'North Korea's Grand Mass Gymnastics and Artistic Performance "Arirang" and Search for Possibilities of National Arts'. *The Korean Literature and Arts* 6 (2010), 161–190.

Information Center on North Korea. 'Summary of North Korean Movie'. *Ministry of Unification*, Accessed August 28, 2023. https://unibook.unikorea.go.kr/data/movie Summary07.

Kang, Hyesuk. 'Mobilization through Nationalism in North Korea: the Multi-part Art Film Nation and Destiny and The Large Scale Mass Game and Performing Art Arirang'. *Review of North Korean Studies* 20 (3) (2017), 138–179.

Kim, Jong-il. *On Further Developing Mass Gymnastics: Talk to Mass Gymnastics Producers*. (Pyongyang: Foreign Languages Publishing House, 1987).

Kim, HwaJung. 'A New Approach to Sport Public Diplomacy through National Role Conceptions in Governance Networks: A Case Study of the 2018 PyeongChang Winter Olympics'. *Korea Observer* 51 (4) (2020), 589–628.

Kim, HwaJung. 'The Emotional Dimensions of North Korean Politics through the Lens of Historical Institutionalism'. *Journal of Contemporary Eastern Asia* 21 (2) (December 2022), 13–26.

Kim, HwaJung. 'What Motivates South Korea's Diplomatic Reform and Innovation'. In *The Palgrave Handbook of Diplomatic Reform and Innovation*, eds. Paul Webster

Hare, Juan Luis Manfredi-Sanchez, and Kenneth Weisbrode (New York: Palgrave Macmillan, 2023), 259–314.

Kim, Unbin. 'Tae Young-ho says the return of Hwang Un-mi and Seo Un-hyang'. *The JoongAng*. (February 6, 2019). Accessed August 28, 2023. https://www.joongang.co.kr/article/23348368#home.

KF (Korea Foundation). 'My Life in Korea: 'Thank You!' *KF Newsletter*, (May 2010). Accessed August 28, 2023. https://www.kf.or.kr/kfNewsletter/mgzinSubViewPage.do?mgzinSn=28&mgzinSubSn=2275&langTy=KOR

Kwon, Heonik and Byung-Ho Chung. *North Korea: Beyond Charismatic Politics* (Rowman & Littlefield, 2012).

Lee, Taeho. 'Korea's Candlelight Revolution and Participatory Democracy'. *Asia Leadership Fellow Program e-magazine* 1 (2018), 1–4.

Mearsheimer, John, and Sebastian Rosato. *How States Think: The Rationality of Foreign Policy*. (Yale University Press, 2023)

Medicott, Carol. 'Symbol and Sovereignty in North Korea'. *The SAIS Review of International Affairs* 25 (2) (2005), 69–79.

Melissen, Jan. 'The New Public Diplomacy: Between Theory and Practice'. In *The New Public Diplomacy*, ed. Jan Melissen (London: Palgrave, 2005), 3–27.

Melissen, Jan. *Beyond the New Public Diplomacy*. (Netherlands Institute of International Relations Clingedael, 2011).

MOFA (Ministry of Foreign Affairs). 'Overview of Participatory Diplomacy'. Accessed August 28, 2023. https://deu.mofa.go.kr/www/wpge/m_25585/contents.do.

Park, Sang woo. 'North Korea Arirang Performance'. *Naver Blog*, (June 15, 2020). Accessed August 28, 2023. https://blog.naver.com/kenjisama/222001764921.

Putnam, Robert D. 'Diplomacy and Domestic Politics: The Logic of Two-Level Games'. *International Organization* 42 (3) (Summer, 1988), 427–460.

Riger, Stephanie. 'What's Wrong with Empowerment'. *American Journal of Community Psychology* 21 (3) (1993), 279–292. rfa news. 'North Koreans' Show for Arirang Performance'. (August 9, 2013). Accessed August 28, 2023. https://www.rfa.org/korean/weekly_program/eu_defector/co-dk-08092013132314.html.

Weiss, Thomas. 'Governance, Good Governance and Global Governance: Conceptual and Actual Challenges'. *Third World Quarterly* 21 (5) (2000), 795–814.

Wolf, James F. 'Public Administration's Multiple Institutionalized Frameworks'. *Public Organization Review* 5 (2005), 183–200.

Yonhap. 'Massive Protest against US Beef to Be Held in Seoul'. (July 5, 2008). Accessed August 28, 2023. https://en.yna.co.kr/view/AEN20080705001200315.

CHAPTER 8

Engaging Citizens in a Polarised Society: The Choices for US Diplomacy

Geoffrey Wiseman and Allison Scott

Summary

This chapter examines how the idea and practices of diplomacy's domestic dimension unfolded in the United States over two politically distinct presidential administrations: that of Republican Donald J. Trump (2017–2021) and Democrat Joseph R. Biden, Jr. (2021–2025). We identify two contrasting variants of state-society relations in times of increased politicisation, populism, and polarisation. The first Trump presidency personified *illiberal populist capture*. In this variant, Trump's America-First foreign policy was reflected in a highly personalised and intense form of politicisation of the Department of State and approach to domestic engagement. In contrast, Biden's approach to diplomacy's domestic dimension may be characterised as *liberal internationalist engagement*. Biden's international leaning foreign policy was underscored by support for a more professional foreign service, one that claimed to reflect and engage with a wider spectrum of American society. Biden's Secretary of State, Antony Blinken, pursued a markedly different form of home engagement than did secretaries Tillerson and Pompeo under Trump. The chapter also explores the role of American diplomats in addressing the domestic political alienation so evident during the first Trump and Biden presidencies.

Keywords

US diplomacy – Department of State – politicisation – populism – polarisation – Donald J. Trump – Joseph R. Biden, Jr.

1   Introduction

In times of increased politicisation, populism, and polarisation in functioning liberal democracies, the domestic engagement policies and practices of their diplomatic institutions are significantly and negatively impacted. Focussing on the United States, we consider how former and current professional American diplomats expressed their views on the 2017–2021 Donald J. Trump presidency and the subsequent 2021–2025 Joseph R. Biden, Jr. administration. Specifically, we examine some of the measures and strategies professional diplomats adopted to counter what they perceived as politicisation and populist pressures thought to polarize and de-democratize US diplomacy's domestic engagement with the American public. More broadly, we explore whether US diplomats and the institutions they serve can contribute in any meaningful ways to assuage domestic political alienation and societal polarisation pressures, thus promoting more informed and inclusive public engagement.

Our argument rests on the assumption that the nature of diplomacy's domestic engagement is highly dependent on the strength of a country's commitment to democratic or pluralist norms. Thus, when those norms are undermined by a populist government, as they were in the years after the election of Republican president Donald Trump in November 2016, the character of diplomacy's domestic engagement is fundamentally altered. In other words, the nature of engagement was as much influenced by Trump's populist 'worldview' as it was by geo-political determinants, such as China's rising power, Russia's annexation of Crimea, or the large-scale flow of 'illegal' migrants into the United States. In this chapter, then, we first evaluate the many ways that diplomats in and around the US State Department orbit, or community of practice, 'resisted' the Trump administration's politicisation and populist practices from 2017–2021. We then ask how those diplomats wrote about 'recovery' from Trump's personalised brand of populism, through domestic engagement, during the more 'normal' presidency of Democrat Biden from 2021–2025.

The United States is different in many ways from other contemporary, functioning liberal democracies that have had populist leaders with illiberal leanings – such as Hungary, Poland, Italy, India, the Philippines, and Brazil. Its geographically dispersed 50-state federal structure, system of checks and balances, and constitution that shares, if unequally, authority over foreign policy between the executive, legislature, and judiciary, produce differences with other democracies. Moreover, the US remains the major stakeholder in the international system and so what happens there has reverberations in many parts of the world.[1] However, while the US political system is distinctive in

---

1   Lake, Martin, and Risse 2021, 252.

many ways, we suggest that the US case provides insights into global debates about politicisation, populism, and polarisation.[2]

In less-politicised and less-populist times, non-American diplomats have commented on the relatively high degree of influence that domestic politics has on the formulation of US foreign policy and conduct of diplomacy.[3] Congressional influence famously attracted the world's attention in 1920 when the Senate declined to ratify the Treaty of Versailles despite President Wilson's attempts to win public support that notably included an 8,000 mile-tour across the country in September 1919 to promote US membership of the League of Nations. From that landmark moment, 'the American Congress probably has greater influence on foreign policy than any other legislature in the world'.[4] Moreover, the US Senate's action also set in motion a closer public interest in the legislative treaty-ratification norm in other pluralist societies. Ratification came to be seen as another manifestation of wider public demands for democratic institutions to represent 'the people' in foreign affairs following the devastation wrought by opaque 'old diplomacy' widely seen to have led to the First World War.

Examining diplomacy's domestic dimension in the United States during President Trump's first term and then Biden's, we see two contrasting variants. The first, personified by Trump, may be characterised as *illiberal populist capture,* in which the political elite sought to direct the public, or rather its 'base' of sympathetic segments of the wider public.[5] In this variant, Trump's personalised, polarising, inward-looking foreign-policy rhetoric was underscored by his unapologetic politicisation – and sidelining – of the Department of State under two secretaries of state Rex Tillerson and Mike Pompeo. While this approach delivered a favourable electoral result for the Republicans under Trump in 2016 and again in 2024, it was accompanied by significant disinformation and a range of undemocratic practices – notably voter suppression measures denying certain citizens a key opportunity to engage with, if indirectly, international issues at the ballot box. We depict the Trump variant of engaging with the public on diplomatic matters as being based on explicitly partisan and selective assumptions about the state-society relationship.[6]

The second variant, generally exemplified by the Biden presidency, may be characterised as *liberal internationalist engagement,* in which political elites

---

2   Biegon and Hamdaoui 2024, 1861.
3   Wiseman 2011, 242–245.
4   Solomon and Quinney 2010, 130.
5   On diplomatic 'capture' by populist governments, see Lequesne 2021.
6   On politicisation of the Department of Justice under Trump, see Rohde 2024.

engaged with domestic publics in a largely more open, transparent manner. In this approach, Biden's assuasive, international-minded foreign policy was reinforced by the Administration's promotion of a more professional and diverse foreign service, one that sought to draw on a wider spectrum of American society. This approach was led by Biden's Secretary of State Antony Blinken, who promoted a markedly less politicised form of domestic engagement than did Tillerson and Pompeo under Trump, declaring at the end of his term, 'As secretary of state, I don't do politics, I do policy'.[7] We depict the Biden-Blinken variant of managing the State Department and engaging with the public on diplomatic matters as being premised on more 'traditional' and notionally inclusive assumptions about the state-society relationship.

In short, the *illiberal-populist* option is broadly critical of America's terms of engagement with the world at large. The Trump variant had the effect of constricting rather than expanding participatory home-based practices between the dwindling number of professional US diplomats and American society. In some contrast, under Biden's *liberal-internationalist* approach, the United States participated more willingly in international institutions, from the United Nations to the G7 and G20, participation that in turn required a high degree of deliberative and participatory public engagement not only by Secretary of State Blinken but also by State Department staff.

We develop our argument as follows. First, we discuss briefly the key theoretical, definitional, and methodological considerations anchoring the chapter's empirical questions about the first Trump and one-term Biden administrations. Second, we reflect on whether the United States has undergone decades-long politicisation and polarisation accelerated by Trump's surprise victory in 2016 and his continued political influence during the Biden presidency. Third, we review a range of public sources and published comments by State Department officers, former and current, regarding Trump's foreign policy and diplomacy, looking for commonalities and strategies held by professional diplomats as to how to mitigate Trump's attempt at politicisation and populist 'political capture'. Fourth, we review a range of State Department views under Biden, looking for commonalities and strategies held by professional diplomats as to how to resist and reverse Trump's populist challenge, namely through public engagement. Finally, we offer our conclusions on the qualities of diplomacy's domestic dimension under two different administrations and on the wider question of the role of American diplomats in ameliorating or contributing to domestic political alienation and societal polarisation.

---

7   Blinken 2024, 76.

2   Theory, definitions, and method

2.1   *Theory*

In an increasingly politicised and polarised American political system from 2016 to 2024, accelerated – but not originated – by Trump's personalised, rather than 'thick', ideological brand of populism, and slowed – but not reversed – by Biden's more conventional brand of democratic politics, our interpretation of the domestic dimension of diplomacy is informed by several theoretical contributions, many of which are elaborated by the editors in their Introduction. We align with the editors' criticism that many theories do not take seriously enough domestic factors in the study of international relations and diplomacy. Most notable in this regard is the influential neo-Realist view that the key determinant of foreign policy is a country's relative power capabilities within the international system (Waltz's 'Third Image') and that foreign policy is not determined or heavily influenced by domestic structures (Waltz's 'Second Image') nor by key individual political leaders (Waltz's 'First Image').[8] Our analysis of the United States under presidents Trump and Biden clearly gives more emphasis to the home dimension – domestic structures, individual leaders and diplomats, and socio-political groups. Indeed, we suggest that the populist trend in the US suggests an almost inverted understanding of international relations in which, in Paul Sharp's words, 'world politics are increasingly domestic politics played out on the international stage'.[9]

For the US case, we re-deploy James Der Derian's argument that 'diplomacy is demarcated by alienation' and his conception of diplomacy as the 'mediation of estrangement'.[10] Der Derian famously argued for reconceptualisation of how these ideas operate at the international level, thus offering 'a better understanding of diplomatic theory'.[11] Exploring modern understandings of 'alienation' as separation, he writes, 'The English term has expanded to include, among its meanings, the separation between individuals; between individuals and society, supernatural beings, and states of mind; between peoples; and more importantly ... *between states*'.[12] Politicisation, populism, and polarisation surged in the United States following Trump's election in 2016 and those developments are clear expressions of deep alienation and estrangement within American society.

---

8   Waltz [1959] 2001.
9   Email correspondence, 20 August 2024.
10   Der Derian 1987, 8.
11   Der Derian 1987, 10–11.
12   Der Derian 1987, 14. Italics in original.

Thus, building on Der Derian's focus on diplomacy's role in mediating estrangement at the international level (which can involve diplomacy creating and maintaining differences even as it mediates between them), we consider whether US diplomats play some kind of mediating role in terms of estrangement and alienation at the domestic level. Noé Cornago also points in this direction when he suggests that 'it is particularly important to emphasize the enduring relevance of diplomacy not only for shaping the international order but for political order within States'.[13] While our argument implies that winning the support of citizens on foreign policy issues raises the stakes and accentuates the domestic arena as a competitive battleground, populism and diplomacy intersect in different ways and are context dependent. Thus, as Jens Meijen has shown in relation to the Flanders case in Belgium, 'the idea of populism as a challenge to diplomacy does not necessarily hold up for regional sub-state diplomacy'.[14] Our concern is that if diplomats are increasingly engaging with their domestic publics – as this volume posits – and if some of those publics are increasingly alienated from each other – as we argue next has occurred in the United States – then what role, if any, have diplomats played in addressing those tensions in domestic society?

In short, our theoretical focus is on how the traditional machinery of official, state-based diplomacy in the United States – the Department of State, its personnel, and networks – articulates its engagement with American society during a time of increased social alienation, negative partisanship, and destabilising populist polarisation.

2.2   Definitions

Politicisation, populism, and polarisation have complex and contested meanings. *Politicisation* occurs in pluralist liberal democracies when political leaders apply direct or indirect pressure on the civil service to gain partisan advantage – stretching the norms and boundaries of 'normal' politics – in ways that incentivise or put pressure on officials to ignore the evidence and legal merits of an issue or to tailor their advice to curry favour or satisfy their political masters.[15] In their comparative study of the politicisation of ambassadorial appointments, Niklasson and Jezierska define politicisation as the 'variety of practices that seek to favourably influence different arenas of decision-making to steer the final outcome towards a political objective'. They contrast politicisation with 'the Weberian ideal of modern bureaucracy', exploring its deval-

---

13   Cornago 2013, 51. See also Huju and Lequesne 2025.

14   Meijen 2023, 35.

15   On politicisation and diplomacy, Wiseman 2022; and Kerr 2023.

uation of 'the professional competences of civil servants and the overall quality of public administration and democracy'.[16]

Drawing on Ruth Cole's work in public administration, Pauline Kerr applies three types of domestic politicisation literature to Australian diplomacy. Cole's first type is *formal or partisan politicisation*, 'whereby merit-based criteria in recruitment and reward is replaced by political criteria'; second, *functional (or behavioural) politicisation*, 'whereby some public servants overstep their neutral expertise, or when public servants become responsive to politicians rather than maintaining neutrality'; and *administrative politicisation*, 'where political advisors intervene in the relationship between the Minister and the public service and obstruct or disrupt the delivery of free and frank advice'.[17] Each of these types of politicisation is observable in the US case. However, we highlight Cole's formal or partisan politicisation as well as the compact definition advanced by Peters and Pierre, who see politicisation of the bureaucracy as 'the substitution of political criteria for merit-based criteria in the selection, retention, promotion, rewards, and disciplining of members of the public service'.[18]

In most liberal democracies, a change of government sees minimal changes of senior personnel across government and in the foreign ministry and foreign service. However, in the United States, an incoming president may fill some 4,000 political appointments across government agencies, including hundreds in the Department of State and roughly 200 ambassadorial appointments. This is a normal part of the US political system and not considered politicisation *per se*. Politicisation occurs when the usual transfer of power is impeded or manipulated, for example by installing putatively 'temporary' political appointments (loyalists) to permanent bureaucratic positions when the sitting president has lost office in an election, as was attempted during President Trump's final months in office in 2020. Typically, politicisation is a nonviolent phenomenon, that can also occur less ostensibly, even surreptitiously, in liberal democracies. Politicisation can occur without populism. Loosely speaking, 'politicisation' is a form of political pressure intended to win partisan political advantage, undermining the neutral professionalism of the bureaucracy, or civil service. It is the opposite of 'professionalisation'.

Populism is an acute form of politicisation that utilises illiberal strategies such as promoting a cult of personality around the leader, developing an ideology – thick or thin – based on anti-elitism and anti-pluralism, packing the

---

16   Niklasson and Jezierska 2024, 1658.
17   Kerr 2023, 119 citing Cole 2020.
18   Peters and Pierre 2004, 2.

judiciary with partisans, culling the bureaucracy for perceived critics, and –
importantly for this chapter – targeting its communications to sympathetic
segments of the wider public rather than to society as a whole. For Destradi
and Plagemann, while populist politicians claim 'to be the only true representatives of "the people" and to embody the popular will', a typical feature of
populist behaviour when in power is 'the continuous mobilisation of their
support base'.[19] In other words, populists do not seek to 'engage' citizens in a
whole-of-society, or whole-of-nation, approach involving meaningful two-way
interaction, as expected in democracies, but aim to direct and mobilise, in a
one-way sense, those segments of society that putatively or potentially support them. And, as Destradi and Plagemann further argue, 'While the politicization of foreign policy does not make it more conflictive per se, the way
populists mobilize support suggests a greater likelihood of escalation [of international disputes]'.[20] A key difference between politicisation and populism, then, is that politicisation does not necessarily involve any direct connections with the public, whereas populism does, even if connections are
highly selective. In democracies, most diplomats will at some time disagree
with government policy writ large as distinct from tactical disagreements on
how to handle a specific issue, but that problem falls under the 'policy dissent'
rubric which, depending how it is addressed by the political leadership, is one
indicator of populist pressures on diplomats.[21]

Political Polarisation can emerge from politicisation but surfaces more seriously and quickly from populist politics. For Andreas Schedler, it is 'collective conflict at the highest level: a rift dividing the entire political community,
the nation'. In his ideal-typical terms, polarisation consists of four essential
features: first, 'extraordinary conflicts, rather than the ordinary quarrels of
democratic competition'; second, conflicts that 'hold the entire polity in
their grip'; third, 'bipolar conflicts among two dominant camps' rather than
among 'a fragmented field of actors'; and, fourth, a sharp 'dividing line' in
society between 'Them' and 'Us'.[22] As we argue in the next section, American
polarisation has been notably exacerbated by the third feature: the overwhelming national dominance of the political coalitions of the Republican
and Democratic parties. Against that wider contextual factor of the dominant
US binary, two-party system, Trump's populist takeover of the Republican

---

19   Destradi and Plagemann 2019, 724, 717.
20   Destradi and Plagemann 2024, 1923.
21   On leadership-centric populism in the United Kingdom, the United States, China, India,
      and Brazil, see Cooper 2022. See also Bartels 2024.
22   Schedler 2023, 343.

Party is widely seen as being the main factor driving this polarisation. It is difficult to predict whether 'polarization's self-perpetuating cycle' of misperception will continue as Heltzel and Laurin caution.[23] With Der Derian's estrangement concept in mind, we note Monika De Silva's conclusion from her study of gender rights diplomacy among embassies in the Warsaw diplomatic corps that 'diplomacy can be a *depolarizing* tool', especially in a bilateral context.[24] We consider whether the US professional diplomatic community can temper some of the excesses and misperceptions of polarisation at the policy level and in society at large.

In sum, we see politicisation, populism, and polarisation through a diplomatic lens, one that traditionally emphasises the institutions and processes that underpin relations *between* polities of various kinds, and, as this volume suggests, increasingly *within* those polities.

2.3   *Method*

In keeping with this book's exploration of diplomacy's domestic dimension, our focus is to compare how the first 'populist' Trump and the 'conventional' Biden administrations interreacted with the State Department and its diplomatic network in their respective 'domestic engagement' policies and practices. To develop this comparison, we assess how State Department-related personnel wrote about the two presidencies. Exploring that question empirically, we reviewed the website of the State Department's professional association, the American Foreign Service Association (AFSA), and the contents of AFSA's *Foreign Service Journal,* covering the period from late 2016 to late 2024. AFSA is the professional association and trade union of US foreign service officers with 16,800 members and The *Foreign Service Journal (FSJ)* is AFSA's flagship outreach platform with a circulation of 18,000.[25] We also drew on writings by former diplomats and others in policy and academic outlets, individuals that broadly speaking are linked to the State Department orbit, what others call the 'foreign policy establishment' (FPE)[26] or the US 'national diplomatic system' (NDS).[27]

---

23   Heltzel and Laurin 2020, 181.

24   De Silva 2024, 1. Emphasis added.

25   The Journal, established in 1919, is free online 'to be a consistently accessible resource for students, IR enthusiasts, educators and researchers', AFSA staff email correspondence with Wiseman, 13 August 2024.

26   Biegon and Hamdaoui 2024, 1863.

27   Hocking, 2018.

3   **Is the United States Increasingly Politicised, Populist, and Polarised?**

To explore our two main research questions – (1) how professional diplomats in the US diplomatic establishment responded to the 2017–2021 Trump administration's populist politics and their 'recovery' efforts during the 2021–2025 Biden administration, and (2) more broadly in terms of this book's societisation-of-diplomacy thesis, whether and, if so, how US diplomats contributed to mediating or ameliorating domestic political alienation and estrangement – we now consider in more detail the question of whether the United States has in fact become more politicised, populist, and polarised. We argue that it has. Moreover, while all four elements of Schedler's political polarisation described above were clearly present in the US context from early 2017 to early 2025, we stress that the US differs from other populist cases in that it demonstrably revolves around two dominant party camps, which makes 'cordoning' populists from power harder than in multi-party systems.[28]

As for whether the United States has in fact become more partisan and polarised in recent times, on the one hand, sociologist Zeynep Tufekci argues that 'there have been many periods in US history when things were worse'. We need not go back to the Civil War, Tufekci argues, but to the 1960s and 1970s, when the civil rights movement, though 'celebrated' today, 'at the time ... was deeply unpopular', the country was 'deeply divided over the Vietnam War', and '[p]olitical violence of all forms was on the rise'.[29]

On the other hand, in their analysis of four political institutions (the presidency, the executive branch, Congress, and the Supreme Court) and sixteen nonpolitical ones (e.g., banks, the media, the police, the military, medicine, and the law), Brady and Kent found that 'confidence in most American political and non-political institutions has fallen precipitously over the past fifty years'.[30] Their survey results, which do not cover the Department of State, show that major institutions have become identified with political parties.[31] Moreover, 'compromises now seem less attainable because powerful interest groups on the left and right are especially entrenched in their positions... . There does not appear to be any middle ground'.[32] They conclude, 'It is hard to bridge these divides, especially when almost every ostensibly authoritative

---

28   Bartels 2024, 119–122.

29   Tufekci 2024.

30   Brady and Kent 2022, 44.

31   Brady and Kent 2022, 43.

32   Brady and Kent 2022, 61, 62.

institution is identified with one side or the other on most issues'.[33] Similarly, Hawkins et al. found that, 'More Americans than ever perceive deep conflicts between Democrats and Republicans: split-ticket voting is at its lowest on record; political beliefs are increasingly divided along party lines; and growing numbers of Americans are expressing extreme distrust of members of other political groups and of governmental institutions'.[34] The clear two-party divide is at the centre of growing polarisation in the United States.

Following Trump's electoral victory over Democrat Hillary Clinton in 2016, populism and partisanship surged,[35] fast evolving into full-blown mutual contempt.[36] Then, with Trump's refusal to accept the results of the 2020 elections and his support for the storming of the US Capitol building on 6 January 2021, it was hard to deny that Americans were profoundly divided.[37] Such extreme polarisation is less conducive to 'normal' domestic engagement in policy issues, as top-down, populist leaders do not encourage genuine citizen participation in most sectors, much less foreign affairs when such issues as immigration are often exploited and contrived, 'rather than responding to public opinion'.[38] And from a bottom-up perspective, lack of trust in institutions decreases the likelihood of positive commitments from citizens.

While Trump was a key accelerant adding fuel to the polarisation fire in the United States with his brand of personalist populism, he was by no means the sole source. Some political analysts point to 'elite' behaviour in general to explain rising partisanship. For Mark Brewer, there is a cyclical effect in which 'elites polarize on issues, causing increased polarization among the mass on these same issues, which in turn fuels further elite polarization as politicians (who are after all elites) react to the views and demands of constituents and voters'.[39] Thus, de-polarising solutions would need to be directed to both political elites and their engagement with the general citizenry, a task arguably suited to the professional mediating strategies – explicit and implicit – of diplomats.

In democratic politics, political parties and leaders are, in theory, accountable to their voting base during elections and then, once elected, to all citizens. However, because of the increasing partisan divide between the two US

---

33   Brady and Kent 2022, 62.

34   Hawkins et al. 2018, 18.

35   Abramowitz and McCoy 2018, 137.

36   Drutman 2020.

37   Abramowitz and Webster 2016, 14.

38   Bartels 2024, 117.

39   Brewer 2005, 220.

major political parties, this sense of democratic responsibility-to-all declined. Consider the 'populism paradox', described by Porcile and Eisen (using examples of Donald Trump, Jair Bolsonaro in Brazil, and Rodrigo Duterte in the Philippines) as the tendency of populist leaders who campaigned on anti-corruption and democratisation platforms to then engage in corrupt and exclusivist practices once in office.[40] In terms of both representation and engagement, populist leaders find ways to control and manipulate their public base.

For populists, political power has thus become less about effective policy and domestic engagement and more about demonising the domestic 'Other' (Schedler's fourth feature), with the consequence that American politics is more a zero-sum game than ever. In the United States, there is electoral benefit in stoking polarisation and partisanship to maintaining populist power. As Achenbach writes, 'In this political environment, a candidate who picks up the banner of 'us versus them' and 'winning versus losing' is almost guaranteed to tap into a current of resentment and anger across racial, religious, and cultural lines, *which have recently divided neatly by party*'.[41] In this climate of populist threat and increased polarisation, there are fewer political opportunities to promote domestic mediation or inclusive engagement.

For others, this narrative too quickly writes off the American public as trapped in alienation. As Packer argues, Americans are 'sick of the political divisions.... The majority hates polarization and wants more compromise'.[42] Moreover, Pollard, Ries, and Amiri find that overall public impressions of diplomacy and American diplomats are generally favourable, with little variation across party lines.[43] They acknowledge underpinnings of polarisation, arguing that 'When issues become contested among partisan elites, Americans more easily form opinions about those issues, and they internalize their party's position as their own preferred position'.[44] However, they maintain the need for and possibility of an engaged and informed public, emphasizing the key role of diplomats and the State Department in that process.

There is historical evidence that professional diplomats recognize their role mitigating both immoderate international and domestic politics. Such a role has grounding in diplomacy's humanist tradition that emerged in early Re-

---

40   Porcile and Eisen 2020.
41   Achenbach 2024. Emphasis added.
42   Packer 2018.
43   Pollard, Ries, and Amiri 2022, 52.
44   Pollard, Ries, and Amiri 2022, 5.

naissance Europe,[45] in the exchange of permanent embassies in Renaissance Italy,[46] in Cardinal Richelieu's institutionalisation of the idea of continuous dialogue in early 17th century French diplomacy,[47] and in US diplomat George Kennan's early Cold War 'Long Telegram'. State-based diplomatic culture has long been infused with the fundamental norm of continuous dialogue, of engaging with friend and foe alike. While US presidents since the Russian Revolution have generally not endorsed the European practice of diplomatically engaging with their international adversaries, American professional diplomats tend to be more inclined to see the advantages of engaging them constantly.[48] In this vein, we argue below that US diplomats translate their commitment to the international norm of continuous dialogue to their own domestic context.

In sum, we find that 21st century politicisation and hyper-partisanship in the United States is more destabilising than in earlier decades of relatively straight-forward 'divided government' in which considerable bipartisan understandings operated, although more so in the US Senate than in the House of Representatives.[49] With those arguments in mind, we consider next whether the professional diplomats in the State Department orbit promoted the established diplomatic norm of continuous dialogue in their approach to engaging the wider American public, thus resisting more narrow populist 'outreach'. We ask whether a State Department deeply committed to professionalism and diplomatic ideals could not only resist Trump-like politicisation of the institution itself but also help in some small way to mediate and mitigate the contemporary estrangement in US domestic politics. We now consider how career American diplomats responded to the first Trump administration.

4 The 2017–2021 Trump Presidency

4.1 Trump's America-First Worldview

The Trump administration's worldview was marked in *substance* by a brand of neo-isolationism and in *style* by a general unpredictability and hostility towards the idea of diplomacy itself. Regarding substance, Trump's *America-*

---

45   Constantinou 2013.
46   Mallett 1994.
47   Hill 1961.
48   Wiseman 2011, 251–253.
49   Fiorina 2013, 58.

First mind-set was astutely labelled by Richard Haass as the 'Withdrawal Doctrine'.[50] Under Trump, the United States withdrew, threatened to do so, or backed away from several international pacts and institutions, including the Paris Agreement on climate change, the Iran nuclear agreement, and the World Health Organization (WHO). Moreover, Trump spoke often about the US withdrawing from NATO, the West's bedrock military alliance that had served the United States well since 1949.

Regarding Trump's style – and general disregard for diplomatic norms of civility – his trademark abrasive language was evident before his presidency began. In office, Trump rarely promoted his ideas with domestic US audiences via professional experts in the State Department. Rather, as Destradi and Plagemann conclude about all populist leaders, he put great stock in his own 'perceptions of popular sentiments'.[51] Trump's extensive, unfiltered use of social media was illustrative of his unique brand of hyper-personalised public engagement, one that involved the President communicating directly with the American public (albeit mostly his own base and the media), but more significantly one that highlighted his unwillingness to use State Department professionals and experts to implement (or mediate) such engagement.

During his 2017–2021 presidency, Trump's regular displays of disrespect for many traditional US allies and friends, juxtaposed to his intermittent respect for autocrats and dictators such as Russia's Vladimir Putin and North Korea's Kim Jong-un, illustrated how the Trump administration leaned toward an illiberal populist approach to foreign policy and diplomacy. In his unorthodox appointments, such as selecting his son-in-law Jared Kushner as special envoy to the Middle East peace process, Trump relied on 'personal trust and intimacy that he could not find in a faceless bureaucracy. In doing so, he [acted] less like a politician in a modern democracy and more like the patriarch of a business family'.[52] While conservative intellectual Jacob Heilbrunn argues that the American right has long flirted with foreign dictators,[53] historian Beverly Gage discerned the difference that, under Trump, this predilection 'captured a US president, along with one of the country's two major political parties'.[54] As argued above, the dominance of the two major political parties is key to understanding populist US dynamics.

---

50   Haass 2020.
51   Destradi and Plagemann 2019, 724.
52   Lutfi et al. 2021, 2.
53   Heilbrunn 2024.
54   Gage 2024.

4.2   *Resisting Populist Capture*

Reviewing articles in the *Foreign Service Journal* (*FSJ*) from 2016–2021, we watched for comment on how career Foreign Service Officers (FSO's) and their network responded to Trump and how they engaged with the Washington DC foreign policy establishment, civil society organizations, and the wider public. Several clear strategies emerged, one of which could be described as indirect criticism and messaging about the perils of illiberal populism abroad. A harbinger of this strategy was *FSJ*'s October 2016 edition entitled 'The U.S. Election Through a Foreign Lens'. Published weeks prior to Trump's electoral victory, the issue addressed the rise and risks of illiberal populism in Austria, Brazil, India, and Mexico, featuring three foreign correspondents and a retired diplomat, Xenia Wilkinson – who had served at the US embassy in Mexico City.[55] Retired and former diplomats have long written for *FSJ*, but their use under Trump became especially pertinent and prominent. In general, erstwhile diplomats add an important perspective on diplomacy's domestic dimension, not only in the United States.[56]

In addition to ex-diplomats, *FSJ* published articles by other career professionals, academics, and even members of Congress, again with the likely intent of challenging the assumption of populist leaders that only they know what the people want and that they have an indisputable electoral mandate to speak on their behalf, while also messaging to the administration and public elites about reasons to avoid populist sidelining and capture of diplomacy. In their response to President Trump directly, authors ranged from critical to supportive, with the latter pointing out to the President and his advisers that the State Department had much expertise to offer the administration, including when it came to domestic engagement. For example, an article published in early 2017 by Keith Mines, a serving diplomat on secondment at the bipartisan US Institute of Peace, was a direct invitation to the newly inaugurated president to enlist the State Department in the challenge that Mines described as 'engaging an ambivalent U.S. public to take on the task of sustaining American leadership in an increasingly unhinged world'.[57] *FSJ*'s 'Notes to the New Administration' extended a similar, yet more strongly-worded olive branch imploring Trump to avoid marginalising the Foreign Service, limit political appointments, and bridge divisions.[58] As seen with Trump's deteriorating relationship with State, however, these peace offerings seemed to go unnoticed.

---

55   See Gleitsmann 2016; Silva 2016; Joshi 2016; Wilkinson 2016.
56   On India, Brazil, and other cases, see Huju and Lequesne 2025.
57   Mines 2017, 18.
58   'Notes to the New Administration' 2017.

Overall, these early, more deferential appeals were not typical. Take, for example, *FSJ* Editor in-Chief Shawn Dorman's piece supporting 220 bipartisan career diplomats who signed an election letter opposing Trump,[59] or long-serving diplomat T. J. Lunardi's resignation letter explaining how he 'cannot in good conscience serve in the Department of State under the incoming president, a man I believe to be a threat to our constitutional order'.[60] It is clear that many State Department officers were aware early on of the threat posed by Trump to their professional autonomy, with some criticising and some communicating to the President as best they could.

Another path of resistance taken by *FSJ* contributors was to criticise, directly or indirectly, US foreign policy rather than Trump himself. This category of articles offers an interesting authorial mix of FSO's and outsiders. For example, the Scholl Chair in International Business at CSIS (the Center for Strategic and International Studies) William Reinsch adopted a business-friendly perspective to critique the administration's foreign policy.[61] This less direct approach often came in the form of persuasion via a dexterous appeal for the US to maintain leadership on the international stage. In one case, former Deputy Special Envoy for climate change Karen Florini and climate scholar Ann Florini penned an article denouncing US withdrawal from the 2015 Paris Climate Agreement.[62] In another, Yale law professor and former State Department official Harold Hongju Koh wrote a piece on the administration's erosion of America's leadership in promoting human rights.[63] And AFSA President Barbara Stephenson wrote several appeals for the administration to reinstate US global leadership.[64] Direct or indirect, supportive or critical, these appeals were largely ignored, although they revealed active efforts by US diplomats to resist or at least moderate Trump's populist capture.

4.3   *Building Relations with Congress*

A notable strategy in Trump's first term was the *Journal's* effort to enhance a longstanding State Department desideratum to establish a constituency in Congress. This endeavour was evidenced in the form of the 'Message from the Hill' section beginning in 2018. Noteworthy was a contribution by Democratic Congressman, later Vice-Presidential Candidate, Tim Walz with the aptly titled 'Dear Foreign Service: We've Got Your Back', calling for stronger

---

59   Dorman 2017, 13.
60   Lunardi 2017, 23.
61   Reinsch 2019.
62   Florini and Florini 2017.
63   Koh 2020.
64   Stephenson 2017, 7.

networks of domestic engagement between the State Department and Congress, a return to normal diplomatic capacity, and, pointedly, for general support for career diplomats.[65] Another example was Democratic Congressman Joaquin Castro, who criticised the Trump administration for gutting the State Department and called for increased public engagement. In Castro's words, 'Only by giving *Americans from all walks of life* a direct say and participation in our country's engagement with the rest of the world can we build a durable constituency at home for diplomacy and American global leadership'.[66] This new Journal section also seemed designed to garner Congressional support from both parties, not only to strengthen State against perceived politicisation but also to widen the Department's domestic support as both a diplomatic outreach and democratising imperative.

4.4   *Career vs. Political Appointments*

Compared with other Western countries, US presidents appoint a relatively higher proportion of non-career ambassadors and senior officials at home.[67] This aversion to entrust the nation's diplomatic representation to a separate class of trained professional diplomats has its origins in the country's historical dread of foreign entanglements and wariness of diplomacy's elitist connotations; but also in the idea that political appointees will be closer to 'the people' than professional diplomats. As a generalisation, US conservatives tend to be more suspicious of diplomacy and diplomats than are US liberals.[68] And this was a sentiment that Trump could easily mine in his politicisation of the State Department. In US practice, following a presidential inauguration, all US ambassadors are required to submit their resignation, thus vacating around 200 ambassadorial positions for the president to fill. By convention in recent decades, the incoming president (new or re-elected) should appoint senior officers of the foreign service ('career' appointees) to some 70 percent of ambassadorial positions, and individuals from outside the foreign service ('political appointees') to the other 30 percent. According to AFSA's online 'Ambassador Tracker' (a fascinating example of diplomats publicly monitoring a key indicator of politicisation), 56.5 percent of ambassadors at the end of Trump's term were career appointments, compared to 43.5 percent political appointments, well above the 30 percent 'norm'.[69]

---

65   Walz 2018, 13–14.
66   Castro 2018, 16. Emphasis added.
67   On the US, see Scoville, 2019. For a comparative study, see Niklasson and Jezierska 2024.
68   Wiseman 2011, 239–242; 253–4.
69   Statistics accessed at https://afsa.org/appointments-donald-j-trump.

In response to strong evidence of this politicising trend with ambassadorial appointments, in May 2019 AFSA president Stephenson strategically conveyed the critical views of highly influential voices such as former State Department deputy secretary William Burns and respected print journalist David Ignatius to note the significant lack of well-trained, professional diplomatic capacity in Trump's first term.[70] Criticism focused on the 'glaring incompetence'[71] of some of Trump's non-career ambassadors and on the troublingly high proportion of political appointments at senior levels in the Department where, by 2020, 'only one of the 28 positions at the assistant secretary level at the State Department [was] filled by an active-duty career officer confirmed by the Senate – the lowest number ever'.[72] These numbers were yet another clear example of Trump's populist capture of career diplomacy and 'demolition' of the State Department.[73] Despite the populist narrative, there is evidence that the promotion of political appointments does not reflect the actual will of the people. In RAND surveys, participants viewed political appointees as less effective than career diplomats.[74] We also note a normative dilemma: is the concept of diplomacy's domestic dimension strengthened by elected *illiberal populists* who engage primarily with some groups in society (and indeed denigrate other groups, often in misogynistic and racist terms), or is it strengthened by unelected *liberal professionals* – apolitical experts and civil servants – who engage putatively more neutrally with wider groups in society? It is to that dilemma that we now turn.

4.5   *Diversity*

While claiming to represent American society, Trump's public outreach typically targeted an assortment of socio-political and religious demographic groups, from evangelical Christians to non-college educated 'low information' white males. His 'American society', however, excluded many other social groups, notably migrants, minorities, indigenous, and LGBT people. This exclusion also played out in foreign affairs. A good example was the administration's antipathy towards the hot-button issue of Diversity, Equity, and Inclusion (DEI), policies and practices that had generated, over time, a consensus supporting internal DEI practices and a foreign policy that reflected those values.

---

70   Stephenson 2019, 7–8.
71   Goldfien 2023, 20.
72   Burns and Thomas Greenfield 2020, 108.
73   Burns and Thomas Greenfield 2020, 101.
74   Pollard, Ries, and Amiri 2022, 54. Cf. Goldfien 2023.

This pro-DEI sentiment within State was voiced publicly in 2020 by retired senior diplomats William Burns and Linda Thomas-Greenfield in an article in *Foreign Affairs*. They observed that the Department had suffered from a lack of diversity under Trump with only 10 percent of staff being people of colour and 25 percent being women. As they argued, 'At the very moment when American diplomacy could benefit most from fresh perspectives *and a closer connection to the American people*, the [foreign service] is becoming increasingly homogeneous and detached, undercutting the promotion of American interests and values'.[75] Further reflecting our contention that American diplomats were increasingly seeing their role as not only representing the US abroad but also at home is Burns and Thomas-Greenfield's view that State Department reform would 'help shape a style of diplomacy that is fit for an increasingly competitive international landscape and *better equipped to serve the priority of domestic renewal*'.[76] *Journal* contributors defended DEI not only as a workforce equity issue but as a critical element of how the US is represented to the world via its diplomats. As retired diplomat Peter Romero wrote, 'As I see it, we have two choices. We can either recommit to our diversity and inclusiveness as a nation, the "American Idea"; or we can avert our eyes and hope that somehow the country will snap back to its senses'.[77] Here again, we see former diplomats speaking up against the Trump administration on behalf of their beleaguered, serving colleagues in the State Department in favour of a more inclusive and diverse foreign service that is more representative of – and connected to – American society.

4.6   *Internal Criticism and Dissent*

The quality of any foreign ministry's domestic engagement will be impacted by the extent to which policy is shaped by internal agency, disagreement, even dissent. A key formal, internal mechanism in this regard is the State Department's official Dissent Channel, set up in 1971–1972 during the Vietnam War, when officers at the US Embassy in Saigon 'saw their reporting cables edited to remove negative information'.[78] The Dissent Channel subsequently allowed State Department and USAID staff 'to express dissenting views in a privileged and confidential way to senior leadership … without fear of retaliation or exposure'.[79] Over the decades, the Channel's immediate impact on changing

---

75   Burns and Thomas-Greenfield 2020, 106. Emphasis added.
76   Burns and Thomas-Greenfield 2020, 111. Emphasis added.
77   Romero 2020, 33.
78   Naland 2024. AFSA had created its own dissent awards four years earlier, in 1967.
79   Berndt and Holzer 2023.

contested policies under both Republican and Democratic administration was decidedly mixed, especially in the face of determined political leadership.[80]

Still, the Dissent Channel had become an established feature in the State Department until it came under early attack from the Trump administration. When the administration imposed a controversial travel ban on citizens from seven Muslim-majority countries in 2017 and reports surfaced of widespread opposition to the ban from State Department officers, Trump's White House spokesman, Sean Spicer, responded to a media question with, 'Those career bureaucrats have a problem with it? They should either get with the program, or they can go'. Note the term 'career bureaucrat' being cast in a pejorative sense. A former Deputy Assistant Secretary of State, Harry Kopp, subsequently reported Spicer's response in the *FSJ*.[81] By then, the Trump administration had effectively frozen the Dissent Channel.

The Dissent Channel was a distinctive, if imperfect, feature of American diplomatic practice for half a century, and the Trump administration's silencing of it represented an approach that went beyond simple politicisation in the direction of illiberal populist capture. Without over-stating the impact of the Dissent Channel as an effective mechanism for constructive dissent nor understating its failures, our conclusion is that its existence and occasional successes set a normative, aspirational standard not only for other US government agencies but also for all foreign services in plural political systems.

While State's Dissent Channel is relatively well-known to the Washington policy world, and therefore allows for a degree of elite public accountability, better known to the wider public via the media were cases where the Trump administration vilified individual government officials and diplomats for speaking out about the implementation of the administration's foreign policy and of resistance to some of Trump's instructions to diplomats in the field. Perhaps the best publicised example was the case of the former US ambassador to Ukraine Marie Yovanovitch, who was recalled by Trump from her ambassadorship in Kyiv under highly politicised circumstances. Yovanovitch, a respected career diplomat, was later publicly denigrated by Trump, his allies in Congress, and public enablers such as former New York City mayor Rudolf Giuliani over testimony she gave during Trump's first impeachment trial regarding alleged political interference in Ukraine. Expressions of public support for Yovanovitch by former career diplomats and others were noteworthy for their recognition of the dilemma faced by diplomats who are professionally unwilling to implement unambiguously politicised instructions and

---

80   E.g., on South Sudan policy under Obama, see Shackelford 2020.

81   Kopp 2017, 45.

pressure from a populist leader.[82] Under populist conditions, the societisation of diplomacy will be selective, as it will be managed by political loyalists rather than foreign-ministry professionals and experts.

4.7   Promoting Expertise for the Wider Public

What is constant in *FSJ*'s commentary and articles is the overall message of the need for professional competence and expertise. This is entirely consistent with diplomacy's centuries-long quest to replace elite connections with merit-based criteria in diplomatic work, a process known as professionalisation. Professional diplomats tend to gravitate in their work towards others in the profession or those with comparable social standing. Thus, the *FSJ's* public engagement inclines towards professional 'policy and opinion elites' and the 'attentive public' at the top of the societal pyramid and less so towards the 'general public'. Nonetheless, during the first Trump administration we see in *FSJ's* strategic authorships' – influential members of Congress, journalists, and academics – recognition of the need for State to reach domestic publics through a strategy of *authorial mediation* of the estrangements wrought by Trumpism. These mediations included *olive branching* articles directed at the incoming Trump administration and at his two secretaries of state, offering often polite suggestions for changes in policy and practice. Such recommendations were an acknowledgement of the need for the Department to reform and modernise itself, and the need to encourage vigorous internal debate and constructive dissent – all forms of resistance to populist capture by a democratically challenged administration moving away from professional diplomacy and leaning into personalisation, politicisation, populism, and polarisation.

While the Trump administration both sidelined and politicised the State Department, the contributions to the *FSJ* and the work of AFSA reveal a strong trade-union ethic of resistance to political capture and deep support for a more professional diplomatic service. This resistance was not cloaked in a call to the picket lines but in a range of persuasive strategies, befitting diplomatic culture's longstanding professional commitment to the art of persuasion. Both current and former American diplomats remained deeply invested in America's international standing and the diplomatic capacity required to maintain reputational status. To that end, serving and retired diplomats pursued a multitude of strategies to resist Trump's anti-elitist populism. While this resistance may be seen to have had limited success resisting Trumpist

---

82   Yovanovitch 2022, 338.

politicisation from 2017-2021, one positive unintended consequence was how Trump engendered a sense of urgency in the State Department for the need to supplement its international diplomatic competencies with new domestic-engagement competencies at home, not only via well-connected networks in the Washington Beltway, but also beyond to wider publics. In a functioning democracy, however, the critical element is elections, and it is to the 2020 election and its outcome that we now turn.

5   The 2021–2025 Biden Presidency

5.1   *Biden's Internationalist Worldview*

In stark contrast to Donald Trump's 'America-First' worldview and populist-base approach to domestic politics, Joe Biden can be broadly classified as a moderate Democrat in domestic politics with a liberal internationalist world-view.[83] Before becoming president in early 2021, Biden had long worked closely with the State Department and its embassies abroad in his roles as US Senator, Chairman of the powerful Senate Committee on Foreign Relations and as Vice-President. Biden signalled how his foreign policy goals differed from his predecessor in a 2020 *Foreign Affairs* article titled 'Why America Must Lead Again: Rescuing U.S. Foreign Policy After Trump'.[84] On assuming the presidency, Biden nominated Antony Blinken as his secretary of state. Blinken, whose public service began at the State Department, was a strong supporter of restoring the State Department to its more traditional professional role, giving considerable attention to rebuilding the Department's reputation as a well-respected government agency defending American interests and values abroad while also engaging more inclusively with the American people than his predecessors – Rex Tillerson and Mike Pompeo – under Trump.

5.2   *Blinken: Restoring the State Department*

In a major speech titled the 'Modernization of American Diplomacy' in October 2021 (significantly delivered at the US Foreign Service Institute, where State Department personnel are trained), Blinken noted that President Biden had 'pledged to put diplomacy at the center of [US] foreign policy'

---

83   Mathews 2024.

84   Biden 2020. For a critique that Biden struggled to find a convincing post-Trump strategic narrative, see Miskimmon et al. 2024.

and to increase the State and USAID budget by 10 percent.[85] In a clear attempt to communicate bipartisanship in that speech, Blinken offered encomia for two former Republican secretaries of state, George Shultz and Colin Powell (remarks that can also be interpreted as oblique criticism of Tillerson and Pompeo). Especially noteworthy in the speech was the attention Blinken gave to the importance for State to 'hear more from the American people'. Blinken's motives were likely driven by his own professional diplomatic background and moderate politics, but also by the rude awakening the diplomatic establishment experienced from Trump's populist foreign policy, much of which was grounded in domestic grievances – some of it authentic, some of it manufactured. As implied above, after Trump's 2017–2021 term, diplomats were likely to pay far more attention to the home front than previously. Thus, in one striking paragraph in his October 2021 speech, Blinken said: 'I'll be asking all senior officials to *make domestic travel and engagement a greater priority...* . We're going to reach out much more regularly to civil society groups, private companies, state and local governments, community organizations, universities, and we'll make sure that we're connecting with people from different parts of the country – *urban and rural* – because our mission isn't to serve some Americans, but all Americans. We're diplomats, and *we're going to focus more of our diplomacy here at home* to make sure our policies reflect the needs, the aspirations, the values of the American people'.[86] There is little doubt that these words were intended to convey to US diplomats that their job is to represent – and engage with – a broad cross-section of American society.

In addition, Blinken explicitly endorsed the diversity, equity, and inclusion principle, announcing that the President's budget increases for State and USAID would lead to increased hiring of staff, more broad-based recruitment, improved training at all levels, and more placement opportunities in other agencies, the private sector, and Congressional offices. These initiatives portended closer connections between the State Department and a wider range of American social sectors than had been the case under Trump's selective, populist mobilisation strategies.

In short, Blinken was clearly aiming to re-claim and re-professionalise the State Department, and the contrast with Trump's first term was plain. For example, in Trump's fourth year as president in 2020, high-profile public commentary by former career US diplomats reflected a strong consensus around the need to recover the Department's reputation for professionalism. In addi-

---

85   Blinken 2021.
86   Blinken 2021. Emphases added.

tion to the influential *Foreign Affairs* article by William Burns and Linda Thomas-Greenfield cited above, Burns wrote in *The Atlantic* that 'The style and substance of our polarized politics have infected American diplomacy.... The inability to compromise at home is becoming the modus operandi overseas'. Robert Putnam's depiction of diplomacy as a 'two-level game' was never more acutely obvious. Burns, a former Deputy Secretary of State, directed substantial blame for 'reflexive' partisanship at Trump and his second Secretary of State Pompeo, whom Burns described as 'the most partisan secretary of state in living memory – systematically sidelining career professionals in favor of political allies'.[87] In his memoir *The Back Channel*, Burns – who subsequently became Biden's CIA Director – criticised the Trump administration's 'hollowing out of the State Department' and Trump's 'dismissiveness toward professional diplomats'. Moreover, Burns wrote, 'if anything, career foreign and civil service officers at State are almost loyal to a fault, eager for the opportunity to deliver for a new administration, and hopeful that their expertise will be valued, if not always heeded'.[88] In arguing that a foreign policy that represented the concerns of the American public, and not those of an 'inbred elite', would be 'a good start toward depolarization',[89] we see a clear belief by a former senior diplomat that a strong professional foreign service could help moderate politicisation in Washington and mediate wider domestic estrangement.

We now report our findings from articles published in the *FSJ* during the Biden presidency, which, with some caveats, reinforce the general picture described above in statements and actions by Biden, Blinken, and Burns. They further help our comparison of the domestic engagement approaches of the first Trump and Biden presidencies.

5.3   *Re-professionalising the State Department*

While it is customary for AFSA to welcome an incoming administration *inter alia* via the *Foreign Service Journal*, the congratulatory statement by AFSA president Ambassador Eric Rubin in January 2021 conveyed a deep sense of relief with Biden's victory over Trump and with Blinken's appointment as secretary of state. Careful to re-affirm that AFSA, as the professional association and labour union for the Foreign Service, was 'fundamentally nonpartisan and nonpolitical', Ambassador Rubin noted that both domestic and foreign observers had confirmed the election as 'free and fair',[90] an unmistakable rebut-

---

87   Burns 2020.
88   Burns 2019, 399; see also 400, 410.
89   Burns 2020.
90   Rubin 2021.

tal of Trump's spurious claims that the 2020 election had been stolen from
him. Further, Rubin criticised a public reference by the President to the department as 'The Deep State Department', a moment that was captured in a
photo of Trump with Pompeo 'the Secretary of State [standing] next to him,
smiling'.[91] Rubin lamented, as did many others in public, how respected US
diplomats such as Ambassador Yovanvitch had been 'abandoned' by their
superiors during the Trump impeachment hearings at a time of 'hyper-
polarization and politicization of US foreign policy'.[92]

Ambassadorial and senior appointments under Biden and Blinken reversed
Trump's politicisation push in favour of more career/professional appointments, including bringing back some of the best diplomatic talent that had
resigned or retired during the Trump presidency. As mentioned above, at the
end of Trump's term in January 2021, of 191 ambassadors, 56.5 percent were
career appointments with 43.5 percent political appointments. By contrast, as
of August 2024, 64.1 percent of President Biden's ambassadors were career
appointment and 35.9 percent other/political. The latter figure can be seen
in an even more positive light given Biden's appointment of eight highly qualified former FSO's, such as Nicholas Burns appointed as ambassador to Beijing,
Linda Thomas Greenfield as Permanent Representative to the United Nations,
and Christopher Hill as ambassador to Belgrade. Thus, Biden's record is significantly closer to the 70:30 norm than was Trump's. Career diplomats have
traditionally regarded this ratio as still too heavily weighted with political
appointees and, as mentioned above, still high compared with other liberal
democracies.

5.4   *Internal Constructive Dissent as Public Reassurance*

From early in his term as secretary of state, Blinken announced that dissent
would not only be tolerated but encouraged, an approach that was in conspic-
uous contrast to Tillerson and Pompeo. In testimony to the Senate Committee
on Foreign Relations, he stated, 'This Dissent Channel is something that I
place tremendous value and importance on. It is a way for people in the
State Department to speak the truth, as they see it, to power'.[93] At his October 2021 Foreign Service Institute speech, Blinken announced that he had
'revitalized' the Dissent Channel because, he explained, in reassuring words
that clearly differentiated his view from that of Trump, 'dissent is patriotic.

---

91   For a different, arguably professional 'loyalty to a fault', view of Pompeo, see Sullivan
      2024, 33–34.
92   Rubin 2021.
93   Quoted in Berndt and Holzer 2023.

And it shouldn't just be protected. It should be and it will be welcomed. I'm reading and responding to every dissent that comes through the channel. And I hope the dissent channel will encourage a culture of constructive, professional dissent, more broadly throughout the department, because dissent makes us stronger'.[94]

These admirable commitments were dramatically put to the test following the Hamas-led terrorist attack on Israel of 7 October 2023 – resulting in a death toll of some 1,200 and the kidnapping of over 200 hostages – and Israel's subsequent retaliatory war in Gaza that in under a year led to the killing of more than 41,000 Palestinians and inflicted massive infrastructure damage.[95] Scores of State Department officers and career diplomats were highly critical of President Biden's seemingly unquestioning public support for Israel's military actions that most legal experts agreed contravened international humanitarian law, even when considering the October 7 attack and Hamas's violations of international law such as hostage taking and its extensive use of civilian facilities for military purposes.[96] Notwithstanding what one official reportedly called a 'mutiny' at the State Department,[97] Blinken told staff that 'we're listening' to those 'who disagree with approaches we are taking'.[98] While it was in Secretary Blinken's interests to contain internal dissent 'in house', as contributors to the *FSJ* note, his loyalty to President Biden and to the norm of ministerial responsibility did not lead him to disavow dissenting State Department career officers as both Tillerson and Pompeo had done under Trump. For the attentive public, including commentators in the serious media, the State Department was recovering its reputation for considering dissenting views. Under these conditions, when America's professional diplomats speak to wider public audiences at home, they are more likely to be seen as representing policies and positions that are arrived at after careful consideration rather than imposed by populist whim.

5.5   *Reflecting Public Diversity*
Yet another attempt by the Biden administration to reverse Trump's populist politicisation of government in general – which carried special significance for the State Department's own efforts to undo four years of sidelining and cap-

---

94   Blinken 2021.

95   Farge and Al-Mughrabi 2024.

96   For a critical view of the US's role in the 'breakdown' of international law in the Gaza conflict, see Hathaway 2024.

97   The Economist 2023.

98   Birnbaum and Hudson 2023.

turing – related to 'the comprehensive internal adoption of and adherence to principles of diversity, equity, inclusion, and accessibility' (DEIA, hereafter DEI, the more commonly used term in public discourse).[99] The State Department embraced the administration's DEI policies, pursuant to a June 2021 Executive Order, not only for their perceived inherent organisational value but also to signal that the nation's diplomats should represent the broadest possible spectrum of society. Moreover, diversity in diplomatic representation can also, for example, reinforce the perception of a country's commitment to open immigration policies and societal multiculturalism.[100] In a bold attempt to link US domestic politics and its international relations – in sharp contrast to Trump's hostility to DEI – the Department actively worked to help 'overseas audiences better understand' diversity and inclusion through public diplomacy programmes at diplomatic missions abroad.[101] Additionally, Blinken's October 2021 Foreign Service Institute speech signalled more diverse society-wide recruitment, efforts that were followed up in practice.[102]

We highlight two significant points flowing from DEI debates for the theme of domestic engagement. First, as Popkova and Michaels have argued, state-supported citizen diplomacy such as international exchange programmes at the local level reflect a 'more inclusive and authentic diplomacy globally'.[103] Second, commitment to the general principle of DEI offers a clear litmus test as to whether any US administration conceives of domestic engagement in 'whole-of-society' terms or in 'select-sectors-of-society' terms. The Biden administration largely falls in the former category and the first Trump administration the latter.

5.6   *Building Domestic Constituencies*

With few exceptions, foreign services worldwide suffer from a dearth of domestic constituencies willing to support them politically. A widespread view inside the US State Department, described by serving FSO Joel Ehrendreich in 2021, was that 'the lack of a recognizable domestic constituency harms the Department of State, both in building support for policies and in the battle for resources from Congress'.[104] It is therefore understandable that the State

---

99   Walker and Kirkpatrick 2023, 6.

100   For an informative, comparative discussion on this topic, see Lequesne et al. 2022, 68-88.

101   Walker and Kirkpatrick 2023, 23.

102   The authors observed the DEI approach to recruitment in the outreach work of the State Department's Mid-West Diplomat in Residence, Susan Falatko.

103   Popkova and Michaels 2022, 669.

104   Ehrendreich 2021.

Department 'has long endeavoured to build its domestic constituency, reaching out to the American people to better explain why and how its work is relevant to them'.[105] Two programmes that address this 'domestic constituency deficit', according to Ehrendreich, are the Diplomats in Residence programme that assigns some 20 senior officers each year to American universities and the Department's Hometown Diplomats programme that encourages a smaller number of officers each year to reach out to their hometown or community.

In January 2023, Blinken launched Welcome Corps, an initiative to encourage US citizen groups to sponsor and assist new refugees.[106] The initiative was led by the Department of State's Refugee Admissions Program, in collaboration with the Department of Health and Human Services and community organisations. In addition, the programme included higher education institutions and private sector employers through the subsidiary Welcome Corps on Campus and Welcome Corps at Work, respectively. The former provided a path to permanent legal status in the United States for refugee students, with participating higher education institutions enrolling refugee students in degree programmes and campus sponsor groups committing to supporting their resettlement through private sponsorship.[107] In 2024, the programme received over 13,000 applications from all 50 states, demonstrating willingness by the State Department to engage with and respond to domestic civil society organisations on sensitive political issues. Despite these efforts, their impact was overshadowed by public perceptions of ineffective security at the Mexican border, exacerbated by Trump's anti-immigrant campaign rhetoric that included his promotion of false claims that Haitian immigrants were eating domestic pets in Springfield, Ohio, and his pledge to deport 11 million illegal migrants.

The Biden administration's aim of developing domestic support for its diplomacy on the migration/refugee issue via higher education institutions was understandable – given their historical role recruiting for such popular programmes as Fulbright scholarships and the Peace Corps. However, by 2024, many universities had been successfully portrayed by Trump and his supporters as elitist, 'woke' institutions out of touch with the growing public concern about such issues as illegal migration. Many of those institutions, especially Ivy League universities, were controversially branded as anti-Semitic by Trump surrogates as Israel's war in Gaza unfolded. In retrospect, Biden and

---

105   Ehrendreich 2021.
106   US Department of State.
107   WelcomeCorps.

Blinken's efforts to engage wider publics via established nongovernmental organisations and higher-education institutions constituted a reasonable re-sponse to Trump's populist 'suspicion that expert authority hides elite power'.[108] However, as discussed next, these efforts were not nearly as success-ful reaching beyond those social sectors predisposed to listen to expert voices, leaving open the question of the actual scope and efficacy of the Biden-Blinken 'whole-of-society' approach.

5.7   States and Cities

A significant Biden administration initiative designed to boost its domestic engagement was the establishment of a new office for subnational diplomacy, headed by a Special Representative for City and State Diplomacy. This signa-ture programme, announced by Blinken in October 2022, was tasked to 'fun-damentally strengthen the Department's ties to [American] cities and com-munities' and to integrate their ideas 'into our policymaking'.[109] This new office inter alia supported US cities and states in their ongoing international engagement activities, such as overseas trade missions, tourism, and interna-tional student promotion. A consequential issue further illustrating foreign-policy synergy between Blinken's Department of State and American cities was climate change: 14 US cities were part of the C40 Cities Climate Leader-ship Group, a global network of 100 world city mayors who had committed to measures aimed at reducing their fair share of global-heating emissions by 2030.

Nina Hachigian, a former first Deputy Mayor for International Affairs in Los Angeles who also served as the US ambassador to ASEAN under President Obama, was appointed to lead the new office. At a conference panel on 'Cities as Guardians of Democracy', Hachigian described the role of the new office as being, 'to ensure that local leaders, mayors, governors, city council members, and county officials in the United States are connected to the benefits of our foreign policy, to their counterparts around the world, and to the US Depart-ment of State'.[110] A noteworthy Biden initiative under the cities rubric was the city of Denver, Colorado and the US Department of State's co-hosting of the inaugural Cities Summit of the Americas in April 2023. The Summit discussed shared commitments to issues ranging from democratic governance to orderly migration and was attended by a range of city mayors, government officials, and community stakeholders. Moreover, Blinken was the first Secretary of

---

108   Mills 2024.
109   Blinken 2022.
110   Hachigian 2023.

State to address the US Conference of Mayors. The City-State initiative was in many ways a strong renunciation of Trump's years-long racially charged and polarising rhetoric that maligned big US cities governed by Democrats as ravaged by crime and corruption. In announcing Hachigian's appointment, Blinken stated that the 'Department continues to pursue the implementation of a foreign policy for *all Americans*', including on 'climate change, economic justice, and *democratic renewal*'. In effect, Blinken was promoting a robust form of liberal internationalist domestic engagement with the American public.[111]

Unlike Trump, who put great faith in his own perceptions of popular sentiment – but often manufactured it, as noted above – Biden and especially Blinken relied heavily on the expertise of officials in the State Department who engaged with the American public in a generally even-handed, professional manner consonant with the ideal of a non-partisan civil service. As laudable as these initiatives were, they were unable to overcome the key urban-rural gap that Blinken had identified in 2021. And the priority given to *cities* was unlikely to bridge the gap with rural America that so heavily buttressed US polarisation, an issue that carried into the November 2024 presidential election and presaged an unresolved question: was the Biden administration's domestic engagement on diplomatic issues too heavily weighted towards sectors of the population already well disposed towards them and reached too few others?

6   Conclusion

In this chapter, we examined how the idea and practices of diplomacy's domestic dimension unfolded in the United States over two politically distinct presidential administrations: that of Republican Donald J. Trump (2017–2021) and Democrat Joseph R. Biden, Jr. (2021–2025). Our examination assumed that the nature of diplomacy's domestic engagement is highly dependent on the strength of a governing administration's commitment to democratic or pluralist norms. Thus, when those norms are undermined and authentic domestic engagement is flouted by a populist leader, such as Donald Trump, we considered how the professional diplomatic community, defined here loosely as the network in and around the State Department, responded in its work on the home front. We then explored how this diplomatic network countered when

---

111   Blinken 2022. Emphasis added. See also Blinken 2024, which has a concluding section on 'The Home Front'.

Trump's first administration was succeeded by the Biden administration, a presidency with more conventional views of diplomacy and of how leaders should engage with their own public on international matters.

Comparing the first Trump and Biden administrations when the American zeitgeist was widely characterised by increased politicisation, populism, and polarisation, we identified two contrasting variants of state-society relations. President Trump personified what we depict as *illiberal populist capture.* In this variant, Trump's inward-looking, Make-America-Great-Again foreign policy approach was reflected directly in the intense politicisation – and sidelining – of the Department of State and its efforts at domestic engagement on diplomatic matters. Under secretaries of state Rex Tillerson and then Mike Pompeo, the State Department leadership pursued highly selective domestic engagement largely directed at groups of Americans perceived to be sympathetic to the President's agenda. As described above, the State Department was heavily politicised – and *deprofessionalised* – under Trump. Thus, if career diplomats were not seen as – or did not become – sufficiently loyal to President Trump, they resigned, retired, or sought refuge in the private, non-profit, and think-tank sectors.[112] Trump appointed a higher proportion of non-career, often unqualified ambassadors and loyalists to senior positions at home. Moreover, the Department's Dissent Channel was discontinued. Based on Trump's unprecedented, personalised deployment of social media and his privileged access to many conservative news outlets, we conclude that Trump himself – rather than the State Department – was the key driver of his first administration's domestic engagement on international issues, representing a highly personalist, populist leadership style that exacerbated social and political polarisation. We see this approach as essentially exclusionary and manipulative of diplomacy's domestic dimension.

In contrast, we characterise Biden's approach to diplomacy's domestic dimension as reflecting *liberal internationalist engagement.* His outward-looking Wilsonian worldview was underscored by support for a more professional foreign service, one that would serve any administration with equal dedication and that would engage with a wider spectrum of American society than had Trump. Biden's Secretary of State, Antony Blinken, pursued a different form of State Department engagement with US society than did Tillerson and Pompeo under Trump. Blinken aimed to *reprofessionalise* the State Department, urging it to engage with a varied cross section of US society. He re-activated the Department's Dissent Channel and embraced DEI policies

---

112   Cooper 2022.

within the Department, at overseas posts, and as a core element in the Department's engagement with domestic society, even though DEI was sharply opposed by Trump and his supporters, as they conceived it. Blinken's State Department also advanced several home-front initiatives such as Welcome Corps and programs under the new Office for City and State Diplomacy. In sum, there was a clear difference in the character of the domestic public engagement policies and practices of the US State Department under President Trump (and his secretaries of state Rex Tillerson and Mike Pompeo) and under President Biden (and his secretary of state, Antony Blinken). However, for all their seriousness of purpose, Blinken's efforts appear not to have reached sufficiently beyond liberal-centrist leaning sectors of US society already well disposed to them – at least on the evidence so far.

On the thorny question we posed, building on Der Derian's work, about the role of American diplomats in ameliorating domestic political estrangement so evident in the United States over the eight-year period covering the first Trump and Biden presidencies, our conclusions are tentative and require further research. To his credit, Biden went to considerable lengths to *depolarise* a divided country – through his generally measured public persona and official statements – following his November 2020 election win and the 6 January 2021 attack by Trump supporters on the US Capitol. However, based on our review of professional diplomatic responses by former and current US diplomats, a counter-factual case can plausibly be made that had it not been for Trump's populist excesses from 2017–2021, professional diplomats in the State Department orbit may well have been slower at acknowledging – and acting on, as they did under Blinken – the growing need for the US diplomatic establishment to take the domestic side of their work more seriously than it had in the past.

In terms of intent, Blinken's engagement programs with the American public were commendable in that they tended to allow for dissenting internal and diverse public voices on issues. However, while those efforts contributed to a sense of a return to governance-as-usual under Biden, they do not appear to have mitigated wider public schisms on such issues as DEI. That Biden's State Department took up this divisive issue at the international *and* internal levels is a clear example of diplomats' attempts to mediate estrangement at home. In short American diplomats are even less than ever transfixed on the 'international' and recognize that – under certain political conditions – they can promote healthy, 'whole-of-society' imaginings of the relationship between the state and the public it represents.

Finally, taking the US case from late 2016 to early 2025 overall, it is hard to find support for the thesis that 'moderate degrees of polarization' effectively revitalise 'the incentives for popular participation ... and broad-based political cooperation'.[113] Electorally, Trump's unique brand of populism held sway with a plurality of the American voting public in his 2024 election victory. Only evidence arising from Trump's second term will reveal more clearly if the work of America's professional diplomats – at home – can resist or mitigate, over the medium-to-long-term, further Trump-led domestic polarisation. Future research will no doubt reveal the extent of democratic backsliding in the United States, which in turn will cast light on the evolving nature of diplomacy's domestic dimension, a factor that will undoubtedly weigh heavily on assessments of the country's soft power and status in world affairs. Moreover, new research on diplomacy's home front will need to do more than assess election outcomes for the important reason that 'while vast numbers of Americans participate in presidential elections, only small minorities of voters actually stay engaged.'[114] In sum, US diplomats will need to find more effective ways to manage populist capture and engage with all of American society not only to promote wider, more informed, and inclusive public engagement but as a potentially meaningful contribution to mediating domestic political alienation in a highly polarised society.

Acknowledgements

The co-authors are deeply grateful to the editors, Paul Sharp and Pauline Kerr for their astute comments and to Juliana Zanubi for valuable research assistance.

Bibliography

Abramowitz, Alan and Jennifer McCoy. 'United States: Racial Resentment, Negative Partisanship, and Polarization in Trump's America'. *The ANNALS of the American Academy of Political and Social Science* 681 (1) (2018), 137–156. doi:10.1177/00027 16218811309.
Abramowitz, Alan and Steven Webster. 'The rise of negative partisanship and the nationalization of U.S. elections in the 21st century'. *Electoral Studies* 41 (2016), 12–22. https://doi.org/10.1016/j.electstud.2015.11.001.

---

113 Sarsfield et al., 10.
114 French 2024.

Achenbach, Joel. 'Science is revealing why American politics are so intensely polarized'. *The Washington Post*, 20 January 2024.

Bartels, Larry M. 'The Populist Phantom: Threats to Democracy Start at the Top'. *Foreign Affairs*, (November/December 2024), 108–125.

Berndt, Sara and Holly Holzer. 'The State Department Dissent Channel: History and Impact'. *Foreign Service Journal* (December 2023), 22–29.

Biegon, Rubrick and Soraya Hamdaoui. 'Anti-populism and the Trump trauma in US foreign policy'. *International Affairs* 100 (5) (September 2024), 1857–1875, https://doi.org/10.1093/ia/iiae174.1

Birnbaum, Michael and John Hudson. 'Blinken confronts State Dept. dissent over Biden's Gaza policy'. *The Washington Post*, 14 November 2023.

Blinken, Antony J. 'America's Strategy of Renewal: Rebuilding Leadership for a New World'. *Foreign Affairs*, (November/December 2024), 62–76.

Blinken, Antony J. 'Naming Ambassador Nina Hachigian as Special Representative for Subnational Diplomacy'. *Department of State* Press Statement, 3 October 2022.

Blinken, Antony J. 'On the modernization of American Diplomacy'. Speech at the U.S. Foreign Service Institute, 27 October 2021.

Biden, Joseph R., Jr. 'Why America Must Lead Again: Rescuing U.S. Foreign Policy After Trump'. *Foreign Affairs* (March/April 2020).

Brady, Henry E. and Thomas B. Kent. 'Fifty Years of Declining Confidence & Increasing Polarization in Trust in American Institutions.' *Daedalus*, 15 (4) (Fall 2022), 43–66.

Brewer, Mark D. 'The Rise of Partisanship and the Expansion of Partisan Conflict within the American Electorate'. *Political Research Quarterly* 58 (2) (2005), 219–229. https://doi.org/10.1177/106591290505800203.

Burns, William J. and Linda Thomas-Greenfield, 'The Transformation of Diplomacy: How to Save the State Department,' *Foreign Affairs* (November/December 2020), 100–111.

Burns, William J. 'Polarized Politics Has Infected American Diplomacy'. *The Atlantic*, 6 June 2020.

Burns, William J. *The Back Channel: A Memoir of American Diplomacy and The Case for its Renewal* (New York: Random House, 2019)

Burns, Nicholas. 'The Future of the Foreign Service: A Discussion with Nicholas Burns, Marc Grossman, and Marcie Ries'. *Foreign Service Journal* (January/February 2021), 19–24.

Castro, Joaquin. 'A Foreign Service for America'. *Foreign Service Journal* (September 2018), 15–16.

Cole, Ruth. 'Maintaining neutrality in the Minister's office'. *Australian Journal of Public Administration* 79 (4) (2020), 495–513. https://onlinelibrary-wiley-com.virtual.anu.edu.au/toc/14678500/2020/79/4.

Constantinou, Costas M. 'Between Statecraft and Humanism: Diplomacy and Its Forms of Knowledge.' *International Studies Review* 15 (2013), 141–162.

Cooper, Andrew. 'The Impact of Leader-Centric Populism on Career Diplomats: Tests of Loyalty, Voice, and Exit in Ministries of Foreign Affairs'. In *Ministries of Foreign Affairs in the World. Actors of State Diplomacy*, ed. Christian Lequesne (Leiden: Brill, 2022), 150–171.

Cornago, Noé. *Plural Diplomacies* (Leiden: Brill, 2013).

De Silva, Monika. 'Gender Wars? Diplomacy as a Depolarizing Practice in International Politics of Gender and Sexuality'. *International Studies Quarterly* 68 (3) (2024), 1–13.

Der Derian, James. *On Diplomacy: A Genealogy of Western Estrangement* (Oxford: Blackwell, 1987).

Destradi, Sandra and Johannes Plagemann. 'Populism and International Relations: (Un)predictability, personalisation, and the reinforcement of existing trends in world politics'. *Review of International Studies* 45 (5) (2019).

Destradi, Sandra and Johannes Plagemann. 'Do populists escalate international disputes?' *International Affairs* 100 (5) (September 2024), 1919–1940.

Dorman, Shawn. '220 Career Diplomats Sign Election Letter Opposing Trump'. *Foreign Service Journal* (November 2017), 13.

Drutman, Lee. 'How Hatred Came to Dominate American Politics'. *FiveThirtyEight*, 5 October 2020.

Ehrendreich, Joel. 'State U–A Proposal for Professional Diplomatic Education and Outreach to America'. *Foreign Service Journal* (July/August 2021), 47–50.

Farge, Emma and Nidal Al-Mughrabi. 'Gaza death toll: how many Palestinians has Israel's campaign killed?' *Reuters*, 1 October 2024. https://www.reuters.com/world/middle-east/gaza-death-toll-how-many-palestinians-has-israels-campaign-killed-2024-07-25/.

Fiorina, Morris P. 'America's Missing Moderates: Hiding in Plain Sight'. *American Interest* 8 (4) (2013), 58–67.

Florini, Karen and Ann Florini. 'It's Not Just about Paris: International Climate Action Today'. *Foreign Service Journal* (July/August 2017), 26–31.

French, David. 'Donald Trump Is Already Starting to Fail'. *The New York Times*, 17 November 2024.

Gage, Beverly. 'The Autocratic Allure: Why the Far Right Embraces Foreign Tyrants'. *Foreign Affairs*, 103 (5) (September/October 2024), 199–204.

Gleitsmann, Verena. 'You Are Not Alone, Believe Me'. *Foreign Service Journal* (October 2016), 31–34.

Goldfien, Michael A. 'Just Patronage? Familiarity and the Diplomatic Value of Non-Career Ambassadors'. *Journal of Conflict Resolution* (2023), 1–26.

Haass, Richard. 'Trump's Foreign Policy Doctrine: The Withdrawal Doctrine'. *The Washington Post*, 27 May 2020.

Hachigian, Nina. 'Why City and State Diplomacy Matters to Our Foreign Policy'. *US Department of State*, 25 February 2023. https://www.state.gov/why-city-and-state-diplomacy-matters-to-our-foreign-policy/.

Hathaway, Oona. 'War Unbound: Gaza, Ukraine, and the Breakdown of International Law'. *Foreign Affairs* 103 (3) (May/June 2024).

Hawkins, Stephen et al. 'Hidden Tribes: A Study of America's Polarized Landscape'. *More in Common* (2018).

Heilbrunn, Jacob. *America Last: The Right's Century-Long Romance with Foreign Dictators* (New York: Norton, 2024).

Heltzel, Gordon and Kristin Laurin. 'Polarization in America: two possible futures'. *Current Opinion in Behavioral Sciences* 34 (2020), 179–184.

Hill, Betram, ed. *The Political Testament of Cardinal Richelieu: The Significant Chapters and Supporting Selections* (Madison: University of Wisconsin Press, 1961).

Hocking, Brian. 'The Ministry of Foreign Affairs and the National Diplomatic System.' In *Diplomacy in a Globalizing World*, eds. Pauline Kerr and Geoffrey Wiseman (Oxford: Oxford University Press, 2018, 2nd ed.), 129–150

Huju, Kira and Christian Lequesne. 'Career Diplomats and Populist Leaders: Mediating or Marketing Estrangement?'. In *Routledge Handbook of Populism and Foreign Policy*, eds. David Cadier, Angelos Chryssogelos, and Sandra Destradi (London: Routledge, 2025), 289–307.

Joshi, Ruchir. 'How India Sees U.S. Elections'. *Foreign Service Journal* (October 2016), 35–38.

Kerr, Pauline. 'Diplomats and Politicization'. In *The Palgrave Handbook of Diplomatic Reform and Innovation*, eds. Paul Webster Hare, Manfredi Sanchez, Juan Luiz, and Kenneth Weisbrode (Cham: Palgrave Macmillan, 2023), 111–131.

Kim, Hwajung and Jan Melissen. 'Engaging Home in International Diplomacy'. *The Hague Journal of Diplomacy* 17 (2022), 611–613.

Klein, Ezra. 'Trump Turned the Democratic Party into a Pitiless Machine'. *The New York Times*, 18 August 2024.

Koh, Harold Hongju. 'Why U.S. Leadership Matters for the Global Defense, Protection and Promotion of Human Rights'. *Foreign Service Journal* (June 2020), 31–34.

Kopp, Harry. 'The State of Dissent in the Foreign Service'. *Foreign Service Journal* (September 2017), 41–45.

Lake, David A., Lisa L. Martin, and Thomas Risse. 'Challenges to the Liberal Order: Reflections on International Organization'. *International Organization* 75 (2021), 225–257.

Lequesne, Christian. 'Populist governments and career diplomats in the EU: the challenge of political capture'. *Comparative European Politics* 19 (6) (2021), 779–795.

Lequesne, Christian et al. 'Ethnic Diversity in the Recruitment of Diplomats: Why Ministries of Foreign Affairs Take the Issue Seriously'. In *Ministries of Foreign Affairs in the World. Actors of State Diplomacy*, ed. Christian Lequesne (Leiden: Brill, 2022).

Lunardi, TJ. 'With Deep Regret'. *Foreign Service Journal* (March 2017), 23–24.

Lutfi, Ameen, Nisha Mathew, and Serkan Yolacan. 'Strongmen and informal diplomats: Toward an anthropology of international relations'. *History and Anthropology* (2021). https://doi.org/10.1080/02757206.2021.1946050

Mallett, Michael. 'Ambassadors and Their Audiences in Renaissance Italy'. *Renaissance Studies* 8 (3) (1994), 229–43.

Mathews, Jessica T. 'What Was the Biden Doctrine? Leadership Without Hegemony'. *Foreign Affairs*, 103 (5) (2024), 38–51.

Meijen, Jens. 'Rethinking the Tensions between Populism and Diplomacy: A Case Study of Regional Sub-State Diplomacy as Populist Image-Building Strategy in Flanders'. *The Hague Journal of Diplomacy* (18) (2023), 35–63.

Mills, M. Anthony. 'The MAGA Science Agenda Reveals America's Future'. *New York Times*, 27 November 2024.

Mines, Keith. 'Mr. President, You Have Partners at State to Help Navigate the World's Shoals'. *Foreign Service Journal* (January/February 2017), 18–22.

Miskimmon, Alister et al., 'Repairing the United States' reputation? The US strategic narrative and the Biden administration'. In *Soft Power and the future of US foreign policy*, ed. Hendrik W. Ohnesorge (Manchester, UK: Manchester University Press, 2024).

Naland, John K. 'AFSA's Constructive Dissent Awards'. *Foreign Service Journal* (April 2024), 53.

Niklasson, Birgitta and Katarzyna Jezierska. 'The Politicization of diplomacy: a comparative study of ambassador appointments'. *International Affairs*, 100 (4) (2024), 1653–1673.

'Notes to the New Administration'. *Foreign Service Journal* (January-February 2017), 33–43.

Packer, George. 'A New Report Offers Insights into Tribalism in the Age of Trump'. *The New Yorker*, 12 October 2018.

Peters, B. Guy and Jon Pierre. 'Politicisation of the civil service: concepts, causes, consequences'. In *Politicisation of the civil service in comparative perspective: The quest for control*, eds. Peters, B. Guy and Jon Pierre (London: Routledge, 2004).

Pollard, Michael S. Charles P. Ries and Sohaela Amiri. 'The Foreign Service and American Public Opinion'. *Research Report, Rand Corporation*, Santa Monica, 2022.

Popkova, Anna and Jodi Hope Michaels. 'Who Represents the Domestic Voice? Diversity, Equity and Inclusion in Citizen Diplomacy'. *The Hague Journal of Diplomacy* 17 (2022).

Porcile, Lica and Norman Eisen. 'The Populist Paradox'. Brookings (28 October 2020), available at: https://www.brookings.edu/articles/the-populist-paradox/.

Reinsch, William. 'U.S.-China Trade: If We Get to Yes, Will It Make Any Difference?' *Foreign Service Journal* (July-August 2019), 32–36.

Rohde, David. *Where Tryanny Begins: The Justice Department, the FBI, and the War on Democracy* (New York: Norton, 2024).

Romero, Peter. 'Living Up to the American Idea'. *Foreign Service Journal* (September 2020), 33–34.

Rubin, Eric. 'A Moment of Hope and Possibility'. *Foreign Service Journal* (January/February 2021), 7.

Sarsfield, Rodolfo, Paolo Moncagatta, and Kenneth M. Roberts, 'Introduction: The New Polarization in Latin America'. *Latin American Politics and Society*, vol 66, no. 2 (May 2024), 1–23.

Scoville, Ryan. 'Unqualified Ambassadors'. *Duke Law Journal* 69 (71) (2019), 71–196.

Shackelford, Elizabeth. *The Dissent Channel: American Diplomacy in a Dishonest Age* (New York: Public Affairs, 2020).

Silva, Carlos Lins da. 'The U.S. Election Through Brazilian Eyes'. *Foreign Service Journal* (October 2016), 28–30.

Solomon, Richard H. and Nigel Quinney. *American Negotiating Behavior: Wheeler-Dealers, Legal Eagles, Bullies, and Preachers* (Washington DC: United States Institute of Peace, 2010).

Schedler, Andreas. 'Rethinking Political Polarization'. *Political Science Quarterly* 138 (3) (Fall 2023), 335–359.

Stephenson, Barbara. 'Sustaining America's Global Leadership'. *Foreign Service Journal* (July-August 2017), 7.

Stephenson, Barbara. 'The State of State: Putting the Back Channel Up Front'. *Foreign Service Journal* (May 2019), 7–8.

'Subnational Diplomacy with Ambassador Nina Hachigian', *Council on Foreign Relations* transcript of remarks, 14 February 2023.

Sullivan, John J. *Midnight in Moscow: A Memoir from the Front Lines of Russia's War Against the West* (New York: Little, Brown and Company, 2024).

The Economist (online). 'What is the American State Department's "dissent channel"?' 9 November 2023.

Tufekci, Zeynep. 'Politicians Say We're More Divided Than Ever: It Could Be Worse'. *The New York Times*, 31 July 2024.

US Department of State. 'Welcome Corps'. https://www.state.gov/welcome-corps/.

Walker, Vivian S. and Deneyse A. Kirkpatrick. 'Public Diplomacy and DEIA Promotion: Telling America's Story to the World'. Washington DC: A Special Report by the US Advisory Commission on Public Diplomacy (November 2023).

Waltz, Kenneth N. *Man, the State, and War: A Theoretical Analysis* (New York: Columbia University Press, [1959] 2001).

Walz, Tim. 'Dear Foreign Service: We've Got Your Back'. *Foreign Service Journal* (January/February 2018), 13–14.

WelcomeCorps. 'About the Welcome Corps'. https://welcomecorps.org/about/.

Wilkinson, Xenia. 'Mexico, NAFTA and Election 2016'. *Foreign Service Journal* (October 2016), 39–42.

Wiseman, Geoffrey. 'Distinctive Characteristics of American Diplomacy'. *The Hague Journal of Diplomacy* 6 (3–4) (December) 2011, 235–259.

Wiseman, Geoffrey. 'Where are the diplomats in Trump's Sidelined State Department?' *Australian Outlook*, 16 May 2017.

Wiseman, Geoffrey. 'Expertise and Politics in Ministries of Foreign Affairs: The Politician-Diplomat Nexus', in Christian Lequesne (ed.), *Ministries of Foreign Affairs in the World. Actors of State Diplomacy*, Leiden: Brill, 2022, 119–149.

Yovanovitch, Marie. *Lessons from the Edge: A Memoir* (New York: Mariner Books, 2022).

Zeya, Uzra S. and Jon Finer. 'Revitalizing the State Department and American Diplomacy'. *Council on Foreign Relations*, Council Special Report No. 89 (November 2020) accessed on *FSJ* (January/February 2021) at: https://afsa.org/boosting-us-diplomacy-and-national-security-three-new-reports. This and two other reports are summarized in this *FSJ* link.

CHAPTER 9

United States Citizen Diplomacy and the Domestic Publics

Navigating the Contested Terrain of Diversity, Inclusion and Representation in State-Supported Programmes

Anna Popkova[1]

Summary

This chapter examines the domestic dimension of citizen diplomacy by analysing the efforts to make U.S. state-supported citizen diplomacy programmes more representative and inclusive of the diversity of the U.S. domestic publics. Drawing on the critical scholarship that analyses the role of identity, power, access, and voice in civil society, this chapter explains that meaningful engagement with the domestic publics must consider the complex relationships of negotiation, collaboration, and contestation between marginalized and dominant groups in socio-political environments marked by power imbalances rooted in histories of inequalities. Intentionally developing, incorporating and sustaining policies and programmes that advance the inclusion and participation of different groups and individuals, especially those with historically limited participation opportunities, is at the core of diversity, equity, inclusion and accessibility (DEIA) work. This chapter examines the DEIA efforts of Global Ties U.S. – the U.S.'s largest and oldest citizen diplomacy organization and network. The findings discuss the three core themes: representation and inclusion for greater authenticity; intentionality; and respect for local communities. Each theme reveals how engaging in meaningful DEIA work brings citizen diplomacy closer to diplomacy's humanistic roots, making citizen diplomacy a "humanistic knowledge practice" concerned with mutual learning and relationship-building – both much-needed approaches to finding solutions to humanity's shared problems. The chapter also discusses challenges, such as overcoming systemic barriers to shifting the perception of citizen diplomacy from an elite activity to one accessible to all, and navigating the development of DEIA projects in a political climate influenced by conservative and far-right forces.

---

1 Western Michigan University

Keywords

citizen diplomacy – domestic publics – representation – diversity – inclusion – humanism – U.S. foreign policy

1   Introduction

Citizen diplomacy is frequently defined as the right, ability and even responsibility of ordinary people to affect foreign policy and international relations by "engaging across cultures, and creating shared understanding through meaningful person-to-person interactions."[2] Because of its "people-to-people" relationship-building component, citizen diplomacy tends to get romanticized by scholars and practitioners alike. Scholars ground citizen diplomacy in the relational approach to diplomacy that rejects the "diplomacy-as-propaganda" view and instead emphasizes the active role of publics in diplomacy, and the authentic relationship-building that frequently results from such interactions.[3] Practitioners always have an abundance of heartwarming stories that show how cross-national friendships and partnerships emerge from many citizen diplomacy initiatives and some indeed have an impact on foreign and domestic policies worldwide.

While citizen diplomacy indeed has many strengths and a robust history of successes, this chapter aims to take a deeper and more critical look at the domestic dimension of U.S. state-supported citizen diplomacy programmes by analysing the opportunities and challenges associated with the ongoing process of trying to make citizen diplomacy more representative and inclusive of the wide variety of people comprising the U.S. domestic publics. Domestic publics have always been instrumental in implementing the state-supported citizen diplomacy programmes; citizen diplomats in local communities open the doors of their businesses, organizations and homes to visitors from all over the world, welcoming them and engaging with them in many different ways. Yet no close attention has been paid to who exactly these citizen diplomats are and the extent to which they reflect the diversity of the local communities they represent. Domestic diversity and representation are important to address because if the strength of citizen diplomacy lies in its power to build relationships in genuine ways and to "tell the American story" authentically,

---

2 The Center for Citizen Diplomacy, n.d.
3 Cull 2009; Fitzpatrick 2007; Fitzpatrick 2010; Kruckeberg and Vujnovic 2005; Vanc and Fitzpatrick 2016; Yun 2006.

domestic diversity – in all its beauty but also complexity and tensions – is an integral part of this story.

The history of the U.S. state-sponsored citizen diplomacy programmes in part explains the lack of attention to domestic publics and further lack of critical engagement with domestic diversity as a key component of citizen diplomacy. In the United States, the power of the ordinary people – not only the political leaders – to affect foreign affairs was formally recognized and institutionalized during the Cold War. The first citizen diplomacy and international exchange programmes supported and funded by the Department of State, such as, for example, the International Visitor Leadership Program (IVLP) trace their roots to the 1950s. While the program was established to "build global alliances," the "us versus them" Cold War foreign policy framework inevitably impacted the goals and the design of the programmes. "Telling the American story" to the world while promoting the American values and "way of life" was a priority and a strategy for winning "the battle for hearts and minds." It was assumed that "the American people" shared the government's foreign policy goals when it came to the larger aim of "winning the Cold War." In turn, the involvement of "the American people" in citizen diplomacy programmes was viewed as a way to showcase the U.S.'s openness to sharing the lives of its ordinary people with others from around the world, and, most importantly, showcasing "democracy at work" as a key American value. Yet the concept of democracy and democratic representation has been treated uncritically in the context of citizen diplomacy by scholars and practitioners. What does "the American story" and the story of the American democracy look like when one takes into consideration the fact that throughout the U.S. history many domestic populations and communities were denied opportunities for democratic participation? What does the American story look like when one highlights the stories of conquest, settler colonialism, slavery, and the resulting systemic injustices but also the stories of resistance that continue shaping the U.S. life and politics? This chapter argues that telling the story of American democracy while building relationships cross-nationally continues to be important, particularly at a time when democratic values are being seriously challenged in the U.S. and around the world. But telling this story authentically means engaging more deeply and critically with the notions of domestic diversity and representation in citizen diplomacy.

Representation is central to both diplomacy and democracy. Just like career diplomats act as representatives of their countries in the international arena, citizen diplomats represent – intentionally or unintentionally – their countries and their communities in the interactions with the foreign peers. Scholars and practitioners frequently talk about the authenticity of citizen diplomat representation because, in contrast to official diplomacy and diplomats, ordinary citizens are viewed as "not having [political] agendas"[4] because "they are just people talking to other people."[5] Another aspect of authentic representation relates to diversity where "ordinary people" are often seen as a more genuine reflection of what a country is like, as opposed to career diplomats who are seen as representing only a fraction of society, usually that connected to political elites and power and thus more privileged in many ways. Representation is also key for democracy – a system that is based, at least in theory, on the idea of ordinary people's political agency and participation in the political process. However, both in democracy and citizen diplomacy, representation is a contested issue. In case of citizen diplomacy, given the history of state-supported citizen diplomacy programmes in the U.S. rooted in the Cold War politics, the organizational practices shaping citizen diplomacy programmes, the larger systemic issues within the U.S. that determine, for example, who has and who does not have the privilege to volunteer for nonprofit organizations, or who does and does not see themselves as a potential "citizen diplomat," what kind of United States of America do the foreign visitors see and experience during their exchange program visits? In turn, what kinds of people and organizations within the U.S. get to benefit from these exchanges? These questions are central to this chapter, which examines the various efforts to make citizen diplomacy more diverse and inclusive by Global Ties U.S. – the largest and oldest organization and a network of community partners that implement state-supported citizen diplomacy programmes throughout the U.S. This chapter argues that in order to represent local communities more authentically, in all of their diversity, one needs to reexamine citizen diplomacy more critically and engage more intentionally and meaningfully with the local, hosting communities. In the past few years, Global Ties U.S. and its network members have been doing so through a variety of DEIA (diversity, equity, inclusion, and accessibility) projects and initiatives. Many of these projects resulted in meaningful changes in structures and policies, as well as in a significant shift in the conversation around citizen diplomacy's purpose and meaning. At the same time, all of these changes have been happening in the environment marked by the growing influence of the radical right in the U.S. politics, the introduction and in some cases passing of the bills targeting DEIA efforts in several states, and the return of Donald Trump to power in 2025. This chapter examines Global Ties U.S.'s DEIA efforts to better understand their purpose and meaning, the key opportunities and challenges asso-

---

4   Popkova 2022, 270.
5   Ibid.

ciated with the process, particularly in the context of the current turbulent
political environment in the U.S., and to enrich our understanding of citizen
diplomacy's domestic dimension as it relates to domestic diversity and representation. This chapter will also argue that meaningful engagement with DEIA
initiatives brings citizen diplomacy closer to diplomacy's humanistic roots,
making citizen diplomacy a "humanistic knowledge practice"[6] concerned
with mutual learning and relationship-building – a critical aspect that brings
diplomacy to the forefront of the much-needed solutions to the shared global
problems humanity faces today.

This chapter begins by discussing the links between the domestic dimension of citizen diplomacy in the U.S., representation, authenticity, and democracy. It then discusses the concept of "humanity-centred diplomacies" and the
concept of diplomacy as humanistic knowledge practice, poses the chapter's
key research questions and discusses the study's methodology. Next, the chapter provides relevant background on Global Ties U.S. and its network and their
recent and ongoing DEIA projects and initiatives. Finally, the chapter presents
the findings, linking them to the theoretical insights discussed in the first two
sections. The chapter concludes by summarizing the key findings and reflecting on their implications for citizen diplomacy as a practice and an area of
academic inquiry.

2   Representing Domestic Society: In Diplomacy and Democracy

Authenticity is considered one of the key strengths of citizen diplomacy. As
Sherry Mueller noted, "citizen diplomacy ... allows the world a genuine insight
into American character, values, and institutions."[7] Indeed, citizen diplomacy
programmes, including state-supported ones, rely on networks of dedicated
volunteers in local communities to make the programmes happen and to
"build relationships and friendships in genuine ways."[8] This authenticity is
often contrasted with traditional diplomacy or state-centred public diplomacy, which is frequently accompanied by "public scepticism" and the perception that "governments always have agendas."[9] In the U.S., involving local
communities also allows showcasing "democracy at work," demonstrating to

---

6 Constantinou 2013.
7 Mueller 2020, 113.
8 Popkova 2022, 270.
9 Ibid.

the world how the democratic values the U.S. promotes worldwide play out domestically.

Representation is critical both for diplomacy and democracy. Citizen diplomats represent their local communities to foreign visitors. But who exactly gets to represent the domestic society? Who gets to be the citizen diplomat and who does not? If citizen diplomacy "allows the world a genuine insight into American character, values, and institutions,"[10] what is an "American character," what are the "American values and institutions" and who represents them to the foreign visitors? Questions of representation and inclusion are equally important for democracy, particularly under the framework of participatory democracy, which emphasizes the importance and the impact of citizens' active involvement in the political decision-making process.[11] Related to participatory democracy is a concept of deliberative democracy, which states that political decisions should be made as a result of reasonable and fair discussion and debate among citizens.[12]

Drawing on the concepts of participatory and deliberative democracy, recent conversations on the role of domestic society in public diplomacy emphasized the importance of "deliberative public diplomacy,"[13] defining it as "people's" or participatory diplomacy where domestic publics actively engage in the foreign policy development process. Such approach implies that members of the domestic publics would be involved in the decision-making process, including on topics like national security or economic priorities.[14] It also shifts the focus from separating domestic and international engagement to viewing them as inherently interrelated. Importantly, deliberative public diplomacy is also defined as a "representative, consultative and inclusive"[15] process, in alignment with the scholarship on democratic theory, as well as progressive thinking about democratic practice that has been wrestling with issues of representation and inclusion for a long time. Yet what has been missing from these early conversations on deliberative public diplomacy is a more nuanced and critical engagement with the question of who exactly these domestic publics are and what historical, cultural, political and systemic circumstances determine whose voices are more or less likely to be included in deliberative public diplomacy. Insights from scholarship on democratic theory

10   Mueller 2020, 113.
11   Bherer, Dufour and Montambeault. 2016.
12   Eagan 2016.
13   Walker, Fitzpatrick, and Wang 2022.
14   Ibid.
15   Walker, Fitzpatrick, and Wang 2022.

that focus on the role of identity, power, voice and inclusion in civil society provide helpful analytical tools for deeper engagement with the question of representation and inclusion of domestic publics in public diplomacy and state-supported citizen diplomacy as one of its elements.

In the U.S. context, the initial debates that raised the questions of democratic representation and inclusion were in part spurred by the English translation of Jürgen Habermas's *The Structural Transformations of the Public Sphere* in 1989. In the book, Habermas introduced the concept of the bourgeois public sphere – a realm in which civil society members came together as private persons to debate and deliberate the activities of the state, acting in an advisory capacity and holding the state accountable through the power of public opinion. Having emerged as a counterweight to absolutist states of early modern Europe, the bourgeois public sphere flourished in the seventeenth and eighteenth centuries and operated through a network of coffeehouses and the production of political pamphlets. Central to the functioning of the bourgeois public sphere was the agency of citizens, and their engagement in rational discussion to which all citizens would have unrestricted access and that would be free of economic and political control. Shortly after the publication of the English translation of *The Structural Transformations of the Public Sphere,* several U.S. theorists pointed out a significant flaw in the concept of the bourgeois public sphere – its exclusion of women, marginalized minorities and labourers. As one of the major critics of the concept Nancy Fraser pointed out, "despite the rhetoric of publicity and accessibility, [the] official public sphere rested on, indeed was importantly constituted by, a number of significant exclusions."[16] The recognition of these exclusions prompted efforts to re-examine the public sphere concept and paved the way for more scholarship that examined the role of identity, power, access and voice in civil society.[17] As Asen and Brouwer noted in their introduction to the volume *Counterpublics and the State*, these efforts resulted in three key areas of inquiry: the analysis of the multiplicity of the public sphere(s), the loosening of boundaries and appreciation of the permeability of borders, and the reconsideration of the separation of the public sphere and the state. Insights from each of these lines of inquiry have direct relevance for today's emerging conversation on greater inclusion of the domestic publics in diplomacy, public diplomacy and foreign policy matters in general. For example, reconsideration of the separation of the public sphere

---

16   Fraser 1990, 67.

17   Asen and Brouwer 2001; Black Public Sphere Collective 1995; Dean 1992; Goodnight 1997; Houser 1998; Jackson 2014; Squires 2002.

and the state is at the core of the very concept of citizen diplomacy, which asserts that ordinary citizens have the ability – and even a responsibility – to shape international affairs and foreign policy. Similarly, the loosening of boundaries and appreciation of permeability of borders is what fuels the increasing efforts to engage domestic publics in public and citizen diplomacy work. Given the focus of this chapter on representation, diversity and inclusion, the first line of inquiry – the analysis of the multiplicity of the public sphere(s) – deserves particular attention and will be discussed next.

Nancy Fraser's term "subaltern counterpublics" became central to the idea of recognition of the multiplicity of publics. Drawing on feminist scholarship and revisionist historiography that demonstrated how women participated in public life despite being formally excluded from the bourgeois public sphere, Fraser introduced the term subaltern counterpublics, defining it as "parallel discursive arenas where members of subordinated social groups invent and circulate counterdiscourses [and] formulate oppositional interpretations of their identities, interests, and needs."[18] Importantly, subaltern counterpublics are not always functioning separately or in opposition to the dominant, mainstream public sphere (although they often do). Instead, as another theorist Jane Mansbridge noted, they "oscillate" across varying spaces. As Asen and Brouwer pointed out, "the emancipatory potential of counterpublics emerges in this dialectical movement of withdrawal and reengagement with wider publics."[19] A scholar of media, race, gender and politics Catherine Squires discussed extensively the various modes of participation by subaltern counterpublics in her work. Subaltern counterpublics can oscillate, act as counterpublics disrupting the state actions and making demands, or they can hold a "parallel" status, "working in conjunction with others on equal footing."[20] These insights illuminate the complexity of interactions between marginalized and dominant groups in socio-political environments marked by power dynamics rooted in histories of inequalities, such as the U.S. Understanding and acknowledging these dynamics is crucial for citizen diplomacy that strives to engage domestic publics more meaningfully while aiming to represent domestic communities authentically and in all of their diversity. Thinking of domestic societies as made up of many diverse publics engaged in complex relationships of negotiation, collaboration, and contestation that are mediated by historical, structural and systemic power imbalances and inequalities is critical for making citizen diplomacy more inclusive and representative. At

---

18   Fraser 1990, 67.
19   Asen and Brouwer 2001, 7.
20   Squires 2001, 132. See also Squires 2002 for additional in-depth analysis of the framework.

the level of citizen diplomacy practice, intentionally developing, incorporating and sustaining policies and programmes that advance the inclusion and participation of different groups and individuals, especially those whose opportunities for participation have been historically limited, as at the core of diversity, equity, inclusion and accessibility (DEIA) work. Focusing on inclusion and diversity is also a progressive, forward-looking approach to diplomacy, which, as Rhonda Zaharna notes in her recent book *Boundary Spanners of Humanity*, is increasingly tasked with "address[ing] the wicked problems that humanity and the planet face."[21] Addressing these problems requires collaboration, collective problem-solving, and creativity borne out of multiplicity of experiences and perspectives – all characteristics of what Zaharna terms "humanity-centred diplomacies." The next section discusses this concept, centring on the notion of humanism and explaining how focusing on diversity and inclusion brings citizen diplomacy closer to diplomacy's humanistic roots.

3   Citizen Diplomacy as Humanistic Knowledge Practice

Asking questions about representation and inclusion in domestic societies engaged in citizen diplomacy takes us to the foundational ideas on the nature of diplomacy, its historical and conceptual roots and, consequently, its purpose and goals. Costas Constantinou discusses diplomacy and its humanistic roots, arguing that complex global problems require solutions that combine "statecraft and humanism."[22] Constantinou argues that statecraft – an approach that is based on prioritizing state interests, foreign policy goals, and the "technical know-hows" of negotiation and advocacy to advance state interests – dominates and in many ways defines modern diplomacy. While this approach "remains crucial and valuable,"[23] its dominance leaves little room for humanism, which is critical for diplomacy's central goal of "mediating estrangement."[24] Constantinou argues that "humanism brings to diplomatic practice the search for *other knowledge* (not merely foreign interest), learning to appreciate and incorporate *rival perspective* (not just rhetorical skill), and on the whole *thinking outside the box* and *rethinking the given*."[25] Drawing on

---

21   Zaharna 2022.
22   Constantinou 2013.
23   Constantinou 2013, 142.
24   Der Derian 1987.
25   Constantinou 2013, 143.

historical examples of diplomatic modes, roles and institutions that had humanism at its core, Constantinou emphasizes the importance of diplomacy as
a humanistic knowledge practice that is detached from politics and independent from the state, and that considers the process of knowledge discovery as
important (if not more important) as the results.

Acknowledging the problematic legacy of the Western humanist project,
which was "used to eradicate alternative ways of living and colonize indigenous polities, languages, and memories" and "to empower the Western/impe-
rial diplomatic subject in highly problematic ways,"[26] Constantinou notes,
echoing Edward Said's view, that documenting and critically re-thinking this
past is very much the purpose of humanism. This perspective on humanism is
important for this chapter because, as will be shown further, meaningful DEIA
initiatives (including those happening in the field of citizen diplomacy) aim to
accomplish just that: to continuously reassess the past, and think creatively,
independently and compassionately about what can be done in the current
moment and for the future to make societies and communities more "human-
centred."

In line with Constantinou's ideas, Rhonda Zaharna's forward-thinking book
Boundary Spanners of Humanity emphasizes the importance of "humanity-
centred diplomacies" as critical for addressing the challenges of today's
world and "the wicked problems of humanity." Zaharna identifies three functions of humanity-centred diplomacies. The first is collaborative problem-
solving. Drawing on insights from traditional diplomacy and referencing Jönsson's work, Zaharna points out that diplomatic studies distinguish between
bargaining and problem solving. The former "involves manipulative tactics in
order to secure relative advantages",[27] while the latter is "associated with creativity and the search for new, inventive solutions" and "implies information
sharing and a joint search for common interests."[28] Jönsson discusses international negotiations that led up to the Ottawa Treaty banning landmines in
1997 and the creation of the International Criminal Court in 2002 as some of
the prominent examples of negotiations that incorporated problem-solving.
This critical difference between bargaining and problem solving aligns with
Constantinou's discussion of the difference between statecraft and humanism
in diplomacy. It also aligns with the concept of power sharing and the notion
of abundance central to meaningful DEIA work.[29] Just like Jönsson contrasts

---

26   Ibid.
27   Zaharna, 162.
28   Jönsson 2015, 14.
29   Cortes and Krzanowski 2019.

bargaining, where negotiating parties focus on "claiming value" or "maximiz-ing one's own utility" while problem-solving involves "creating value" or "ex-panding the pie", scholars and practitioners of DEIA initiatives similarly dis-cuss power sharing as a key principle for problem-solving. Moreover, the concept of power sharing in fact comes from the field of conflict mediation, including mediation of violent ethnic conflicts[30] and civil conflicts.[31]

The second function of humanity-centred diplomacies is "mediating human diversity." Indeed, when one wants to engage in collaborative prob-lem-solving and draw on a multiplicity of views, perspectives and back-grounds, mediation of human diversity becomes a key function but also a skill. Political theorist Iris Marion Young who wrote extensively on the nature of justice and social difference noted that difference is "a necessary resource for a discussion-based politics in which participants aim to cooperate, reach understanding and do justice."[32] Meaningful DEIA initiatives are grounded in evidence-based research from various fields on mediation of difference and on using diversity and difference as valuable resources for effective collabora-tions and creative breakthroughs. Applying these insights to concrete practi-ces in citizen diplomacy can help make the practice more humanity-centred and move it closer to its humanistic roots. Finally, the third function Zaharna discusses is "the need for public diplomacy to respond to the needs of humans, most prominently emotional and spiritual needs."[33] As Zaharna further notes, "the practice of empathetic public diplomacy elevates public diplomacy prac-tice from the *battle* for hearts and minds to the *care* for hearts and minds"[34] – a distinction that aligns with Constantinou's "statecraft versus humanism" dis-cussion. Similarly, empathy and emotional intelligence are at the core of any meaningful and effective DEIA initiatives.

This chapter connects the ideas that emerge in conversations about diver-sity, equity, inclusion, accessibility and justice in citizen diplomacy to critical scholarship on the role of subaltern counterpublics in civil society, and to the fundamental principles of humanism and humanity-centred diplomacies. To this end, this chapter is guided by the following research questions: What are the key themes and principles that define DEIA work in citizen diplomacy context, particularly in its domestic dimension? What are the opportunities and challenges – cultural, systemic, and political – associated with imple-

---

30   Sisk 1996.
31   Gates, n.d.
32   Young 1997, 385.
33   Zaharna, 162.
34   Ibid.

menting DEIA initiatives in citizen diplomacy programmes at the local level? To what extent do the key principles that define DEIA work in citizen diplomacy's domestic dimension bring citizen diplomacy closer to diplomacy's humanistic roots and align with the principles of humanity-centred diplomacies?

The sources for this study were collected in three primary ways: participant observation, institutional analysis of a variety of documents and reports by Global Ties U.S. and its network members, and in-depth semi-structured interviews with staff members and volunteers involved in implementing DEIA initiatives at Global Ties U.S. and across the network.

The author of this study has been involved with Global Ties for over six years, initially as a volunteer and then as a Board Member of one of the network members – a Michigan-based citizen diplomacy organization Global Ties Kalamazoo. In addition, the author attended three Global Ties U.S. National Meetings – in 2019, 2021 (virtual), and 2024 – as well as several network member virtual events and webinars devoted to DEIA initiatives. At Global Ties Kalamazoo, the author has been closely involved with the development and implementation of DEIA initiatives and thus has been at the centre of the discussions on the opportunities and challenges associated with such work.

To supplement and enrich this locally-based participant observation experience, the author conducted ten interviews with staff members and volunteers involved in DEIA initiatives at Global Ties U.S. and its network members across the U.S.[35] In addition to the interviews and participant observation, the author also analysed a variety of reports and documents produced by Global Ties U.S. and its networks members relating to DEIA work. Triangulating evidence from participant observation, interviews and content analysis of the reports and documents allowed identifying the key themes that characterize DEIA work in citizen diplomacy context, and specifically in the work of the Global Ties U.S. and its network members.

4   Global Ties U.S. and Global Ties Network

Global Ties U.S. is the largest and oldest citizen diplomacy network in the U.S. Founded in 1961 by President John F. Kennedy Administration, Global

---

35   The study was approved by the University's Institutional Review Board (IRB project number 19-03-11). The names of interview participants in all direct quotes featured in this chapter were replaced by pseudonyms to protect participants' privacy.

Ties U.S. was originally created to support the International Visitor Leadership Program (IVLP), the State Department's flagship international exchange program focused on building stronger global alliances through citizen diplomacy. The founding of Global Ties U.S., initially called the National Council for Community Services to International Visitors, was a response to the need to create an organization that would connect the independent nonprofit citizen organizations across the country that were already providing the infrastructure and logistical support for the IVLP and other exchange programmes. These community-based organizations relied on the networks of local volunteers who organized professional meetings, hospitality and informal events for the visitors. The organizations are private nonprofit entities, independent of the State Department, with their own governance models and operation practices. Global Ties U.S. connects them all with each other, fosters learning and sharing of best practices, and helps coordinate the work between them and the exchange program agencies in Washington DC. The relationship between Global Ties U.S. and the U.S. State Department is a public sector-private sector partnership where the Department of State relies on already existing citizen diplomacy organizations across the country to implement exchange programmes and citizen diplomacy initiatives and Global Ties U.S. makes coordinating the work of several dozen of such organizations in all 50 U.S. states easier. In this partnership process, the Department of State determines the policy objectives and manages the programmes' balance while the nonprofit partners implement and administer the programmes. However, even at the program development stage, the Department of State and the implementing partners collaborate closely because the implementing partners have the knowledge of the local details and context that are critical for designing successful programmes. Like in any partnership, this process is not always smooth and flawless; tensions and negotiations are a part of it as partners inevitably bring in their different institutional practices, values, viewpoints, and individual and organizational interests.[36] This partnership model has three key benefits. First, local nonprofits are deeply connected with their local communities and thus can draw on robust local networks and resources to implement the programmes successfully – something the State Department is not able to do. Second, the local implementing partners are non-state actors completely independent of the government and thus can serve as a buffer between the government that sponsors the programmes and the program participants. As Sherry Mueller notes, "this arrangement preserves the credibility

---

36   For a detailed discussion of the dynamic of public-private partnership in the context of
      state-supported citizen diplomacy and exchange programmes, see Pisarska 2015.

of the program by keeping the government at arm's length. It signals that exchange programmes are authentic two-way educational experiences rather than purveyors of brainwashing propaganda."[37] Third, contracting the implementation of the programmes to nonprofits is considerably less expensive for the State Department than maintaining its own staff specifically for implementing programmes across the country. The local implementing partners rely on networks of local volunteers to run the programmes and also raise additional funds locally and internationally on their own.

The importance, impact and benefits of the public-private partnerships for citizen diplomacy and exchange programmes were recognized early in the history of state-supported exchanges. This recognition and subsequent effectiveness of the partnership allowed Global Ties U.S. to grow and thrive. Throughout its six decades of existence, Global Ties U.S. has expanded to include more than 120 organizations representing all U.S. states. It also established partner organizations outside the United States in more than 20 countries through networks of exchange program alumni. In addition to continuing to implement the IVLP, Global Ties has been implementing various other international exchange programmes in almost 90 communities across the U.S.

The very nature of the public-private partnership that defines the relationship between Global Ties U.S. and the U.S. State Department assumed active engagement of the domestic publics in citizen diplomacy programmes. Local, U.S.-based volunteer citizen diplomats have always been essential to the functioning and success of the programmes. Yet throughout the history of these programmes most attention of the practitioners and scholars has been directed at the experiences of foreign visitors and the impact of programmes on them. As was mentioned earlier in this chapter, state-supported citizen diplomacy programmes were first designed to support the U.S. foreign policy objectives during the Cold War. This historical context explains many of the built-in assumptions that guided these initiatives. For example, even though the programmes were designed to "increase mutual understanding,"[38] the focus more often was on "telling the American story" to the visitors, and on the visitors' perception of the U.S. and Americans.[39] Winning the Cold War battle for hearts and minds was the primary goal and thus "put[ing] Uncle

---

37   Mueller 2020, 114.
38   US Information and Educational Exchange Act n.d.
39   See Popkova 2022 for a more detailed discussion of this aspect of state-supported citizen diplomacy programmes.

Sam's best foot forward"[40] was particularly important. Indeed, as articulated in the United States Information and Educational Exchange Act of 1948, known as the Smith-Mundt Act, U.S. government exchange programmes were important because they offered visitors a "full and fair picture of American life and institutions so that they could disseminate accurate, and presumably mostly favourable, information about America to their fellow citizens upon their return home."[41] Over the years, as historical and political circumstances have been changing both worldwide and in the U.S., it became clear that greater attention to domestic publics and their involvement in citizen and public diplomacy would benefit diplomacy's goal of reaching mutual understanding. Two key points of transformation have been particularly influential. First, the failures of U.S. public diplomacy in the post-9/11 years demonstrated that the quality of communication was more important than quantity and thus relationship-building and listening were paramount to public diplomacy's success.[42] Second, the political climate in the U.S. has been changing in profound ways. Specifically, the progressive steps toward greater recognition of systemic racism and other forms of injustice against marginalized communities have been accompanied by the rise of conservative forces and activities of far-right groups. The growing influence of movements like *Black Lives Matter* or *MeToo* has been matched in strength by a simultaneous rise to power of right-wing groups and leaders, the subsequent presidency of Donald Trump in 2016–2020, and his return to the White House in 2025. The COVID-19 pandemic and the resulting social, economic, political and cultural consequences intensified these clashing trends. In particular, 2020 was a critical year for racial and social justice initiatives in the United States. The initiatives gained critical momentum after the mass protests in response to George Floyd's murder in May of 2020. Many organizations in virtually all industries and public and private sectors launched diversity, equity, inclusion, and accessibility (DEIA) initiatives – some more superficial and others more meaningful and effective – to respond to what seemed like a significant shift in public understanding of the importance of addressing systemic racial injustice. In 2020, Global Ties U.S. partnered with Nonprofit HR – the country's leading and oldest consulting firm specializing in the organizational needs of nonprofits and other social impact organizations – to conduct a comprehensive DEIA assessment.

---

40   Mueller 2020, 118.
41   US Information and Educational Exchange Act n.d.
42   Fitzpatrick 2011.

Building on the assessment's outcomes in early 2021, Global Ties U.-S. created a DEIA Working Group. The working group's initial statement declared that "as international exchange professionals who work to reflect the United States to the world, we must look inward to ensure that we are aiming to be diverse, equitable, and inclusive – and actively be part of the solution for racial justice that is long overdue within the United States."[43] The group articulated its commitment to "more intentionally approach issues of diversity, equity, inclusion, and justice in the international exchange field"[44] and to "move values of diversity, equity, inclusion, and justice to the centre of international exchange programming [as it is] essential to building trust with individuals, communities and nations that our mission demands."[45] The support of the federal government, with President Joe Biden signing the Executive Order 13985 on his first day in office in early 2021 that outlined a "whole of government approach" to advancing racial equity and support for underserved communities through the federal government, including both domestic and foreign policy, also played a critical role in enabling Global Ties U.S. to launch this comprehensive DEIA initiative and to plan for it to be an ongoing effort. As articulated in the concluding section of the Global Ties U.S. Statement on diversity, equity, inclusion, accessibility, and justice, "we have begun to better educate ourselves and break down barriers for a truly open and inclusive society. We have a lot of listening and work to do. The work will be iterative. This is not a one-time project; we are committed to changing norms."[46] As these initiatives commenced, however, many DEIA projects across the country came under threat as the far-right groups grew their influence and multiplied their activities in the courts, social and traditional media, municipal governments, public school boards and other areas of U.S. society. This dynamic of clashing progressive and conservative political forces in a deeply polarized society makes up an important socio-political context that affects how Global Ties U.S. and its network members in various states approach the issues of equity, diversity, inclusion, accessibility and justice in their work. The next section will dive deeper into this process, discussing more specifically the nuances, opportunities and challenges that accompany this work.

---

43   Diversity Statement n.d.
44   Ibid.
45   Ibid.
46   Diversity Statement n.d.

5   DEIA in Citizen Diplomacy

When Global Ties U.S. created the DEIA Working Group, it also created three Task Force groups, each focusing on applying the DEIA lens to a specific aspect of citizen diplomacy work: the Programmatic Change Task Force, the Organizational Change Task Force and the Why Task Force. The sub-sections below draw on themes that emerged from the analysis of DEIA activities and conversations that have been occurring across all three areas. Before moving on to the discussion of these themes, it is important to briefly describe the purpose and central goals of each task force (see Table 9.1 for a summary).

The Programmatic Change Task Force examines all elements of international exchange programming from the DEIA lens. Programming is at the core of state-supported citizen diplomacy programmes. It includes professional meetings and events, informal interactions with volunteers and host community members, and informal social events. How can programming be made more inclusive and representative? What would it take to engage the local communities in all of their diversity in citizen diplomacy? These and many related questions drive the work of the Programmatic Change Task

TABLE 9.1   Global Ties U.S.: DEIA task forces

Task force name	Purpose
The Why Task Force	Focuses on the larger questions of the meaning, importance and purpose of DEIA in citizen diplomacy and international exchanges. The group's goal is to keep the larger DEIA Working Group on track by reminding why DEIA in citizen diplomacy matters and what else can and should be done.
Programmatic Change Task Force	Examines all elements of international exchange programming from DEIA lens, focusing on such components as home hospitality, federalism briefings, professional resource recruitment, and professional meeting management, among others.
Organizational Change Task Force	Develops specific steps to make international exchange workspaces more inclusive, just, and more reflective of the diversity of the communities these workplaces represent and serve.

Force. The Organizational Change Task Force is driven by the idea that those who run the organizations – staff, board members, volunteers – have to model the DEIA values. The Task force members focus on developing specific steps to make international exchange workspaces more inclusive, just, and more reflective of the diversity of the communities these workplaces represent and serve.

The Why Task Force tackles the larger questions of the meaning, importance and purpose of DEIA in citizen diplomacy and international exchanges. While its work has fewer tangible outcomes and direct applications to the day-to-day operations that drive international exchanges and citizen diplomacy, the Why Task Force's goal is to keep the DEIA Working Group on track by reminding why DEIA in citizen diplomacy matters, what else can and should be done, and, as one of the Task Force's leaders put it, "by encouraging people to question and push into discomfort but also comfort."[47]

The sub-sections below discuss the key themes that emerged from the analysis of activities, outcomes and deliverables of the three Task Forces of the DEIA Working Group, combined with a number of informal conversations, formal interviews, and many hours of participant observation by the author. The discussion of each theme also examines the opportunities and challenges associated with implementing DEIA initiatives in citizen diplomacy, and connects them to the conceptual foundations of this chapter.

5.1   Representation and Inclusivity for Greater Authenticity

The interconnected notions of representation and inclusivity define much of the DEIA work and the conversations that surround it at Global Ties U.S. The idea that greater inclusion is key to better and more authentic representation of local U.S. communities, and the country as a whole, is central to the DEIA efforts discussed and implemented by Global Ties U.S. and its network members. All three DEIA task forces address the questions of representation and inclusion. For example, from the programmatic perspective, the critical question becomes, how does one create programmes for international visitors and local communities that are inclusive and representative of the local communities? The Toolkit developed by the Programmatic Change Task Force and distributed across the network in 2023 directly engages with this question, offering concrete approaches to assessing existing programming resources from DEIA lens and engaging new resources by cultivating relationships with various community organizations and thus broadening the pool of resources.

---

47   Interview with Sarah, August 2023.

For example, some interviewees mentioned that taking visitors to the same places and people because "if things worked well in the past, why not use it again" had the downside of being "boxed in." As one participant emphasized, "I think it is incredibly important to involve organizations and community members we haven't worked with in the past, even if it's more work and an 'unknown territory' because this is what ensures inclusion and diversity, which ultimately benefits us all."[48] Moreover, this approach also ensures that more people and organizations of various kinds from the local communities benefit from citizen diplomacy by engaging with foreign visitors. One of the questions driving this approach is, what types of people and organizations even see themselves as citizen diplomats? As one interview participant noted, "there is this notion that citizen diplomacy and international exchanges are these 'higher-level', 'elite' experiences that are only accessible and, frankly, only useful for people [who are] upper-class, white-collar professions, etc. and only they can truly benefit [from exchanges]."[49] Yet, as the participant emphasized, exchanges are for everybody and the greater the diversity of participants, the better it is both for the international participants who get to see the U.S. in all of its diversity, and for the local community members who "feel seen and respected and valued when asked to share their expertise."[50]

The idea of "de-elitization" of citizen diplomacy as key to making it more inclusive came up frequently – particularly in informal conversations, workshop discussions and formal interviews conducted for this project. It is important to note, however, that the idea that "exchanges are for everyone" still remains aspirational, with some Global Ties network members having made greater progress on diversifying their volunteer base and others still working towards it. The systemic issues rooted in the history of international exchanges and state-supported citizen diplomacy projects continue to influence the experiences of participants and the design of programmes. Interview participants noted that it is hard to "get populations to be involved with citizen diplomacy if they inherently don't feel represented within the description."[51] Some interviewees brought up classism, noting that very few middle-class families host international visitors, which is "reflecting the historical population of those who have been involved in international affairs."[52]

---

48   Interview with Susan, July 2023.
49   Interview with Helen, September 2023.
50   Ibid.
51   Interview with Sarah, August 2023
52   Interview with Sarah, August 2023

At the same time, there is a widespread recognition that these dynamics need to change. To this end, the Programmatic Change Task Force also came up with recommendations to create inclusive meetings that facilitate more authentic two-way experiences where international participants and local professional hosts have equal opportunities to engage and where their conversations go beyond the surface of "we do this and we do this wonderfully."[53] As one of the study participants noted, "we do our best to make sure that [the meetings we arrange] are with people who have critical viewpoints [and are] interested in a more in-depth exchange, in sharing what the challenges they face are."[54] This approach helps get to "a certain level of authenticity" where" people get to know the communities they visit better but also "everybody gets to learn about themselves ... because you find commonalities."[55]

Representation and inclusivity are also central to programmatic changes that get at broader perspectives on diversity, equity and inclusion. For example, many programmes include formal City Tours, and programming for the International Visitor Leadership Program (IVLP) also includes Federalism Briefings – meetings where various local leaders provide an overview of U.S. federalism, focusing on inter-relationships among the government's branches in decentralized U.S. system. Both the City Tours and Federalism Briefings are important events where those who lead them can either rely on the "grand narratives" of U.S. history and politics or use the occasion to provide a more nuanced perspective that discusses the problematic aspects of history and politics along with the points of pride. Presenters can praise the U.S. political system and brag about the city's strengths, "showing off the best" to the international visitors and taking what Constantinou terms an "advocacy" approach that strategically highlights the strengths and overlooks or minimizes the challenges of those being represented by the diplomatic actors. Alternatively, one can take a "reflexive" approach and structure the Federalism Briefing as a conversation that does not shy away from criticism, encourages reflection and brings in multiple, and sometimes conflicting, perspectives to the U.S. political system and history. Program managers and directors interviewed for this study talked about intentionally reaching out to community leaders who could run a Federalism Briefing either specifically with DEIA lens or from a critical perspective that goes beyond the grand narratives of history and politics.

---

53   Interview with Kate, October 2023.
54   Ibid.
55   Interview with Kate, October 2023.

Similarly, the Why Task Force launched an initiative of revising city descriptions that are included in the program books that visitors receive upon arrival to the U.S. One of the people central to this initiative explained that the city descriptions were "a false representation of [local] communities."[56] Giving the example of Cleveland, Ohio, the interviewee pointed out how Cleveland's description started with the statement that the city was founded by General Cleveland, which "didn't provide any context on indigenous communities [who are] such an important component of America."[57] The interviewee emphasized the importance of being respectful of "where the history actually started" rather than "wip[ing] it clean and hav[ing] it be a representation [of history]."[58] Something as small as a city description in a programme book can send a powerful message about how the community that "represents the Unites States" to the visitors understands their own history and, by extension, its contemporary state. Whose voices are included in historical narratives about the city? Whose voices tell the story of the city as it lives today? Who is included and excluded and why? City descriptions, when composed with these questions in mind, can become the launching pads for deeper conversations, mutual learning and discoveries that make citizen diplomacy and international exchanges so valuable. Such deeper conversations also move citizen diplomacy closer to diplomacy's humanistic roots, where "rethinking the given" and "searching for other knowledge"[59] become the driving forces of diplomacy as a humanistic knowledge practice.

Interestingly, the project of revising city descriptions presents a fascinating case where the autonomy of individual network members clashes with the rules and regulations imposed by the State. As Constantinou noted, autonomy and independence are crucial for engaging in diplomacy as a humanistic knowledge practice. Given the structure of the Global Ties U.S. network, its members indeed enjoy a great deal of autonomy from the State Department even when running exchange programmes sponsored and supported by it. When the initiative of revising the city descriptions started, many community members across the U.S. embraced it and were eager to get started. Yet, because the city descriptions are included in the formal booklets, they have to be reviewed and approved by the State Department. One of the participants interviewed for this project discussed the pushback – "because of the systems

---

56   Interview with Sarah, August 2023.
57   Ibid.
58   Ibid.
59   Constantinou, 2013.

and the bureaucracy of the State Department"[60] – they received despite the support for the initiative from community-based members of the Global Ties network. The interviewee pointed out that "convincing the State Department to agree to allow them to actually update and make city descriptions more relevant and inclusive [is] ... the biggest accomplishment."[61] It is important to note that this was happening under the Administration that was openly and explicitly supportive of the DEIA efforts. Yet this dynamic is a vivid illustration of a classic tension in public-private partnerships where the bureaucratic structures of the state are resistant to change, are cautions to take quick action and are risk averse. As Pierre Bourdieu noted, a change of status does not necessarily imply the immediate changing of "one's system of acquired dispositions."[62] The U.S. Department of State's newly adopted language of diversity and inclusion thus does not imply that it will be immediately and decisively followed by corresponding action, especially on matters of racial justice – an area where the State has been one of the enablers of injustice for most of the U.S. history.

Similarly, the topic of offering local hosts participating in citizen diplomacy programmes compensation came up in a number of discussions around inclusion and representation. One of the barriers to implementing this idea is the requirement, especially for some of the State-supported programmes, that all local hosts participate as volunteers. Yet volunteering is a privilege that only certain types of people and organizations have, resulting in most volunteers being "while, wealthy, older and often retired men and women."[63] Some network members found creative ways of providing stipends to the hosts but, like with city descriptions, there is still much work to be done at the systemic, policy and bureaucratic levels to get a higher-level buy-in for the idea and to reexamine the tension between volunteerism and privilege.

Finally, a significant aspect of Global Ties U.S. DEIA work aimed at more authentic representation and inclusivity in citizen diplomacy centred on organizational changes. Key to these efforts was examining the extent to which the leadership – Boards of Directors, staff, volunteers – of the Global Ties U.S. and its network members were representative of their communities. To this end, the Organizational Change Task Force developed a set of recommendations and best practices on Board recruitment and diversification, inclusive and equitable hiring practices, and creating an inclusive culture. Just as with

60   Interview with Sarah, August 2023.
61   Ibid.
62   Bourdieu 1990, 11.
63   Interview with Shannon, August 2023.

programmatic changes, some network partners have made progress in implementing these changes. Some abolished unpaid internships and/or partnered with local universities to recruit and hire students from historically marginalized populations for their internship positions. Others stopped requiring formal degrees for their staff positions. Some network members established anti-racism and DEIA committees and task forces of their own to address these questions locally, and required that their Board members and staff regularly participate in anti-racism and DEIA trainings. Many questions continue to be discussed and debated. For example, does requiring annual monetary contributions – and especially requiring specific (frequently quite high) amounts – automatically exclude some people? What is the best approach to diversifying Boards without tokenizing potential and actual Board members? These and related questions get at the broader question: How does one ensure authenticity, inclusion, and representation in citizen diplomacy? This question brings us to the next core theme.

5.2   *Intentionality*

Intentionality emerged as one of the most critical components of the DEIA-focused work at Global Ties U.S. The first step of such intentional approach involved an internal review of organizational resources and practices with a critical eye for the extent to which underrepresented voices and perspectives were included in existing programmes. Many Global Ties network members have conducted such reviews since 2020 – some on their own, some with the help of facilitators, depending on the size of the organization and the resources at their disposal.

Global Ties U.S. has also been providing resources, support and facilitation of such conversations since 2020. For example, in the summer of 2020, Global Ties U.S. hosted a virtual National Programmers Workshop that featured the Social Justice Series – a keynote and three thematic sessions focused on education, housing and health – that sparked critical conversations about racism and inequality in the United States, their historical roots and harmful consequences affecting present-day situations. Participants reflected on what they learned, and discussed how the insights from the sessions could be applied to citizen diplomacy programming. Building on these reflections, in 2021, Global Ties U.S. organized a virtual Programmers Workshop titled "Diversity in Exchanges," which took place over the course of three days and was devoted entirely to discussing the approaches to embracing diversity and equity in programming. The events inspired members across the country to engage in their own, local, community-specific DEIA activities. For example, some network members established anti-racism and DEIA committees tasked with brainstorming and implementing DEIA initiatives in their specific citizen diplomacy organizations in their specific communities. Some revised their organizational policies with DEIA lens; some completed DEIA trainings by partnering with local organizations offering such trainings. As one of the participants interviewed for this project noted, "at its core, the role of DEIA initiatives is to be intentional."[64] The interviewee stressed the importance of intentionality in building local networks and choosing participants for specific projects, and the importance of asking, on a regular and systematic basis, "is equity in the centre of what we are doing, is justice anywhere in what we are doing, is there diversity in representation?"[65] Most importantly, sustaining these practices through developing intentional structures "where you are looking at your policies, at how you do what you do, who does it, all of those things, just as part of your regular process"[66] is particularly critical. Global Ties U.S. has been working on providing its member organizations with the tools that would help sustain such intentional engagement. The Toolkit developed by the Programmatic Change Task Force, the Organizational Change Matrix developed by the Organizational Change Task Force, and the revised city descriptions discussed above are all examples of such tools.

Intentionality is key to mediating human diversity – a critical function of humanity-centred diplomacies. While Zaharna'a discussion focuses more on the global dimension of human diversity, in the context of humanity-centred diplomacies the distinction between "global" and "local" diversity in fact becomes irrelevant. Intentionality is also at the core of diplomacy as humanistic knowledge practice because "familiarizing themselves with the wide spectrum of human relations, escaping the dominant perspective, and connect[ing] to diplomacy not merely as passive observers or public servants but as active humans" only happens when the intention is in place because of "the hard labour required" to "look critically and self-critically at diplomatic action on all fronts."[67]

Intentionality is also what connects the efforts for greater inclusion and representation in diplomacy and democracy. At the 2023 Global Ties U.S. National Meeting, the U.S. Department of State Senior Advisor for Racial Equity and Justice Jessica Huber emphasized this connection and noted that inclusion and democracy "both require constant maintenance and a commitment

---

64   Interview with Kate, October 2023.
65   Ibid.
66   Ibid.
67   Constantinou 2013, 144.

to open and inclusive societies."[68] As some of the progressive practices of democratic assemblies – and the scholarship that analyses them – demonstrates, effective representation and inclusion in the democratic process can only be achieved through intentional, carefully planned and well-facilitated practices.[69] This is a challenging process, and one of the challenges to intentionality in the citizen diplomacy context frequently brought up was what one of program managers called "time and falling into patterns."[70] Programmes run smoothly when there are true and tried ways of running them, including reliable volunteers, venues, programming partners, vendors and others involved. Yet the danger of such smooth operations is in "falling into patterns," meaning relying on the same resources instead of seeking new ones, and operating with the same mindset instead of challenging yourself to expand it. Falling into patterns happens even more frequently when one is pressed by time. When we need something to be done quickly, we go to who/what we know. There is a recognition of this danger, however. As one program manager noted, "you keep trying to create new patterns because you know you are going to fall into patterns."[71] She stressed that "the idea is to make sure that ... when you need to do something really fast, you already have the lens through which you are planning in a way that's fair, [inclusive and just].[72]

Some program managers also talked about intentionally making time in their weekly schedules to search for new resources, foster new relationships with people and organizations that can help make citizen diplomacy more representative, inclusive and thus more authentic, and to reassess the lens through which they do their work.

Another challenge related to the intentional implementation of DEIA initiatives that came up frequently referred to the broader political climate in the United States, the possible return of Donald Trump to the White House in 2025 and what this might mean for DEIA work in general across the country and in the citizen diplomacy and international exchanges in particular. When answering the question "are you worried about 2025?" one of the participants said that they were "terrified" and yet also emphasized that it was especially important "to dig our heels into [why DEIA work matters]."[73]

---

68   Zheng and Kratz 2023.
69   Lacelle-Webster and Warren 2021.
70   Interview with Kate, October 2023.
71   Ibid.
72   Interview with Kate, October 2023.
73   Interview with Sarah, August 2023.

There is a recognition at Global Ties U.S. that DEIA terminology has a problematic reputation, mainly among those on the political right but not only. Many superficial DEIA initiatives undertaken by various organizations in the last few years have contributed to this reputation as well. The current position among the people committed to DEIA work at Global Ties U.S. and across the network is that it is important to get as much as possible done, so that the results of this work are as hard to overturn as possible. In the most recent moves to "future proof" this work, the DEIA group changed its name to Community of Practice for Diversity. The new name is less politically charged than the DEIA term has become, yet it still allows to engage in initiatives that would enable greater and more equitable inclusion of individuals and resources representing local communities in citizen diplomacy. One could argue that the name change reflects the beginning of self-censorship, even complicity in the political environment where the far-right political forces are making gains, including the growing success of anti-DEIA legislations in several states across the country. Others, however, would point to the importance of the work itself and even a natural evolution of the terms and labels attached to it, where Community of Practice for Diversity in fact sounds more "grassroots" than the DEIA term that over the years has become part of "corporate speak." It remains to be seen how the larger political dynamics, especially following the U.S. 2024 Presidential election, will impact the work itself and the language surrounding it.

5.3   *Respect*

A critical piece of the meaningful DEIA work in citizen diplomacy is respect for the host communities. As much as the programmers of state-supported citizen diplomacy programmes may be eager to diversify their programmes, volunteer networks, boards and staff in order to represent their communities more authentically, this work takes time that is needed to build relationships and trust with various communities. When working with communities that have been historically underrepresented in international exchanges and mainstream public life in general, it is critical to be aware of the history of the relationship between the U.S. government and many of these groups. This history has been marked by oppressive policies and practices, heavy surveillance and physical violence,[74] and the attempts by the U.S. government to exploit marginalized groups to achieve its domestic and foreign policy goals.[75]

---

74   Dawson 1995.

75   Von Eschen 2004.

As a result, members of the marginalized groups tend to distrust the government and perceive any state-supported initiatives with suspicion.

In some ways, community-based citizen diplomacy organizations like the ones comprising the Global Ties Network are well-positioned to engage various publics, including those from underrepresented populations, in citizen diplomacy work. While they implement state-supported programmes, they are still independent non-profit organizations who are "deeply immersed in the public life of their communities."[76] In a way, they themselves are the diplomats engaged in diplomacy as humanistic knowledge practice because of the "critical distance from the state"[77] they have and because in their work they do not seek "to affirm the sovereign certainties of states and the prioritizing agendas of their policies."[78] Precisely because community-based members of the Global Ties Network are in a position to be trusted by their local communities, the stakes of maintaining that trust through respecting and, when needed, protecting their communities are high. This idea of respecting and protecting communities came up frequently in formal interviews and informal conversations. Participants mentioned how on a number of occasions visitors wanted to "see the real America" by requesting to drive through the poor neighbourhoods. These requests struck the interview participants as deeply problematic and representing a form of poverty tourism, which exploits the local communities and does not provide a chance for the visitors to truly get to know the communities either. Similarly, many mentioned a great interest from the visitors in visiting the Native American reservations but discussed how important it was to include the indigenous history and the indigenous communities in programming but do it on these communities' terms, with respect for their voice and agency.

In another example, one of the interview participants shared a story from 2015 when the city of Baltimore was under curfew for a few days after mass protests erupted in response to the murder of an African-American man, Freddie Gray, by the police. The national program agency the interview participant worked for asked if a group of visitors could drive through the community where Freddie Gray was murdered. This request struck the interview participant as inappropriate. She recalled asking: " ... for what reason? Why do you want to do this? What is the purpose of this? Is it just to say 'oh, look at all the poor people, look at all the mad Black people, look at all the people who are

---

76   Popkova and Michaels 2022, 676.

77   Constantinou 2013, 142.

78   Ibid., 142-143.

angry!' Why is this something that you think is ok to do?"[79] This participant emphasized that it is important to do work that challenges the misconceptions and implicit biases and showcases all aspects of the U.S. society but that it is also important "to allow people to push back and keep [their] community safe."[80] Similarly, after the George Floyd murder in Minnesota in 2020, members of the Minnesota-based citizen diplomacy organization remarked on how "everybody wants to come to Minnesota now to talk about race relations but we are healing, we are not ready to have these conversations."[81] As another participant noted when discussing this topic, "it's the re-triggering of trauma, and that is something that we as professionals and event planners and storytellers have to be respectful of, [respectful] of our communities."[82]

The idea of respect and care for the local communities and the local realities these communities exist in and live through connects well with Zaharna's point about humanity-centred diplomacies responding to humans' emotional needs. As Zaharna noted, the practice of empathetic public diplomacy elevates public diplomacy practice from the *battle* for hearts and minds to the *care* of hearts and minds. Observing, analysing and reflecting on the work that has been happening across the Global Ties U.S. citizen diplomacy network reveals that DEIA-centred conversations steer citizen diplomacy toward such humanity-centred model, particularly when they emphasize respect for the local communities as a critical component of citizen diplomacy work.

6   Conclusion

Citizen diplomacy, including state-supported citizen diplomacy programmes, is considered one of the most authentic and effective forms of public diplomacy because of its capacity to build relationships through direct people-to-people interactions. In the U.S. context, it is also considered an effective way to showcase "democracy at work" by demonstrating how the democratic values the U.S. promotes worldwide play out domestically. Yet a big question of who exactly, and in what ways, gets to represent the domestic communities during the state-supported citizen diplomacy programmes remains underexplored in citizen diplomacy scholarship. This chapter brought in theoretical insights from scholarship on democracy and civil society to explore the no-

---

79   Interview with Sarah, August 2023.
80   Ibid.
81   Interview with Joan, September 2023.
82   Interview with Sarah, August 2023.

tions of representation and inclusion in citizen diplomacy's domestic dimension. The chapter further connected these insights to scholarship in diplomatic studies and public diplomacy that views diplomacy as a "humanistic knowledge practice" that is first and foremost "humanity-centred."

By focusing on the notions of representation and inclusion in citizen diplomacy's domestic dimension while connecting these ideas to the broader understanding of the purpose and functions of diplomacy in today's world, this chapter pursued two central goals. First, to argue that in order to represent local communities more authentically, in all of their diversity, one needs to reimagine citizen diplomacy and engage more intentionally and meaningfully with the local, host communities. Such meaningful engagement must be rooted in recognition of the role that histories of inequalities and systemic injustice in the U.S. play in making U.S. citizen diplomacy what it is, with its practices, defining principles and expectations. Second, the chapter aimed to demonstrate that paying closer attention to the notions of representation and inclusion in citizen diplomacy's domestic dimension brings citizen diplomacy closer to diplomacy's humanistic roots.

To accomplish the first goal, the chapter used empirical insights to demonstrate how Global Ties U.S. and its network members strive to implement specific and meaningful DEIA initiatives to make citizen diplomacy more inclusive and representative of various U.S. communities in all of their diversity. The analysis of these insights demonstrated that the three core themes – representation and inclusion for greater authenticity, intentionality, and respect for local communities – defined DEIA work at organizational and programmatic levels and also at the broader and more conceptual level of why DEIA work matters in citizen diplomacy. Each core theme reflected the opportunities and challenges associated with meaningful implementation of DEIA projects in citizen diplomacy. Each theme also showcased how applying DEIA lens to citizen diplomacy, especially to its domestic dimension, helps reimagine citizen diplomacy as first and foremost a humanistic knowledge practice – independent from the state, intentional in its search for other knowledge and rival perspectives, and constantly rethinking the given. Similarly, applying DEIA lens to citizen diplomacy allows embracing the functions of humanity-centred diplomacies: collaborating (rather than bargaining), managing human diversity, and centring empathy and care as driving forces behind citizen diplomacy.

Analysing citizen diplomacy and its domestic dimension through DEIA lens helps take a more critical – and realistic – look at the existing citizen diplomacy practices. As citizen diplomacy gets contrasted with traditional, state-led diplomacy, it is frequently perceived as by definition more authentic, more

empathetic, more human-centred and inclusive. However, scrutinizing existing citizen diplomacy structures and practices from DEIA lens demonstrates
that this is not always and necessarily the case. As many of the insights discussed above show, citizen diplomacy often functions as an "exclusive club"
for people and organizations with numerous social, economic and political
privileges. Shifting the narrative from citizen diplomacy as an "elite thing
that fancy people do" to "citizen diplomacy is for everyone" remains to be
one of the most challenging tasks for practitioners. As this chapter discussed,
the challenge traces its roots to systemic inequalities that have been defining
the U.S. history and politics. These inequalities had been reinforced by the
traditional separation of the foreign and domestic spheres in the U.S. politics.
Who represents the communities participating in citizen diplomacy – an activity historically relegated to the sphere of foreign politics and thus to those
privileged enough to participate? Relatedly, whose voices have been included,
excluded, and why? Which community members have even considered themselves "qualified" to participate in citizen diplomacy and international exchanges? All these questions point to the need to examine more thoroughly
the history of citizen diplomacy and international exchanges and the ways in
which this history reflected and shaped the power dynamics defining the relationships between dominant and marginalized groups in the U.S. society.
This work might be especially challenging to do – both for academics and
practitioners – in the current polarized political environment, where conservative and far-right forces are increasingly gaining more power. Yet it is important to remember that making citizen diplomacy more accessible for local
communities, growing and diversifying citizen diplomacy networks, and
transforming organizational practices within citizen diplomacy organizations
to make them fair, just, and human-centred can help make citizen diplomacy –
and citizen diplomats – key players in addressing the shared problems of humanity that transcend national politics and populist agendas.

Bibliography

Asen, Robert and Daniel C. Brouwer, eds. *Counterpublics and the State* (Albany: State
    University of New York Press, 2001).
Bherer, Laurence, Pascale Dufour and Françoise Montambeault. 'The Participatory
    Democracy Turn: An Introduction'. *Journal of Civil Society* 12 (3) (2016), 225–30.
Black Public Sphere Collective. *The Black Public Sphere: A Public Culture Book* (Chi-
    cago, IL: University of Chicago Press, 1995).

Bourdieu, Pierre. *In Other Words: Essays Towards a Reflexive Sociology* (Stanford, CA: Stanford University Press, 1990).

Constantinou, Costas M. 'Between Statecraft and Humanism: Diplomacy and Its Forms of Knowledge'. *International Studies Review* 15 (2) (2013), 141–62.

Cortes, Antonio and Steven Krzanowski. 'Power Sharing – An important part of Integrating DEI'. *Nonprofit HR Blog*, 22 June 2019. https://www.nonprofithr.com/keys -to-integrating-dei-transparency-power-sharing-and-accountability-2/.

Cull, Nicholas. 'Public Diplomacy Before Gullion'. In *Routledge Handbook of Public Diplomacy*, eds. Nancy Snow and Philip M. Taylor (New York: Routledge, 2009), 19–23.

Dawson, Michael. 'A Black Counterpublic? Economic Earthquakes, Racial Agenda(s), and Black Politics'. In *The Black Public Sphere*, eds. The Black Public Sphere Collective (Chicago, IL: University of Chicago Press, 1995).

Dean, Jodi. 'Including Women: The Consequences and Side Effects of Feminist Critiques of Civil Society'. *Philosophy and Social Criticism* 18 (1992), 379–406.

Derian, James Der. *On Diplomacy: A Genealogy of Western Estrangement* (Oxford: Blackwell Pub, 1987).

Diversity Statement. *Global Ties U.S.* https://www.globaltiesus.org/our-story/diver sity-equity-and-inclusion/

Eagan, Jennifer. L. 'Deliberative Democracy'. *Encyclopedia Britannica*, May 17, 2016. https://www.britannica.com/topic/deliberative-democracy.

Fitzpatrick, Kathy. 'Advancing the New Public Diplomacy: A Public Relations View'. *The Hague Journal of Diplomacy* 2 (3) (2007), 187–211.

Fitzpatrick, Kathy. *The Future of U.S. Public Diplomacy: An Uncertain Fate* (Boston, MA: Martinus Nijhoff, 2010).

Fitzpatrick, Kathy R. 'U.S. Public Diplomacy in a Post-9/11 World: From Messaging to Mutuality'. *CPD Perspectives* 6 (2011).

Fraser, Nancy. 'Rethinking the Public Sphere: A Contribution to the Critique of Actually Existing Democracy'. *Social Text* 25-26 (1990), 56–80.

Gates, Scott. 'Power-Sharing, Democracy and Civil Conflict'. *Peace Research Institute Oslo*. https://www.prio.org/projects/1559.

Goodnight, Thomas G. 'Opening Up "the Spaces of Public Dissention"'. *Communication Monographs* 64 (1997), 270–275.

Houser, Gerard A. 'Civil Society and the Principle of the Public Sphere'. *Philosophy & Rhetoric* 31 (1) (1998), 19–40.

Jackson, Sarah J. *Black Celebrity, Racial Politics, and the Press: Framing Dissent* (New York: Routledge, 2014).

Jönsson, Christer. 'Relationships between Negotiators: A Neglected Topic in the Study of Negotiation'. *International Negotiation* 20 (2015), 7–24.

Kruckeberg, Dean and Marina Vujnovic. 'Public Relations, not Propaganda, for US Public Diplomacy in a Post-9/11 World: Challenges and Opportunities'. *Journal of Communication Management* 9 (4) (2005), 296–304.

Lacelle-Webster, Antonin, and Mark E. Warren. 'Citizens' Assemblies and Democracy'. *Oxford Research Encyclopedia of Politics*, 2021. https://doi.org/10.1093/acre fore/9780190228637.013.1975.

Mueller, Sherry L. 'The Nexus of US Public Diplomacy and Citizen Diplomacy'. In *Routledge Handbook of Public Diplomacy*, eds. Nancy Snow and Nicholas J. Cull (2nd edition, New York: Routledge, 2020), 112–119.

Popkova, Anna. 'Exploring Citizen Diplomacy's Local Impact: The Case of Global Ties Kalamazoo'. *The Hague Journal of Diplomacy* 17 (2) (2022), 248–276.

Popkova, Anna, and Jodi Hope Michaels. 'Who Represents the Domestic Voice? Diversity, Equity and Inclusion in Citizen Diplomacy'. *The Hague Journal of Diplomacy* 17 (4) (2022), 669–678.

Pisarska, Katarzyna. 'The Role of Domestic Public Engagement in the Formulation and Implementation of US Government-Sponsored Educational Exchanges: An Insider's Account'. *Place Branding and Public Diplomacy* 11 (1) (2015), 5–17.

Sisk, Timothy D. *Power Sharing and International Mediation in Ethnic Conflicts* (US Institute of Peace Press, 1996).

Squires, Catherine. 'The Black Press and the State: Attracting Unwanted (?) Attention'. In *Counterpublics and the State*, eds. Robert Asen and Daniel C. Brouwer (Albany: State University of New York Press, 2001), 111–136.

Squires, Catherine. "Rethinking the Black Public Sphere: An Alternative Vocabulary for Multiple Public Spheres'. *Communication Theory* 12 (4) (2002), 446–468.

The Center for Citizen Diplomacy. *About us.* https://www.centerforcitizendiplomacy .org/about-us/

US Information and Educational Exchange Act of 1948. *US Agency for Global Media.* https://www.usagm.gov/who-we-are/oversight/legislation/smith-mundt/.

Vanc, Antoaneta M. and Kathy R. Fitzpatrick. 'Scope and Status of Public Diplomacy Research by Public Relations Scholars, 1990-2014'. *Public Relations Review* 42 (3) (2016), 432–440.

Von Eschen, Penny. *Satchmo Blows Up the World: Jazz Ambassadors Play the Cold War* (Cambridge, MA: Harvard University Press, 2004).

Walker, Vivian S., Kathy R. Fitzpatrick and Jay Wang. 'Exploring U.S. Public Diplomacy's Domestic Dimensions: Purviews, Publics, and Policies'. Report by the United States Advisory Commission on Public Diplomacy and the USC Center on Public Diplomacy, April 2022.

Young, Iris Marion. 'Difference as a Resource for Democratic Communication'. In Deliberative Democracy: Essays on Reason and Politics, eds. James Bohman and William Rehg (Cambridge: Massachusetts Institute of Technology Press, 1997), 383–406.

Yun, Seong-Hun. 'Toward Public Relations Theory-Based Study of Public Diplomacy: Testing the Applicability of the Excellence Study'. *Journal of Public Relations Research* 18 (4) (2006), 287-312.

Zaharna, R. S. *Boundary Spanners of Humanity: Three Logics of Communications and Public Diplomacy for Global Collaboration* (Oxford, New York: Oxford University Press, 2022).

Zheng, Angela and Isabelle Kratz. 'Global Ties U.S. 2023 National Meeting Plenary Session: (Re)Building Community Through Intentional DEIA'. *Exchange Matters*, 5 May 2023. https://members.globaltiesus.org/global-ties-u-s-2023-national-meet ing-plenary-session-rebuilding-community-through-intentional-deia/.

CHAPTER 10

Democratic Diplomatic Middle Grounds: Theorising and Expanding the Role of Domestic Societies in Paradiplomatic Relations

Scott Michael Harrison and Quinton Huang

Summary

The field of diplomatic studies has seen a surge of interest in the role of non-central government and domestic society actors in international relations. Still, the functions of these actors and their relationships with traditional diplomatic actors, such as national governments, foreign ministries, embassies and consulates, and multilateral institutions, have been under-theorised. Drawing on the concepts of co-production and policy assemblage, we propose a novel framework of the 'democratic diplomatic middle ground' formed by the interactions of state, non-central government, and domestic society actors. This 'middle ground' moves the locus of agency away from official government actors and recentres international relationships in the shared space among diplomatic stakeholders. Using the case study of Canada-Asia Pacific municipal twinning (also known as sister city or friendship city relationships), we demonstrate how the 'democratic diplomatic middle ground' helps explain how various actors influence the evolution of identities, capacities, and conceptions inherent to these diplomatic ties. Expanding beyond the non-central government level, we reinterpret recent literature on interstate diplomacy and international organisations using the 'democratic diplomatic middle ground' framework to reveal new insights about how non-central government and domestic society actors exert agency and are themselves transformed through diplomatic activities. Finally, we consider how the 'democratic diplomatic middle ground' analytical framework can be identified in other paradiplomacies, including city, provincial, and Indigenous diplomacy and deployed as a policy model for governments of all levels and domestic society actors to develop more synergistic international policies and relationships.

Keywords

city diplomacy – citizen diplomacy – democratic diplomacy – municipal twinning – sister cities – paradiplomacy – subnational diplomacy – Indigenous diplomacy

1   **Reconsidering the 'Democratic Deficit' of Foreign Policy from the Inside Out**[1]

The twenty-first century has seen widespread concern over global 'democratic backsliding,' epitomised by the rise of authoritarian figures amidst increasing populism, militarism and securitization around the world. Such a panic, however, is not necessarily new. In the wake of the so-called end of the Cold War, a substantial problem for the study of democracy has been the 'democratic deficit'. This deficit, characterised by the widening gap between public opinion and state policies, was not limited to domestic policy. Instead, the rise of increasingly complex international institutions, such as the European Union, and a wave of unpopular Western wars in the Persian Gulf, Iraq and Afghanistan prompted stark debates over the undemocratic nature of international relations. As the renowned theorist of democracy Robert Dahl once remarked, 'probably no important area of public policy presents such a daunting challenge to the theory and practice of democracy as foreign policy'.[2] This challenge has become even more dire in the context of the democratic backsliding of this century within a global landscape increasingly characterised by armed conflict and hegemonic rivalry. Consequently, there are mounting efforts by academics, policymakers and other stakeholders to democratise the practice of foreign policy through a variety of means, including deliberative democratic exercises and direct participatory assemblies.[3]

Equally transformative, however, has been the rise of new kinds of diplomacy in both prominence and practice: the international relations of non-central governments (NCGS). Though this is not a new phenomenon, there is growing attention by policymakers toward the global engagements of local governments on the one hand, and an expanding academic literature on NCG and non-state diplomacies on the other hand.[4] These trends have sub-

---

1   This chapter is a revised, updated, and expanded version of Harrison and Huang 2022.

2   Dahl 1999A, 110; Dahl 1999B.

3   Canada International Council 2021; Geis, Opitz, and Pfeifer 2022.

4   For example, the 'City and State Diplomacy Act' was introduced in the U.S. Congress in 2021, the Biden Administration created the first Special Representative for Subnational Diplomacy within the Department of State in 2022, and in May 2024 the State Department announced it will deploy officers to select U.S. cities to advise on foreign policy in support of Biden's concept of 'a foreign policy for the middle class'. Each of the Australian states have developed their own international trade and / or tourism strategies or programs that speak to the importance and priority of international engagement. Australian states maintain 63 trade and investment offices and 33 tourism offices abroad. Many Canadian provinces have international strategies and collectively have 93 offices abroad. Japan's Council of Local Authorities for International Relations was established in 1988 to support interna-

stantially changed our understanding of what diplomacy is and have flipped traditionally state-oriented international relations thinking on its head. Increasingly, scholars – including contributors to this volume – have complicated this new landscape further by emphasising the influence of domestic society actors in international relations, either through their own efforts or in their constitutive roles within other forms of diplomacy. Domestic society's diplomatic interventions can be seen in contexts ranging from municipal twinning and trade agreements to the chambers of multilateral institutions.

Our earlier contribution in a *Hague Journal of Diplomacy* forum theorised the concept of the 'diplomatic middle ground' to explain the co-produced nature of these paradiplomatic spaces. In this chapter, we further refine this concept by building off various fields of literature, and we use our examination of municipal twinning relationships as a springboard for engaging with other types of paradiplomacy. Here, we use 'democratic diplomatic middle ground' in both descriptive and prescriptive terms to describe our observations of real life paradiplomatic activities, first in municipal twinning and then in other forms of city diplomacy, provincial diplomacy, and Indigenous diplomacy. In other words, we use this concept to name a component of what already occurs in practice in various forms of engaging home in diplomacy and as a mechanism for action and policy development to bolster democratic practices in international relations and foreign policy beyond the state.

What does the rise of 'democratic diplomatic middle grounds' mean for the worsening 'democratic deficit' in foreign policy? This chapter attempts to articulate the relationship between domestic society involvement in diplomacy on the one hand, and democratic practice in foreign affairs on the other hand. In doing so, we bridge two fields that on the surface bear little to no relation with each other: paradiplomacy and deliberative democracy. As we will argue, many of deliberative democracy's ideals are the most apparent at the level of actors beyond the central government, and the increasing role that these actors play in international relations opens up a channel for the democratisation of foreign policy. We demonstrate the concordance between concepts and practices in deliberative democracy to those we identify in the everyday practice of paradiplomatic relations.

---

tional activities of local governments, China's Belt and Road Initiative and its Associations for Friendship with Foreign Countries have strong subnational components, meanwhile South Korean local governments have been gaining autonomy over the last three decades. Harrison and Huang 2023. See footnotes in subsequent sections for other relevant references.

This chapter proceeds in six parts. In Section 2, 'Bridging Theories of Diplomacy and Democracy', we provide an overview of current related theories, highlighting the need to address their intersections and non-Western contexts such as those in Northeast Asia. In Section 3, we briefly define the 'democratic diplomatic middle ground'. In Section 4, 'The Principal-Agent Problem in the Democratic Diplomatic Middle Ground', we reintroduce the diplomatic middle ground as a model and discuss how the co-produced nature of identity and agency at the diplomatic middle ground complicates the idea of democratic representation in foreign relations. In Section 5, 'Everyday Deliberation and Democratic Praxis in Municipal Twinning', we draw from our empirical evidence from municipal twinning to sketch out the deliberative democratic practices that sustain the diplomatic middle ground and outline a framework for the democratisation of foreign policy through them. Finally, in Section 6, 'Foreign Policy and Diplomacy beyond the State', we expand this framework to paradiplomatic practices beyond municipal twinning to other forms of paradiplomacy. We conclude in Section 7, 'Conclusion', by outlining the main limitations to our framework as well as identifying pathways and opportunities for the implementation of our insights by policymakers.

2   Bridging Theories of Diplomacy and Democracy

This section critically examines the existing approaches, theories, and findings of two fields – deliberative democracy and paradiplomacy – to highlight the need for a more comprehensive understanding of how democratic practices shape the activities and policies of subnational governments and other representative groups of domestic society on the international stage. It argues that while some scholars and practitioners have already fruitfully identified possible applications of deliberative democracy to the practice of foreign policy, much of these interventions have occurred at the level of the sovereign nation-state (through its foreign ministry) and operate using formalised deliberative systems that neglect the more quotidian, subnational ways in which domestic society engages in international relations.

On the other hand, the rise in paradiplomatic relationships, agreements, and institutions – such as municipal twinning relationships – demonstrates the powerful role that local communities have in shaping subnational entities' foreign relations, and also shows potential for influencing national level policies. However, the degree to which such paradiplomatic activities can present opportunities for the democratisation of foreign policy remains underscrutinised. This section aims to shed light on this potential by laying the groundwork for our investigation of Canada-Asia Pacific municipal twinning relationships as an empirical base for the conceptualisation of a 'democratic diplomatic middle ground'. Here we make use of two sets of related data. The first is a first-of-its-kind broad, longitudinal dataset we compiled and analyzed with all 249 nominally active Canada-Asia Pacific municipal and provincial twinning relations.[5] The second is a set of eighteen informal, anonymised, and semi-structured interviews with municipal officials and domestic society actors involved in Canadian twinning relations with China, Japan, South Korea and Taiwan,[6] regions which account for most (227) of Canada's twinning agreements in the region. The concept of a democratic diplomatic middle ground holds promise for a more inclusive and participatory approach to international relations.

Deliberative democracy has become an increasingly influential approach for understanding and revitalising democracy amidst declining confidence and participation in formal, representative democratic institutions (such as elections). It examines the ideals and aspirations of the process of how discussion and debate among citizens can and should contribute to the public good through procedures, decision-making, or policy.[7] The field has dissected the intricacies of why deliberation is a 'critical component of democracy',[8] what it entails, and how it can be effectively utilised to increase societal and citizen agency, policy efficacy and legitimacy, and build trust.[9] There is also a growing body of literature that addresses shortcomings relevant to our chapter, such as the relationship between deliberation and imbalances in equality in voice, power and ability to influence outcomes since processes are often driven by elites and politics and how the theory has generally overlooked legacies of colonisation.[10] It is a flexible theoretical concept that has the ability to expand and reshape driving concepts and definitions of how deliberation should ideally work in democracies. Overall, we think that these theoretical and empiri-

---

5   Harrison and Huang 2023.
6   Among the eighteen interviews, two touched on Canada–China relationships, seven on
    Canada–Japan relationships, two on Canada–Korea relationships and twelve on
    Canada–Taiwan twinning relationships. Some interviews touched on relationships
    with twinning partners from two or more countries. Eleven of the interviews were
    with individuals and groups in Canada, while the other seven were with individuals
    and groups in the other economies.
7   Geis, Opitz, and Pfeifer 2022; Mansbridge 2019; Parkinson and Mansbridge 2012; Elster
    1998.
8   Mansbridge 2019.
9   Parkinson and Mansbridge 2012; OECD 2020.
10 Curato, Hmmond, Min 2019; Johnson 2015; Ryfe 2005; Mutz 2008; Mansbridge 2019.

cal findings from deliberative democracy can help inform general best practices for citizen-paradiplomatic engagement domestically in a democracy.

Several key concepts from deliberative democracy bear relevance to our discussion of the democratic diplomatic middle ground. Firstly, deliberative democratic theory emphasises the role of 'communicative power' or 'everyday talk' between individual members of a society as a key component of deliberative democracy.[11] This communicative power forms the basis of the 'public sphere', which exists alongside and legitimises the formal political system. Second, the systemic turn in deliberative democracy has emphasised the creation of mechanisms or sites where deliberation can be formalised and sustained.[12] These sites are often framed as 'mini-publics,' often designed in such a way for representativeness or maximum interaction between participants. Thirdly, however, more recent theorists have argued a more expansive view of deliberative democracy's role in a wider landscape or ecosystem of democratic practices. For example, some have proposed a rethink of the relationship between deliberative systems and mini-publics on the one hand, and the formal representative institutions of liberal democracy on the other.[13] Others have concentrated on the organic nature of deliberation in everyday life, emphasising the role of spontaneously created sites of deliberation as opposed to formally systematised ones.[14]

The relationship between democracy (deliberative or otherwise) and diplomacy, on the other hand, has been less well-developed. As many scholars of foreign policy and domestic public opinion have shown empirically across liberal democratic societies, there exists a concerning and widening gap between the views and preferences of domestic publics and the foreign policies pursued by governments and enacted by parliaments.[15] Furthermore, the rise of international organisations and multilateral institutions, such as the European Union and the World Trade Organization, has generated considerable debate about their potentially corrosive effect on the power of the public to impact their government's foreign policies.[16]

One potential factor in the weak ties between democracy and foreign policy could be the abstract nature of foreign policy as compared to other policy areas in government. Consequently, deliberative democracy, with its empha-

---

11   Habermas 1996; Mansbridge 1999; Flynn 2004.

12   Mansbridge 2019; Owen and Smith 2015; Beauvais and Warren 2019.

13   Vitale 2006; Felicetti, Niemayer and Curato 2016.

14   Mansbridge 1999; Tanasoca 2020; Asenbaum 2022.

15   Page and Barabas 2000; Page and Bouton 2006.

16   Moravcsik 2002, 2004; Omelicheva 2009.

sis on collective discussion and learning, has the potential to rectify this. Several scholars, including other authors in this volume, have demonstrated how this could work in cases such as the German foreign ministry.[17] Experimental deliberative discussions on foreign policy in Canada and other places have also demonstrated the potential of ordinary citizens and other members of domestic society to participate and shape foreign policy conversations.[18] However, such studies and pilots have often focused on the level of foreign ministries, which are far away from the local communities that form the most organic connection to the domestic society from which democratic foreign policy must draw its legitimacy.[19]

In the past several decades, the field of diplomatic studies has moved away from a singular focus on the sovereign state to examine a broader range of diplomatic actors, including subnational governments, domestic society and citizen-diplomats. Collectively, these diverse forms of diplomatic activities beyond the state are known as 'paradiplomacy.' Much of the early work on paradiplomacy focused on the foreign relations of provinces and municipalities that worked either in tandem or at odds with the central government's agenda. The predominant thrust of the provincial and municipal diplomacy field has been towards the actions of city governments as directed by premiers, governors, mayors and other subnational government officials.[20] Later scholarship expanded this by examining the evolving variety of subnational diplomatic institutions, such as city twinning, networks, and summits, as well as subnational trade agreements.[21] Largely on separate lines, the fields of citizen and diaspora diplomacy have interrogated how ordinary people and diasporic groups utilise personal, kinship, business and affective ties to influence the foreign relations of their countries.[22] More recently, some scholars

---

17   Cameron 1998; McCormick 2006; Geis, Opitz, and Pfeifer 2022.
18   Canadian International Council 2021; Government of Canada 2022B.
19   Melo and Baiocchi 2006; Crowley 2009.
20   van der Pluijm and Melissen 2007.
21   Acuto 2013; Tavares 2016; Davidson et al. 2019; Amiri and Sevin 2020; Acuto and Leffel 2021; Marchetti 2021; Acuto, Kosovac and Hartley 2021; Groen 2022; Amiri 2022; Pipa and Bouchet 2020; Bouchet 2022; Haddad 2022; Clarke 2009, 2011; Jayne, Hubbard and Bell 2013; Laguerre 2019.
22   In using the terms 'citizen diplomacy' and 'diaspora diplomacy', we do not mean to distinguish between formal citizens (i.e., those who hold the nationality of the host country) and other domestic society actors such as international students, permanent residents, immigrants and visitors (both documented and undocumented). Rather, we invoke these concepts to intervene in these currently existing academic fields and to make use of terminology in popular usage, while acknowledging the exclusionary logics that 'citizen' and 'diaspora' can connote. When referring to individual actors, we use

have also explored the diverse relationships that citizen and diasporic diplomats have with state and local governments' diplomacies, from different starting points and scales, ranging from city government strategies to diasporic
'ethnopreneurs'.[23]

Finally, many critics of deliberative democracy have noted the Eurocentric
bias of deliberative democratic theory and have argued for more culturally
specific study of actually existing deliberative democracy.[24] A similar charge
could be levied against the study of paradiplomacy, which has often emphasised relationships between communities in the Global North. In recent years,
however, studies of subnational relations in the Asia/Indo-Pacific, particularly
regarding China, Japan, Korea, Indonesia, and India, have reflected the diversity of forms of paradiplomatic engagement, and the range of constitutional
structures currently extant that put domestic societies and local governments
on the global stage.[25]

The introduction of two substantially different geopolitical contexts –
North America and Northeast Asia – introduces another set of considerations:
the diversity of forms and conceptions of sovereignty, democracy, diplomacy,
and international relations in these two regions. The Asia/Indo-Pacific domestic and international engagement contexts that form the underlying backbone
of the research for this chapter offer further pause for reflection on deliberative democracy as a theory and a practice when different types of democracies
engage or when democracies engage with states run by non-democratic governments.[26] In each case, just as citizen participation can be used to advance
public concerns or challenge hegemonic governments, it can also be used as a
means of 'authoritarian renewal'.[27] Many of the relationships we examined
also included engagement between democratic and non-democratic societies
and government bodies. In some instances, we saw democratic central governments that took steps to limit citizen and NCG engagement in the name of
foreign policy to protect the state and its people and others that touted the
importance of whole-of-society engagement in foreign policy but with reservations. Municipal twinning agreements and their citizen and city actors that

---

'domestic society actors' to refer to what other scholars have previously referred to as
'citizens' or 'diasporas'.

23   Sharp 2001; Henders and Young 2016; Young and Henders 2012, 2016; Ho and McConnell
      2017; Brinkerhoff 2019; Alejo 2022; Lee 2019, 2020; Hubbert 2020.
24   Gunaratne 2006; Bailey 2022; Deveaux, 2006.
25   Tavares 2016; Jackson 2018; Pietrasiak et al. 2018; Jain 2005; Surwandono and Maksum
      2020; Liu and Song 2020; Ramraj 2023.
26   Banerjee 2022; He, Breen, and Fishkin 2022; Leib and He 2006; Fan 2021; Ishikawa 2002.
27   He, Breen, and Fishkin 2022; He and Curato 2022.

drive them could be a part of one or more of these types of international engagements.

3 Defining the Democratic Diplomatic Middle Ground

We build on the interventions of such studies by moving the centre of analysis away from individual actor categories to what we call the 'democratic diplomatic middle ground' of paradiplomacy. As previously mentioned in our *Hague Journal of Diplmacy* forum essay, we draw from the literatures on assemblage theory and co-production in conceptualising this middle ground. Furthermore, we were inspired by historian Richard White's concept of the 'middle ground' that sought to name a particular mode of Indigenous-settler relations in the Great Lakes region in the eighteenth century.[28]

This middle ground refers to the spaces where these various actors intersect and overlap to co-produce a new, distinct diplomatic terrain that shapes and structures these relationships more than any single actor, and in turn transforms the actors themselves. The middle ground does not rely on assumptions or ideals that there is equality of status, power or voice within the spaces, or even that they are or need to be fully democratic. By spaces, we mean not only the physical spaces where twinning actors meet and events occur, but also the discursive spaces produced by ongoing policies, connections and narratives that form paradiplomatic relationships.

We suggest that the democratic diplomatic middle ground has the following characteristics:

- It decenters formal governing institutions like city halls and regional councils, instead modelling an assemblage of diverse actors with blurry boundaries.
- It defines societies and communities not as discrete actors or units, but rather as spheres or assemblages that contain sometimes consonant, sometimes dissonant actors who work together or vie for representation.
- It identifies a space shared between the two international communities and the various actors that represent them as the space where diplomacy functions and where democratic deliberation occurs.

---

28   White 1991. As White emphasised, the 'middle ground' denotes a contingent time-space where two groups' power relations are such that they are forced to work together, creating opportunities for misunderstandings and cultural transformation. We are mindful of Philip Deloria's (2006) and other scholars' cautions about hollowing out the specificity of this term.

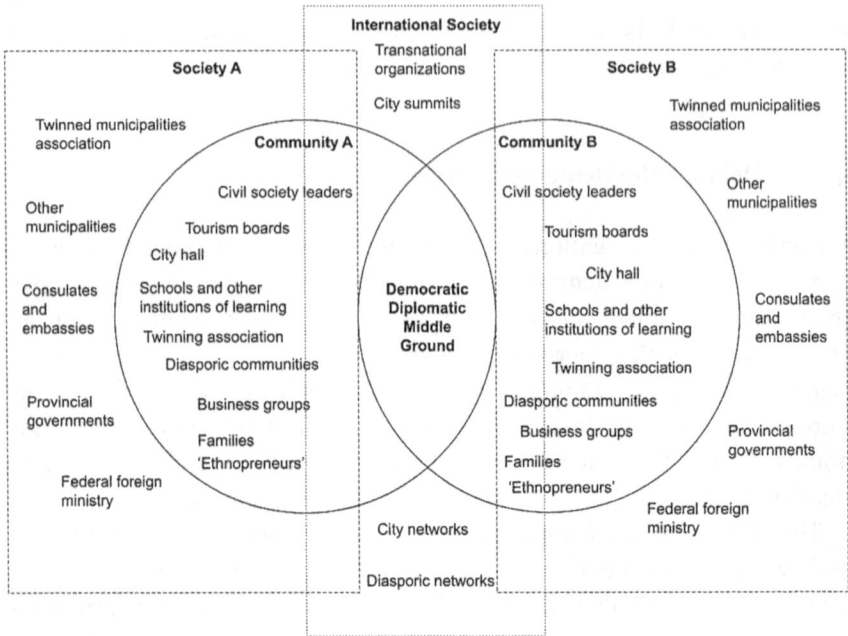

FIGURE 10.1 Visualising the democratic diplomatic middle ground

- This space is not dependent on particular institutions or agreements, but rather flexibly adapts to changing conditions within the two communities and interacts with ongoing dynamics at the societal and international levels.
- It acknowledges that, while a greater proportion of each community is involved in the democratic diplomatic middle ground, this only represents a limited percentage of the actual communities.

The exact configuration of this middle ground often varies, particularly between different countries and jurisdictions and even particular twinning relationships. But rather than highlight such variations or disaggregate government and domestic society into smaller components, our focus is to name and map the concept of a democratic diplomatic middle ground as another means for understanding and supporting engaging home in diplomacy. In sections 4 and 5 we use examples from municipal twinning to map out different aspects of the democratic diplomatic middle ground, before considering a sample of other forms of paradiplomacy of which this concept applies in section 6.

4   The Principal-Agent Problem in the Democratic Diplomatic Middle
       Ground

We understand the democratic diplomatic middle ground as a lens to conceptualise how identities and categories such as 'citizen', 'city', 'government' and
'domestic society' are constructed in the interaction between different actors
through paradiplomatic practices. Embedded in our use of the middle ground
is the term co-production, which draws on the field of science and technology
studies and its insights into the co-production of knowledge and 'sociotechni-
cal objects'.[29] Alexander Buhmann's discussion on how states and cities can
variably construct and perform joint attribution also informs our interpretation of how cities and domestic society actors can become identified collectively or separately.[30]

    From our previous research on Canada's municipal twinning with coun-
terparts in the Asia/Indo-Pacific and interviews with people involved in municipal twinning on both sides of the Pacific, we found that it was difficult to
separate identities cleanly into 'official' and 'domestic society actor'. Consider, for example, the nature of 'twinning societies', which are civic associations composed of private citizens involved in twinning relationships. In
some towns, like the Shiraoi Sister City Association in Japan, twinning societies are housed under the municipal government; in others, such as the
Lethbridge Twinning Society in Canada they are completely independent
civil society organisations. Yet, other twinning societies, like the Alberta /
Japan Twinned Municipalities Association and the Hokkaido Canada Society, include multiple cities or even provinces where city representatives
could be either city officials or private citizens. However, the membership
of twinning societies often includes current and former city officials and
mayors. In these cases, the identity of a civil society group can blur into an
official one through the mingling of official and domestic society actors.
These co-produced identities become more apparent if our analytical focus
travels with the evolution of a particular activity.

    For example, we spoke to diasporic leaders in Canada involved in cam-
paigns to donate personal protective equipment (PPE) from their country of
origin during the COVID-19 pandemic. Though these PPE campaigns were
branded as part of a public diplomacy push by the country of origin, the diasporic leaders ultimately sourced the PPE shipments and identified recipients in Canada through connections made as part of sister city relationships.

---

29   Jasanoff 2004b, 42.
30   Buhmann 2022.

The donations were publicly celebrated as diplomatic gifts from the country of origin, but they were also understood as the result of personal connections between diasporic groups and civic institutions and part of attempts to assert diasporic citizenship in a hybridised Canadian multicultural identity. These PPE donations were thus simultaneously represented as state-led, city-led and diaspora-led diplomacy through deliberative interactions between government and diasporic actors.

Even more fundamentally, however, the question of who has the authority to represent the 'city' in international settings can arise from the interaction between different actors and specific economies. For example, we encountered several twinning relationships and twinning negotiations where municipalities in Canada were primarily represented by a twinning society, non-governmental organisation, or civil society actor, while their counterparts in Japan, China, South Korea, or Taiwan were primarily represented by the municipal government. This often had to do with differences in city-level resources, and conceptions of city-level internationalisation, such as what aspects of international engagement a city should spend its resources and prioritise, and in the case of China included how officials in cities implemented overarching priorities from Beijing.[31] The different degree or style of democracy in each country also affects who represents a municipality and in what capacity. Several domestic society interviewees from various municipalities in Canada told us how surprised they were at being treated as formal municipal government representatives when they visited their counterparts. When their counterparts from one of those economies reciprocated, they were apparently taken aback at how Canadian city officials greeted ordinary citizens accompanying their official city delegation in a similar manner. Throughout the development of several sister city relationships we examined, the municipal governments in Canada and their counterpart governments in China, Japan, South Korea, and Taiwan adapted to each other's expectations of who was supposed to 'represent the city' and brought both official and domestic society actors in equal standing on municipal twinning delegations.

Thus, we suggest that the democratic diplomatic middle ground involves different actors and conceptions of legitimacy from both sides. The deliberation on this middle ground defines and transforms who is worthy of being a representative of the 'city', thus highlighting how deliberative interactions and outcomes can take precedence or at least stand parallel to official notions of diplomatic representation.

---

31   Harrison and Huang 2023, 30–32; Acuto et al. 2016; Yan 2021; Han, Wang, and Wei 2022; Zhou and Cao 2024.

5   Everyday Deliberation and Democratic Praxis in Municipal
         Twinning

We also understand the democratic diplomatic middle ground as an interpretative framework that can help explain how different actors collaboratively produce diplomatic relations at the local level. In this, we are inspired by the increasing application of assemblage thinking in the urban policy and international relations fields. While the concept of 'assemblage' and our concept of middle ground are not congruent, we see usefulness in the 'flat ontology' of assemblage theory that conceives of individual units coming together as coherent 'assemblages' that can in turn disassemble and reassemble into new forms.[32] By redirecting attention away from individual actors towards the democratic diplomatic middle grounds at the intersection of their interactions, we can see how municipal twinning relationships are made of various types of assemblages of capacities and power dynamics, continuities and change, and criteria and conceptions of twinning over time.

5.1   *Capacities and Power Dynamics of Actors*
In our interviews, we often heard about the crucial roles that domestic society actors played due to their unique capacities compared with government officials. The most common theme raised was that citizens had situated knowledge that city officials lacked. For example, councillors and civil society leaders in a highly multicultural Canadian city on the west coast highlighted how diasporic leaders' knowledge and connections with local consulates of countries where the city had twinning relations made them the key conduit for interactions between the city government and local consulates. Being able to equally bridge and smoothly navigate linguistic, cultural, and political barriers are rare but valuable traits when they are recognised and utilised by governments, businesses, and/or communities. But acquiring such bi-cultural (or multicultural) knowledge and insights can place individuals outside particular domestic norms and often go underappreciated and underutilised. Such challenges mean that such people reach these opportunities by a series of unforeseen paths and opportunities. They may also restrict only those with sufficient entrepreneurial energy to seek out such paths. Yet city officials on both sides of the Pacific also told us they believed that civil society and business groups could have more sustainable and active relationships in their twinned counterparts' societies than bureaucrats were able to achieve. They explicitly and

---

32   McCann and Ward 2012; Acuto and Curtis 2014; Dittmer 2014.

implicitly mentioned how those outside government had the flexibility to work around certain political or bureaucratic constraints and better maintain relationships exceeding political terms.

But city governments also have essential capacities and power that domestic society members and the private sector lack. One civil society leader in Canada, who was proposing a friendship city relationship with his hometown in Northeast Asia, argued that the reputation and authority conveyed in an official twinning agreement was more valuable than any funding that would arise from it. They had already amassed their own resources over decades of successful arts and cultural programming but said they needed the convening power of an official designation and (even nominal) participation from municipal governments to open doors that their own network could not. They proposed a reconceptualised version of city-to-city agreements which, after securing the cities' official seals, would be driven by and paid for by the very communities and businesses they were trying to connect. They argued that this would ultimately help the cities grow, expand, and deepen cultural and business connections. The programmes that are now being worked out based on this idea could help the city and domestic society actors navigate a variety of international political and diplomatic tensions, city budgetary constraints, and civil society international engagement limitations.

By contrast, in the case of a town in British Columbia, Canada, whose sister city relationship in Hokkaido, Japan was anchored in a decades-long student exchange, it was precisely municipal funding and human resources that were desired as the volunteer-run twinning society was responsible for all the details of the exchange programme. Both the twinning society chair and the mayor of the town felt that having the logistics of the exchange funded by the city and handled by municipal staff, as their twinning counterpart did, would alleviate an unfair burden on volunteers and improve the sustainability of the programme. The twinning society also discussed how the school district and other organisations charge a significant amount of money to facilitate international school exchanges. While this may help offset costs, create new business ventures and mitigate some challenges, the chair argued that as soon as a programme becomes a paid, for-profit initiative, it risks treating those involved as commodities. In addition, they argued that for-profit exchanges could easily lose some of its "soft" benefits including participants (from both countries) being held to higher standards to act as representatives from their respective countries and cities and developing closer family and community relationships that often last years after the exchange. In this case, even while the civil society organisers often struggled with funding, the value of the decades-long personal relationships between citizens in Canada and Japan devel-

oped through the municipal twinning programme appeared to draw a boundary about how far they would want to go in securing public funds and support
without going private.

Most twinning relationships we encountered within our dataset and via
interviews combined the unique capacities and power dynamics of domestic
society actors and local governments to varying degrees. For each twinning
relationship, available capacities and power dynamics between city officials
and civil society leaders on each side of the relationship impacted the formation and evolution of the activities and scope of the relationship, which often
ebbed and flowed over the course of years. Understanding how capacities and
power dynamics influence potential equalities and inequalities within the
collaborative process could help create practices and policies to support
more equitable and inclusive approaches to diplomatic engagement.

5.2   *Continuities and Change over Time*

The concept of democratic diplomatic middle grounds of municipal twinning
allows us to follow relationships and programmes as 'middle grounds' that
reassemble over time, instead of focusing on governments or individual actors
at a specific point in time. This foregrounds the importance of taking a longer-
term view of citizen-city democratic diplomacy that may outlast any one single or small group of individuals and a particular city government or political
party, better accounting for ebbs and flows of activity. For example, student
exchange programmes often require individuals, twinning societies, school
boards and cities to work together. In practice, the core responsibility of maintaining these exchange programmes shifts between these actors in response to
changes in interest, capacity and power, and politics by all stakeholders over
the course of years, if not decades. A schoolteacher initially founded the student exchange programme in one town in Ontario, Canada in a private capacity. Over three decades, the exchange programme moved from being under
the schoolteacher's personal responsibility to that of a newly founded twinning society, and then to the administration of a single high school. Throughout this evolution, the actors involved and the scope of the exchange itself
changed significantly, but the representation of the exchange continued to
be that of a programme under the twinning relationship.

Another middle ground of continuity and change can be a historical legacy
grounded in initial civil society connections that inspires and embeds itself in
a later twinning city relationship. For example, we spoke with officials and
community leaders from municipalities in Canada and Taiwan that became
sister cities in the early 2000s in the wake of an anniversary celebration of a
Canadian missionary from one of the municipalities who had set up a Chris-

tian mission and a host of other institutions, most notably schools and hospitals, in the other municipality and the surrounding region over a century ago. Interviewees spoke about how, despite such longstanding ties, it was a conference that brought together scholars, leaders from schools and churches, and officials and community members from both cities where the idea was borne to create more exchanges, which eventually led to the city twinning agreement. Both before and after the twinning agreement was signed, there was an assemblage of interactions involving the two municipal governments and a diverse set of civil society actors. Our interviewees in both cities cited the central role of the original historical legacy in informing and motivating their interactions with the twinning counterpart, though they drew different meanings from the legacy depending on the focus of their activities. Leaders from churches and schools, city officials, and community members all proudly claimed a stake in making it happen, meaning that they could all claim some degree of ownership of the partnership and its evolution. Though the relationship between the two localities spanned over a century and a half, the forms of the relationship changed as new actors, joining as part of the twinning agreement, added new motivations and outcomes (such as student exchanges and tourism promotion) to existing religious, humanitarian and diasporic ties. Centring this legacy as a 'middle ground' allows us to see the formal twinning agreement between the two municipal governments as merely a component of a broader, older assemblage of diplomatic interactions between the two communities.

5.3   Criteria and Conceptions

Focusing on the democratic diplomatic middle ground of municipal twinning relationships also prompts us to consider the different criteria for success and conceptions of municipal twinning (and other forms of paradiplomacy for that matter) that various actors might have, and how these might interact, conflict and overlap with each other in a co-productive process.[33] Success for a domestic society actor involved in twinning, for example, may be different than for a government institution. Local governments and domestic society are also made up of diverse actors and groups that may have divergent intentions and values, which will influence their goals, activities and assessments of twinning. In our interviews we heard about how a former Canadian school principal who started a student exchange programme described how they clashed with the local school district on how to measure the success of

33   Ryan and Mazilli 2021.

the programme. The principal focused on building a strong relationship with the twinned counterpart and involving a wide range of students and teachers in the programme. The school district, however, was primarily concerned with how the exchange would fit into the rest of the school district's programming. Reflecting on the matter after retirement, the principal regretted not engaging the school board more and better integrating the exchange into existing school board activities.

Conceptions of twinning have been and are based on a variety of motivations such as supporting citizen diplomacy to foster global peace, build unity or regional integration within certain international blocs (such as the former Communist bloc or the European Union), to promote North-South exchange to enhance development and economic growth, promote global justice, and boost private sector growth and trade and investment.[34] Domestic society actors may also have conceptions of twinning that are distinct from those of local governments. For example, a civil society leader in Western Canada who was proposing a friendship city relationship with their hometown told us that their main motivation was to promote the value of multiculturalism, cultural and artistic exchange and related dialogue in both their hometown and the city where they live, and to foster dialogue on these issues in and between Canada, Taiwan, and multiple other countries in Europe and Southeast Asia, all the while highlighting the positive local economic impact of such initiatives. In this sense, their conception of the proposed twinning relationship as a vehicle for social advocacy complicated nuanced, and expanded the cultural and business partnerships envisioned by both cities' friendship city programmes. But by emphasising the possible cultural industry connections that the relationship could engender, the civil society leader also demonstrated how their vision could adapt to meet the expectations, such as business and trade, that others might have for the twinning relationship. Many other agreements between Canada and China, Japan, South Korea and Taiwan have also changed their focus and goals, sometimes over the course of decades. Some, like the Alberta-Hokkaido relationship, began after developing education, culture and sports linkages, but expanded to include business and trade in sectors such as agriculture, energy, and forestry.

Noting how different actors perceive and interpret criteria and conceptions for success over time and geography can help foster more productive democratically co-produced policy and programmes by making more transparent links between specific actors, their main interests and what they may value in

---

34 Harrison and Huang 2023, 28–29.

the endeavor. For example, city officials could place more value in political aspects of twinning, such as addressing taxpayers' concerns about spending on foreign relations, supporting twinning-related best practices, or highlighting big picture items such as business deals or internationalisation of their municipality, that help create positive public perceptions. They could even be swayed or influenced by international geopolitical considerations and pressures in how they manage existing twinning relationships and consider new agreements or cancel old agreements. Meanwhile, domestic society actors may privilege positive contributions to communities, including business, cultural and education ties, and people-to-people connections and dialogue. The exact mix may depend on the specific city government and domestic society actors involved in the assemblage at a given time. Being more attuned to the changing dynamics of criteria of success and conceptions of a particular para-diplomatic activity may boost communication and relationship building.

We invoke the democratic diplomatic middle ground as a normative model of diplomatic urban governance where government officials and domestic society actors collectively design and implement policy. Here, we incorporate ideas from the literature of urban planning and policy studies that emphasise the growing role of public participation in policy-making and advocate for the intentional involvement of local communities (either through 'top-down' inclusion by the state or 'bottom-up' assertion by civil society) in the design of government programming.[35] While we suggest that democratic co-production in twinning already exists, taking active measures to foster it would allow municipalities to better take advantage of the synergies between local governments and domestic society and reinforce democratic deliberative practices.

A democratic diplomatic middle ground approach to understanding and managing municipal twinning moves the focus of the twinning relationship away from an agreement signed between two city halls or a particular year of events, for instance, towards an enduring and evolving relationship between two communities over time. Local governments should take advantage of the wide array of domestic society actors that have unique capacities and opportunities to contribute to twinning, and they should be aware of their diverse interests, criteria for success and conceptions of twinning relationships. We also suggest going beyond traditional models of citizen engagement in policy-making to embrace the democratic diplomatic middle ground model of municipal twinning. Such a model would require the local government to share with various civic institutions and groups not only the 'ownership' of the twin-

---

35   Watson 2014; Voorberg, Bekkers and Tummers 2015; Sorrentino, Sicilia and Howlett 2018; Galuszka 2019; Rosen and Painter 2019.

ning relationship, but also the process of designing, reforming and implementing twinning policy and programming. In actual practice, this may require a
degree of humility, transparency, trust, sharing, cultural sensitivity, and security clearance (where applicable), as well as the promotion of democratic
practices that necessitates investment and commitment to foster.

6   Foreign Policy and Diplomacy beyond the State

The above examples and analysis revolve around municipal twinning relationships in general with specific examples from those between Canada and counterparts in China, Japan, South Korea, and Taiwan. However, our theoretical
contribution extends beyond those geographies or diplomacies as the concept
of a democratic diplomatic middle ground (and the associated assemblages of
capacities and power dynamics, continuities and change, and criteria and
conceptions) also applies to other forms of paradiplomacy. Countries are divided into an array of government levels and jurisdictions such as regions,
provinces/states, metropolitan areas, local authorities (cities, towns, villages,
counties and the like), and Indigenous nations, many of which actively participate in international relations and diplomacy. Literature and analysis of other
types of paradiplomacies, similar to that of twinning literature, often focus on
actors rather than democratic diplomatic middle grounds. Below, we briefly
address how other types of diplomacy by cities, provinces, and Indigenous
Peoples are often overshadowed by the study of state diplomacy and relate
them to the middle ground concept.

6.1   *Other City Diplomacies*
Despite there being over 10,000 cities worldwide which are home to more
than half the world's population, city diplomacy, similar to other paradiplomacies, remains overshadowed by that of states. Michele Acuto, for instance,
argues that '[c]ities are the invisible gorillas of international studies' because, in '[f]ocusing too much on the presence of nation-states and intergovernmental relations on this scene, scholars have failed to perceive the
relevance of other elements in world politics'.[36]
    In addition to municipal twinning, cities are engaged in a variety of diplo-
matic and international activities that often involve civil society actors, including city networks, city summits, and trade missions. Many city govern-

---

36   Acuto 2013, 1–2.

ments also maintain branches dedicated to international trade and invest-ment or have city councilors tasked with such initiatives that engage with non-government actors such as civil society organisations, businesses, and Indigenous communities, as well as other cities and provincial and central governments, to meet their international engagement goals and objectives. They may work with central governments, follow their lead, or even compete with them as they pave their own paths to engage with the international com-munity in the pursuit of various goals and objectives, such as real estate and development investment, and co-operation on greening and climate action, international development, smart cities, and responses to health crises as we saw during the COVID-19 pandemic. Acuto and Benjamin Leffel suggest that there are more than 300 city networks advancing discussion, policy, and ac-tion related to such goals, including C40 Cities, the Federation of Canadian Municipalities, the World Bank's Global Smart City Partnership Program, Local Governments for Sustainability, United Cities and Local Governments, and OECD Champion Mayors for Inclusive Growth.[37] As Raffaele Marchetti argues, 'cities are where the action is'.[38]

Similar to municipal twinning, each of these networks and initiatives rely on a convergence of actors over time that create their own kinds of democratic diplomatic middle grounds with varying capacities and power dynamics, con-tinuities and changes over time, and criteria and conceptions of success re-garding their end goals. To varying degrees, these municipal middle grounds respond to and influence domestic and international government and non-government actors to drive policy, programmes, and change.

6.2   *Provinces*

Similar to cities, provinces[39] also engage in international diplomacy and for-eign policy. Provinces/states often create their own international engagement strategies, participate in provincial twinning relationships, engage with vari-ous international organisations, and set up offices abroad in pursuit of their economic, cultural, political, and/or image-related interests.[40] All of these ac-

---

37   Acuto and Leffel 2021, 1759; C40 Cities 2024; Federation of Canadian Municipalities 2024;
        World Bank; Interviews 2021.

38   Marchetti 2021, 1–2.

39   I.e., the level of government immediately under the central government that is indepen-
        dently elected and has some degree of autonomy and jurisdiction. Country-specific
        terms also include prefectures, states, territory, and a variety of special city categories.

40   Tavares 2016; Paquin 2018, 2019; Aldecoa and Keating 1999; Jain 2005; Schiavon 2019;
        Harrison and Huang 2023, 42.

tivities include deliberative processes with an array of government and non-government partners and stakeholders.

For example, the Canadian provinces of Alberta, British Columbia, Ontario, Quebec, and Saskatchewan all currently maintain overseas offices. Since Canadian provinces first began opening offices in the late 1960s, there have been expansions and contractions of these efforts. These are due to changes of provincial governments that lead such initiatives, periodic internal reviews, budget constraints, changing government priorities, input from province-based businesses and diaspora, the electorate which may change support for overseas initiatives, changes in provincial-central government relations as well as changes in the international political economy and geopolitics.[41] We are currently witnessing an expansion of Canadian provincial international offices and initiatives. Similar to past growth periods since the 1980s, the Asia/Indo-Pacific remains the geographic focal point of these provincial international efforts. Perhaps coincidentally, this began shortly before the Canadian federal government released its November 2023 Indo-Pacific Strategy, which aims to be a whole-of-society, whole-of-government strategy to engage with the region.[42] The story about how this strategy will influence relationships and dialogue between various levels of government, among ministries in the same government level (e.g. various federal government ministries), civil society and Indigenous nations is still unfolding, but will no doubt provide a rich area for discussion and analysis on paradiplomacy in general and the changing shape of democratic diplomatic middle grounds in practice.

Provincial offices abroad are meant to serve the specific interests of a province. They focus on providing more in-depth and province-specific guidance to both province-based and international stakeholders and partners than their central government counterparts. But the activities of provincial offices abroad and their engagement with and awareness by civil society, non-government actors vary significantly as many limit their activities to 'core' sectors and related businesses. Yet, even though their activities and outcomes may be relatively and perhaps broadly unknown within a province, the partners and stakeholders they do engage with at home in their initiatives abroad form what we see as a familiar blurring of official and unofficial boundaries in a democratic diplomatic middle ground. For example, in a provincial-led initiative abroad, there could be times when a province-based business, an NGO,

---

41   Labreque and Harrison 2018; Harrison 2018; Harrison and Jin 2020; Kukuchka 2008, 2009; Jacomy-Millette 1976.

42   Government of Canada 2022A, 2024A, 2024B.

or a provincial official come to represent Canada despite not being a federal government official.

In host countries unfamiliar with Canada's unique federal-provincial jurisdiction divide, provincial offices can risk confusing or complicating international engagement with Canada, especially when each province's international offices are resourced differently, have their own mandates, and networks that may overlap or differ from the federal government and its associated ministries engaged abroad. In other words, each province has its own peculiar capacities and power dynamics, continuities and change over time, and criteria and conceptions of success and what they ought or ought not to be doing according to set key performance indicators and evaluations. Despite the potential to confuse or complicate a national brand or bilateral engagement, they offer potential for deepening and strengthening international relations that can often continue to function during times of diplomatic tensions between central governments. Viewing these activities as democratic diplomatic middle grounds can help clarify these non-central government-led diplomatic practices and help both provincial and federal governments create more effective policies and programmes.

6.3   *Indigenous Diplomacies*

Indigenous diplomacies is a category of paradiplomacy that does not fit neatly within substate or non-central government diplomacy. Yet, it is intricately related to our discussion about the democratic diplomatic middle ground and engaging home in diplomacy. Indigenous Peoples have been involved in transnationalism, diplomacy, foreign policy, and international trade activities for thousands of years. Yet while recognition of the role of Indigenous Peoples in international relations is increasing across various disciplines and fields, the study of Indigenous diplomacy remains relatively new.[43] Indigenous diplomacies are and will arguably be an increasingly critical component for the field of diplomacy and for broadening our understanding of what it means to be 'engaging home in diplomacy'. Central government foreign policy and diplomacy were and arguably in many cases are still driven by states that were colonial powers or created through colonisation and decolonisation processes. As such, colonial perspectives are embedded to varying degrees in diplomatic practices, policies, institutions, and nation-states themselves (and the academic fields that study them). Indigenous Peoples have engaged with various actors ranging from individuals, NGOS, and international organisations to

---

43   Beier 2005, 2009; Henderson 2008; Lackenbauer and Cooper 2007; Montsion 2015, 2016; Christmas 2012; Brigg and Graham 2023; Ryser 2012.

multiple levels of central and non-central governments at their home and abroad. In their deliberative processes, they have and continue to show how they represent themselves as distinct entities rather than as a 'domestic society' within colonial states and are also shaping diplomatic practices and outcomes. Upon close inspection, we can see similar democratic diplomatic middle grounds at work.

The global Indigenous population includes approximately 476 million people, comprising roughly 5,000 distinct groups, living in around (and sometimes across border areas of) 90 countries, in areas that account for significant portions of global biodiversity. About 70 per cent of the global Indigenous population call some part of the Asia/Indo-Pacific home.[44] In comparison, the Indigenous population in Canada is 1.8 million, which includes 630 First Nations communities, 53 Inuit communities in the north that encompass over a third of Canada's territory, and various Métis communities across the country. What often gets missed in citing such numbers is that multiple layers of democratic diplomatic middle grounds over the course of generations have shaped these formations and their internationally focused activities.

While Indigenous diplomacies were always a part of Indigenous nation-nation relations and Indigenous nation-colonial power relations, Indigenous diplomacies as a global phenomenon surged from the 1970s. Since then, Indigenous governments, organisations, and individuals have built global networks with each other, with central and non-central governments, international organisations, NGOS, and non-Indigneous individuals, in the pursuit of their interests. These include the revitalisation of their political, economic and cultural rights and livelihoods, recognition, and reconciliation.

Numerous Indigenous-led initiatives have contributed to creating and maintaining global Indigenous diplomatic networks and organisations since the 1970s that embody the democratic diplomatic middle ground. For example, George Manuel, an Indigenous political leader from Canada, spearheaded the creation of the World Council of Indigenous Peoples, which sought to build an international Indigenous organisation in the pursuit of having Indigenous rights recognised globally.[45] Activities by Inuit, Sámi and Russian Indigenous Peoples of the North and deliberation with central governments culminated in their inclusion and full participation in all dialogue at the Arctic Council, alongside the five littoral states of the Arctic.[46] An example of Indig-

---

44   United Nations, Indigenous Peoples; World Bank, Indigenous Peoples; IWGIA 2023.

45   Sanders 1977; Manuel and Posluns [1974] 2018; McFarlane and Manuel 2020; Library and Archives Canada, R9349; Laenui 1990; Crossen 2014.

46   Bloom 1999; Koivurova and Vanderzwaag 2007.

enous diplomacy involving extensive international deliberation that has received almost no attention in academic literature is how the Indigenous Ainu of Japan began purposefully engaging internationally. Since the 1970s, many Ainu began organising and participating in delegation trips abroad and, since 1989, Ainu have been hosting gatherings of Indigenous Peoples from around the world. In these activities, they have aimed to build solidarity and to learn from the experiences of other Indigenous Peoples to inform their own domestic and international activities to represent themselves and revive their rights.[47]

Indigenous diplomacies also expanded into international organisations made up of internationally recognised states. Indigenous leaders and non-Indigenous allies, for example, were able to insert Indigenous Peoples' issues and gain accreditation in the United Nations (unlike how Indigenous Peoples' attempts to gain audiences in the League of Nations, the UN's predecessor, were unsuccessful). José R. Martinez Cobo's global study about discrimination against Indigenous Peoples helped pave the path for the creation of the UN Working Group on Indigenous Populations in 1982, which provided a platform for Indigenous Peoples to directly address and raise their concerns within the UN.[48] The UN expanded this initiative by continuing to work with with Indigenous organisations to create the Permanent Forum on Indigenous Issues in 2000, the Special Rapporteur on the Rights of Indigenous Peoples in 2001, the UN Declaration on the Rights of Indigenous Peoples in 2007, and the Expert Mechanism on the Rights of Indigenous Peoples in 2007.[49] These mechanisms continue to the present. Much of the present debate is about how Indigenous Peoples can work with central and non-central governments and domestic societies to implement inherent Indigenous rights and agreements to which states have historically committed.

While Indigenous Peoples-related deliberations at the UN are wide-ranging, there are more focused Indigenous initiatives that also depend on engaging home in diplomacy. The creation of the Indigenous Peoples Economic and Trade Cooperation Agreement (IPETCA) sheds light on how Indigenous leaders from several countries worked with each other, an international organisation focused on economic policy issues, and state-level ministries to create an international agreement aimed at fostering Indigenous inclusion in

---

47   Harrison 2025; Harrison 2021; Hara and Harrison 2022; Tsutsui 2018, 26–81.

48   Martínez Cobo Study; Sanders 1989.

49   Henderson 2008; Lightfoot 2016; Niezen 2003; Tsutsui 2018; Uemura 2013; Rombouts 2017; Charters and Stavenhagen 2009; Anaya 2004.

international trade and investment.[50] This agreement came out of deliberations at the Asia-Pacific Economic Cooperation, a 21-member regional economic forum established in 1989 to leverage the growing interdependence of the Asia-Pacific, when New Zealand-Aotearoa was its chair in 2021 at the height of the COVID-19 pandemic. As host, New Zealand/Aotearoa created an all-Māori 'Indigenous Taskforce' charged with including and elevating Indigenous economic and trade policy discussion within the work of APEC. Multiple virtual meetings were held with Indigenous business leaders from APEC member countries throughout the year to discuss Indigenous involvement in shaping and advancing trade policy. By the end of the year, the task force was able to have a set of priorities included in the organisation's year-end reports. They also worked with central governments and Indigenous leaders in New Zealand, Canada, Australia and Taiwan to create the IPETCA. At the time of writing, implementation of the agreement remains in its early stages. Even so, we can already see that its creation of the nascent Partnership Council resembles and is unfolding as a democratic diplomatic middle ground. Each participating economy has created a team of four individuals, comprising two representatives from the government and two representatives from Indigenous communities, to discuss domestic priorities. These teams then report as a group at APEC meetings.[51]

Indigenous diplomacies have and continue to shape issues both at home and abroad in diverse areas such as human rights, traditional and non-traditional security (climate action, food security, health), trade and investment, tourism, data sovereignty, intellectual property, artificial intelligence, reconciliation, and law.[52] Assemblages of Indigenous and non-Indigenous individuals, communities, non-governmental organisations, lawyers, scholars, and multiple levels of governments and international organisations have been convening, discussing, and engaging at home and abroad over decades. Recognising the democratic diplomatic middle ground at work in Indigenous diplomacies could open more effective and targeted forms of collaboration between Indigenous Peoples and non-Indigenous allies and accomplices in advancing decolonisation.

---

50   New Zealand Foreign Affairs and Trade.

51   Harrison active participation ABAC Indigenous Leaders Dialogues in 2021. APF Canada 2021A, 2021B, 2021C; APEC 2021, 2022; APEC Business Advisory Council 2021, p. 14, 29, 55–56. On Indigenous international trade and business also, see Harrison and Norris 2019; Harrison and Asgari 2020; Burrows and Schwartz 2020; Hilton 2021; Colbourne and Anderson 2020.

52   Ryser 2012.

7   Conclusion

This chapter examined engaging home in diplomacy via municipal twinning, other city diplomacies, provincial diplomacy, and Indigenous diplomacy. We identified and described everyday practices of paradiplomacy as a democratic diplomatic middle ground. Naming existing paradiplomatic practices helps both to understand engaging home in diplomacy in a new light. It will also stimulate evidence based-policy analysis and development to support and enhance democratic practices in foreign policy.

However, theorising and examining engaging home in diplomacy is anything but simple. Naming democratic diplomatic middle ground as a critical feature of diplomacy requires painting a broad brush over many complexities and variations within paradiplomatic practices. As with simplifying complexities and nuances in any field, especially those of a global nature, there are limitations, caveats, and exceptions. We will leave scrutiny of these pitfalls for future debate, as our goal herein has been to highlight that while there may be a worsening 'democratic deficit' in foreign policy led by states, the broad existence (and perhaps rise) of democratic diplomatic middle grounds in a variety of paradiplomacies is a beacon of hope in an era of general global dissatisfaction of democracy that has been termed a 'global democratic recession.'[53]

Central governments often espouse concepts like whole-of-government and whole-of-society, and words such as collaborative, co-operative, co-ordinated governance, in relation to their diplomacy and foreign policy. Such framing often has non-central government and citizen (and occasionally Indigenous Peoples) participation in mind. This signals that many central governments are seeing engaging home in foreign policy and diplomacy as critical. But in these contexts, it is often implied that, while central governments will engage with home, it will remain the central government that will drive diplomatic and foreign policy efforts. However, when we make paradiplomacies the central launching place for examining diplomacy, other possibilities emerge beyond the objective of strengthening central governments' foreign policy and diplomatic efforts. Engaging home can also create new paths that may contradict or push central governments on their foreign policy, or change the way they support or constrict paradiplomatic actors and activities. While paradiplomacy can and does complement and strengthen a coun-

---

53   Foa et al. 2020

try's foreign policy, a democratic diplomatic middle ground framework foregrounds paradiplomacy's democratic promise and emphasises its role in mitigating against democratic deficits in international relations.

A democratic diplomatic middle ground should not be conflated with an
equal ground. Power structures, resources, politics, and types of political systems will influence the components of the democratic diplomatic middle
ground, including capacities and power dynamics, continuities and change,
and criteria and conceptions that will change over time and require ongoing
negotiation. For example, if one country is more aware and strategic of utilising paradiplomacy for its diplomatic goals than another country, it could sup-
ply resources for non-central governments to engage with counterparts internationally that may gain local support but could undermine or threaten
another country. Being out-strategised and out-resourced by another country
could also lead to below-the-radar risks. Paradiplomatic efforts could potentially heighten the challenges of misinformation, disinformation, foreign interference, and trust in institutions in democratic societies. Countering these
potential pitfalls could encourage a central government to take on a stronger
top-down approach that muzzles non-central governments or Indigenous-led
initiatives that it may see as undermining a state's written or implied foreign
policy, security, values, or interests.

However, rather than thinking of paradiplomatic activities as potential
threats to state sovereignty, our focus on the participatory democratic
potential of these sites of paradiplomacy suggest a different frame: that of
democratic legitimation of the foreign policy of the central government (i.e.,
increasing domestic society buy-in, creating infrastructure for intergovernmental relations, channeling internal conflict into practicable fora, etc.).
This helps put meat on the bones for 'whole-of-government' or 'whole-of-
society' endeavours, which usually strain to be perceived or implemented
as such. Encouraging and supporting democratic diplomatic middle grounds
requires resources for municipalities, provinces, Indigenous Peoples, and
civil society to be direct leaders, partners and contributors in international
diplomatic initiatives that matter locally. Deeper and more effective paradiplomacy will inevitably reshape the way we think about diplomacy in a
traditional sense away from the perspective that sees states as the sole actors and arbitrators of diplomacy and foreign policy. However, it also has
significant potential to strengthen democratic principles. They also have
the potential to help states more effectively deal with the global challenges
of our time, including climate change, loss of biodiversity, disaster mitiga-
tion and recovery, social and gender inequality, peace and stability, health
crisis, and ungoverned next-generation technologies like artificial intelli-

gence.[54] Without understanding and valuing the intricacies of the democratic diplomatic middle grounds in which paradiplomacy occurs, it remains
unclear what putative whole-of-government and whole-of-society policies
mean in practice.

Each paradiplomatic activity includes the intention of a government, a civil
society organisation, an NGO, or an Indigenous nation to represent itself and
its interests internationally. But in doing so, they inevitably engage with civil
society, NGOS, and other levels of government in their home country and in
other countries. We can look at each of these levels of paradiplomacy separately, with each as having their own particular type of democratic diplomatic
middle ground. Yet, none of them operate in a vacuum. For example, as we
argued, when cities engage in municipal twinning relations, they create a distinct middle ground with citizens. But they may also interact and deliberate to
varying degrees with provincial governments, Indigenous nations, and central
government officials at home and abroad. Exploring diplomacy from the perspective of such an integrated ecosystem of middle grounds requires new theoretical framing and empirical research. They will equally require attending to
the actors, sites and scales of paradiplomacy and the middle grounds where
they intersect. This new research agenda will undoubtedly require more interdisciplinary research on paradiplomacy, particularly from anthropological
and historical perspectives.[55]

We hope this chapter sparks ideas for future research, particularly to move
beyond broad overviews to address the actors, sites and scales of paradiplomacy and the middle grounds where they intersect. This is not merely an
exciting and stimulating academic endeavor, as these findings are intricately
related and (we think) valuable for a variety of policymakers and diplomatic
actors. But our initiatives and findings risk being confined to a small segment
of the academy already convinced of the importance of paradiplomacy unless
we do more. In addition to researching and writing on the intricacies of paradiplomacy and what it means for democratic practices in foreign policy, we
need to communicate our findings beyond academia to support and work
with the paradiplomatic actors about which we write.

---

54   Harrison and Huang 2023, 38–41; Bouchet 2022; Truman Centre.
55   Hubbert 2020.

Bibliography

Acuto, Michele. *Global Cities, Governance and Diplomacy: The Urban Link* (New York: Routledge, 2013).

Acuto, Michele and Simon Curtis. 'Assemblage Thinking and International Relations'. In *Reassembling International Theory*, eds. Michele Acuto and Simon Curtis (London: Palgrave Macmillan, 2014), 1–15.

Acuto, Michele, Anna Kosovac and Kris Hartley. 'City Diplomacy: Another Generational Shift?'. *Diplomatica* 3 (1) (2021), 137–146. DOI 10.1163/25891774-03010007.

Acuto, Michele and Benjamin Leffel. 'Understanding the Global Ecosystem of City Networks'. *Urban Studies* 58 (9) (July 2021), 1758–1774. DOI 10.1177/0042098020-929261.

Acuto, Michele, Mika Morissette, Dan Chan, and Benjamin Leffel. '"City Diplomacy" and Twinning: Lessons from the UK, China and Globally'. Future of Cities: Working Paper, Foresight, Government Office for Science, 2016.

Aldecoa, Francisco and Michael Keating, eds. *Paradiplomacy in Action: The Foreign Relations of Subnational Governments* (New York: Routledge, 1999).

Alejo, Antonio. 'Diasporas as Actors in Urban Diplomacy'. *The Hague Journal of Diplomacy* 17 (2022), 138–150. DOI: 10.1163/1871191X-bja10094.

Amiri, Sohaela. 'City Diplomacy: An Introduction to the Forum'. *The Hague Journal of Diplomacy* 17 (1) (2022), 91–95. DOI: 10.1163/1871191X-bja10090.

Amiri, Sohaela and Efe Sevin, eds. *City Diplomacy: Current Trends and Future Prospects* (Cham: Springer, 2020).

Anaya, James. *International Peoples in International Law* (Oxford: Oxford University Press, 2004).

APEC. 'Case Studies on Advancing Inclusive Economic Growth: Understanding and Valuing Indigenous Economies within APEC'. APEC SOM Committee on Economic and Technical Cooperation, April 2021.

APEC. 'Unlocking Indigenous Peoples' Economic Potential in the Asia-Pacific Region for a More Inclusive Recovery'. APEC Economic Committee, January 2022.

APEC Business Advisory Council (ABAC). 'Report to APEC Economic Leaders: People, Place and Prosperity – Tāngata, Taiao me te Taurikura', 2021.

Asenbaum, Hans. 'Doing Democratic Theory Democratically'. *International Journal of Qualitative Methods* 21 (2022). DOI 10.1177/16094069221105072.

Asia Pacific Foundation of Canada. 'Asia-Pacific Economic Cooperation Takes Steps Toward Indigenous Inclusion'. 8 July 2021A. https://www.asiapacific.ca/asia-watch/asia-pacific-economic-cooperation-takes-steps-toward.

Asia Pacific Foundation of Canada. 'Asia-Pacific Economic Cooperation Hosts Indigenous-focused Dialogues'. 21 October 2021B. https://www.asiapacific.ca/asia-watch/asia-pacific-economic-cooperation-hosts-indigenous-focused.

Asia Pacific Foundation of Canada. 'New Zealand Concludes Year as APEC Host.' 16 November 2021C https://www.asiapacific.ca/asia-watch/new-zealand-conclu des-years-apec-host.

Bailey, Tom. (Ed.). *Deprovincializing Habermas: Global Perspectives* (2nd ed.) (London: Routledge, 2022).

Banerjee, Subhabrata Bobby. 'Decolonizing Deliberative Democracy: Perspectives from Below'. Journal of Business Ethics 181 (2022), 283–299. DOI 10.1007/s10551-021-04971-5

Beauvais, Edana and Mark Warren. 'What Can Deliberative Mini-publics Contribute to Democratic Systems?' *European Journal of Political Research* 58 (3) (2019), 893–914.

Beier, Marshall J. *International Relations in Uncommon Places: Indigeneity, Cosmology, and the Limits of International Theory* (London: Palgrace Macmillan, 2005).

Beier, Marshall J., ed. *Indigenous Diplomacies* (London: Palgrave Macmillan, 2009).

Bloom, Evan T. 'Establishment of the Arctic Council'. *The American Journal of International Law* 93 (3) (1999), 712–22. DOI 10.2307/2555272.

Brigg, Morgan and Mary Graham, eds. 'Toward Indigenous Diplomacy: Relational challenges to International Relations and foreign policy survivalism', special issue, *Australian Journal of International Affairs* 77 (6) (2023).

Bouchet, Max. 'Strengthening Foreign Policy through Subnational Diplomacy'. *The Hague Journal of Diplomacy* 17 (1) (2022), 96–108. DOI 10.1163/1871191X-bja10091.

Brinkerhoff, Jennifer M. 'Diasporas and Public Diplomacy: Distinctions and Future Prospects'. *The Hague Journal of Diplomacy* 14 (1–2) (2019), 51–64. DOI 10.1163/1871191X-14101015.

Buhmann, Alexander. 'Unpacking Joint Attributions of Cities and Nation States as Actors in Global Affairs'. *The Hague Journal of Diplomacy* 17 (1) (2022), 109–122. DOI: 10.1163/1871191X-bja10092.

Borrows, John, and Risa Schwartz, eds. *Indigenous Peoples and International Trade: Building Equitable and Inclusive International Trade and Investment Agreements* (Cambridge: Cambridge University Press, 2020).

C40 Cities. https://www.c40.org/

Cameron, Maxwell A. 'Democratization of Foreign Policy: The Ottawa Process as a Model'. *Canadian Foreign Policy Journal* 5 (3) (1998), 147–65. DOI 10.1080/11926422.1998.9673154.

Canada International Council. 'Foreign Policy By Canadians.' 2021. https://thecic.org/research/foreign-policy-by-canadians/

Charters, Claire and Rodolfo Stavenhagen, eds. *Making the Declaration Work: The United Nations Declaration on the Rights of Indigenous Peoples* (Copenhagen: IWGIA, 2009).

Chrismas, Robert. 'Multi-Track Diplomacy and Canada's Indigenous Peoples'. *Peace Research* 44/45 (2/1) (2012), 5–30.

Clarke, Nick. 'In What Sense "Spaces of Neoliberalism"? The New Localism, the New Politics of Scale, and Town Twinning'. *Political Geography* 28 (8) (2009), 496–507. DOI: 10.1016/j.polgeo.2009.12.001.

Clarke, Nick. 'Globalising Care? Town Twinning in Britain since 1945'. *Geoforum* 42 (1) (2011), 115–125. DOI: 10.1016/j.geoforum.2010.10.006.

Cohn, Theodore H. and Patrick J. Smith. 'Subnational Governments as International Actors: Constituent Diplomacy in British Columbia and the Pacific Northwest'. *BC Studies* 110 (1996), 25–59. DOI: 10.14288/bcs.v0i110.1339.

Colbourne, Rick and Robert Anderson, eds. *Indigenous Wellbeing and Enterprise: Self-Determination and Sustainable Economic Development* (London: Routledge, 2020).

Cremer, Rolf D., Anne De Bruin and Ann Dupuis. 'International Sister-Cities: Bridging the Global–Local Divide'. *American Journal of Economics and Sociology* 60 (1) (2001), 377–401.

Crossen, Jonathan. 'Decolonization, Indigenous Internationalism, and the World Council of Indigenous Peoples'. PhD dissertation, University of Waterloo, 2014).

Crowley, Kate. 'Can Deliberative Democracy Be Practiced? A Subnational Policy Pathway'. *Politics & Policy* 37 (5) (2009), 929–1188. DOI 10.1111/j.1747-1346.2009.00208.x.

Curato, Nicole, Marit Hammond, and John B. Min, eds. *Power in Deliberative Democracy: Norms, Forums, Systems* (London: Palgrave MacMillan, 2019).

Dahl, Robert A. 'Democracy Deficits and Foreign Policy'. *Dissent* 46 (1) (Winter 1999A), 110–113.

Dahl, Robert A. 'Can International Organizations Be Democratic? A Skeptic's View.' In *Democracy's Edges*, edited by Ian Shapiro and Casiano Hacker-Cordón, 19-36. Contemporary Political Theory (Cambridge: Cambridge University Press, 1999B). DOI: 10.1017/CBO9780511586361.003.

Davidson, Kathryn, Lars Coenen, Michele Acuto and Brendan Gleeson. 'Reconfiguring Urban Governance in an Age of Rising City Networks: A Research Agenda'. *Urban Studies* 56 (16) (2019), 3540–3555.

Deveaux, Monique. *Gender and Justice in Multicultural Liberal States* (Oxford: Oxford University Press, 2006).

Deloria, Philip J. 'What Is the Middle Ground, Anyway?'. *William and Mary Quarterly* 63 (1) (Jan. 2006), 15-22. DOI 10.2307/3491723.

Dittmer, Jason. 'Geopolitical Assemblages and Complexity'. *Progress in Human Geography* 38 (3) (2014), 385–401. DOI 10.1177/0309132513501405.

Elster, Jon, ed. *Deliberative Democracy* (Cambridge: Cambridge University Press, 1998).

Fan, Mei-Fang. *Deliberative Democracy in Taiwan: A Deliberative Systems Perspective* (London: Routledge, 2021).

Federation of Canadian Municipalities. 'International Programs.' https://fcm.ca/en/programs/international-programs.

Felicetti, Andrea, Simon Niemeyer, and Nicole Curato. 'Improving Deliberative Participation: Connecting Mini-Publics to Deliberative Systems'. *European Political Science Review* 8 (3) (2016), 427–48. DOI 10.1017/S1755773915000119.

Flynn, Jeffrey. 'Communicative Power in Habermas's Theory of Democracy'. *European Journal of Political Theory* 3 (4) (2004), 433–454. DOI 10.1177/1474885104045914.

Foa, Roberto Stefan, et al. 'The Global Satisfaction with Democracy Report 2020' (Cambridge: Centre for the Future of Democracy, 2020).

Galuszka, Jakub. 'What Makes Urban Governance Co-Productive? Contradictions in the Current Debate on Co-Production'. *Planning Theory* 18 (1) (2019), 143–160. DOI 10.1177/1473095218780535.

Geis, Anna, Christian Opitz, and Hanna Pfeifer. 'Recasting the Role of Citizens in Diplomacy and Foreign Policy: Preliminary Insights and a New Research Agenda'. *The Hague Journal of Diplomacy* 17 (4) (2022), 614–627. DOI https://doi.org/10.1163/1871191x-bja10136.

Government of Canada. 'Canada's Indo-Pacific Strategy: IPS Implementation Progress Report', APFC Roundtable, 5 February 2024A.

Government of Canada. 'Canada's Indo-Pacific Strategy 2022 to 2023 Implementation Update'. Ottawa: Global Affairs Canada, 2024B.

Government of Canada. 'Canada's Indo-Pacific Strategy.' Ottawa: Global Affairs Canada. November 2022A https://www.international.gc.ca/transparency-transparence/indo-pacific-indo-pacifique/index.aspx?lang=eng

Government of Canada. 'Minister Joly announces new Indo-Pacific Advisory Committee'. Ottawa: Global Affairs Canada, 9 June 2022B. https://www.canada.ca/en/global-affairs/news/2022/06/minister-joly-announces-new-indo-pacific-advisory-committee.html

Groen, Rosa S. 'Understanding the Context for Successful City Diplomacy: Attracting International Organisations'. *The Hague Journal of Diplomacy* 17 (1) (2022), 123–137. DOI 10.1163/1871191X-bja10095.

Gunaratne, Shelton. A. 'Public Sphere and Communicative Rationality: Interrogating Habermas's Eurocentrism'. *Journalism & Communication Monographs* 8 (2) (2006), 93–156. DOI 10.1177/152263790600800201.

Habermas, Jürgen. *Between Facts and Norms: Contributions to a Discourse Theory of Law and Democracy* (MIT Press, 1996).

Haddad, Mary Alice. 'City Networks in East Asia: A New Dimension to Regional Politics'. *Asia Policy* 29 (1) (2022), 190–193. DOI 10.1353/asp.2022.0012.

Han, Yonghui, Hao Wang, and Dongming Wei. 'The Belt and Road Initiative, Sister-city Partnership and Chinese Outward FDI'. *Economic Research-Ekonomska Istraživanja* 35 (1) (2022). DOI: 10.1080/1331677X.2021.1997618.

Hara, Kimie and Scott Harrison. 'The Cold War, the San Francisco System, and the Rise of Indigenous Rights Movements in Japan'. *Rivista italiana di storia internazionale* (2022), 217-240. DOI 10.30461/106161.

Harrison, Scott. 'Celebrating Friendship across the Pacific: The 50th Anniversary of the Burnaby – Kushiro Sister City Relationship'. Asia Pacific Foundation of Canada, 2015. https://www.asiapacific.ca/blog/celebrating-friendship-across-pacific -50th-anniversary.

Harrison, Scott. 'Enhancing Trans-Pacific People-to-People Ties: Japan–Canada Twinning (Sister) Relationships'. Asia Pacific Foundation of Canada, 2018. https://www .asiapacific.ca/canada-asia-agenda/enhancing-trans-pacific-people-people-ties-ja pan-canada.

Harrison, Scott. 'Indigenous Historical Reconciliation in Canada, Taiwan, Japan'. In *Reconciliation and Symbiosis in East Asia from Comparative Perspectives*. Edited by Kimie Hara (Kitchener, ON: Pandora Press, 2025).

Harrison, Scott. 'Ainu of Japan Hosting the World: Ainu-led International Conferences'. Virtual paper presentation at Japan Studies Association of Canada, Thompson Rivers University, 2021.

Harrison, Scott and Dakota Norris. 'Guidebook for Doing Business in the Asia Pacific: A Resource for Indigenous Businesses'. APF Canada, 2019, https://www.asiapacific .ca/publication/guidebook-doing-business-asia-pacific-resource-indigenous.

Harrison, Scott and Robin Asgari. 'International Trade Inclusivity: The CPTPP and Indigenous International Trade and Investment'. APF Canada, 2020, https://www .asiapacific.ca/publication/international-trade-inclusivity-cptpp-and-indigenous.

Harrison, Scott and Yiwei Jin. 'A Case for Provincial Offices in Asia – and How to Make Them Better', Asia Pacific Foundation of Canada, 2020. https://www.asiapacific. ca/publication/case-provincial-offices-asia-and-how-make-them-better.

Harrison, Scott and Quinton Huang. 'Canadian Twinning in the Indo-Pacific: The Agency of Subnational Actors in Present Relationships and Future Strategies'. *Canadian Political Science Review* 17 (1) (2023), 25–56. DOI 10.24124/c677/2023 1863.

Harrison, Scott, Quinton Huang, Natasha Fox, and Amy Zhou. 'Toward an Ecosystem Approach: COVID-19, Canada-Asia Pacific Relations, and International Organizations'. Asia Pacific Foundation of Canada, March 2022. https://www.asiapacific.ca/ sites/default/files/inline-files/PHAC-Paper4_MARCH_V2_0.pdf.

He, Baogang and Nicole Curato. 'Deliberative Democracy in Southeast Asia'. Deliberative Democracy Digest, 14 October 2022. https://www.publicdeliberation.net/de liberative-democracy-in-southeast-asia/

He, Baogong, Michael Breen, and James Fishkin, eds. *Deliberative Democracy in Asia* (London: Routledge, 2022).

Henders, Susan J. and Mary M. Young. '"Other Diplomacies" of Non-State Actors: The Case of Canadian–Asian Relations'. *The Hague Journal of Diplomacy* 11 (4) (2016), 331–350. DOI 10.1163/1871191X-12341351.

Henderson, James (Sa'ke'j) Youngblood. *Indigenous Diplomacy and the Rights of Peoples: Achieving UN Recognition* (Saskatoon, SK: Purich Publishing, 2008).

Hilton, Carol Anne. *Indigenomics: Taking a Seat at the Economic Table* (Gabriola, BC: New Society Publishers, 2021).

Ho, Elaine and Fiona McConnell. 'Conceptualizing "Diaspora Diplomacy": Territory and Populations betwixt the Domestic and Foreign'. *Progress in Human Geography* 42 (3) (2017), 235–255. DOI 10.1177/0309132517740217.

Hubbert, Jennifer. *Scaling Paradiplomacy: An Anthropological Examination of City-to-City Relations* (Los Angeles, CA: Figueroa Press, 2020). https://uscpublicdiplomacy .org/sites/default/files/useruploads/u47441/Scaling%20Paradiplomacy_2.6.21.pdf.

Ishikawa Yuki. 'Calls for Deliberative Democracy in Japan'. *Rhetoric & Public Affairs* 5 (2) (2002), 331–345. DOI 10.1353/rap.2002.0031.

IWGIA. *The Indigenous World 2023* (Copenhagen: IWGIA, 2023).

Jacomy-Millette, Anne-Marie. 'International "Diplomatic" Activity of Canadian Provinces, with Emphasis on Quebec Behaviour.' *Revue générale de droit* 7 (1) (1976), 7–23. DOI 10.7202/1059653ar.

Jackson, Thomas. 'Paradiplomacy and Political Geography: The Geopolitics of Substate Regional Diplomacy'. *Geography Compass* 12 (2) (2018) https://doi.org/10.1111/gec3.12357

Jain, Purnendra. *Japan's Subnational Governments in International Affairs* (London: Routledge, 2005).

Jasanoff, Sheila. 'The Idiom of Co-Production'. In *States of Knowledge: The Co-Production of Science and Social Order*, ed. Sheila Jasanoff (New York: Routledge, 2004a), 1–12.

Jasanoff, Sheila. 'Ordering Knowledge, Ordering Society'. In *States of Knowledge: The Co-Production of Science and Social Order*, ed. Sheila Jasanoff (New York: Routledge, 2004b), 13–45.

Jayne, Mark, Philip Hubbard and David Bell. 'Twin Cities: Territorial and Relational Geographies of "Worldly" Manchester'. *Urban Studies* 50 (2) (2013), 239–254. DOI 10.1177/0040980124504080.

Jin, Yiwei. 'Reimagining Canada–China Twinning amidst Diplomatic Tensions'. Asia Pacific Foundation of Canada, 2020a. https://www.asiapacific.ca/publication/reimagining-canada-china-twinning-amidst-diplomatic-tensions.

Jin, Yiwei. 'Toward a Canadian Twinning Strategy: Lessons from South Korea'. Asia Pacific Foundation of Canada, 2020b. https://www.asiapacific.ca/publication/toward-canadian-twinning-strategy-lessons-south-korea.

Jin, Yiwei and Scott Harrison. 'Rainy Day Connections: Sister Cities during COVID-19'. Asia Pacific Foundation of Canada, 2020. https://www.asiapacific.ca/publication/rainy-day-connections-sister-cities-during-covid-19.

Johnson, Genevieve Fuji. *Democratic Illusion: Deliberative Democracy in Canadian Public Policy* (Toronto: University of Toronto Press, 2015).

Kading, Terry and Aliesha Thomas. 'The Indo-Pacific Region, Immigration, International Students and Small Mid-Sized Cities in the BC Interior – Policy and Capacity Issues'. *Canadian Political Science Review* 17 (1) (2023), 57-76. DOI 10.24124/c677/20231868.

Koivurova, Timo and David L. Vanderzwaag. 'The Arctic Council at 10 years: Retrospect and Prospects'. *University of British Columbia Law Review* 40 (1) (2007), 121–94.

Kukuchka, Christopher J. *The Provinces and Canadian Foreign Trade Policy* (Vancouver: UBC Press, 2008).

Kukuchka, Christopher J. 'Dismembering Canada: Stephen Harper and the Foreign Relations of Canadian Provinces'. *Review of Constitutional Studies* 14 (2009), 21-52.

Labrecque, Charles-Louis and Scott Harrison. 'Canadian Provinces and Foreign Policy in Asia'. *International Journal* 73 (3) (September 2018), 429–448. DOI 10.1177/0020702018791583.

Lackenbauer, P. Whitney and Andrew F. Cooper. 'The Achilles Heel of Canadian International Citizenship: Indigenous Diplomacies and State Responses'. *Canadian Foreign Policy Journal* 13 (3) (2007), 99-119. DOI 10.1080/11926422.2007.9673445

Laenui, Pōkā and Hayden Burgess. "The World Council of Indigenous Peoples An Interview with Pōkā Laenui (Hayden Burgess)." *The Contemporary Pacific* 2 (2) (1990), 336–348.

Laguerre, Michel S. *Global City-Twinning in the Digital Age* (Ann Arbor: University of Michigan Press, 2019).

Lecours, André. 'Paradiplomacy: Reflections on the Foreign Policy and International Relations of Regions'. *International Negotiation* 7 (1) (January 2002): 91–114. DOI 10.1163/157180602401262456.

Lee, Kian Cheng. 'Re-Envisioning Citizen Diplomacy: A Case Study of a Multifaceted, Transnational, People's Republic of China "Ethnopreneur"'. *Journal of Current Chinese Affairs* 48 (2) (2019), 127–147. DOI 10.1177/1868102620907240.

Lee, Kian Cheng. 'Neglected Agents: Elucidating Chinese Social Actors' Role in Thai–Sino Smart City Diplomacy'. *International Journal of Chinese Studies* 11 (1) (2020), 1–20. https://icsum.org.my/wp-content/uploads/2020/08/IJCS-111-1KC-Lee-for-website.pdf.

Leib, Ethan and Baogang He, eds. *The Search for Deliberative Democracy in China* (New York, NY: Palgrave Macmillan, 2006).

Library and Archives Canada. World Council of Indigenous Peoples, R9349.

Lightfoot, Sheryl. *Global Indigenous Politics: a Subtle Revolution* (London: Routledge, 2016).

Liu,Tianyang and Yao Song. 'Chinese Paradiplomacy: A Theoretical Review'. *SAGE Open* 10 (1) (2020).

Madison, Ian and Emmanuel Brunet-Jailly. 'The International Activities of Canadian Cities: Are Canadian Cities Challenging the Gatekeeper Position of the Federal Executive in International Affairs?'. In *The Power of Cities in International Relations*, ed. Simon Curtis (London: Routledge, 2014), 107–131.

Mansbridge, Jane "Everyday talk in the deliberative system (1999)" in *Jane Mansbridge: Participation, Deliberation, Legitimate Coercion*, edited by Melissa Williams (London: Routledge, 2019), 101–120.

Manuel, George and Michael Posluns. *The Fourth World: An Indian Reality* (Minneapolis: University of Minnesota Press, 1974, 2018).

Marchetti, Raffaele. *City Diplomacy: From City-States to Global Cities* (Ann Arbor: University of Michigan Press, 2021).

'Martínez Cobo Study'. United Nations. https://www.un.org/development/desa/indig enouspeoples/publications/2014/09/martinez-cobo-study/.

McCann, Eugene and Kevin Ward. 'Assembling Urbanism: Following Policies and "Studying Through" the Sites and Situations of Policy Making'. *Environment and Planning A: Economy and Space* 44 (1) (2012), 42–51. DOI 10.1068/a44178.

McCormick, James M. 'Democratizing Canadian Foreign Policy'. *Canadian Foreign Policy Journal* 13 (1) (2006), 113–131. DOI 10.1080/11926422.2006.9673422.

McFarlane, Peter, and Doreen Manuel. *Brotherhood to Nationhood: George Manuel and the Making of the Modern Indian Movement* (Toronto: Between the Lines, 2020).

McHugh, James T. 'Paradiplomacy, Protodiplomacy and the Foreign Policy Aspirations of Quebec and Other Canadian Provinces'. *Canadian Foreign Policy Journal* 21 (3) (2015), 238–256. DOI 10.1080/11926422.2015.1031261.

Melo, Marcus Andre and Gianpaolo Baiocchi. 'Deliberative Democracy and Local Governance: Towards a New Agenda'. *International Journal of Urban and Regional Research* 30 (2006), 587–600. DOI 10.1111/j.1468-2427.2006.00686.x.

Montsion, Jean Michel. 'Diplomacy as Self-Representation: British Columbia First Nations and China'. *The Hague Journal of Diplomacy* 11 (4) (2016), 404–425. DOI 10.1163/1871191X-12341333.

Montsion, Jean Michel. 'Disrupting Canadian Sovereignty? The 'First Nations & China' Strategy Revisited'. *Geoforum* 58 (2015), 114–121. DOI 10.1016/j.geoforum .2014.11.001.

Moravcsik, Andrew. 'In Defence of the Democratic Deficit: Reassessing Legitimacy in the European Union'. *Journal of Common Market Studies* 40 (4) (2002), 603–624.

Moravcsik, Andrew. 'Is there a "Democratic Deficit" in World Politics? A Framework for Analysis'. *Government and Opposition* 39 (2004), 336-363. DOI 10.1111/j.1477-7053.2004.00126.x.

Mutz, Diana C. 'Is Deliberative Democracy a Falsifiable Theory?' *Annual Review of Political Science* 11 (1) (2008), 521–538. DOI 10.1146/annurev.polisci.11.081306.070308.

New Zealand Foreign Affairs and Trade. 'The Indigenous Peoples Economic and Trade Cooperation Arrangement'. https://www.mfat.govt.nz/en/trade/nz-trade-policy/the-indigenous-peoples-economic-and-trade-cooperation-arrangement/.

Niezen, Ronald. *The Origins of Indigenism: Human Rights and the Politics of Identity* (Berkeley: University of California Press, 2003).

OECD. 'Innovative Citizen Participation and New Democratic Institutions: Catching the Deliberative Wave'. Paris: OECD Publishing, 2020. DOI 10.1787/339306da-en.

Omelicheva, Mariya Y. 'Global Civil Society and Democratization of World Politics: A Bona Fide Relationship or Illusory Liaison?' *International Studies Review* 11 (1) (2009), 109–132.

Owen, David and Graham Smith. 'Survey Article: Deliberation and the Systemic Turn.' *Journal of Political Philosophy* 23 (2015), 213–234. DOI 10.1111/jopp.12054.

Page, Benjamin and Jason Barabas. 'Foreign Policy Gaps between Citizens and Leaders'. *International Studies Quarterly* 44 (3) (2000), 339–364. DOI 10.1111/0020-8833.00163.

Page, Benjamin and Marshall Bouton. *The Foreign Policy Disconnect: What Americans Want from Our Leaders but Don't Get* (University of Chicago Press, 2006).

Paquin, Stéphane. 'Identity Paradiplomacy in Québec'. *Quebec Studies* 66 (December 2018), 3–26. DOI 10.3828/qs.2018.14.

Paquin, Stéphane. 'Paradiplomacy'. In *Global Diplomacy: An Introduction to Theory and Practice*, eds. Thierry Balzacq, Frédéric Charillon, and Frédéric Ramel (London: Palgrave Macmillan 2019), 49–61.

Parkinson, John, and Jane Mansbridge, eds. *Deliberative Systems: Deliberative Democracy at the Large Scale. Theories of Institutional Design*. Cambridge: Cambridge University Press, 2012. DOI 10.1017/CBO9781139178914.

Pietrasiak, Małgorzata et al. *Paradiplomacy in Asia. Case Studies of China, India and Russia* (Łódź: Łódź University Press, 2018).

Pipa, Anthony F. and Max Bouchet. 'Multilateralism Restored? City Diplomacy in the COVID-19 Era'. *The Hague Journal of Diplomacy* 15 (4) (2020), 599–610.

Ramraj, Victor Vridar. 'Global Challenges and Plurilateral Engagement in the Indian Ocean World'. *Canadian Political Science Review* 17 (1) (2023), 10-24. DOI 10.24124/c677/20231867.

Rosen, Jovanna and Gary Painter. 'From Citizen Control to Co-Production: Moving Beyond a Linear Conception of Citizen Participation'. *Journal of the American*

Planning Association 85 (3) (3 July 2019), 335–347. DOI 10.1080/01944363.2019.16-18727.

Rombouts, S.J. 'The Evolution of Indigenous Peoples' Consultation Rights under the ILO and U.N. Regimes', *Stanford Journal of International Law* 53 (2) (Spring 2017), 169–224.

Ryan, Holly Eva and Caterina Mazzilli. 'Debating the Value of Twinning in the United Kingdom: The Need for a Broader Perspective'. *British Politics* (2021). DOI 10.1057/s41293-021-00163-x.

Ryfe, David M. 'Does Deliberative Democracy Work?', *Annual Review of Political Science* 8 (1) (2005), 49-71. DOI 10.1146/annurev.polisci.8.032904.154633.

Ryser, Rudolph C. *Indigenous Nations and Modern States: The Political Emergence of Nations Challenging State Power* (London: Routledge, 2012).

Sanders, Douglas. *The Formation of the World Council of Indigenous Peoples.* IWGIA Document 29 (Copenhagen: IWGIA, 1977).

Sanders, Douglas. 'The UN Working Group on Indigenous Populations.' *Human Rights Quarterly* 11 (3) (1989), 406–433.

Sharp, Paul. 'Making Sense of Citizen Diplomats: The People of Duluth, Minnesota, as International Actors'. *International Studies Perspectives* 2 (2) (2001), 131–150. DOI 10.1111/1528-3577.00045.

Schiavon, Jorge. *Comparative Paradiplomacy* (New York: Routledge, 2019).

Sister Cities International. *Peace through People: 50 Years of Global Citizenship* (Louisville, KY: Butler Books, 2006).

Sorrentino, Maddalena, Mariafrancesca Sicilia and Michael Howlett. 'Understanding Co-Production as a New Public Governance Tool'. *Policy and Society* 37 (3) (2018), 277–293. DOI 10.1080/14494035.2018.1521676.

Surwandono and Ali Maksum. 'The Architecture of Paradiplomacy Regime in Indonesia: A Content Analysis'. *Global: Jurnal Politik Internasional* 22 (1) (2020), 77–99.

Tanasoca, Ana, *Deliberation Naturalized: Improving Real Existing Deliberative Democracy* (Oxford, 2020).

Tavares, Rodrigo. *Paradiplomacy: Cities and States as Global Players* (New York: Oxford University Press, 2016).

Truman Centre. 'City and State Diplomacy Toolkit'. https://www.trumancenter.org/issues/city-and-state-diplomacy-toolkit?trk=public_post_comment-text.

Tsutsui, Kiyoteru. *Rights Make Might: Global Human Rights and Minority Social Movements in Japan* (Oxford: Oxford University Press, 2018).

Uemura Hideaki. *Shimin no gaikō: Senjūminzoku to ayunda 30 nen* [Citizen Diplomacy: 30 Years with Indigenous Peoples] (Hōsei University Press, 2013).

United Nations. Fight Racism. 'Indigenous Peoples'. https://www.un.org/en/fight-racism/vulnerable-groups/indigenous-peoples

United Nations. Indigenous Peoples at the United Nations. https://social.desa.un.org/issues/indigenous-peoples/indigenous-peoples-at-the-united-nations.

van der Pluijm, Rogier and Jan Melissen. *City Diplomacy: The Expanding Role of Cities in International Politics* (The Hague: Netherlands Institute of International Relations 'Clingendael', 2007).

Vitale, Denise. 'Between deliberative and participatory democracy: A contribution on Habermas'. *Philosophy & Social Criticism* 32 (6) (2006), 739–766. DOI 10.1177/0191453706064022.

Voorberg, W. H., V. J. J. M. Bekkers and L. G. Tummers. 'A Systematic Review of Co-Creation and Co-Production: Embarking on the Social Innovation Journey'. *Public Management Review* 17 (9) (2015), 1333–1357. DOI 10.1080/14719037.2014.930505.

Watson, Vanessa. 'Co-Production and Collaboration in Planning – The Difference'. *Planning Theory & Practice* 15 (1) (2014), 62–76. DOI 10.1080/14649357.2013.866266.

White, Richard. *The Middle Ground: Indians, Empires, and Republics in the Great Lakes Region, 1650-1815* (Cambridge: Cambridge University Press, 1991, 2011).

World Bank. 'Global Smart City Partnership Program.' https://www.worldbank.org/en/programs/global-smart-city-partnership-program

World Bank. 'Indigenous Peoples'. https://www.worldbank.org/en/topic/indigenous peoples

Yan, Flora. 'PRC Perspectives on Subnational Diplomacy in China-US Relations'. *The Diplomat*. December 16, 2021. https://thediplomat.com/2021/12/prc-perspectives-on-subnational-diplomacy-in-china-us-relations/.

Young, Mary M. and Susan J. Henders. '"Other Diplomacies" and the Making of Canada–Asia Relations'. *Canadian Foreign Policy Journal* 18 (3) (2012), 375–388. DOI 10.1080/11926422.2012.742022.

Young, Mary M. and Susan J. Henders. '"Other Diplomacies" and World Order: Historical Insights from Canadian–Asian Relations'. *The Hague Journal of Diplomacy* 11 (4) (2016), 351–382. DOI 10.1163/1871191X-12341352.

Zelinsky, Wilbur. 'The Twinning of the World: Sister Cities in Geographic and Historical Perspective'. *Annals of the Association of American Geographers* 81 (1) (1991), 1–31. DOI 10.1111/j.1467-8306.1991.tb01676.x.

Zhou, Jianjun and Tingting Cao. 'International Friendship Cities, Spatial Spillover Effect and Urban Export Growth: Evidence from China'. *Australian Economic Papers* (2024), 1–27. DOI 10.1111/1467-8454.12331.

CHAPTER 11

The Benefits and Pitfalls of Engaging Youth in Diplomatic Affairs: A Case Study of the Junior Diplomat Initiative

Štěpánka Zemanová

Summary

The democratisation of diplomacy in recent years opened new opportunities for non-state actors' engagement and activities in the public interest or on behalf of governments. A wide variety of practices emerged at the domestic and international levels of how the non-state actors involved in national and global policy-making conduct and shape international affairs worldwide. The scholarly literature has extensively reflected the inclusion of civil society into governance frameworks, non-state public diplomacy, non-governmental institutions and so forth. Nevertheless, due to the complexity of these issues, their dynamics and rapid innovations, many blind spots remain.

The chapter explores the potential of youth grassroots initiatives to assist in shaping various national and international agendas through interactions with political and diplomatic elites. Drawing on the concepts of deliberative engagement and 'coupling' of public and diplomatic elites, it examines the Junior Diplomacy Initiative (JDI) activities of Prague, Geneva, Paris and Tbilisi. The chapter aims to analyse how an initially modest student activity translates into an international grassroots diplomacy project and what the benefits and pitfalls of such youth initiatives are. Lessons for diplomatic practice and incentives for future research are also addressed.

Keywords

democratisation of diplomacy – deliberative engagement in diplomacy – youth in diplomacy – youth grassroots initiatives – Junior Diplomacy Initiative (JDI)

1 Introduction[1]

In the last two decades, diplomacy has evolved towards more inclusive practices, greater interconnection with the public and, thus, progressive societisation.[2] A combination of top-down initiatives by governments and international bodies aimed at collaboration and bottom-up calls for engagement of the public propelled the change. Consequently, the participation of the public in various national and international agendas, previously the exclusive domains of officials and diplomats, expanded significantly. Nowadays, diplomacy encompasses a broad spectrum of actors, from influential non-governmental organisations (NGOs) to networks of experts to small grassroots initiatives and individuals.[3]

Concurrently, the way policy-makers and diplomats perceive the collaboration with these actors has also become more differentiated and nuanced.[4] Increasingly, these actors are seen as valuable allies in achieving policy and diplomacy goals.[5] Their involvement when addressing, pursuing or improving national and international diplomacy agendas has almost become a norm.[6] In a number of documented cases, these actors enhance their impact independently of states or international organisations,[7] sometimes performing diplomatic functions even unconsciously, without being aware of it.[8]

The existing literature points to impressive skills, constructiveness, innovativeness and creativity that allow the public to shape policies from the micro level of local problems faced, for example, by dissent or indigenous groups, up to the macro level of global challenges such as climate change.[9] It shows how

1 The author gratefully acknowledges institutional support from the Faculty of International Relations, Prague University of Economics and Business. Her thanks also go to the editors of the Hague Journal of Diplomacy Forum on 'Engaging Home in International Diplomacy' (vol. 17, no. 4) and of this volume for their guidance and valuable suggestions on how to develop the chapter; Jeremy Alan Garlick for his insightful comments on earlier versions of the text; as well as Věra Jeřábková, Jan Bondy, Ludvík Eger, Ondřej Wágner, Markéta Haase and the JDI members whom she consulted for their openness and willingness to share experiences.
2 Melissen 2011; Fitzpatrick 2012; Kelley 2014.
3 Cull 2019; Gerodimos 2013; Huijgh 2019.
4 Zaharna 2011; Attias 2012.
5 Hocking 2006, 2011.
6 Hocking 2006, 2011; Gregory 2016; Modaber 2016; Wiseman 2004, 2010; Geis, Opitz and Pfeifer 2022.
7 Anton and Moise 2022.
8 Badie 2018.
9 Fulda 2019; Kelley 2010.

their involvement helps expand the traditional policy and diplomacy toolkit through innovative strategies, tactics and methods, such as new approaches to interconnectedness, networking or cross-border people-to-people and peer-to-peer interactions.[10] However, despite the rapid development of knowledge in this field, some significant segments of the public remain neglected. These include, among others, youth.[11]

Scholarly reflections of young people's interactions with foreign policy and diplomacy to date have focused primarily on their opinions and attitudes,[12] educational mobility and exchange programmes.[13] This sharply contrasts with the dynamics of youth as a demographic cohort and the growing interest in involving youth in diplomatic practice, evidenced, for example, by the UN 2030 Strategy calling for 'regular online and offline engagements' between young people and foreign policy and diplomacy professionals,[14] or the EU Youth Action Plan,[15] which provides a policy framework for a strategic partnership with young people in EU external action.

This chapter therefore discusses the potential of youth grassroots initiatives to assist in shaping various national and international agendas through interaction with politics and diplomacy elites. The aim is to show that even a small-scale youth activity, initially created as a supplement to the university curriculum, can engage in a deliberative way in diplomacy at the national and international levels. However, establishing such co-operation is not entirely straightforward and requires overcoming several obstacles and pitfalls.

To fulfil the aim, the empirical example of the Junior Diplomat Initiative (JDI), a youth organisation established in 2011 at Prague University of Economics and Business (VŠE), is employed. The organisation can be considered a less likely case of deliberative diplomacy engagement, as it was founded with a different purpose, has always been run by small teams and is targeted primarily within the home university. Nevertheless, it represents a success story of creating avenues to integrate youth into foreign and international policy- and

---

10   Bolewski 2018; Gerodimos 2013; Melissen and Wang 2019; Norris 2002; Constantionou, Cornago and McConnell 2016.
11   Acosta, Szlamka and Mostajo-Radji 2020; Barber and Mostajo-Radji 2020.
12   Ciftci 2013; Davies, Kingsley and Wang 2023.
13   See Bislev 2017; Frominykh 2017; Snow 2020; McCann 2021; Tiessen 2007; Laqua 2023; Graziani 2017; Jain 2020; Scott-Smith 2020.
14   United Nations 2018, 6.
15   European Commission and the High Representative of the Union for Foreign Affairs and Security Policy 2022.

diplomacy-related deliberative systems (hereafter diplomacy-related deliberative systems).[16]

The chapter proceeds as follows. Section one puts the JDI project into the broader context of youth in diplomatic affairs. Section two provides the theoretical background for the study of youth's interaction with diplomacy elites. Section three traces the growth of JDI Prague from the classroom to a partner of the Ministry of Foreign Affairs of the Czech Republic (MFA CR) and its contribution to Czech foreign policy-making and implementation. Section four focuses on the internalisation of the JDI through foreign offices and contacts with many partners in international relations, foreign policy and diplomatic practice. Section five analyses the JDI's contribution to key functions of diplomacy-related deliberative systems. Section six discusses the weaknesses and constraints of this type of youth engagement in diplomacy.

As Prague University of Economics and Business is the home institution of the author, the chapter is partly based on her long-term experience and contact with the JDI. Thus, in a sense, it could be considered a result of participant observation. However, the analysis draws rather on primary data collected in two waves. Initially, documentary evidence of the JDI's activities and events was gathered from the JDI's founders, their website and social media during the period February–May 2022. This was supplemented by the author's correspondence with two representatives of the MFA CR.[17] In the second phase in April–November 2023, the research was expanded mainly with additional data from the MFA CR and other parties (e.g. embassies). Finally, the analysis was completed with semi-structured interviews with JDI founders, alumni and supporters.

2   Involving Youth in Diplomatic Affairs: A Broader Context

According to the United Nations' demographic definition, youth consists of people between the ages of 15 and 24.[18] Numbering approximately 1.2 billion, this cohort accounts for 16 per cent of the global population and is steadily growing.[19] More than half of the youth are in formal or non-formal education

---

16   See Mansbridge et al. 2012, 4–7.

17   The research resulted in The Hague Journal of Diplomacy article Zemanová 2022.

18   However, as Perovic (2016, 3) points out, the concept of youth differs in different policies and legislations. For example, in Europe they range between 12 and 35 years old; in some cases, they are merged even with children, that is, between 0 and 35 years old.

19   United Nations 2022.

and training.[20] Around 220 million currently attend tertiary education world-wide, a number that has more than doubled in the last two decades.[21] Further-more, a substantial number of young people are in their first job(s). Thus, besides youth as a whole, the figures imply at least two important sub-groups: students and emerging professionals in various occupations.

Nevertheless, through the lens of the social sciences, youth is seen rather as the social construct of a life stage characterised by transition between child-hood and adulthood, during which people undergo rapid development and extensive changes.[22] Although they move from dependence on adults to inde-pendence, they may still rely on adult support or interventions.[23] At the same time, they mature physically and mentally and form their own worldviews, including political attitudes. Therefore, youth is considered a distinct social group with its own opinions and subculture,[24] capable of complete apathy and disinterest in politics on the one hand, and direct and radical activism at the national and international levels on the other.[25] This implies the need for a specific approach in many fields, including diplomacy.

In international politics and diplomacy, young people's engagement reaches back to the late 19th century, when the first youth organisations emerged.[26] These organisations gradually became both political actors and foreign policy and diplomacy tools. As a result, there have been many cases of them functioning in both democratic and non-democratic settings, with stances ranging from very moderate to revolutionary and militant ones. Many youth organisations and their international associations continued to exist even though their activities were significantly affected by the two world wars.[27] Their meetings then became a space for debates on pressing international issues from various perspectives, such as peace and war, colo-nialism, armament, racism, environmental problems, global warming and so on.[28]

---

20   Fifty-six per cent in 131 countries with recent data, according to UNESCO 2023.
21   World Bank 2022. Note that this is the total number of tertiary students regardless of
      their age.
22   Jones 2009.
23   Bersaglio, Enns and Kepe 2015, 59–60.
24   Bersaglio, Enns and Kepe 2015.
25   Leuscher 2018; Rosenmayr 1972.
26   The origins of international student organisations date back to the mid-19th century with
      the formation of the World Student Christian Federation and the Young Men's Christian
      Association (YMCA). Altbach 1970.
27   Altbach 1970.
28   Roberts 2015; Stone 2021.

Since the interwar period, these organisations have been functioning as partners to international bodies, assisting youth in preparing for future diplomatic careers, among others.[29] Many episodes of youth involvement and youth-oriented diplomacy initiatives also emerged during the Cold War,[30] despite the ideological cleavages and the tendencies of superpowers to involve youth in their ideological rivalry.[31] They include, for example the Experimental Youth Centre, established in 1960 by the Council of Europe,[32] and the Ship for Southeast Asian and Japanese Youth Program, backed since the mid-1970s by the Association of Southeast Asian Nations.[33]

The new international political conditions in the 1990s and 2000s enabled the turn to youth in the development agendas of global agencies.[34] The turn was boosted with the adoption of the World Programme of Action for Youth in 1995 as well as the creation of the Inter-Agency Network on Youth and Development and the global Youth Employment Network. In the 2010s, it culminated in the preparation of the UN's Sustainable Development Goals (SDGs), which, unlike its Millennium Development Goals (MDGs), reflected extensive consultation with youth as one of the strongest advisory voices among the various demographics.[35]

Simultaneously, opportunities for young people's engagement and platforms for co-operation with youth have been established in other parts of the UN system and in other international bodies.[36] Prominent examples today include Y7 and Y20, which are fora bringing together young leaders from across the globe to formulate policy recommendations to be presented to the official G7 and G20 summits.[37] There is also the EUs Youth Sounding Board to advise on youth empowerment in EU external action.[38]

---

29   This is documented by the examples of European Confédération Internationale des Étudiants' alumni who joined national diplomacies or the League of Nations. Other similar examples include the University Federation for the League of Nations or European Student Relief (later International Student Service). Laqua 2017, 609–610.

30   Independence of peoples, anti-war and peace initiatives, disarmament, solidarity, eradication of poverty, human rights, anti-apartheid, etc. Harrison 1989.

31   Altbach 1964; Koivunen 2020.

32   Eberhard 2002.

33   Government of Japan, Cabinet Office n.d.

34   Besides the UN, this relates, for example, to the World Bank and the International Labour Organization.

35   Bersaglio, Enns and Kepe 2015; Acosta, Szlamka and Mostajo-Radji 2020; Hujo and Carter 2019.

36   United Nations n.d.

37   Future Leaders Network 2022.

38   European Commission n.d.

With the rise of public diplomacy, states followed international organisations in connecting their foreign policies and diplomacies with young people,
both domestically and abroad.[39] For example, the Dutch Ministry of Foreign
Affairs appoints an Ambassador for Youth, Education and Work, has recently
set up a Youth Advisory Commission, and involves youth in development cooperation within the Youth at Heart programme.[40] The Ukrainian Ministry of
Foreign Affairs has been trying to involve talented young people directly in
national diplomacy through its newly created Youth Council.[41] At the same
time, there has been a boom in various exchange programmes worldwide,
expected to spread awareness of individual countries, their values, culture
and so on.

Finally, many NGOs, such as Save the Children and the World Economic
Forum,[42] have significantly intensified their work with youth. Youth themselves have begun to create their own infrastructure to deal with international
political and diplomatic issues, although not always successfully, as evidenced
by the efforts to create the UN Youth Assembly in the late 1990s. Currently,
these initiatives range from large platforms for co-operation between youth
organisations, such as the Global Youth Action Network supporting youth
participation in the UN, with over 1,200 members,[43] up to small, intimate
initiatives with benefits primarily at local levels.[44]

Within the broad spectrum of youth organisations, those bringing together
students and young professionals form two specific segments. In relation to
diplomatic affairs, students have long worked to spread awareness of the international governance architecture, starting with the interwar models of the
League of Nations, to the 'Model United Nations' since 1947, and more recently
to the World Trade Organization (WTO),[45] NATO, the Arab League, the African
Union and the Organisation of American States.[46] At the same time, many
student organisations and groupings have been able to engage in expert policy

---

39   The former engagement takes place both in international organisations and, for exam-
      ple, in development policy. It is also evidenced by the initiatives of development agen-
      cies in several developed countries, most recently USAID, the Canadian Development
      Agency and the UK Department of International Development. Modaber 2016.

40   Youth at Heart n.d.

41   Ministry of Foreign Affairs of Ukraine 2022.

42   Sukarieh and Tannock 2008.

43   Global Youth Action Network n.d.a, n.d.b.

44   Salazar et al. 2022; Zemanová 2022.

45   Model WTO 2023.

46   Dunn 2019.

– and diplomacy-related debates,[47] as well as to deploy various forms of domestic and international activism. As a result, it has been widely recognised that they can exercise political influence, both domestically and at the international level.[48]

Young professionals are a kind of transitional group among youth in general, or students specifically, and professional communities. Related initiatives include specialised training, information and opinion sharing as well as networking in the late stages of studies or the first few years after entering the workforce. Although these initiatives are also quite widespread,[49] a more systematic mapping of their significance in diplomacy is still lacking. This applies to both diplomatic services and other professions.[50]

3   Democratic Engagement of Youth in Diplomacy: A Theoretical Background

Young people have a wide range of tools at their disposal for participating in politics and diplomacy. Primarily, provided they have already reached the required age, they can influence the direction of national foreign policies and diplomacies in conventional ways as voters, petitioners, members of political parties and so on. While this remains stable over time, they are also able to develop and expand an unconventional non-electoral repertoire dynamically, often on a do-it-ourselves basis.[51]

Nowadays, the unconventional toolkit ranges from diplomats' participation in youth-organised events to publishing and participating in public consultations,[52] contacting political representatives and campaigning, and engaging in collective protest actions and riots. Their innovativeness can even result in unexpected contributions to the achievement of international or foreign policy goals through novel initiatives, such as the recent viral branding of Israel in the 'The Hot Dudes and Hummus – Israel's Yummiest' Instagram campaign.[53]

---

47   Dunn 2019; Muldon 1995.
48   Leuscher 2018; Altbach 1989.
49   The European Diplomatic Programme (European Union External Action 2023), Young Diplomats Forum (Global Diplomats Forum n.d.), Professional Course for Foreign Diplomats (Ministry of Foreign Affairs, Government of India 2023) and Young Diplomats (n.d.) are a few examples.
50   A few exceptions include Stein (2007) and Šime (2023).
51   Bárta and Lavizzari 2021; van Deth 2001.
52   Bátora 2005.
53   Samuel-Azran et al. 2019.

The dynamics of unconventional engagement make youth an attractive target of cultural, educational and public diplomacy, a soft-power tool, and sometimes even a valued partner in advancing various agendas and solving problems.[54] However, this does not translate automatically into youth exercising influence and taking an active part in co-creating decisions. According to the existing scholarly literature, such engagement requires the existence of relevant democracy environments – deliberative, participatory or counter-democracy ones.[55] This applies to both domestic politics and foreign policy (including diplomacy).[56]

The democracy environments differ in terms of mechanisms, means and the quality of engagement they enable. In a deliberative environment, decision-making reflects public discussions. Youth can thus exercise influence through opinion and recommendations articulated in public debates. A participatory environment enables them to take part directly in the decision-making process and make their suggestions through public participation platforms. This can simultaneously increase their interest in specific issues and support for solutions that youth are involved in formulating. In contrast, the counter-democracy mode insists on activism and external pressure on elites through collective actions.[57]

While youth's domestic and international counter-democracy activism has attracted attention for decades,[58] knowledge about their representation in decision-making has been limited mainly to national politics and policies, in particular educational ones.[59] Nevertheless, the broader study of democratic deliberation suggests that the first two modes closely correspond with different ways that elites co-opt the public in decision-making.[60]

At the foundational level, elites create only unidirectional communication streams and disseminate information about policies and decisions without expecting feedback. At a higher stage of consultation, they selectively determine the audience and scope of the debate. Although it allows for some degree of public input, the process remains tightly controlled by official authorities, limiting the breadth of participation. Only at the advanced, participatory level is the two-way relationship between elites and public (including youth)

---

54   Bu 1999; Huber 2017; Pate 2016; Tiessen 2007.
55   Gutmann and Thompson 2004; Gretschel et al. 2014; Elstub, Ercan and Mendonça 2019.
56   Rask and Wortinghton 2015; Pfeifer, Opitz and Geis 2020.
57   Bárta and Lavizzari 2021.
58   Altbach and Lipset 1969; Altbach 1989; Sherrod, Flanagan and Kassimir 2006.
59   Klemenčič and Park 2018.
60   Arnstein 1969; Gramberger 2001.

robust, empowering public actors to take a significant role through the generation of proposals and direct involvement in policy and decision shaping. In terms of quality, all these stages can include both fair approaches and malpractices such as manipulation through information or tokenism – a merely symbolic or superficial involvement to show a willingness to collaborate.[61]

Thus, to gain a voice in public debates and diplomacy-related deliberative systems, youth must engage with both formal and informal elites in arenas that facilitate discursive interactions. The arenas can be informal public spaces with few restrictions on who participates and what can be said (cafés, classrooms, the Internet, public hearings, etc.).[62] However, their claims will not be heard if they are not transmitted to empowered fora – the places where decisions are made.[63]

To capture the process of connecting non-state actors with elites (or public spaces with empowered ones), the scholarly literature introduces the concept of 'coupling'. According to Mansbridge et al., this requires 'convergence, mutual influence and mutual adjustment', in which each party considers the reasons and proposals of the others.[64] To make coupling work, there should be a flexible connection, ensuring that participants on the public side, such as youth, are neither disregarded nor co-opted by elites as the more influential party.[65] Moreover, elite domination in these debates, which is a risk given their expertise in rhetoric and argumentation, should be prevented.[66]

Maintaining a looser coupling allows public actors and elites to interact, respond and adapt to each other. Such a connection arises when the frequency of mutual interactions remains low, these interactions are of an indirect nature, a high degree of causal indeterminacy is maintained in the relationship, or one coupled party does not respond immediately to the other party's impulses.[67]

Finally, coupling with elites gives public actors, including youth, the opportunity to propose solutions to political problems through arguing, demonstrating, expressing and persuading. If successful, these actors become nodes of the deliberative systems and can contribute to their essential functions: epistemic, ethical and democratic. The epistemic function involves forming

---

61   Varwell 2022.

62   Dryzek 2009.

63   Ercan, Hendriks and Boswell 2018; Hendriks 2016.

64   Mansbridge et al. 2012, 23.

65   Parkinson 2012.

66   Setälä 2021.

67   Mansbridge et al. 2012; Rasche 2012.

opinions, preferences and decisions based on sound information and relevant reasoning; the ethical function fosters mutual respect among participants; and the democratic function promotes equality and inclusiveness in political processes.[68]

The remainder of this chapter shows how these processes work in the bottom-up direction. It captures how the JDI, a small organisation at the crossroads of youth, students' and young professionals' bodies, founded in Prague 2011, engaged first in Czech foreign policy and diplomacy and then, through its branches in France, Switzerland and Georgia, deliberatively coupled with international diplomatic elites. At the same time, it seeks lessons from the JDI's successes and failures.

4   JDI Prague and Its 'Diplomatic Salons' as an Example of Youth's Deliberative Engagement in Diplomatic Affairs

Within the broad spectrum of possible youth engagement patterns, the JDI started quite traditionally as a project of three undergraduate International Studies and Diplomacy programme students to build a platform where they and their classmates could 'confront their theoretical knowledge with the practice of the contemporary world of diplomacy'.[69] The initial idea was to add value to the introductory classes they took during their first year at university through direct contact with the diplomatic service and to complement the issues they studied with practical insights into what diplomacy really means at seminars, occasional practitioners' lectures and visits to embassies. This plan was greeted with enthusiasm by the university. From the very beginning, the JDI enjoyed the support of teachers and the university administration.[70]

However, although the founders came up with the JDI project more than twenty years after the Velvet Revolution in the former Czechoslovakia, they entered an environment in which youth organisations were still being (re-)formed. Thus, as an early bird focused on International Relations and Diplomacy, the JDI had to overcome the barrier of distrust and aloofness with which initially almost all the representatives of the MFA CR and the embassies in Prague responded to their invitations. To do so, they used the experience and contacts they had already gained through the 'Prague Student Summit'

---

68   Mansbridge et al. 2012.
69   Junior Diplomat Initiative n.d.
70   Interview 5 and author's experience.

and 'Model UN' some time earlier,[71] when they were attending secondary school.[72] This suggests that there is a potential for inspiration and know-how to spill over among various youth organisations.

The coupling with Czech foreign policy elites started when Věra Jeřábková, a prominent Czech diplomat and then director of the Diplomatic Academy at the MFA CR,[73] agreed to take over patronage of the JDI. The support the JDI gained from the former director of the Diplomatic Academy, and from Jan Bondy, then director of the Public Diplomacy Department at MFA CR, also played an important role.[74] With Jeřábková's and Bondy's assistance, the JDI was soon able to hold several successful events and increase interest in their activities among other ministerial officials and foreign diplomats accredited in Prague.

Nevertheless, even though the JDI created in this way an informal public space to debate foreign policy and diplomacy issues, information flowed through it mainly in a one-way direction, from elites to youth, in the initial phase. Moreover, the young participants observed a certain detachment or caution when diplomats were speaking about political issues, in sharp contrast to their honesty in telling them what the diplomatic agenda looks like, what skills diplomats need for successful careers and how diplomatic service potentially affects their private lives, including family members.[75]

As the JDI founders were unwilling to settle for that, they sought a more balanced two-way discursive interaction. They wanted officials and diplomats to approach the meetings as a form of brainstorming and not only to impart something, but also to take something away from JDI events. The young audience was then to become a source of fresh and innovative perspectives on a range of contemporary diplomatic issues, although only sometimes immediately applicable in practice.[76] Therefore, the founders introduced the principle of interactivity: a relatively quick shift from a short introduction by the

---

71   Prague Student Summit n.d.

72   Interview 2.

73   Prior to 2024, the unit prepared future diplomats for their career in the Czech foreign service and provided further professional training of career diplomats. However, since the beginning of the year it has been undergoing a transformation to become an independent organisation.

74   Interview 2.

75   Interviews 1, 3 and 4. A JDI France co-founder stated that she would retrospectively address this by introducing a Chatham House Rule at JDI events to make the speakers more comfortable in speaking openly. Interview 3.

76   Author's informal conversation with Věra Jeřábková, 7 June 2023.

guest to a discussion and dialogue with space for questions and the opinions of the youth.[77]

This interactivity soon became the core of the JDI's most significant project in the Czech Republic, the 'Diplomatic Salons', a long-lasting series of bi-annual meetings designed to allow youth 'to meet representatives of Czech diplomacy directly on the premises of the Ministry of Foreign Affairs of the Czech Republic and discuss with them various topics of international relations'.[78] Moreover, these were complemented by other measures designed to attract a wider audience and increase the deliberative potential. These included an attempt by the JDI to involve experts from academia, the private sphere and the non-profit sector and thus to bring together a wide range of perspectives besides those of the youth and the MFA CR.[79] At the same time, the MFA CR facilitated the streaming of several 'Salons' to the public and provided regular updates about the 'Salons' on its website.[80]

According to Jan Bondy, receiving feedback on foreign policy agendas from participants during the debates is one of the important benefits of the 'Salons' for the MFA CR.[81] Moreover, the 'Yearbook of Czech Foreign Policy 2012'[82] considers the 'Salons' 'an important contribution ... to opening debates on crucial foreign policy to the public'.[83] This confirms that the second direction of communication was indeed established.

However, opening a new direction of discursive interaction (from the audience to the ministry) by no means implies that the youth and other participants in the 'Salons' would be directly involved in decision-making. Furthermore, the ability of the audience to raise issues in debates remained constrained. Over time, the practice became established that the choice of the theme and guests of the 'Salon' was based on a consensus between the JDI and the Public Diplomacy Department. The JDI team members thus could choose the topics and try to cover the widest possible range of fields and subfields of contemporary diplomacy.[84] However, the Public Diplomacy

---

77   Interview 1.

78   Ministry of Foreign Affairs of the Czech Republic 2012.

79   Nováková 2022.

80   See Mansbridge et al. 2012, 9.

81   Author's email correspondence with Jan Bondy, 7 July 2022.

82   An expert analysis produced by the Institute of International Relations, Prague, a research organisation linked to the MFA.

83   Peterková and Tomalová 2013.

84   The 26 events so far (as of April 2024) covered a variety of topics, from the priorities of Czech foreign policy to 'The Young Generation and 75 Years of the United Nations'; see, for example, Ministry of Foreign Affairs of the Czech Republic 2019, 2021, 2022.

Department maintained a space for correction and could thus veto topics sensitive or problematic from the perspective of contemporary Czech national interests.[85]

Similar limitations on youth's coupling with Czech foreign policy elites is also evident in the 'Memorandum on Cooperation' concluded by the MFA CR and the JDI in 2016 'to seek cooperation for the benefit of the Foreign Service of the Czech Republic'.[86] The JDI promised to promote a positive image of the MFA CR and spread awareness about the MFA's activities.[87] In turn, the MFA CR pledged to assist in JDI events through expert advice, communication support, the provision of venues for events and enabling youth participation in selected activities of the Diplomatic Academy and other professional events hosted by the Academy or the MFA CR.[88] There was no indication that the collaboration would go beyond information or consultation or that the JDI would get more space in some areas of Czech foreign policy-making.

5   The Internationalisation of the JDI's Involvement in Diplomacy-Related Deliberative Systems

Over more than a decade of JDI's existence, its ability to create informal spaces for coupling with elites has expanded. Just two years after it was formed, it extended beyond the borders of the Czech Republic. This happened first through the 'Youth Dialogue' conferences of 2013–2015. Through the speakers, the JDI connected to the international diplomacy-related decision spaces, for example those at the level of the EU.[89] As the 'Dialogues' (unlike the 'Diplomatic Salons') were held in English, they attracted a mixture of nationals and foreigners studying in Prague. In this way, the JDI also started to promote understanding at the international level.[90]

Furthermore, thanks to educational mobility, JDI activities and the organisational model soon spread from the Czech Republic to several universities abroad – the Graduate Institute of International and Development Studies (IHEID), Geneva, in 2013; Sciences Po Paris in 2015; the Moscow State Institute

---

85   Interview 1.

86   Ministry of Foreign Affairs of the Czech Republic and Junior Diplomat Initiative 2016, article 1.

87   Ibid., article 4.

88   Ibid., article 3.

89   Eger 2013; Junior Diplomat Initiative 2013, 2014.

90   See Payne 2009, 579–580; Payne, Sevin and Bruya 2011, 45–46.

of International Relations and the Diplomatic Academy Moscow in 2018; and Tbilisi in 2019.[91] The direction of the initial expansion from the Czech Republic to Switzerland and France is quite atypical for a model that originated in a country trying to move closer to the West for more than three decades and widely adopting Western patterns in many areas of its political, economic and social life.[92] The JDI's professional orientation, or focus on diplomatic practice and more professional discussions, provided a clear path for them to navigate this difficult environment. Their success shows that the focus on diplomacy and diplomatic practice occupies a niche and adds value even in the substantially more developed and busier ecosystem of Western youth organisations.[93]

Compared with those in Prague, the founders of the JDI chapters in France and Switzerland considered it easier to interact with diplomacy elites in the two Western cities, as the representatives of states and international institutions in Geneva and Paris are more familiar with this collaboration mode.[94] Furthermore, the JDI's association with well-known educational institutions, which have long co-operated with diplomatic corps, helps to open gates.[95] Even so, one of the founders of JDI France says that it was not easy in the beginning and that a senior supporter like Věra Jeřábková at JDI Prague probably would have helped them a lot.[96]

As grassroots initiatives with the potential to gain more credibility among recipients than official channels,[97] and with their unique mix of youth, knowledge, know-how and online presence, JDI affiliates gradually became attractive partners for various representatives of international diplomacy. Thus, they were able to get involved in several diplomacy-related deliberative systems and connect with a growing number of nodes through formal and informal political talks about issues of common concern that far exceed the borders of the JDI home states.[98] This happened primarily through the 'Youth Dialogue', which moved from Prague to Geneva in 2016, and the annual conventions of JDI France since 2021.

---

91   Interview 1. However, JDI Georgia's social media activity ceased at the turn of 2021 and 2022. Neither the author of this chapter nor anyone from JDI Prague was able to contact the organisers. Thus, the Tbilisi chapter may no longer be active or even exist.

92   See Jacoby 2001, 171.

93   Interview 3.

94   Interview 1.

95   Interviews 2 and 3.

96   Interview 3.

97   See Payne 2009.

98   Mansbridge et al. 2012, 8.

These events bring together not only state officials and career diplomats from all over Europe, but also researchers from various academic institutions and think tanks. In addition, it has become standard that the events attract speakers from intergovernmental bodies, such as the UN, WTO, World Health Organization, EU, Organisation for Security and Co-operation in Europe and International Telecommunication Union; NGOs such as the International Committee of the Red Cross, DiploFoundation and Independent Diplomat; and companies including Microsoft.[99]

Moreover, as repeatedly demonstrated in the scholarly literature, new media are increasingly crucial in diplomacy to set agendas, promote discourse and work with public opinion.[100] Young people, who have grown up with these media as an integral part of their lives, become, thanks to their online presence and user literacy,[101] important targets of digital diplomacy as well as valuable allies. The online presence of JDI teams has always represented an added value for possible partners from national and international diplomatic services.

Today, JDI affiliates reach hundreds and even thousands of followers. Their virtual presence extends from social media to other online tools, including announcements and reports from events on various websites (JDI Prague), blogs (JDI France) and YouTube videos (JDI Switzerland). Even though the main communication channels mostly disseminate invitations to JDI events, the promotion of the thematic focus also contributes to the agenda-setting and framing of current diplomatic and political topics among youth. These topics broadly correspond with the crucial agendas of global institutions and/or JDI home countries' governments.

However, this advantage of JDI may gradually deplete as communication through social media becomes more complicated compared with the early days of the organisation. With the growing tide of information, it is harder to overcome the attention scarcity of the youth audience. Furthermore, the dynamics of social media require constant adaptation of the communication style and use of newly emerging social platforms.[102] Initially, the websites, Facebook profiles and personal interactions of the JDI team with other young people were the main communication channels, but their importance has declined over time. To maintain its impact, the JDI had to extend their promotional efforts to X (formerly Twitter), LinkedIn and especially Insta-

---

99   Junior Diplomat Initiative 2015.
100   See, e.g., Manor 2019.
101   See Collin 2015; Ward 2013; Xenos, Vromen and Loader 2014.
102   Interview 1.

gram, which currently seems to play a prominent role among its information channels.

Moreover, despite the wider possibilities of JDI branches outside the Czech Republic, the lack of control by their partners over the content of individual actions means they have not yet expanded into a participatory mode of involvement in the decision-making process either. It is generally not the JDI's ambition to promote its own proposals for the direction of international politics and diplomacy. Nor do their official partners seek this type of engagement.

Thus, the JDI remains in a deliberative mode and primarily opens the way for the dissemination of information to the young audience. Although the principle of interactivity ensures that information also flows in the opposite direction, the impact of youth opinions in the reverse direction depends entirely on the readiness and willingness of their official counterparts to reflect them in relevant decision-making spaces. A direct relationship between the views expressed in the youth debate and the subsequent decisions can hardly be proven.

However, many young people previously involved in the JDI have gone on to become diplomacy professionals. Some of the interviews for this chapter confirm that they promote the attitudes they formed during their time in JDI in their current practice.[103] A striking example of this is the co-operation with youth, of which they are generally enthusiastic proponents and which they find stimulating. Examples of this include the extension of the Czech youth delegates' visits to the UN from Washington to Geneva, the dissemination of information about internship opportunities in international and European institutions, support for interns and support for study trips. Moreover, JDI alumni and former participants declare their readiness to continue the dialogue with youth and listen to their perspectives. They attach considerable importance to youth in fields such as green diplomacy.[104] As one of the interviewees nicely put it, 'they can learn something from me or from my organisation, but we can learn a lot from them'.[105]

6 The Contribution of the JDI to the Key Functions of Diplomacy-Related Deliberative Systems

Through their deliberative engagement, whether it is the facilitation of one-way information flows or a two-way interactive dialogue, the JDI network

---

103   Interviews 1, 2 and 3.
104   Interview 1; Junior Diplomat Initiative Switzerland 2023b.
105   Interview 4.

contributes one of the basic features of deliberative systems: the epistemic function, which consists mainly in the production of appropriately informed opinions and preferences. At the very beginning, this function was shaped by the young people themselves. The university and diplomatic actors primarily assisted them in fulfilling their educational goals. The JDI concentrated mainly on topics relevant to Czech foreign policy and, with embassy visits, also touched upon the foreign policies and diplomacy of other countries.

The expansion of the JDI to Geneva and Paris shifted the emphasis to global diplomacy.[106] In Geneva, where the JDI was linked to a relatively small institution with approximately 700 students, the founders sought from the beginning to engage students at other universities. Combined with the orientation on the graduate level, this meant a broader thematic scope, including many more technical issues, such as the relationships between diplomacy and technology or cybernetics.[107]

The JDI partners soon discovered that they could also profit from cooperation by spreading awareness of their own goals and activities. As a result, together with four other youth organisations,[108] JDI Prague obtained financial support from the Visegrad Fund, an intergovernmental donor organisation established by Visegrad Group (V4) countries, with its 'Visegrad Group + Serbia Simulation' introducing the international negotiations between the V4 and the Serbian MFA to students from all five countries concerned. The simulation, which took place at the Czech Embassy in Belgrade, became an official part of the 2016 Czech Visegrad Four Presidency programme.[109]

Similarly, in 2021, despite its short institutional history, JDI Georgia was awarded a grant from NATO's Public Diplomacy Division for its JDI4NATO campaign. This time, the aim was to spread information about NATO's role in Black Sea security among Georgian youth.[110] The campaign included events such as essay competitions related to NATO activities and membership and online seminars, familiarising the participants with how NATO operates and its role in Black Sea security as well as refuting disinformation about NATO.[111]

In the long term, the knowledge and skills that young people develop as both JDI team members and participants in workshops pay off in the real

106   Junior Diplomat Initiative France 2023; Junior Diplomat Initiative Switzerland 2023a.
107   Interview 2.
108   Association of Diplomacy in Practice, Corvinus University Budapest; BEUM Student Association, Belgrade; Euroatlantic Centre, Matej Bel University Banska Bystrica; and Students' Foreign Affairs Club, Warsaw School of Economics.
109   Junior Diplomat Initiative 2016.
110   Junior Diplomat Initiative Georgia 2021.
111   Junior Diplomat Initiative Georgia 2022.

diplomacy world. All JDI founders and several alumni have been recruited by MFAS, the European External Action Service, or international intergovernmental and non-governmental bodies. The JDI-grown professionals value the JDI's contribution to their careers by publicly presenting their work in the organisation, for example on their LinkedIn profiles, but also by continuing to support the JDI and returning to youth to inspire them for either the diplomatic journey or work in international politics in general.[112]

The entire functioning of the JDI executive team has been enriching the CVs of the JDI team members and, thus, the probability of admission to prestigious graduate study programmes and obtaining funding to study abroad. But first, it helps the team members improve their organisation, communication and negotiation soft skills as well as managerial competencies and stress resistance. According to some JDI alumni,[113] this is precisely the skill set they now use every day in their jobs. Thus, if subsequently recruited by MFAS or international intergovernmental and non-governmental organisations, this extracurricular training pays dividends in diplomatic practice.

Second, the networking for future careers made it easier to get started and work with new colleagues they met during their time at the JDI. However, this benefit mainly concerned the Czech branch and future Czech diplomats, who used their mutual ties and contacts with senior officials, especially at the beginning of their careers at the MFA CR. In the Swiss and French JDI chapters, a significant barrier to building a more sustainable network has been the international character of the young audience and, therefore, the considerable geographical dispersion of the alumni and former youth participants after entering practice.[114] The maintenance and use of the interpersonal ties created through the JDI thus seem strongly individual.

Furthermore, thanks to the JDI, both team members and young participants at the JDI events were able to form more realistic expectations of life as a diplomat and better prepare themselves mentally for various challenges.[115] In many cases, the honesty of diplomats in sharing their personal experience with the occupation helped the JDI alumni and event participants rethink their view of diplomacy and their future careers in the field and decide not to join the diplomatic service at all. Some of them concluded that they did not want to deal with the administrative work and bureaucracy, an integral

---

112   For example, see the LinkedIn profiles of Ondrej Wagner, Ludvík Eger, Kamila Harabinova, Lea Ytrehus, Nissi Raja and Alex Lavaud.
113   Interviews 1, 2, 3, 7, 8, 9 and 10.
114   Interviews 1, 2 and 7.
115   Interviews 1, 8 and 9.

part of diplomats' agenda. Others were not ready to combine their personal lives with frequent travel and long-term assignments abroad. As a result, these young people decided on alternative careers. By making the decision in due time, they probably saved themselves and the diplomatic services they would have entered a lot of complications. As one of the JDI's founders noted, based on professional experience in diplomacy, the incompatibility of expectations and reality frequently results in frustration, early departures and workplace tensions.[116]

The educational function has also been strengthened within the JDI framework thanks to some alumni and other former participants continuing to support the organisation long after graduation, having built successful careers.[117] The support includes the willingness to become a guest of the JDI and share with attendees their journey from the university and the JDI to diplomatic practice. For example, the JDI founders are still in contact with the affiliates in Prague, Geneva and Paris and support their work.

With geographic expansion and the ability to engage not only embassies but also international intergovernmental and non-governmental organisations, the focus of the JDI shifted from foreign policy agendas to global issues. Thus, several value-oriented agendas came to the fore. The contribution of the JDI network to the ethical functions of the diplomacy-related deliberative systems became more pronounced. Moreover, it significantly exceeded the norms ensuring mutual respect for the participants involved in the system, which is particularly evident from the focus of the JDI conferences. Nevertheless, one can also find several micro-examples, such as the publication of a letter of congratulations to Ngozi Okonjo-Iweala, the first female and African leader at the head of the WTO, referring to gender equity and sustainability.[118]

The first editions of the 'Youth Dialogue' conferences held in Prague from 2013 to 2015 introduced topics such as preventive diplomacy as a tool for maintaining stability in Europe. The subsequent conferences organised by the Geneva JDI affiliate since 2016 added issues such as ethics and diplomacy, the power of women and inclusivity in diplomacy, and environmental diplomacy – critical voices. A similar normative approach is also characteristic of the JDI France annual conventions, as demonstrated by the 2022 title '#WeCannotWait: Pressing issues of global governance' and the content, focusing on human rights, women in fragile states and communicating climate change.

---

116   Interview 2.
117   Interviews 1, 2 and 3.
118   Junior Diplomat Initiative Switzerland 2021.

Finally, the contribution of the JDI to the democratic function of deliberative democracy systems can also be observed. As the JDI founders stated, JDI
team members wanted to be pro-active and to give themselves and other
young people a voice through their initiative.[119] Thus, as one of the interviewees nicely summarised, the JDI 'has allowed them to seamlessly transition
from observers to active participants in the world of foreign policy, receiving
its impact while also having the unique opportunity to contribute as engaged
citizens, passionate learners, and future professionals'. It was the first time
they could see 'the power of taking initiative – just reaching out, asking a
question, making a proposal'.[120]

At the same time, since the beginning the JDI founders and team members
have always been aware that by choosing a specific topic and a particular
guest, they are already expressing their political opinion and can influence
the opinions of their young colleagues. Therefore, they try to anchor their
choices in democratic values. They attempt to combine many different perspectives in a single event, or to balance the one-sided view offered at one
event in future activities. They have also been supported by the value settings
of their home universities, for example, the solid liberal orientation and strong
support for international law typical of IHEID.[121]

7   The Pitfalls of JDI-Type Youth Diplomacy Initiatives' Involvement in Diplomacy-Related Deliberative Systems

Besides benefits, the coupling of youth-led initiatives such as the JDI with
international politics/foreign policy and diplomacy elites also has its problematic aspects. In addition to those already mentioned in the relationship
between the JDI and its official representatives, there are some difficulties
related to the organisational framework itself. First of all, there is the comparative advantage of JDI chapters in Paris and Geneva, the centres of global
diplomacy, in hosting a richer diversity of guests and audiences for lower operational costs. For JDI events, this raises critical questions about the equity of
such youth diplomacy efforts. The proximity to national and/or international
diplomatic hubs seems to be one of the key prerequisites for the co-operation
of youth initiatives with both foreign policy-makers and diplomats, dictating
the scope and impact of this type of youth project. It largely predetermines

---

119   Interview 3; Interview 2.
120   Interview 3.
121   Interview 2.

youth's ability to create public deliberation spaces and co-shape the related discourse.

Again, this is particularly obvious from the 'Youth Dialogue' example. In Geneva, the annual convention regularly connects youth with the representatives of Geneva-based international bodies in the city, the Delegation of the EU, as well as states' permanent missions to the UN and other intergovernmental organisations. In contrast, despite additional funding for travel, the events of the first few years in Prague welcomed only a handful of international speakers as the increase in budget did not address the time burden related to transfers between various destinations.[122]

It is thus a question of how accessible and attractive those events would be for national and international diplomats in places outside the capitals and major diplomatic centres. The issue has not yet arisen in the JDI's current development, as the project has not yet reached destinations without diplomatic presence. However, it can be assumed that such a situation would make contacts with officials and diplomats even more difficult and their response even less positive. At the same time, there are few ways to overcome these geographical limitations. Perhaps leveraging digital advancements could be a solution for wider and more inclusive participation outside the diplomatic centres.

Moreover, the problem of proximity is intertwined with the choice of working language in youth organisations' activities. Events held in English are widely accessible for international audiences, which multiplies the effect of people-to-people interaction and the opportunities to deliberate on international issues. For example, larger gatherings of the JDI held in Geneva attract youth not only from Geneva but also from other Swiss university towns and even from Paris.[123]

The use of local language, meanwhile, allows the deliberations to be focused on the domestic public and national foreign policy issues, and it contributes to the cultivation of local diplomatic vernacular. At the same time, however, it problematises the involvement of foreigners, such as students in international programmes in the case of the JDI, not only at these events but also in organisational teams. If it were to result in a kind of exclusivism (which does not seem to be the case for the JDI so far), it might threaten the credibility of the whole grassroots model and the involvement of individual youth organisations in deliberative systems as well.

---

122   Interviews 2 and 3.
123   Interview 2.

The decision to prefer an international language or to alternate between local and international ones thus reflects a complex negotiation between restricting or broadening access and deliberating on foreign or international affairs. The linguistic dilemma is emblematic of broader tensions between exclusivity and accessibility of events, prompting a reflection on how youth initiatives can navigate these challenges while fostering constructive and inclusive discourse.

Furthermore, as Mansbridge et al. suggest, youth organisations must avoid overly tight coupling with international and foreign policy and diplomacy actors, including the possibility of accepting too generous financial support from them.[124] To remain a credible and independent forum for dialogue and learning, it is essential for a youth initiative to strategically preserve its autonomy and the diversity of perspectives it represents. However, decoupling from these official frameworks also poses a risk because it interrupts the exchange of information and opinions.

In the case of the JDI, the former threatens more locally focused chapters. Specifically, JDI Prague has closely aligned with the Czech Republic's foreign policy focuses, such as the EU, transatlantic relationships, and regional issues in the Western Balkans and the Middle East. Similarly, JDI Georgia has emphasised topics related to NATO, reflecting a significant geopolitical interest of the country. In contrast, chapters in Switzerland and Paris prioritise engagement with permanent missions, embassies and international organisations. However, this gives them little voice in the foreign policies and diplomacies of Switzerland and France.

Additionally, to function as nodes of deliberative systems in the long term, youth initiatives must fulfil certain organisational prerequisites. In particular, they must have the ability to attract the attention of the young audience and the wider public in the context of growing competition from other youth associations and activities. The problem is exacerbated by the fragmentation of information channels and the spillover of young people between them.[125] At the same time, this puts pressure on the quality and innovation of their events and is thus also a stimulus for their further development.[126]

Finally, the creation of a functional internal organisational system that ensures the longevity of the organisation also plays an important role. By definition, the organisations have to deal with the fact that youth is temporal, and their functioning may be disrupted by personnel changes. In this regard, hav-

---

124   Mansbridge et al. 2012, 22–23.
125   Vaid and Harari 2021.
126   Interviews 1 and 3.

ing reached its tenth anniversary in 2021, the JDI's flexible organisational model based on the annual partial renewal of the core team has proved sustainable. In Geneva, where this is not possible due to the design of the study programmes at IHEID, a workable form of know-how transfer between the outgoing and the new team has been found.[127] The only exception in this regard was the Georgia affiliate, which was based on a student who transferred the JDI ways of working from Sciences Po and then worked with the JDI for some time after her studies in a NATO project.[128]

8   Conclusions

The JDI example shows that even youth grassroots initiatives can facilitate deliberation relating to diplomatic affairs and create public spaces for discussion with elites on issues of common concern in this area. To establish such spaces and launch informal discussions, these initiatives need not possess significant strength or experience. Rather, the potential depends on the courage and enthusiasm of both the youth and their political and diplomatic counterparts.

As higher education continues to internationalise and youth mobility increases,[129] the scope of youth initiatives is expanding from the domestic to the international realm and global politics. The coupling then extends from the representatives of states to those of international organisations. Consequently, youth organisations turn into peripheral nodes in various national and international diplomacy-related deliberative systems.

Particularly in these newly appearing deliberative environments, youth play several roles. They provide channels for governments, embassies and representatives of international bodies to inform and raise awareness of various foreign and international political agendas. To some extent, they also open access to youths' fresh ideas, which often sharply contrast with the routine of diplomats' and international servants' work. Nevertheless, the JDI case also suggests that deliberative engagement does not easily translate into participation in relevant decision-making, due to both the lack of such ambition on the part of the organisation and the efforts of the partners to keep cooperation within certain limits and to control its content.

---

127   Interview 1.
128   Interviews 1 and 2.
129   de Wit and Altbach 2021; Tight 2022.

With the growing demographic and political weight of youth, as well as students and young professionals, globally and the growing interest in these groups in some countries and international organisations, new opportunities for politicians and diplomats to establish more such partnerships will arise. Collaboration can occur through top-down engagement with youth bodies or positive responses to their bottom-up initiatives, benefiting all parties involved. However, to make full use of them, it is necessary to know more about their possible forms, benefits and pitfalls, opportunities and constraints.

Paradoxically, the scholarly interest in how these groups approach diplomacy and how diplomacies approach them has been very limited. If citizen participation is to become a new distinctive research agenda in diplomatic studies, the study of youth's, students' and possibly young professionals' engagement must be an integral part of it and must move far beyond the widely recognised significance of youth and student exchanges. The agenda can build both on the parallels with the involvement of other sectors of the public, and on the broad interest in youth, students and young professionals in other disciplines, in particular sociology and education.

Table 11.1 suggests three possible avenues of future research. One should focus on basic forms of interactions between diplomacy and youth. Another should pivot towards a typology of diplomacy-related organisations, initiatives and activities of youth, students and young professionals in terms of participants, agendas, operational patterns, tools, durability and so forth. Furthermore, a deeper understanding of these initiatives' and organisations' evolving roles in the national and international diplomacy-related deliberative systems, their core agendas and the importance and form of more senior partners' (such as career diplomats) support is also desirable.

For the first research avenue, a good starting point for future study might be the distinction between diplomacy for youth, diplomacy through youth and youth diplomacy (with possible analogies for students and young professionals). Diplomacy for youth includes official diplomatic activities aimed at supporting youth internationally. Diplomacy through youth focuses on engaging youth in the creation and/or implementation of diplomacy in various national and international agendas. The concept of youth diplomacy then covers various diplomatic activities of youth to promote their own goals, without organisational links to states or international organisations.

In the latter two cases, the study of youth's coupling with elites and the distinction between deliberative, participatory and counter-democracy environments where it happens provides an appropriate analytical background to identify various mechanisms and methods youth organisations and initiatives use to support or challenge diplomacy elites. They make it possible to capture

TABLE 11.1   Engaging youth in diplomatic affairs: possible future research avenues

Research avenue	Possible focus; conceptualisation
Basic forms of interactions between diplomacy and youth	Passive: – diplomacy for youth – youth as an object of diplomacy, political and diplomatic activities of official actors (MFAs, embassies, international organisations, etc.) aimed at youth as a target group and audience Active: – diplomacy through youth – youth involved by official actors in the development and/or implementation of specific international political foreign policy and diplomatic agendas – youth diplomacy – advocacy by youth for their own goals and interests in the field of international politics, foreign policy or diplomacy that is not primarily initiated by official actors
Typologies of youth initiatives and bodies involved in diplomacy	Participants – youth in general – defined by age only – students – participants in some level(s) of education – young professionals – the early stages of a career in international politics, foreign policy and/or diplomacy or other professions Organisation, durability – informal/formal groups and bodies – ad hoc, temporary, permanent Operational patterns – democratic – indirect or direct involvement in decision-making processes related to international politics, foreign policy and/or diplomacy – counter-democracy – exercising external pressure on elites through collective actions – non-democratic – specifics of youth involvement in foreign policies and diplomacies of authoritarian and totalitarian regimes Agenda – general – not limited to a specific area of international politics, foreign policy or diplomacy – particular – focused on a specific area or areas, for example, peace and war, anti-colonialism, disarmament Tools – the ways and means used by young people to promote goals in the field of international politics, foreign policy and diplomacy

TABLE 11.1   Engaging youth in diplomatic affairs: possible future research avenues (*cont.*)

Research avenue	Possible focus; conceptualisation
Democratic environments enabling youth involvement in decision-making	Specifics and quality of involving youth in different environments: – deliberative – the involvement of youth through information and opinion sharing in public debates – participatory – direct involvement of youth in decision-making processes – activism – indirect involvement of youth through external pressures on decision-makers Patterns of co-operation between youth and official representatives: – the direction of initiative – bottom-up (from youth to elites), top-down (from elites to youth) – the intensity and consequences of coupling youth and elites – loose vs tight coupling Contribution of youth to essential functions of deliberative systems: – epistemic – impact on forming opinions, preferences and decisions based on sound information and relevant reasoning – ethical – fostering mutual respect among participants – democratic – promoting equality and inclusiveness in political processes Pitfalls/risks of youth engagement – problems arising from the specificities of youth as a demographic cohort in general, as well as from different modalities of youth co-operation with international politics, foreign policy and diplomacy elites

different directions of communication between youth and elites (one-way, two-way; top-down, bottom-up) as well as different qualities of their relationship (tight vs loose coupling, de-coupling).

Better knowledge of the differences between deliberative and participatory forms of co-operation between youth and diplomacy elites, as well as related opportunities, possible benefits, constraints, risks and pitfalls, could also help in identifying best practices and striking examples of failures in this area, together with the circumstances in which they appear. The broader impacts of youth involvement in diplomacy-related deliberative systems on the public can then be captured through deeper understanding of youth contributions to the main functions of the diplomacy-related deliberative system – epistemic, educational and ethical ones. Finally, given that the current and next young generations are growing up with new communication technologies and must adapt to an ever-changing media landscape, the consequences of the digital natives' emergence for further developments of diplomacy-related deliberative systems as well as digital diplomacy should also be given adequate scholarly attention.

Bibliography

Acosta, Matias, Zsofia Szlamka and Mohammad A. Mostajo-Radji. 'Transnational Youth Networks: An Evolving Form of Public Diplomacy to Accelerate the Sustainable Development Goals'. *SocArXiv*, 9 March 2020.

Altbach, Philip G. 'The International Student Movement'. *Comparative Education Review* 8 (2) (1964), 131–137.

Altbach, Philip G. 'The International Student Movement'. *Journal of Contemporary History* 5 (1) (1970), 156–174.

Altbach, Philip G. 'Perspectives on Student Political Activism'. *Comparative Education* 25(1) (1989), 97–110.

Altbach, Philip G. and Seymour Martin Lipset, eds. *Students in Revolt* (Boston: Houghton Mifflin, 1969).

Anton, Anca and Raluca Moise. 'The Citizen Diplomats and Their Pathway to Diplomatic Power'. In *Diplomacy, Organisations and Citizens*, eds. Sónia Pedro Sebastião and Susana de Carvalho Spínola (Cham: Springer, 2022), 219–254. DOI 10.1007/978-3-030-81877-7_13.

Arnstein, Sherry R. 'A Ladder of Citizen Participation'. *Journal of the American Institute of Planners* 35 (4) (1969), 216–224.

Attias, Shay. 'Israel's New Peer-to-Peer Diplomacy'. *The Hague Journal of Diplomacy* 7 (4) (2012), 473–482. DOI 10.1163/1871191x-12341235.

Badie, Bertran. 'Transnationalizing Diplomacy in a Post-Westphalian World'. In *Diplomacy in a Globalizing World: Theories and Practices*, 2nd edition, eds. Pauline Kerr and Geoffrey Wiseman (New York: Oxford University Press, 2018), 90–109.

Barber, Kevin and Mohammad A. Mostajo-Radji. 'Youth Networks' Advances toward the Sustainable Development Goals during the COVID-19 Pandemic'. *Frontiers in Sociology* 5 (589539) (2020), 1–5.

Bárta, Ondřej and Anna Lavizzari. *Insights: Meaningful Youth Political Participation in Europe* (Strasbourg: Council of Europe and European Commission, 2021).

Bátora, Jozef. *Public Diplomacy in Small and Medium-Sized States* (The Hague: Netherlands Institute of International Relations 'Clingendael', 2005). https://www.clingendael.org/sites/default/files/2016-02/20050300_cli_paper_dip_issue97.pdf.

Bersaglio, Brock, Charis Enns and Thembela Kepe. 'Youth Under Construction: The United Nations' Representations of Youth in the Global Conversation on the Post-2015 Development Agenda'. *Canadian Journal of Development Studies/Revue canadienne d'études du développement* 36 (1) (2015), 57–71. DOI 10.1080/02255189.2015.994596.

Bislev, Ane. 'Student-to-Student Diplomacy: Chinese International Students as a Soft-Power Tool'. *Journal of Current Chinese Affairs* 46 (2) (2017), 81–109.

Bolewski, Wilfried. 'Corporate Diplomacy as Global Management'. *International Journal of Diplomacy and Economy* 4 (2) (2018), 107–138.

Bu, Liping. 'Educational Exchange and Cultural Diplomacy in the Cold War'. *Journal of American Studies* 33 (3) (1999), 393–415.

Ciftci, Sabri. 'Social Identity and Attitudes toward Foreign Policy: Evidence from a Youth Survey in Turkey'. *International Journal of Middle East Studies* 45 (1) (2013), 25–43.

Collin, Philippa. *Young Citizens and Political Participation in a Digital Society* (New York: Palgrave Macmillan, 2015).

Constantinou, Costas M., Noé Cornago and Fiona McConnell. 'Transprofessional Diplomacy'. *Brill Research Perspectives in Diplomacy and Foreign Policy* 1 (4) (2016), 1–66.

Cull, Nicholas J. 'The Tightrope to Tomorrow: Reputational Security, Collective Vision and the Future of Public Diplomacy'. *The Hague Journal of Diplomacy* 14 (1–2) (2019), 21–35. DOI 10.1163/1871191X-14011014.

Davies, Graeme A. M., Edney Kingsley and Bo Wang. 'Modelling Chinese Youth Support for Military Intervention in the Diaoyu/Senkaku Islands: Beyond Nationalism and Militarism'. *Journal of Conflict Resolution* 67 (7–8) (2023), 1510–1536.

de Wit, Hans and Philip G. Altbach. 'Internationalization in Higher Education: Global Trends and Recommendations for Its Future'. *Policy Reviews in Higher Education* 5 (1) (2021), 28–46.

Dryzek, John S. 'Democratization as Deliberative Capacity Building'. *Comparative Political Studies* 42 (11) (2009), 1379–1402. DOI 10.1177/0010414009332129.

Dunn, Joe P. 'A "Model" for Active Learning and Leadership Development: International Model NATO'. *Journal of Political Science Education* 15 (4) (2019), 528–534.

Eberhard, Lawrence. *Council of Europe and Youth: Thirty Years of Experience* (Strasbourg: Council of Europe Publishing, 2002).

Eger, Ludvík. 'První ročník konference JDI Youth Dialogue netradičně propojí diplomaty, akademiky a aktivní studenty' [The first annual JDI Youth Dialogue Conference will bring together diplomats, academics and active students in an

unconventional way]. Adam.cz, 2013. http://www.adam.cz/clanek-2013030043
-prvni-rocnik-konference-jdi-youth-dialogue-netradicne-propoji-diplomaty-akade
miky-a-aktivni-studenty.html.

Elstub, Stephen, Selen A. Ercan and Ricardo Fabrino Mendonça, eds. *Deliberative Systems in Theory and Practice* (London: Routledge, 2019).

Selen A. Ercan., Carolyn M. Hendriks and John Boswell. 'Reforming Democracy in Disconnected Times: A Deliberative Systems Approach'. ECPR *Joint Session Workshop WS05: Can Participatory Reforms Save Representative Democracy*, 10–14 April 2018. https://researchprofiles.canberra.edu.au/en/publications/reforming-de mocracy-in-disconnected-times-a-deliberative-systems-

European Commission, 'Youth Sounding Board. Make Your Voice Heard!'. n.d. https:// international-partnerships.ec.europa.eu/policies/youth/youth-sounding-board_en.

European Commission and the High Representative of the Union for Foreign Affairs and Security Policy. 'Joint Communication to the European Parliament and the Council: Youth Action Plan (YAP) in EU external action 2022–2027, Promoting Meaningful Youth Participation and Empowerment in EU External Action for Sustainable Development, Equality and Peace'. 4 October 2022. https://eur-lex.eu ropa.eu/legal-content/EN/TXT/?uri=CELEX%3A52022JC0053%qid=166636181 8770.

European Union External Action. 'European Diplomatic Programme'. 27 March 2023. https://www.eeas.europa.eu/eeas/european-diplomatic-programme-2_en.

Fitzpatrick, Kathy R. 'Defining Strategic Publics in a Networked World: Public Diplomacy's Challenge at Home and Abroad'. *The Hague Journal of Diplomacy* 7 (4) (2012), 421–440. DOI 10.1163/1871191x-12341236.

Frominykh, Alexey. 'Russia's Public Diplomacy in Central Asia and the Caucasus: The Role of the Universities'. *The Hague Journal of Diplomacy* 12 (1) (2017), 56–85.

Fulda, Andreas. 'The Emergence of Citizen Diplomacy in European Union–China Relations: Principles, Pillars, Pioneers, Paradoxes'. *Diplomacy and Statecraft* 30 (1) (2019), 188–216. DOI 10.1080/09592296.2019.1557419.

Future Leaders Network. 'G7 Youth Summit 2022'. 2022. https://www.futureleaders .network/opportunities-y7.

Geis, Anna, Christian Opitz and Hanna Pfeifer. 'Recasting the Role of Citizens in Diplomacy and Foreign Policy: Preliminary Insights and a New Research Agenda'. *The Hague Journal of Diplomacy* 17 (4) (2022), 614–627. DOI 10.1163/1871191x-bja10136.

Gerodimos, Roman. 'Introducing "Citizen Diplomacy 2.0": A Framework for the Study of Online Civic Engagement with Global Affairs'. In *The Media, Political Participation and Empowerment*, eds. Richard Scullion, Roman Gerodimos, Daniel Jackson and Darren Lilleker (London: Taylor & Francis Group, 2013), 161–174.

Global Diplomats Forum. 'Young Diplomats Forum 2024'. n.d. https://ssifs.mea.gov
.in/?3682?000.

Global Youth Action Network. 'About'. n.d.a. https://gyan.tigweb.org/about/.

Global Youth Action Network. 'Membership'. n.d.b. https://gyan.tigweb.org/mem
bers/.

Government of Japan, Cabinet Office. 'The Ship for Southeast Asian and Japanese
Youth Program'. n.d. https://www8.cao.go.jp/youth/kouryu/en/sseayp/sseayp
.html.

Gramberger, Marc. *Citizens as Partners: OECD Handbook on Information, Consultation
and Public Participation in Policy-Making* (Paris: OECD Publishing, 2001).

Graziani, Sofia. 'The Case of Youth Exchanges and Interactions between the PRC and
Italy in the 1950s'. *Modern Asian Studies* 51 (1) (2017), 194–226.

Gregory, Bruce. 'Mapping Boundaries in Diplomacy's Public Dimension'. *The Hague
Journal of Diplomacy* 11 (1) (2016), 1–25.

Gretschel Anu, Tiina-Maria Levamo, Tomi Kiilakoski, Sofia Laine, Niina Mäntilä, Geo-
frey Pleyers and Harii Raisto. *Youth Participation Good Practices in Different Forms
of Regional and Local Democracy* (Helsinki: Finnish Youth Research Network and
Finnish Youth Research Society Internet Publications, 2014). https://www.youthre
search.fi/images/julkaisuja/youthparticipation_goodpractices.pdf.

Gutmann, Amy and Dennis F. Thompson. *Why Deliberative Democracy?* (Princeton:
Princeton University Press, 2004).

Harrison, Benjamin T. 'Waning of the American Student Peace Movement of the
Sixties'. *Peace Research* 21 (3) (1989), 1–15. http://www.jstor.org/stable/23609947.

Hendriks, Carolyn M. 'Coupling Citizens and Elites in Deliberative Systems: The
Role of Institutional Design'. *European Journal of Political Research* 55 (1) (2016),
43–60.

Hocking, Brian. 'Multistakeholder Diplomacy: Forms, Functions and Frustrations'. In
Multistakeholder Diplomacy: Challenges and Opportunities, ed. Brian Hocking (Geneva: DiploFoundation, 2006), 13–29.

Hocking, Brian. 'Non-State Actors and the Transformation of Diplomacy'. In *The Ash-
gate Research Companion to Non-State Actors*, ed. Bob Reinhara (Farnham: Ash-
gate, 2011), 225–236.

Huber, Daniela. 'Youth as a New "Foreign Policy Challenge" in Middle East and North
Africa: A Critical Interrogation of European Union and US Youth Policies in Morocco and Tunisia'. *European Foreign Affairs Review* 22 (1) (2017), 111–128.

Huijgh, Ellen. *Public Diplomacy at Home* (Leiden: Brill Nijhoff, 2019).

Hujo, Katja and Maggie Carter. 'Transformative Change for Children and Youth in the
Context of the 2030 Agenda for Sustainable Development'. *Innocenti Working Papers*, 15 April 2019. DOI 10.18356/D4BB03EA-EN.

Jacoby, Wade. 'Tutors and Pupils: International Organizations, Central European Elites, and Western Models'. *Governance* 14 (2) (2001), 169–200.

Jain, Romi. 'China's Strategic Foray into Higher Education: Goals and Motivations vis-à-vis Nepal'. *Diplomacy & Statecraft* 31 (3) (2020), 534–556. DOI 10.1080/09592 296.2020.1782677.

Jones, Gill. *Youth* (Cambridge: Polity Press, 2009).

Junior Diplomat Initiative. 'Information in English'. n.d. https://jdi.vse.cz.

Junior Diplomat Initiative. 'Registrace na konferenci JDI Youth Dialogue 2013 zahájena!' [Registration for JDI Youth Dialogue 2013 is now open!], mojeskola.cz 2013. https://www.mojeskola.cz/Sborovna/Akce/jdi.pdf.

Junior Diplomat Initiative. 'Druhý ročník konference JDI Youth Dialogue netradičně propojí diplomaty, akademiky a aktivní studenty.' [The second edition of the JDI Youth Dialogue Conference will bring together diplomats, academics and active students in an unconventional way]. 24 March 2014. https://www.mojeskola.cz/Sborovna/Akce/JDI-Dialog2.pdf.

Junior Diplomat Initiative. 'JDI Youth Dialogue/Annual Conference'. 2015. http://www.jdi-vse.cz/jdiyouthdialogue/.

Junior Diplomat Initiative. 'V4 + Serbia Simulation'. 2016. http://www.jdi-vse.cz/v4/.

Junior Diplomat Initiative France. 'Events'. 2023. https://jdifranceorg.wordpress.com/our-past-events/.

Junior Diplomat Initiative Georgia. 'Raising Awareness in the Role of NATO in the Black Sea Security in Youth'. 2021. https://docs.google.com/forms/d/1aDeOBX WYoyxfIu7A6od4I5K6r2i-7Ss2NtOJYxVHMNE/viewform?edit_requested=true.

Junior Diplomat Initiative Georgia. 'Events'. 2022. https://www.facebook.com/jdigeor gia/past_hosted_events.

Junior Diplomat Initiative Switzerland. 'Our Letter of Congratulations to @NOIweala'. 2021. https://twitter.com/JDI_Switzerland/status/1369560855973625863/photo/1.

Junior Diplomat Initiative Switzerland. 'Events'. 2023a. https://jdi-switzerland.wee bly.com/events.html.

Junior Diplomat Initiative Switzerland. 'Managing Your Career and Care Responsibilities'. 2023b. https://www.instagram.com/jdi_geneve/?img_index=1.

Kelley, John Robert. 'The New Diplomacy: Evolution of a Revolution'. *Diplomacy & Statecraft* 21 (2) (2010), 286–305. DOI 10.1080/09592296.20.

Kelley, John Robert. *Agency Change: Diplomatic Action Beyond the State* (Washington, DC: Rowman & Littlefield, 2014).

Klemenčič, Manja and Bo Yun Park. 'Student Politics: Between Representation and Activism'. In *Handbook on the Politics of Higher Education*, eds. Brendan Cantwell, Harnish Coates and Roger King (Cheltenham: Edward Elgar, 2018), 468–486.

Koivunen, Pia. 'The World Youth Festival as a Soviet Cultural Product during the Cold War'. *Quaestio Rossica* 8 (5) (2020), 1612–1628. DOI 10.15826/QR.2020.5.548.

Laqua, Daniel. 'Activism in the "Students' League of Nations": International Student Politics and the Confédération Internationale des Étudiants, 1919–1939'. *The English Historical Review* 132 (556) (2017), 605–637. DOI 10.1093/ehr/cex153.

Laqua, Daniel. 'The Politics of Transnational Student Mobility: Youth, Education and Activism in Ghana, 1957–1966'. *Social History* 48 (1) (2023), 87–113. DOI 10.1080/03071022.2023.2146902.

Luescher, Thierry M. 'Altbach's Theory of Student Activism in the Twentieth Century: Ten Propositions That Matter'. In *Students in Twentieth-Century Britain and Ireland*, ed. Jodi Burkett (Cham: Palgrave Macmillan, 2018), 297–318.

Manor, Ilan. *The Digitalization of Public Diplomacy* (Cham: Palgrave Macmillan, 2019).

Mansbridge, Jane, James Bohman, Simone Chambers, Thomas Christiano, Archon Fung, John Parkinson, Dennis F. Thompson and Mark E. Warren. 'A Systemic Approach to Deliberative Democracy'. In *Deliberative Systems: Deliberative Democracy at the Large Scale*, eds. John Parkinson and Jane Mansbridge (Cambridge: Cambridge University Press, 2012), 1–26.

McCann, Gerard. 'The Trumpets and Travails of "South–South Cooperation": African Students in India since the 1940s'. In *India's Development Diplomacy and Soft Power in Africa*, eds. Kenneth King and Meera Venkatachalam (Suffolk: Boydell & Brewer, 2021), 169–184.

Melissen, Jan. *Beyond the New Public Diplomacy* (The Hague: Netherlands Institute of International Relations 'Clingendael', 2011). https://www.clingendael.org/sites/default/files/pdfs/20111014_cdsp_paper_jmelissen.pdf.

Melissen, Jan and Jian Wang. 'Introduction'. In *Debating Public Diplomacy: Now and Next*, eds. Jan Melissen and Jian Wang (Boston: Brill, 2019), 1–5.

Ministry of Foreign Affairs of the Czech Republic. 'Ministr Schwarzenberg zahájil pravidelné diplomatické salony' [Minister Schwarzenberg opened regular diplomatic salons]. 27 September 2012. https://www.mzv.cz/jnp/cz/udalosti_a_media/archiv_zprav/rok_2012/x2012_09_27_ministr_schwarzenberg_zahaji_pravidelne_diplomaticke_salony.html.

Ministry of Foreign Affairs of the Czech Republic. 'XIX. Diplomatický salon JDI na MZV ČR: "15 let v EU: Současná role ČR v EU a budoucí výzvy"' [XIX. Diplomatic salon JDI: '15 Years in the EU: Current role of the Czech Republic in the EU and future challenges']. 4 December 2019. https://www.mzv.cz/jnp/cz/zahranicni_vztahy/verejna_diplomacie/aktivity/xix_diplomaticky_salon_jdi_na_mzv_cr_15.html.

Ministry of Foreign Affairs of the Czech Republic. 'XX. Diplomatický salon JDI s Alexandrem Sporýšem, Michalem Brožou a Michaleou Ptáčkovou na téma "Mladá generace a 75 let Spojených národů"' [XX. JDI diplomatic salon with Alexander Sporýš, Michal Broža and Michalea Ptáček on the topic 'The Young Generation and 75 Years of the United Nations']. 31 March 2021. https://www.mzv.cz/jnp/cz/zahra

nicni_vztahy/verejna_diplomacie/aktivity/xx_diplomaticky_salon_jdi_s_alexandr
em.html.

Ministry of Foreign Affairs of the Czech Republic. 'XXIII. Diplomatický salon Junior
Diplomat Initiative na MZV ČR: Ekonomická diplomacie ČR – aktuální výzvy
a priority' [XXIII. Diplomatic salon Junior Diplomat Initiative at the Ministry of
Foreign Affairs of the Czech Republic: Economic diplomacy of the Czech Republic – current challenges and priorities]. 26 April 2022. https://www.mzv.cz/jnp/cz/
vyhledavani/index$219343.html?text=Diplomatický%20salon%20JDi.

Ministry of Foreign Affairs of the Czech Republic and Junior Diplomat Initiative.
'Memorandum o spolupráci mezi Ministerstvem zahraničních věcí České repub-
liky a Junior Diplomat Initiative, z.s.' [Memorandum on Cooperation between the
Ministry of Foreign Affairs of the Czech Republic and Junior Diplomat Initiative,
Registered Association]. 24 October 2016.

Ministry of Foreign Affairs, Government of India, Sushma Swaraj Institute of Foreign
Service. 'Professional Course for Foreign Diplomats'. 24 February 2023. https://
ssifs.mea.gov.in/?3682?000.

Ministry of Foreign Affairs of Ukraine. 'The Ministry of Foreign Affairs of Ukraine Is
Establishing a Youth Council under the Ministry of Foreign Affairs of Ukraine'.
12 August 2022. https://mfa.gov.ua/en/news/ministry-foreign-affairs-ukraine-
establishing-youth-council-under-ministry-foreign-affairs-ukraine.

Modaber, Rohollah. 'Role of Youth Diplomacy in Governments' Foreign Relationships
by Using YNGOs Capacity' (Youth Non-Governmental Organizations)'. *Journal of
Politics and Law* 9 (2) (2016), 219–231.

Model WTO. 'Who We Are?', 2023, https://www.model-wto.org/.

Muldon, James P. 'The Model United Nations Revisited'. *Simulation and Gaming* 26 (1)
(1995), 27–35.

Norris, Pippa. *Democratic Phoenix*: *Reinventing Political Activism* (Cambridge: Cambridge University Press, 2002).

Nováková Bára. 'JDI uspořádalo svůj dvacátý čtvrtý diplomatický salon' [JDI held its
twenty-fourth diplomatic salon]. *iList*, 16 December 2022. http://www.ilist.cz/
clanky/jdi-usporadalo-svuj-dvacaty-ctvrty-diplomaticky-salon.

Parkinson, John. 'Democratizing Deliberative Systems'. In *Deliberative Systems: Deliberative Democracy at the Large Scale*, eds. John Parkinson and Jane Mansbridge
(Cambridge: Cambridge University Press, 2012), 151–172.

Pate, Seth W. 'Taiwanese Youth Nationalism and Its Implications for US Foreign
Policy'. *Fletcher Forum on World Affairs* 40 (1) (2016), 157–172.

Payne, Gregory J. 'Reflections on Public Diplomacy: People-to-People Communication'. *American Behavioral Scientist* 53 (4) (2009), 579–606.

Payne, Gregory J., Efe Sevin and Sara Bruya. 'Grassroots 2.0: Public Diplomacy in the
Digital Age'. *Comunicacao Publica* 16 (3) (2011), 45–70.

Perovic, Bojana. 'Defining Youth in Contemporary National Legal and Policy Frameworks across Europe, Partnership between the European Commission and the
Council of Europe in the Field of Youth'. 2016. https://pjp-eu.coe.int/documents/
42128013/47261653/Analytical+paper+Youth+Age+Bojana+Perovic+4.4.16.pdf/eb59
c5e2-45d8-4e70-b672-f8de0a5ca08c.

Peterková, Jana and Eliška Tomalová. 'Kulturní rozměr české zahraniční politiky'
[The cultural dimension of Czech foreign policy]. In *Česká zahraniční politika v
roce 2012* [Czech foreign policy in 2012], ed. Michal Kořan (Prague: Institute of
International Relations, 2013), 321–336.

Pfeifer, Hana, Christian Opitz and Anna Geis. 'Deliberating Foreign Policy: Perceptions and Effects of Citizen Participation in Germany'. *German Politics* 30 (4)
(2020), 485–502.

Prague Student Summit. 'About Prague Student Summit'. n.d. https://www.student
summit.cz/en/about/.

Rasche, Andreas. 'Global Policies and Local Practice: Loose and Tight Couplings in
Multi-Stakeholder Initiatives'. *Business Ethics Quarterly* 22 (4) (2012), 679–708.

Rask, Mikko and Richard Worthington, eds. *Governing Biodiversity through Democratic Deliberation* (London: Routledge, 2015).

Roberts, Ken. 'Youth Mobilisations and Political Generations: Young Activists in Political Change Movements During and Since the Twentieth Century'. *Journal of
Youth Studies* 18 (8) (2015), 950–966.

Rosenmayr, Leopold. 'New Theoretical Approaches to the Sociological Study of
Young People: Introduction'. *International Social Science Journal* 24 (2) (1972),
216–256.

Salazar, Juan Francisco, Elizabeth Leane, Gabriela Roldán, Caleb Fraser, Katia Macías
Díaz, Chloe Power, Florencia Garro, Rudzani Silima and Elias Barticevic. 'The Ant-
arctic Youth Coalition: An Experiment in Citizen Participation and South–South
Cultural Diplomacy'. *The Polar Journal* 12 (1) (2022), 5–21. DOI 10.1080/
2154896X.2022.2062560.

Samuel-Azran, Tal, Betti Ilovici, Israel Zari and Orly Geduild. 'Practicing Citizen Diplomacy 2.0: The Hot Dudes and Hummus – Israel's Yummiest' Campaign for
Israel's Branding'. *Place Branding and Public Diplomacy* 15 (1) (2019), 38–49.

Scott-Smith, Giles. 'Exchange Programs and Public Diplomacy'. In *Routledge Handbook of Public Diplomacy*, 2nd edition, eds. Nancy Snow and Nicolas J. Cull
(New York: Routledge, 2020), 38–49.

Setälä, Maija. 'Advisory, Collaborative and Scrutinizing Roles of Deliberative Mini-
Publics'. *Frontiers in Political Science* 2 (591844) (2021), 1–10.

Sherrod, Lonnie R., Constance A. Flanagan and Ron Kassimir. *Youth Activism: An
International Encyclopaedia* (Westport, CT: Greenwood, 2006).

Šime, Zane. 'European Diplomatic Practice Seen through the Post-Graduate Lens'. EU Diplomacy Paper 7/2023 (Brussels: College of Europe, 2023). https://www.research gate.net/profile/Zane-Sime/publication/373439607_European_Diplomatic_Prac tice_Seen_through_the_post-Graduate_Lens/links/64ec6b74oacf2e2b521d31e5/Eu ropean-Diplomatic-Practice-Seen-through-the-post-Graduate-Lens.pdf.

Snow, Nancy. 'Academic Exchanges as Good Propaganda'. In *Routledge Handbook of Public Diplomacy*, 2nd edition, eds. Nancy Snow and Nicolas J. Cull (New York: Routledge, 2020), 422–429.

Stein, Ronaldo. 'Diplomatic Training Around the World'. In *Foreign Ministries: Managing Diplomatic Networks and Optimizing Value*, eds. Kishan S. Rana and Jovan Kurbalija (Malta and Geneva: DiploFoundation, 2007), 235–264.

Stone, Linda. 'Youth Power – Youth Movements: Myth, Activism, and Democracy'. *Ethics and Education* 16 (2) (2021), 249–261.

Sukarieh, Mayssoun and Stuart Tannock. 'In the Best Interests of Youth or Neoliberalism? The World Bank and the New Global Youth Empowerment Project'. *Journal of Youth Studies* 11 (3) (2008), 301–312. DOI 10.1080/13676260801946431.

Tiessen, Rebecca. 'Educating Global Citizens? Canadian Foreign Policy and Youth Study/Volunteer Abroad Programs'. *Canadian Foreign Policy Journal* 14 (1) (2007), 77–84.

Tight, Malcolm. 'Internationalisation of Higher Education Beyond the West: Challenges and Opportunities – the Research Evidence'. *Educational Research and Evaluation* 27 (3–4) (2022), 239–259.

UNESCO. 'Education Data Release 2023'. 13 September 2023. https://uis.unesco.org/en/news/education-data-release.

United Nations. 'UN Youth Delegate Programme'. n.d. https://www.un.org/development/desa/youth/what-we-do/what-can-you-do/establish-a-youth-delegate-programme.html.

United Nations. 'Youth 2023 Working With and For Young People.' 2018. https://www.un.org/youthenvoy/wp-content/uploads/2018/09/18-00080_UN-Youth-Strategy_Web.pdf.

United Nations, 'Global Issues: Youth'. 2022. https://www.un.org/en/global-issues/youth.

Vaid, Sumer S. and Gabriella M. Harari. 'Who Uses What and How Often? Personality Predictors of Multiplatform Social Media Use among Young Adults'. *Journal of Research in Personality* 91 (2021), 104005.

van Deth, Jan W. 'Studying Political Participation: Towards a Theory of Everything?'. April 2001. https://www.researchgate.net/publication/258239977_Studying_Political_Participation_Towards_a_Theoryof_Everything.

Varwell, Simon. 'A Literature Review of Arnstein's Ladder of Citizen Participation: Lessons for Contemporary Student Engagement'. *Exchanges: The Interdisciplinary Research Journal* 10 (1) (2022), 108–144.

Ward, Janelle. 'Youth and Websites: Exploring How Young People Use the Internet for Political Participation'. In *The Media, Political Participation and Empowerment*, eds. Richard Scullion, Roman Gerodimos, Daniel Jackson and Darren Lilleker (London: Taylor & Francis Group, 2013), 192–204.

Wiseman, Geoffrey. 'Polylateralism and New Modes of Global Dialogue'. In *Diplomacy*, Volume 3, eds. Christer Jönsson and Richard Langhorne (London: SAGE, 2004), 36–57.

Wiseman, Geoffrey. 'Polylateralism: Diplomacy's Third Dimension'. *Public Diplomacy Magazine* 4 (1) (2010), 24–39.

World Bank. 'Higher Education'. 22 October 2022. https://www.worldbank.org/en/topic/tertiaryeducation.

Xenos, Michael, Ariadne Vromen and Brian D. Loader. 'The Great Equalizer? Patterns of Social Media Use and Youth Political Engagement in Three Advanced Democracies'. *Information, Communication & Society* 17 (2) (2014), 151–167.

Young Diplomats. n.d. https://www.young-diplomats.com.

Youth at Heart. n.d. https://www.youthatheart.nl.

Zaharna, Rhonda S. 'The Public Diplomacy Challenges of Strategic Stakeholder Engagement'. In *Trials of Engagement: The Future of US Public Diplomacy*, eds. Ali Fisher and Scott Lucas (Leiden: Brill/Martinus Nijhoff, 2011), 201–229.

Zemanová, Štěpánka. 'Grassroots Student Diplomacy: The Junior Diplomat Initiative (JDI) in Prague, Geneva, Paris and Tbilisi'. *The Hague Journal of Diplomacy* 17 (4) (2022), 679–691.

Interviews

Interview 1. JDI Founder. Online. 29 September 2023.

Interview 2. JDI Founder. Online. 13 October 2023.

Interview 3. JDI Chapter Founder. Online. 13 October 2023.

Interview 4. JDI Founder. Email correspondence. 22 September–17 October 2023.

Interview 5. Faculty, Prague University of Economics and Business. 16 October 2023.

Interview 6. JDI Alum. Online. 14 October 2023.

Interview 7. JDI Alum. Online. 25 October 2023.

Interview 8. JDI Alum. Email correspondence. 12–29 October 2023.

Interview 9. JDI Alum. Email correspondence. 13–31 October 2023.

Interview 10. JDI Alum. Email correspondence. 13 October–14 November 2023.

CHAPTER 12

Concluding Reflections

Andrew F. Cooper

In the first *Hague Journal of Diplomacy* blog in November 2019,[1] I posited that diplomacy was taking a domestic turn. Although my commentary was abbreviated in content, it reflected a frustration in how diplomatic practices have been traditionally portrayed both in diplomatic studies and International Relations (IR). Using a sports analogy, diplomacy no longer can or should be depicted in the literature (or in operation) as through only 'away' practices matter. 'Home' contests – and contestation – not only exist but play out in a vibrant and impactful manner in which the process and outcomes cannot be taken for granted. Therefore, in terms of overall value, a shift in focus towards 'home engagement' raises highly saliant issues left out of the traditional scholarship. Whose voices are heard? Can those voices be managed or even manipulated? And what is the impact of this wider and deeper recognition of the salience of 'double-edged' diplomacy?[2] Is it simply to embrace and legitimatise more democratic processes? Or is to open the door to a greater intensity of diplomatic practices, with a privileging of impulsive spirits?

With considerable credit, the collection edited by Jan Melissen, HwaJung Kim, and Githma Chandrasekara provide a thicker and more sophisticated analysis of what they term 'Home Engagement in Diplomacy.' In doing so, they provide requisite balance to the international and domestic images of diplomacy.

If expressing admiration about the ambition of this volume, and how it fills a necessary gap, in some areas the book raises more questions than it answers. The most important of these is the tension between the participatory ideals given so much attention in the book and illiberal and autocratic ascendancy.

There is no question that we have to take seriously the optimistic spirit of the participatory ideals animated so explicitly in several in this collection. One of these is Anna Popkova's chapter analysing the efforts to make citizen diplomacy in the United States (US) more inclusive and representative of its diverse domestic publics. Another is Štěpánka Zemanová analysis of the Junior Diplo-

---

1   Cooper 2019b.
2   Moravcsik 1993.

macy Initiative, with a deep investigation of where and how student-led project have evolved into an international platform for grassroots diplomacy.

Anybody who has participated in formal or informal events nationally or globally will appreciate the appetite for participation in diplomatic practices and processes by traditionally under-represented or marginalised groups. However, as Geoffrey Wiseman and Allison Scott convey in their illuminating article, 'Engaging or Manipulating Citizens in a Polarised Society: The Choices for US Diplomacy,' the optimism behind these initiatives lies in the 'assumption that the nature of diplomacy's domestic engagement is highly dependent on the strength of a country's commitment to democratic or pluralist norms.'

As evident by the ascendancy of illiberal and autocratic forces in so many parts of the world, these assumptions cannot be taken for granted. As I referred to in an earlier publication, one of the main causes of the systemic challenge to diplomacy and diplomats is the process of dis-intermediation – with a focus not on 'home engagement' but 'home' disengagement by foreign ministries.[3] Per se, a process in which diplomacy and diplomats appear to be disconnected from the interests and identity of their domestic societies. This dynamic in turn is exacerbated by the ability of hyper-empowered individuals to tap into this feeling of neglect and frustration: with as Wiseman and Scott underscore a highly pessimistic world view.

Using both traditional and social media, these individuals push to make a direct and emotional appeal to their supporters. To some considerable extent the Trump personalist populist challenge exemplifies American exceptionalism. As Wiseman and Scott note, given the connection of the US with forms of liberal engagement over the post-1945 era, 'what happens there has reverberations in many parts of the world.' To be sure, the reactions to the personalist populist challenge located in the US Department of States are far more diverse: extending across the range of 'exit', 'voice,' and 'loyalty.'[4] If the domestic turn with respect to American society at large exhibits deep estrangement, the bureaucratic response has displayed both alienation and mediatory instincts.

At the same time, the image of exceptionalism should not be taken too far. For if the impact of the US centred challenge has a greater seismic effect, both the causation and the techniques associated to this type of challenge are closely aligned in a variety of other countries. Such a shared dynamic makes the chapter by César Jiménez-Martínez highly pertinent in capturing the technological component of this challenge. But in addition to the concentration of Jiménez-Martínez on the role of digital participation in challenging state au-

---

3   Cooper 2019a.
4   Cooper 2022.

thority from the bottom up, there is also the issue of how and where digital media platforms can be used by illiberal and authoritarian forces in a top-down manner. In both cases, the phenomenon accentuates conflict and contestation with respect to national identity and policy.[5] As Jiménez-Martínez concludes in references cited by the editors, future debates should, therefore, address tensions between 'top-down' and 'bottom-up' perspectives, exploring when these approaches may align or conflict.[6]

Nor, for that matter, is the populist ascendancy the only challenge to diplomacy and diplomats. As Popkova suggests, counterpublics 'at home' can allow greater constructive engagement. But they could bring out greater jaggedness, showcasing intensifying opposition to the dominant public sphere.

To return to the sports domain, with the specific illustration of US public diplomacy in mind, it is no longer possible to manage or manipulate the citizen diplomacy of important constituencies such as African American athletes. Consistent with the conceptualisation of sports as a vehicle of diplomatic projection[7] sports stars generally and African American athletes in particular should be vital ingredients for cultivating a positive American citizen brand. Yet, the viability of the model promoted in earlier eras has disappeared. No longer are African- American athletes willing to be mobilised in line with earlier fixed practices with a focus on 'away' engagement. Indeed, in the context of Black Lives Matters protests, even some African American athletes who had participated in earlier State Department tours, questioned this strategy. A weighty example of this thinking came in the reflections of Oscar Robertson, the former National Basketball Association star, who in a carefully crafted article written in 2016, "I hope that both active and retired athletes, and their player associations, will get personally involved ... for starters, maybe we need State Department sports and cultural tours on American soil to change the hearts and minds of our own people'.[8]

With the polarisation around the wars in Ukraine and Gaza, as well as on migration and refugee flows, the accommodation of youth voices will become far more complex. On the one hand, global summits such as the Conference of the Parties (COP) process and the G20, have become more accommodative to this demographic. On the other hand, though, forces of dissent will become more visible and demanding. This is especially so, when campaigners on is-

5　Mihelj & Jiménez-Martínez 2021.
6　Ibid.
7　Murray and Pigman 2014.
8　Robertson 2016, in Cooper 2018, 170.

sues such as climate change and Gaza become intertwined, as profiled in the evolution of Greta Thurnburg's activities.

To pose these questions is not at all to diminish the wider merits of this collection. On the conceptual front, it is worthwhile reflecting on the distance between this work and the traditional literature not only in diplomatic studies but in International Relations more generally. No less than in my own attempts to go beyond the constricted boundaries of mainstream institutionalist IR,[9] the project developed by the editors is animated by a desire to recalibrate analysis towards 'the domestic dimension of diplomatic practice that is begging for better answers than the study of diplomacy and international relations (IR) theory can presently offer.

The collection is explicitly eclectic in approach: with an astute appreciation for the emotional driven elements that are opened up by the domestic turn. Not for Melissen, Kim, and Chandrasekara the rationalistic based analysis offered by mainstream IR. But equally the editors move away from the confinement of realism, with its disciplined fixation on the dictates of the national interest and the confines of 'high politics.' What the book appreciates in a manner that extends its differentiation in analysis from the mainstream is the comprehensive impact of the domestic turn. That is to say, the turn is interpreted as being saliant not just on the basic question of 'home' versus 'away' but in terms of the unique qualities attached to the 'away' dimension: Not only is there a shift away from the logic of rational choice in political economy and on national security. There is a reorientation towards a self-conscious concern regarding the privileging by societal forces of 'their personal sense of safety and their material well-being.'

As such, the collection marks a decisive departure not only from the neo-realists, notably Kenneth Waltz, and liberal institutionalists and neorealists, but classical geo-political driven realism, above all Henry Kissinger, as well.

In declaratory fashion, Kissinger acknowledged the importance of the domestic component of diplomacy: 'What used to be considered domestic events can now have world-wide consequences.'[10] Nonetheless, in operational terms, Kissinger was dismissive of the 'home' arena for diplomacy beyond his control. Steeped in the ethos of state-centrism and national interest, the practices he used were designed explicitly to exclude societal forces. On this theme, it is vital to remember that Kissinger was attacked not by normative oriented critics because of his dismissal of the claims for human rights in

---

9   Cooper 2024.
10   Kissinger 1969, 51.

foreign policy, but by populists for his subordination of American values to 'one world ideologists.'[11]

While distancing the analysis from realpolitik assumptions, there is also some nuanced differences between this collection and other mainstream diplomatic interpretations. Whereas some contributions in the collection offer optimistic scenarios about the trajectory of diplomacy, the overall tenor of the book is a cautionary one. Although some space is allowed for foreign ministries to be 'boundary spanners' this process is not taken to be a smooth one. Borrowing from the earlier contributions of Huijgh,[12] 'home engagement' is interpreted as one that must build in the emotional dimensions showcased in this double-edged diplomacy.

The more elaborate framing chapter, 'Theorising and Debating Diplomacy's Domestic Deficit,' by Melissen and Chandrasekara, extends the analysis both conceptually and operationally in terms of the nature and meaning of what they term the societisation of diplomacy. From my perspective, the most compelling part of this analysis is the focus on what is missing in mainstream IR. This is not to suggest that diplomacy studies is free of 'missing' dimensions. The longstanding neglect of consular activities – the closest component of diplomacy to societal deliverables – is as Melissen and Chandrasekara point out being the most obvious traditional site of neglect.

As in the other areas of the constricted analysis by mainstream IR, targeting 'the abstractions such as the system of states and shared beliefs about state behaviour in the international system,' is at the core of the problem of neglect. Conceptualisation based on assumptions of logical designs lends itself easily to an over emphasis on structure, and the downplay of agency: both individual and collective. But the deficiency in terms of the neglect of societisation is accentuated by the parsimonious nature of the analysis. Anything 'messy' is avoided. Looking outwards, this means that the challenge of the Global South is left out. Looking inwards this approach stymies bringing to the fore any features that showcase societal polarisation.

Here, as signalled by Melissen and Chandrasekara, Hedley Bull's conceptualisation of a society of states presents a valuable potential corrective. Bull is careful with the conflation of domestic analogies. Nonetheless, as Stanley Hoffmann suggests,[13] although Bull's work did not visualise a world moving 'beyond the states system', it at least indicated the possibility of a 'wider world

---

11   Gewen 2020, 334.

12   Huijgh 2013.

13   Hoffmann 1986: 190.

political system' that borrowed elements from the 'domestic model' with space for societal as well as state actors.

Beyond the pivotal conceptual questions, the collection is valuable on several practice dimensions. Having reversed the lens by which diplomacy is analysed, public diplomacy is no longer restricted to the 'away' arena. Rather it becomes 'enmeshed with society' on the 'home' field. What is more, any refutation of the need to reverse this lens is countered by the transformative force of digital diplomacy: with Melissen and Chandrasekara giving pride of place to Ilan Manor's conclusion that: 'Domestic digital diplomacy represents the creation of a new and profound relationship between diplomats and their citizens.'

Reversing the lens brings out a wider spectrum of techniques regarding diplomatic repertoires. There is certainly an impetus towards innovative forms of constructive engagement, with society identified as an asset. One of the most intriguing contributions of the collection is Christian Lequesne's chapter: 'Home Diplomacy Across Borders: Consular and Diaspora Diplomacy in France.' Above all else, Lequesne' chapter demonstrates how the notion of 'home engagement' can be extended to the physically 'away'. Accordingly, in this highly distinctly case, the relationship between inside and outside territoriality is given new meaning: with engagement with national diasporas moved from the inside to the outside.

As Lequesne conveys the extraterritorial dimension of the French consular services' engagement with French citizens living overseas highlights the importance of considering both territorial and non-territorial relationships in any comprehensive analysis of home engagement in diplomacy. As it is, Lequesne's chapter moves into some added questions, with special reference to the implications of privatisation regarding consular services. But, when stretched out in comparative sense, such an interface raises a wider number of sensitive questions about consular management and possible manipulation: in that this expanded domain may extend into question of political surveillance and transactional diplomacy where services are traded for support.

To be sure, other possible studies beyond the array of countries covered in this volume, across a wide spectrum of interpretations, from India, Turkey, to Sri Lanka, to Eretria, await follow up studies. Such an approach in turn implies an emphasis not just on dynamics around innovative forms of constructive 'home' engagement based on society as an asset but forms of 'home' engagement that reflect an identification of domestic forces as a 'problem.'[14]

---

14   Manor, Jiménez-Martínez, and Dolea 2021.

Although far from being the only theme covered, the question of the relationship between diasporic leaders' and local consulates jumps out as well in the contribution by Scott Michael Harrison and Quinton Huang, Democratic Diplomatic Middle Grounds: Theorising and Expanding the Role of Domestic Societies in Paradiplomatic Relations. Namely, with regard to the arena where countries have city to city twinning relation. What is innovative in this contribution, however, is not just the range of snapshots across forms of city diplomacy, provincial diplomacy, and Indigenous diplomacy making up 'paradiplomacy.' Rather it is the attempt to locate this array of activity as a core empirical base for the conceptualisation of a 'democratic diplomatic middle ground.'

Whatever the accuracy of this innovative conceptualisation, it is clear that this set of activities is no longer invisible. Provinces or regional governments impact a wide number of trade deals. From the UN to social summits at the G20, to name the key examples at the apex of diplomacy, Indigenous Peoples have moved out of the margins of global affairs. And cities have taken on a pivotal role at the COP process, as well as an array of social summits. At the recent Rio de Janeiro G20, for instance, there was not only an Urban (U) 20 but a global summit of favelas.

The second practice dimension of note relates to the scope of investigation. A number of the cases focus on the developed industrial world in and apart from the US. Even among these cases, though, the collection shows the enormous variation. In their chapter, The Evolution of Domestic Public Diplomacy in Germany: Engaging the 'Public' at Home on Foreign and Security Policy Since 1990, Opitz, Pfeifer and Geis, depict Germany as a quintessential country epitomising both the dynamics – and the need to analyse – 'domestic public diplomacy'. At the same time, they are cognisant of the complexity that this shift brings with it: with detailed attention to the different types of contestations that have emerged over time (punctuated by a series of critical junctures).

Alternatively, while the role of domestic forces in diplomacy has increasingly been viewed (and engaged with), this shift is far less noticeable in Japan as confirmed by the valuable contribution by Toshiya Takahashi, 'Social Legitimacy, State-Society Relations and Non-State Actor Diplomacy in Japan.' At the core of Takahashi's argument is that non-state actors continue to lack the legitimacy in terms of social standing to allow them inclusion in diplomacy.

These conclusions reinforce the image of Japan as an outlier to the trends situated in a variety of other countries. Yet, although convincing, future research could potentially examine other reasons for this strikingly distinctive pattern. Does the lack of legitimacy for societal groups also reflect a decided sense of insularity in the case of Japan? Or does cultural risk-aversion play an amplified part? On either ground, as Takahashi fully appreciates, the relative lack of domestic input into diplomatic practice cannot be accounted for by a lack of a security dilemma. On this point, as informed by the overview provided by the editors in their Introduction, and the focus in the latter part of Takahashi's chapter, the analysis of Huijgh for example should point in a fuller engagement on the part of the Japanese public, in that they live in an 'environment where domestic (security) concerns are increasingly linked to international events domestic politics.'[15] Certainly, it is intriguing that although Takahashi indicates that change 'is not yet at hand,' there are signs that Japan is 'evolving very slowly to become more diverse, which will eventually require a transformation of Japanese diplomacy.'

The chapter by HwaJung Kim, Diplomacy and People: Contrasting Cases of The Two Koreas' People-Empowerment Approaches to Diplomacy, extends the images of dichotomous dynamics. In the component of the chapter examining North Korea there is a richness of analysis that is welcome, but with an understanding regarding the deep sense of continuity built into the authoritarian structure as exemplified in the process around the *Arirang* Mass Games. While there is an intense degree of coercion, there is also a high level of competence and effectiveness. As Kim concedes after detailed study: 'An authoritarian country such as North Korea has also shown excellent skills in mobilising people, organising and upscaling international events through citizen participation, providing engaged citizens with privileged treatment, and achieving the country's diplomatic goals thereby.'

In contrast to the North Korean model of control, South Korea's Participatory Diplomacy Center does open up to an authentic feature of citizen participation in the democratic process. In doing so, though, Kim also illuminates the extent to which the level of political polarisation served as a backdrop to this innovative dynamic. Arguably the main takeaway from Kim's chapter is the sophistication around the practices developed through the Participatory Diplomacy Center: 'the Center found a way to optimise a process of implementing citizen consultation in diplomacy without provoking public arousal.'

Yun Zhang's contribution elaborates on the theme that predictability about diplomatic practices should not be taken for granted. The chapter by Zhang, 'Internal Societisation of Diplomacy: The Disintegration of State-Society Relations and its Moderating Effects on Japanese Diplomacy toward China,' is one fascinating example. Given the assertiveness of the Chinese party-state (and netizens), it might be expected that there could (or even should) be a similar

---

15   Huijgh 2019, 37 (originally published in 2011).

mode of domestic mobilisation by the Japanese public. But instead of assertiveness, the shift that took place tilted towards 'internal societisation of diplomacy:' with a doubling down of a constraining ethos. As Zhang concludes with conviction: 'In sum, the so-called 'China threat' is not enough to change the very nature of the disintegration of the state–society relationship in Japan, which moderates Japan's diplomacy towards China.'

In rehearsing the essential strengths of the book, at the forefront is the mix of empirical comprehensiveness and conceptual innovation. Certainly, the editors are fully justified in stating that: 'The studies in this volume are a first systematic effort to compensate for what is arguably an impermissible omission in the received wisdom on diplomacy's parameters and potentialities.'

To signal how states engage with their domestic publics on diplomatic matters, or that the themes of the book tap into a 'largely underexplored and yet potentially rich area for the study of diplomacy', is not to suggest that this research agenda will simply one of adding on cases or building on the conceptual logic of expended participation. As noted, the tension between the participatory ideals embedded in the book and the set of challenges in operational practice are not going away. On the contrary, it is likely they will be not only accentuated but diversified.

It is understandable under these conditions why there might be some nostalgia for when diplomacy and diplomats only had to deal with the 'away' dimension. Thankfully, though, this book does not go down this path. It accepts that diplomacy – with special reference to the variation of democratic countries – will be in large number of cases be noisy and messy. But the contributors remain confident that the 'home' crowd is not the problem per se. As such there is an acceptance that even with all the jagged edges, the shift towards navigations of 'home engagement' to complement the 'away' dimension is here to stay. And with this impressive collection, there is a weighty confirmation that this turn is not only necessary and right but one that should be sustained and refined.

Bibliography

Cooper, A.F. 'Adapting Public Diplomacy to the Populist Challenge', *Hague Journal of Diplomacy* 14 (1-2), April 2019: 36–50.

Cooper, A.F. blog for the *Hague Journal of Diplomacy*, the Populist Challenge and the Domestic Turn in Diplomacy 7 November 2019. <https://www.universiteitleiden.nl/hjd/news/2019/blog-post–the-populist-challenge-and-the-domestic-turn-in-diplomacy>

Cooper, A.F. 'The Impact of Leader-Centric Populism on Career Diplomats: Tests of Loyalty, Voice, and Exit in Ministries of Foreign Affairs,' in *Ministries of Foreign Affairs in the World. Actors of State Diplomacy*, ed., C. Lequesne (Leiden: Brill, 2022): 150–171.

Cooper, A.F. *The Concertation Impulse in World Politics Contestation over Fundamental Institutions and the Constrictions of Institutionalist International Relations* (Oxford: Oxford University Press, 2024).

Gewen, B. The Inevitability of Tragedy: Henry Kissinger and His World. New York: W. W. Norton & Company, Inc, 2020.

Hoffmann, S. 'Hedley Bull and His Contribution to International Relations,' *International Affairs* 62 (2)1986, 179–195.

Huijgh, E. 'Introduction: Public Diplomacy in Flux: Introducing the Domestic Dimension'. *The Hague Journal of Diplomacy* 7 (4) (2012), 359–367.

Huijgh, E. *Public Diplomacy at Home: Domestic Dimensions* (Leiden and Boston: Brill Nijhoff, 2019).

Kissinger, H. *American Foreign Policy: Three Essays* by Henry Kissinger. (New York: W. W. Norton, 1969), 51–97.

Manor, I, C. Jiménez-Martínez, and A. Dolea. blog for the Hague Journal of Diplomacy. 'An asset or a hassle? The public as a problem for public diplomats 18 November 2021 <https://www.universiteitleiden.nl/hjd/news/2021/blog-post–an-asset-or-a-hassle-the-public-as-a-problem-for-public-diplomats>

Mihelj, S. and C. Jiménez-Martínez. 'Digital Nationalism: Understanding the Role of Digital Media in the Rise of 'New' Nationalism'. *Nations and Nationalism* 27(2) (2021), 331–346. DOI 10.1111/nana.12685.

Moravcsik, A. 'Introduction: Integrating International and Domestic Theories of International Bargaining,' in *Double-Edged Diplomacy: International Bargaining and Domestic Politics* , eds., P. Evans, H. Jacobson and R. Putnam (Berkeley: University of California Press, 1993), 3–42.

Murray, S., and A.G. Pigman. 2014. Mapping the relationship between international sport and diplomacy. Sport in Society 17 (9): 1098–1118.

Robertson, O. 'The Dream Team you've never heard of,' The Undefeated,' 11 August 2016., in Cooper, A.F. 'U.S. public diplomacy and sports stars: mobilizing African-American athletes as goodwill ambassadors from the cold war to an uncertain future,' *Place Branding Public Diplomacy* 15 (3), 11 December 2018: 165–172.

Index

www.ingramcontent.com/pod-product-compliance
Lightning Source LLC
Chambersburg PA
CBHW020452270326
41926CB00008B/574